*Manifold Destiny*

# Manifold Destiny

Arabs at an American
Crossroads of
Exceptional Rule

## John Tofik Karam

VANDERBILT UNIVERSITY PRESS
*Nashville, Tennessee*

Maps from OpenStreetMap.org are licensed under the OpenDataCommons.org Open Database License (ODbL).

Library of Congress Cataloging-in-Publication Data

Names: Karam, John Tofik, author.
Title: Manifold destiny : Arabs at an American crossroads of exceptional rule / John Tofik Karam.
Description: Nashville : Vanderbilt University Press, [2020] | Includes bibliographical references and index.
Identifiers: LCCN 2020034084 (print) | LCCN 2020034085 (ebook) | ISBN 9780826501332 (hardcover) | ISBN 9780826501325 (paperback) | ISBN 9780826501349 (epub) | ISBN 9780826501356 (pdf)
Subjects: LCSH: Arabs—South America—Ethnic identity. | Arabs—South America—Social conditions. | Arabs—United States—Public opinion. | South America—Politics and government. | South America—Relations—United States. | United States—Relations—South America.
Classification: LCC F2239.A7 K37 2020  (print) | LCC F2239.A7  (ebook) | DDC 327.8073—dc23
LC record available at https://lccn.loc.gov/2020034084
LC ebook record available at https://lccn.loc.gov/2020034085

Para Josephine e Nur

قدري أنتما

El camino es el destino
O caminho é o destino
The Road is Destiny
الطريق هو الوجهة

*Los hijos de los días*, Eduardo Galeano (2012)

# Contents

# Acknowledgments

**One's destination may or** may not be destiny. In Spanish and Portuguese, *destino* can mean destination and destiny. In Arabic, al-wijha is destination whereas al-qadr evokes a pre-determined destiny. Likewise, in English, destination is the end of a journey while destiny suggests one's eventual fate. Notwithstanding the title, this book is neither a literal destination nor an actual destiny but rather a "history of the present" that I hope will soon take another, more progressive, direction that would make the story recounted in these pages the past of a future with greater equity, justice, and belonging. The research that resulted in this book began at a more optimistic time, in 2007 specifically. I completed most of the research by 2011, when it seemed that this hemisphere was headed for somewhere other than the conjunction where we now find ourselves. Over these years, I met and married my wife, and we welcomed into the world our daughter whose vibrant light gives me energy each and every day. I know not where we are bound for, but I am content that we are bound together.

I want to express my deepest gratitude to the entire community in Foz do Iguaçu and Ciudad del Este for making this research possible. Since most have been mentioned in the press, I decided to keep real names, except in cases of some private individuals for whom I use pseudonyms. I will be forever indebted to Mohamad Barakat and Fouad Fakih, who welcomed me at the border and introduced me to many of the protagonists in these pages. I also extend thanks to Mohamad Abu Ali, Adão Luiz Almeida, Amer A. S., Baina, Mihail Meskin Bazas, Rogério Bonato, Nasser Chamseddine, Nabil Chamseddine, Adnan El Sayed, Arialba Freire, Marcelle Ghies, Khaled Ghotme, Hector Guerín, Mhamad Mahmoud Ismail, Ricardo Jimenez, Sheik Taleb Jomha, Sheik Mohamad Khalil, Luiz Francisco Macchioratto, the late Juvêncio Mazzarollo, Yusuf Nassar, Antônio Vanderli Moreira, Aluízio Palmar, Abdul Rahal, Ali Said Rahal, Hamad Rahal, Nadia Rahal, Fawaz Rahal, Ali Hussein Safadi, Faisal Saleh, Juan Carlos Salinas, Isam Saour, Antônio Savaris, Said Taigen, Fawez Tarabain, Wagner, Fatima Yahya, and Yahya. I want to express my sincere appreciation to countless others who I read about in the local border press. A special thanks to Alfredo Jalaf in Puerto Iguazú. In addition, I want to thank interlocutors in Asuncíon and Brasília, including Talal AlDamasi, Coco Arce, Augusto Ocampos Caballero, Coronel Walter Felix Cardoso Junior, Bader Rachid Lichi, the late Dr. Luís Alfonso Resck Haidder, Daniel Nasta, Carlos Nuñez, Carlos Torres, Victor Torres, Reinaldo Penner, Armando Rivarola, and José Vidal.

The research that resulted in this work was funded by the National Endowment for the Humanities, the Fulbright Scholar Program, DePaul University, and the University of Illinois, Urbana-Champaign. At DePaul University, I want to especially thank the Department of Latin American and Latino Studies, which provided institutional and moral support at the very start of this project. At the University of Illinois, Urbana-Champaign, I express my gratitude to the Department of Spanish and Portuguese, the Humanities Research Institute, the Lemann Center for Brazilian Studies, and the Office of the Vice Chancellor for Research, which ensured the support that saw this project to the end. I am deeply grateful for the camaraderie and support of numerous colleagues and friends from both universities, especially

Mary Arends-Kuenning, Raquel Castro Goebel, Camilla Fojas, Glen Goodman, Maria Gillombardo, Waïl Hassan, Marc Hertzman, Stephanie Hilger, Amor Kohli, Kalyani Menon, Chernoh Sesay Jr., and Lourdes Torres. I wish to extend heartfelt thanks to Luiz Loureiro and the entire Fulbright Commission in Brazil. At Vanderbilt University Press, I sincerely thank acquisitions editor Zachary Gresham and managing production editor Joell Smith-Borne for taking on this project and believing in this book. I want to extend my particular debt to the anonymous reviewers whose interventions improved the manuscript. I am especially indebted to Jerry Dávila and Jeff Lesser who read prior parts of this manuscript and who made critiques and gave reassurances without which I would have never persevered. Any shortcomings in the coming pages are of my own doing.

Other debts I owe to friends and colleagues in Argentina, Brazil, Canada, Lebanon, Paraguay, the US, and elsewhere. I thank Christine Folch, Lorenzo Macagno, Silvia Montenegro, Paulo Pinto, Fernando Rabossi, and Caroline Schuster for their camaraderie and support at the border. I thank the staff at the Biblioteca Pública Elfrida Engel Nunes Rios, the Câmara Municipal de Foz do Iguaçu, and the newspaper *A Gazeta do Iguaçu* in Foz do Iguaçu, as well as the staff at the Centro de Documentación y Estudios in Ciudad del Este. I thank Aluízio Palmar for permission to use numerous photographs of the Arab community from the newspaper *Nosso Tempo*. In Brasília, I thank Antonio Carlos Lessa and the Instituto de Relações Internacionais at the Universidade de Brasília for welcoming me in 2019 for the final leg of research. I want to also extend thanks to Rogério de Souza Farias in Itamaraty, Brazil's Ministry of Foreign Relations, for welcoming me into the archive. In Asunción, I am grateful to Rose Palau at the Centro de Documentación y Archivo para la Defensa de los Derechos Humanos (CDyA, better known as the Archivo del Terror), Zayda Caballero Rodríguez at the Biblioteca Nacional del Paraguay, and Adelina Pusineri and Raquel Zalazar at the Museo Andrés Barbero. I express thanks to David Sheinin for showing me the ropes in Buenos Aires and to the Biblioteca Nacional de Argentina. I also want to extend my gratitude to Roberto Khatlab and the Center for Latin American Studies and Cultures at USEK in Lebanon.

I am also grateful for many colleagues who invited me to present parts and synopses of this book. Their engaged comments made this a better work. I thank Martin Slama, Johann Heiss, and participants in the Comparing Arab Diasporas workshop at the Austrian Academy of Sciences. I am indebted to Jeff Lesser, Raanan Rein, the Tam Institute for Jewish Studies, and participants in the Together Yet Apart symposium at Emory University. I thank Tobias Boos, Anton Escher, Paul Tabar, and participants in the conference on Palestinian, Lebanese, and Syrian communities in the World, held at the Institute of Geography at Johannes Gutenberg University. I thank Dwight McBride and the Race and Ethnicity Study Group in Chicago. I am indebted to Akram Khater, Andrew Arsan, the *Mashriq & Mahjar* journal, and the Moise A. Khayrallah Center for Lebanese Diaspora Studies at North Carolina State University. I am indebted to Ellen McLarney, the Brazil Initative, and participants in the Middle East in Latin America symposium at Duke University. I thank Ignácio Corona, Abril Trigo, Jeffrey Cohen, and the Center for Latin American Studies at Ohio State University. I am grateful to Jim Green and the Middle East Studies / Brazil Initiative at Brown University. I am indebted to Amal Ghazal and the Center for Comparative Muslim Studies at Simon Fraser University.

In the nearly decade and a half that it took for this book to come to fruition, family meant everything. I thank my mother, Amelia Karam, and my late father, Maron Karam, my sister Mary Karam Mckey and my brother Joseph Karam, my brother-in-law, John McKey, and my sister-in-law, Marianne Skau, and my nephew, Matthew, and nieces, Tamar, Katherine, and Alia. I owe my cousins— especially Antônio and Nazaré Bichara, Claudine Bichara and the late Rony Oliveira, Bichara Abidão Neto and Ana Paula, Jeff and Isabella Hooker, and Felipe Bichara and Alê. I too owe close friends in São Paulo, Eduardo Chaalan Bitar, Helô Machado, Felipe Machado, Fernando Machado, and Natália, and many others. Words are not enough to express my gratitude to my wife, Josephine Karkafi, who endured years of me writing and rewriting this book. I began to pen these acknowledgments on the day of our daughter's sixth birthday, our destination and destiny in this world. Decades from now, when our daughter flips through the pages of the dusty hardcover or used paperback, or perhaps more likely glances at a digital copy of this book, I hope that the world that she and her generation inhabit will be a better one.

*Urbana-Champaign, September 2, 2020*

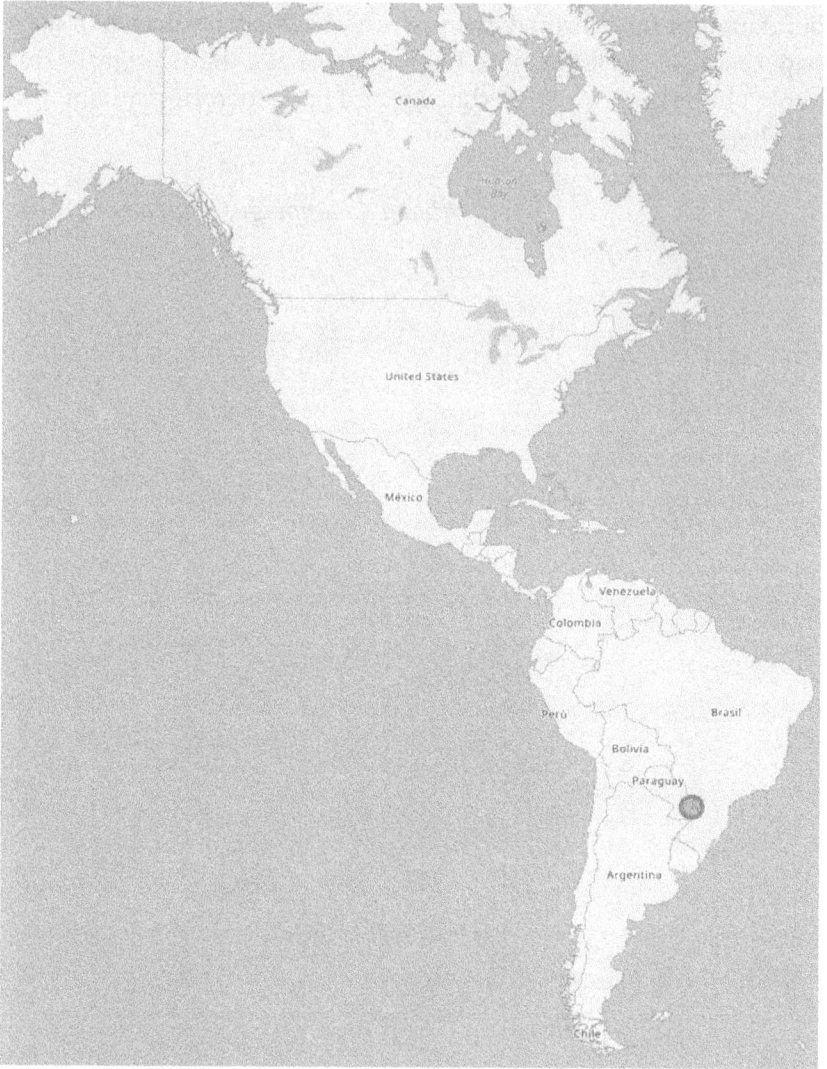

**Figure 0.1.** The border where Brazil, Paraguay, and Argentina meet in hemispheric perspective. © OpenStreetMap contributors

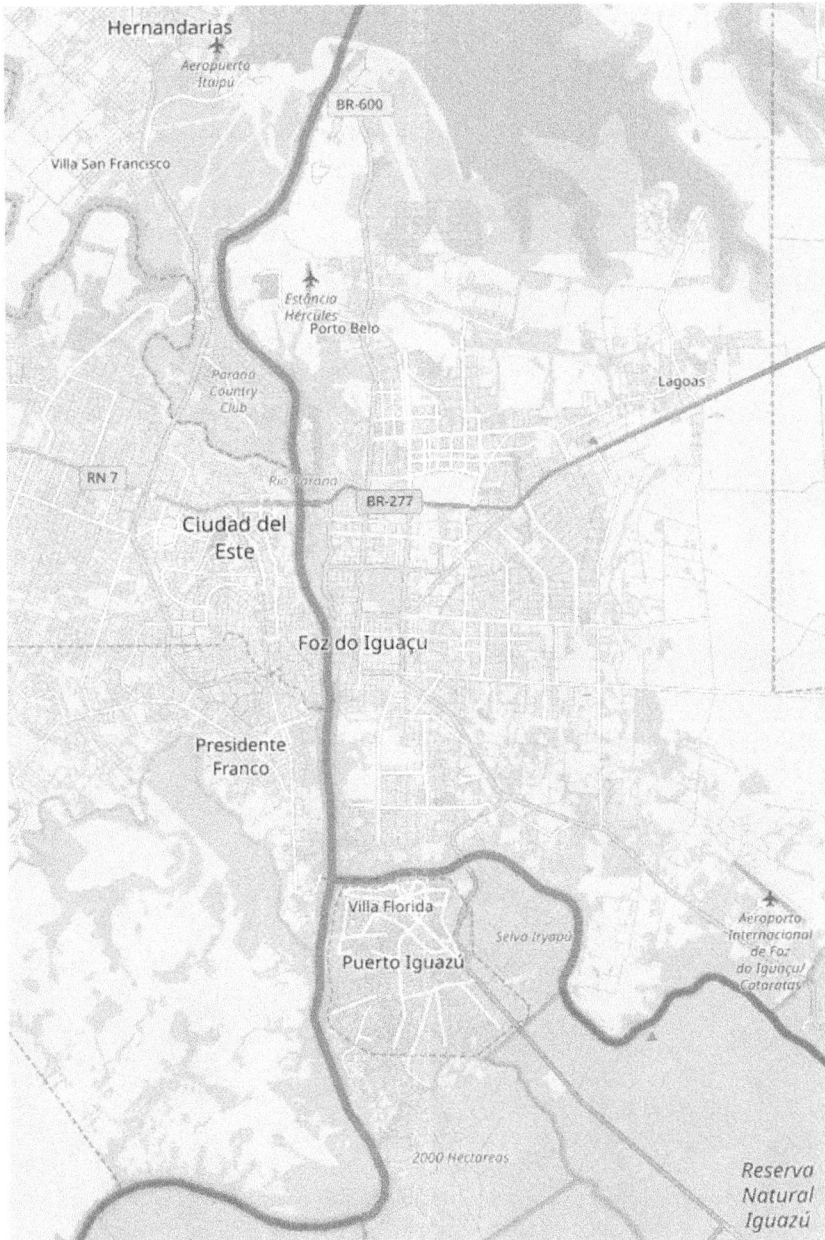

**Figure 0.2.** A map of the border where Brazil, Paraguay, and Argentina meet. On the right is the Brazilian city of Foz do Iguaçu. On the left is the Paraguayan city of Ciudad del Este. At the bottom of the map is the Argentine town of Puerto Iguazú. © OpenStreetMap contributors

# Destined for America

**"I'm American . . . more** American than George W. Bush," declared Mohamad Barakat.[1] Barakat had studied in the United States, visited relatives in Canada, and permanently settled at the border where Brazil, Paraguay, and Argentina meet. On the Paraguayan side of the border, his colleague Said Taijen sent orders to Central and North America. Taijen imported consumer goods through Colón- and Miami-based free trade zones before the establishment of the South American trade bloc, known as Mercosur (the Spanish acronym for the Southern Common Market).[2] Taijen and others continued doing business after the trade accord was ratified by Brazilian, Paraguayan, Argentine, and Uruguayan states. The bloc's motto, "our north is the south" was embodied by Mohamed Ismail, nicknamed Magrão (Big Skinny, in Portuguese), on the Brazilian side of the border. Seeing the hemisphere from his point of view, Magrão granted an interview to the *Washington Post* where he poked fun at what the newspaper cited as "absurd reports of terrorist cells" at the border, much to the chagrin of the US State Department.[3] Such trade and civic affairs concerned Mohamad, Said, Magrão, and other overwhelming numbers of Muslim Lebanese and fewer Muslim Palestinians and Syrians. They self-identified as *árabes* (Arabs) at this hemispheric crossroads, which is usually called the *tríplice fronteira* in Portuguese, the *triple frontera* in Spanish, and the *tri-border* in English.[4]

In the "destiny of America," are Arabs at this border moving "toward continental integration?"[5] In 1965, military heads of state used such language to inaugurate the Friendship Bridge between the Brazilian and Paraguayan sides of the fluvial border.[6] Arabs had already begun settling in the city of Foz do Iguaçu on the Brazilian side, and in Ciudad del Este on the Paraguayan side (which was known as Ciudad Presidente Stroessner until 1989). Hardly any inhabited the town of Puerto Iguazú on the Argentine side of the border. But in the 1990s, the Argentine state distracted attention from unresolved violence in the capital of Buenos Aires by pointing fingers at Arabs on the Brazilian and Paraguayan sides of the border.[7] Without evidence, Mercosur authorities debated while US counterparts framed Arabs at the border as a threat, especially after 9/11. In response, Arabs led tens of thousands of border residents in the event Paz sem Fronteiras / Paz sin Fronteras / Peace without Borders. Arabs later served as witnesses in the Foz do Iguaçu city government-led lawsuit against CNN that portrayed the border as a "terrorist haven." Since that time, predominantly US-based scholars of security studies have voiced suspicions that Arabs at the border harbor terrorist affinities.[8] In this "spurious scholarship," a turn of phrase I borrow from postcolonial critic Edward Said, Arabs at the border trouble a hemispheric America.[9]

My work instead explores how Arabs fold into a hemisphere historically troubled by US power once characterized in extraordinary terms as "manifest destiny." Based in the two main cities of the border, Foz do Iguaçu and Ciudad del Este, I show that Arabs embody and endure a hemispheric America of exceptional rule without a given center. I focus on their "transnational projects," by which I mean "economic enterprises" as well as "political, cultural, and religious initiatives" that "take place on a recurrent basis across national boundaries," borrowing from the work of anthropologists Linda Basch, Nina Glick Schiller, and Cristina Szanton Blanc, as well as that of sociologist Alejandro Portes.[10] The six chapters of this study examine the projects that Arabs undertake at the border in a "multiplication of the Americas," which according to historian Felipe Fernández-Armesto, "makes the present state of the hemisphere seem neither inevitable nor indefinitely sustainable."[11] From the 1960s to the 1990s, Arabs projected their trade and activism in a semiperipheral America, a Third World America, and an Ummah America. From the 1990s to the 2010s, their business and civic networks continued in a free trade America, a war-torn America, and a speculative America. Neither determining nor determined by any given state agenda or central power, Arabs play in what Magrão characterized as a "much bigger game."

Arabs fulfill what I call a "manifold destiny." The figure of speech refers to the many folds or ways Arabs accommodate exceptional or extraordinary measures that state powers enact for an indeterminate time.[12] In this unfinished but not interminable saga, Arabs connect the heretofore separate subjects of authoritarian South America and the counterterrorist US.[13] Arabs opened businesses and community centers at the border during US-backed authoritarian military dictatorships in Brazil (1964–1985), Paraguay (1954–1989), and Argentina (1976–1983). Examining authoritarian and postauthoritarian orders from the 1960s to the 1990s, the book's first half is made up of three chapters that address how Arabs at the border acceded to state exceptions that drew Paraguay toward Brazil and away from Argentina and the US. Considering the counterterrorist orders of ostensible liberal democracies between the 1990s and the 2010s, the book's second half, also composed of three chapters, looks at the ways Arabs at the border grew accustomed to the exceptions made by Mercosur member states and the US, scrutinized in intermittent searches for terrorism that failed to find anything of the kind. The two parts of this book show how over some six decades Arabs came to terms with the authoritarian rise of Brazil over the once Argentine- and US-dominated Paraguay as well as the counterterrorist reach of Mercosur and the US. Witness to authoritarian and counterterrorist measures that twisted or truncated real democratic enfranchisement, their "manifold destiny" reveals a hemispheric history of exceptional rule.

Set on the Brazilian and Paraguayan sides of the border shared with Argentina and subject to Mercosur and the US, this study casts Arab traders and activists as circumstantial protagonists on a hemispheric stage where states suspend or enact law by fiat. Taking my cue from their historically informed understandings of being simultaneously actors and acted upon, I represent Arabs as agents of development and suspects of tax evasion, as activists for solidarity and as persons accused of terrorism. When I undertook the lion's share of the archival and ethnographic work for this book between 2007 and 2011, I often heard the remark, "a colônia é muito acomodada" (the community is well-accommodated / complacent). Arabs felt that their long-time presence on the Brazilian and Paraguayan sides of the border, where they overwhelmingly live and work, neither erased nor were erased by timeless images of them as suspects that they felt were more common in Argentina and the US. Attentive to such tensions and paradoxes, I explore how Arabs drew upon and were drawn into spheres of influence emanating from Brasília, Asunción, Buenos Aires, and Washington, DC, at an American crossroads of authoritarian legacies and counterterrorist liaisons. Arabs point not to liberal democratic fits and starts in Brazil, Paraguay, Argentina, Mercosur, and the US, but rather an illiberal hemispheric experiment whose current equivocation is itself par for the course.

## Transnational Turns at a Crossroads

Moving aside, or decentering, "manifest destiny," this book transposes the "trans-" of transnational Arab projects onto the "trans-" of a "trans-American" scale of analysis.[14] I advance transnational turns in area and ethnic studies that began nearly three decades ago. Since the 1990s, scholars have reconceptualized not only the world areas of Africa, Asia, Latin America, and the Middle East, but also ethnicized and racialized peoples, including African Americans, Asian Americans, Latinas/os, and Arab Americans. This transnational thinking has produced alternative units of analysis such as a Black Atlantic,[15] an American Pacific,[16] Latina/o Americas,[17] and an Arab Atlantic.[18] In this vein, my work draws upon a new understanding of the "Middle East" as "sets of networks holding together, and held together by, people and things, places and practices," as articulated in the *Mashriq & Mahjar* journal and several other books in Middle East migration studies.[19] I extend this transnational approach to the Middle East across three fields with distinct understandings of the hemisphere: American studies, Brazilian studies, as well as Latin American and Latino studies.

My thinking commences with a recent intervention in American studies, a field that historically distanced itself from area and ethnic studies.[20] Since the 1990s, literary critics, historians, and social scientists have redirected the field's object of study from the "United States of America" toward peoples and places straddling its borders.[21] But critics note that this move beyond the nation-state failed to adequately dislodge US-centrism or expose disavowals of exceptionalism.[22] Transnational turns in American Studies left more or less intact US exceptionalist beliefs of being "distinctive," "exemplary," "exempt," or "unique."[23] In one recent corrective, Kristin Hoganson and Jay Sexton brought US history into "trans-imperial terrain" occupied by other expansionist state agendas.[24] In yet another mediation "between the Middle East and the Americas," Ella Shohat interrupted "'an American' nationalist teleology" by proposing a new synthesis of area and ethnic studies where a particular region or geography "constitute not a point of origin or final destination" but rather a "terminal in a transnational network."[25] These approaches guide my analysis of transnational Middle Eastern ties amid rival states and overlapping orders in the hemisphere.

Accordingly, I traverse the field of Brazilian studies, whose object of study, Brazil, took shape in hemispheric debate despite its fraught location within the idea of "Latin America."[26] Scholars mapped Brazilian exceptions, and accompanying discourses of exceptionalism, across territorial boundaries. They focused on Brazilian monarchical and republican distance from the idea of Latin Americanness envisioned by Spanish-speaking counterparts.[27] They looked at the Brazilian state's own engagement with Americanism, which shifted between rapprochement and rivalry with the US.[28] They also followed Brazil's expansive influence leading up to and during the aforementioned period of authoritarian rule.[29] From that time to today, political scientist and anthropologist Paul Amar recently explored how Brazil is "increasingly asserting itself on the world stage" by "reaching out commercially and culturally to the Middle East."[30] His vision of a "new Global South" applied the "polycentric" perspective of cultural critics Ella Shohat and Robert

Stam, which "does not refer to a finite list of centers of power but rather introduces a systematic principle of differentiation, relationality, and linkage."[31] In this regard, to paraphrase Shohat and Stam, my aim is for Brazil and Brazilian studies to "travel more" through a transnational Middle East that decenters the US and American Studies in hemispheric formation.[32]

These current modes of thought dovetail with transnational turns in Latin American and Latino Studies. Moved by Gloria Anzaldúa's *La Frontera/Borderlands* that questioned not only physical but also epistemic borders, Sonia Álvarez, Juan Flores, George Yúdice, José David Saldívar, and others reimagined *las Américas* (the Americas) from the border (*la frontera*, in Spanish).[33] As Latin American studies entered into dialogue with Latino studies, corporations, governments, and universities likewise sought to capitalize on their rapprochement.[34] Attentive to the possibilities and pitfalls of such "turns" beyond the nation, cultural critic Juan Poblete envisioned these fields on a "transamerican and transatlantic scale" across the "whole hemisphere, its political economy, and the interconnectedness of its politics, cultures, and societies."[35] Poblete remarked that the significance of studying "Middle Eastern immigrant populations in the Americas" is not to displace "nation and area-centered paradigms" but rather to emphasize "cross-border processes" in the making of "national and regional geographies."[36] My work advances his insights by mapping Middle Eastern transnational projects on a hemispheric scale.

As an original fusion of American studies, Brazilian studies, as well as Latin American and Latino studies though transnational Middle East studies, this account about Arabs at the border makes headway on José David Saldívar's idea of "trans-Americanity."[37] Saldívar drew upon Aníbal Quijano and Immanuel Wallerstein's idea of "Americanity" that reconceived the "New World" not as a pre-existing space that was brought into the wider world but rather as a sui generis "pattern" of Eurocentric power that expanded globally.[38] Saldívar emphasizes the idea of "Americanity" as a space of not only coloniality, but also subalternity, by which he means "a subjected state of being" among "minoritized" peoples. Rather than the epistemic "delinking" option that Walter Mignolo proposed,

Saldívar opens up a wider range of subaltern possibilities through a transamerican hemisphere. In this way, I approach Middle Easterners as "subaltern elites," below those dominating but above those dominated on the Brazilian and Paraguayan sides of the border marked by Argentina, Mercosur, and the US.[39] Connecting and connected by many Americas, they circulate ideas, goods, and monies at and beyond the hemispheric crossroads under examination here. By way of a transnational Middle East, my goal is to take a first step in broadening the meaning of "trans-" in a "trans-American" hemisphere.

Instead of the "template" of the Mexican-US border that serves as a reminder of the nineteenth-century belief in "manifest destiny," my study is based at a boundary that Iberian empires invented centuries earlier in the Treaty of Tordesilhas (in Portuguese) or Tordesillas (in Spanish).[40] Signed in 1494, this "first division of the world," according to historian Bartolomé Bennassar, still reverberates at the crossroads where Portuguese-dominant Brazil meets Spanish-dominant Paraguay and Argentina, and where the indigenous language of Guarani endures among others.[41] Geographer Adriana Dorfman mapped *estudos fronteiriços* (border studies) on the Brazilian side while anthropologist Alejandro Grimson began theorizing "borderization" from the Argentine side.[42] Meanwhile, sociologists Silvia Montenegro and Veronica Giménez Béliveau led an ever-growing scholarship on identity, belonging, and inequality across the border's cities of Foz do Iguaçu, Ciudad del Este, and Puerto Iguazú.[43] Anthropologists Fernando Rabossi, Rosana Pinheiro Machado, Paulo Pinto, and others joined them in focusing on migrants settling from elsewhere in South America as well as from the Middle East and East Asia.[44] Between 1973 and 1984, the world's largest hydroelectric dam was built on the Paraná River that serves as the border between the Brazilian and Paraguayan sides, a half-hour north of the aforementioned Friendship Bridge. Consequently, the population of Foz do Iguaçu soared from under 34,000 in 1970 to over 136,000 in 1980, and nearly doubled again by 2010.[45] The Paraguayan border city skyrocketed from some 7,000 in 1970 to nearly 50,000 inhabitants in 1980, again doubled by 1990, reaching over 300,000 as the largest urban center at this crossroads by 2002.[46] In contrast, the Argentine town of Puerto Iguazú is three times smaller. It grew from under 3,000 in 1970 to nearly 10,000 in 1980, to some 20,000 in 1990, and just over 80,000 by 2010.[47] Home to the world famous waterfalls, called Iguaçu (in Portuguese), Iguazú (in Spanish), or Iguazu (in English), the Argentine and Brazilian sides of the border are separated by the homonymous river, a tributary of the Paraná. In 1985, this trinational borderland's second and only other bridge was inaugurated between the Argentine and Brazilian sides, officially named Tancredo Neves and sometimes called the Puente de la Fraternidad (Fraternity Bridge, in Spanish).[48] Under scrutiny from Mercosur member states and the US, this crossroads must be understood in not only national or regional but more broadly hemispheric terms.[49]

Locating a transnational Middle East across many Americas, and many Americas across a transnational Middle East, my work contributes to a trans-American configuration of area and ethnic studies amid what anthropologist Bruce Knauft calls the "provincialization of the United States."[50] Toward the end of the George W. Bush era, Knauft argued that US geopolitical influence is not disappearing but rather diminishing relative to rising powers on the periphery. His political-economic prognosis of "manifest destiny" drew upon but also diverged from historian Dipesh Chakrabarty's *Provincializing Europe*, which asked how universalized categories such as capital, the nation-state, and modernity that stem from Europe are both "indispensable and inadequate" to grasp the "margins" of the world.[51] For Knauft, the paradox that peripheral areas and groups "can neither fully escape . . . nor be reduced" to dominant centers and blocs demands not new thinking, but rather "recovered countervoices" that unsettle "larger patterns of political and economic domination."[52] By recovering such voices among Arabs at the border, this book contributes to the provincialization of the US in a hemispheric history of exceptional rule. Over more than six decades, Arabs came to terms with governmental suspensions of rules and rights. Their accommodation of state exceptions continued through the impeachment proceedings that respectively took place in Paraguay (2012), Brazil (2015–16), and the US (2019–20). They and others bore witness to the extraordinary measures that anticipated the right-wing presidencies of Mario Abdo Benítez (2018–present) in Paraguay and Jair Messias Bolsonaro (2019–present) in Brazil and epitomized that of Donald John Trump (2016–present) in the US. The "manifold destiny" that Arabs fulfill at a crossroads sheds new light on this hemisphere's exceptional rule not yet over.

## Transnational Accommodation of State Exceptions

This study points to a heretofore unacknowledged hemispheric trajectory of exceptional rule. I follow anthropologist Aihwa Ong's rethinking of the exception "as an extraordinary departure in policy that can be deployed to include as well as to exclude."[53] Whether enabled or constrained, Arabs came to terms with varying forms of Brazilian, Paraguayan, Argentine, Mercosur, and US exceptional rule. From the 1960s to the 1990s, Arabs traded and mobilized under US-backed authoritarian and post-authoritarian governments in Brazil, Paraguay, and Argentina, which made exceptions that opened markets and sought ties with the Middle East. Between the 1990s and the 2010s, Arab trade and activism continued under Mercosur and US counterterrorism (called *antiterrorismo*, in Portuguese and Spanish), which suspended liberal democratic and market norms in search of terrorism associated with, but not found among, Middle Easterners at the border. Despite the sea-change in "normative orders," Arabs' accommodation of authoritarian legacies and counterterrorist liaisons point to an American epoch of not liberal democratic advances but more equivocally state exceptions.[54]

The liberal economic exceptions made by otherwise illiberal governments brought Paraguay toward Brazil and away from Argentina and the US.[55] The first chapter looks at Lebanese, Palestinian, and Syrian traders in this hemispheric shuffle between the 1960s and the late 1980s. On the Brazilian side of the border, Arabs exported Brazilian-made manufactures to Paraguayan consumers, leveraging Brazil's military government that exempted exportation from some taxes amid the wider suspension of civil rights. Meanwhile, Arabs on the Paraguayan side imported through a simplified tax system at the border set up by the otherwise imperious Paraguayan dictatorship, bringing in East Asian–made merchandise from US-dominated Panama that was sold to Brazilian consumers criss-crossing the bridge. Arabs expanded Brazil's manufacturer and consumer markets over the once Argentina- and US-dominated Paraguay. Through liberal exceptions in illiberal regimes, Arabs animated a semiperipheral America that neither led to nor derived from US influence in the hemisphere.

States with authoritarian legacies curbed liberationist prospects in a hemispheric America as well as made exceptions for a trans-national Middle East.[56] The second chapter asks how Arabs came to terms with Third Worldist agendas at this crossroads. Under the liberal exceptions of illiberal regimes in the 1970s and 1980s, mostly Lebanese but also some Palestinians and Syrians took up Arab and Islamic activism. On the Brazilian side of the border, their advocacy aligned with the military as well as the civilian opposition that eventually took over the state. Meanwhile on the Paraguayan side of the border, they remained in compliance with the regime's party that kept power after an internal military coup ended the dictatorship. But this transition from authoritarian rule was cut short by the unresolved 1992 attack on the Israeli embassy in the Argentine capital of Buenos Aires. Scrutinized but never charged, Arabs at the border faced illiberal exceptions to nascent liberal democratic rule. Arabs responded by mobilizing on the Brazilian side of the border, but not in solidarity with counterparts on the Paraguayan side where the state suspended their rights under post-authoritarian Argentine and US pressures.

In 1994, the Argentine state failed to prevent a second bombing, this time of a Jewish community building in Buenos Aires, testing Arabs' decades-long institution-building of an Ummah, a universal Islamic community. As will be seen in the third chapter, the post-authoritarian Argentine state took exceptional measures to militarize its side of the border against Muslim Arabs on the Brazilian and Paraguayan sides.[57] Under US pressure, Argentine border patrol detained Arabs venturing onto the Argentine side while Argentine government ministers pressured Brazilian and Paraguayan counterparts to scrutinize Arab religious leaders in Foz do Iguaçu and Ciudad del Este. Downplaying Shia and Sunni differences, Lebanese,

Palestinian, and Syrian Muslims condemned anti-Jewish violence and spoke of themselves as scapegoats for Argentina's failure to investigate and prosecute the attack. In this Ummah America, Arabs accused Argentine, US, and other authorities of unduly blaming them and organized through Islam on the Brazilian and Paraguayan sides of the border. Through illiberal exceptions made by liberal democratic rulers, Arabs became the targets of *antiterrorismo*, an authoritarian legacy in post-authoritarian governments.

At this conjuncture, state powers founded Mercosur, which not only standardized tariffs but also stimulated illiberal security.[58] The fourth chapter chronicles Arabs' efforts to accommodate new tariff rates while the democratic norms of the accord were suspended for them. On the Brazilian side of the border, Arabs began to import from outside the bloc by using Mercosur's Common External Tariffs (CETs). On the Paraguayan side, Arabs obtained exemptions to Mercosur CETs, importing from free trade zones in Panama and increasingly from Florida.[59] US and Argentine authorities, however, alleged that their cross-border trade threatened security in Mercosur. Brazilian officials investigated such liaisons to shore up the bloc. The Brazilian state set up additional checkpoints at its border with Paraguay, detaining and releasing migrants of mostly Arab origin who resided in Foz do Iguaçu and ran stores in Ciudad del Este. Arabs at the border sought to accommodate the Mercosur bloc as an economic accord but they became intermittently labeled as "non-Mercosur" residents. Facing illiberal security exceptions in a liberal economic bloc, Arabs faced and followed a free trade America.

In declaring war with no end after September 11, 2001, US government authorities demanded South American counterparts take exceptional measures against Arabs at the border.[60] As will be shown in the fifth chapter, Brazilian officials demurred to US counterterrorism but Paraguayan counterparts deferred, as Paraguayan territory witnessed dozens of US military missions in the next five years.[61] Ensuing debates about whether Arabs at the border were or would be complicit with terrorism distracted attention from prior, decades-long US support of South American dictatorships that alleged to combat terrorism as well. In this war-torn America, Arabs at the border drew upon, and were drawn into, distinct Brazilian and Paraguayan state positions in US-led counterterrorism. Some joined with Brazilian officials wary of US counterterrorist accusations by organizing the aforementioned event, Peace without Borders. Others on the Paraguayan side became duplicitous informants and finger-pointed business rivals as terrorists, later jailed for tax evasion. Under exceptional militarization in civilian rule, Arabs at the border neither openly confronted nor entirely conformed to US-led war.

US officials continued to scrutinize Arabs at the border in what Marieke de Goede called the "extralegal targeting" of "suspect monies."[62] The sixth chapter will examine these speculative accounts that Arabs at the border were cast and performed in, economically and imaginatively. In 2002, Brazilian, Paraguayan, Argentine, and US states established the "3+1 Group on Tri-Border Security" that prioritized the pursuit of terrorist finance. Subsequently, the US Treasury Department blacklisted a handful of Arabs at the border despite finding no traces of terrorist monies while the Brazilian state investigated systemic banking irregularities that laundered billions to Paraguay.[63] Arabs tried to settle accounts in this speculative America. They helped the Foz do Iguaçu government sue CNN for defaming border trade as terrorist finance, curtailed Islamic and Middle Eastern philanthropy in Foz do Iguaçu, and donated to a new mosque in Ciudad del Este, buoyed by sales of name brand East Asian-made imports. Under exceptions to democratic and market norms, Arabs grew accustomed to counterterrorist financial monitoring that still found no such cases at the border.

My account of Arab transnational projects rethinks an American history of exceptional rule. From the 1960s to the 1990s, Arabs traded and mobilized through the liberal exceptions made by illiberal and post-illiberal governments that otherwise guarded domestic markets and suspended legal norms for purported security. From the 1990s through the 2010s, Arabs continued business and civic engagement through the illiberal exceptions of now liberal governments that otherwise opened markets and eschewed military rule. Fouad Fakih bore witness to such state exceptions since migrating from Lebanon to Brazil's side of the border. In the 1970s and 1980s, Fakih was president and served on the board of the

Commercial and Industrial Association of Foz do Iguaçu (known as Acifi), working with authoritarian state officials from Brazil, Paraguay, and elsewhere. From the 1990s to today, he continued to work with state authorities in the Peace without Borders movement, and the Foz do Iguaçu city government lawsuit against US counterterrorist coverage of the border. Accordingly, Fakih voiced an exceptional view of "all that América [*sic*], and especially Brazil, Paraguay, and Argentina, have represented" for Arabs.[64] Having accommodated shifting forms of exceptional rule for decades, Fakih also expressed cynicism about condoning and condemning it, remarking that "when there's a dictatorship, 80 percent of people approve of it. And when the dictatorship ends, 80 percent of people disapprove of it."[65] Mindful of his and others' uncommitted view toward exceptional rule in the hemisphere, my study casts Arabs with circumstantial roles in the authoritarian past and counterterrorist present of America.

## Arabs in and beyond "Our América"

Arabs at the border extend the boundaries of what Cuban intellectual José Martí called *nuestra América*.[66] In 1895, Martí spoke of "our América" in reference to what is now usually denominated as Latin America and the Caribbean and warned of incipient US interventionism. Not using his distinction between "our America" and "the America that is not ours," Middle Easterners as well as Muslims were already migrating across what they designated as *Amrika* (America, in Arabic).[67] A century or so later, Martí's vision inspired the aforementioned hemispheric turn in American studies.[68] And again, case studies of Middle Easterners as well as Muslims appeared in circuitous hemispheric trajectories.[69] Accommodating but not seamlessly fitting into any given hemispheric vision, Arabs inhabit and transcend "our América."

In 1892, the grandfather of Mohamad Barakat, introduced at the start of this book, headed to "América," because "era tudo América" (it was all America), whether north or south of the equator.[70] Departing the village of Baaloul in the Beqaa Valley, then part of the Ottoman Empire, he settled in the Brazilian city of São Paulo, with an intermittent stint in Argentina. After some time, the grandfather's brothers moved to Ontario, Canada, while the grandfather himself returned to Baaloul. Subsequently, the grandfather sent two sons to live with his brothers in Canada. By 1900, other villagers from Baaloul arrived in Argentina. By 1920, their sales routes led them to Colombia, with many converging in Maicao, a Colombian town bordering with Venezuela in La Guajira peninsula, where their descendants thrive today.[71] They and other Arabs also moved westward from Barranquilla to Santa Marta as well as eastward to the island of San Andrés. In 1945, Ahmad Mattar listed villagers from "Balloul" in these and other Colombian towns.[72] Soon after, some migrated to US-dominated Panama when the "largest free trade zone of Americas" opened in Colón, a commercial boon to their ties across the hemisphere.

Arising from the Eastern Mediterranean, these patterns of chain, step, and circulatory migration merged and merged with America. Interrupted by World War I and the Interwar years, migration from the Eastern Mediterranean resumed after World War II, the moment that the Arab border presence began in earnest.[73] In 1951, the father of Mohamad Barakat departed the same village of Baaloul and settled in Foz do Iguaçu on the Brazilian side of the border, around the time that the Nasser, Osman, and Rahal families started settling and trading too. With his father's remittances, Mohamad Barakat himself left Baaloul for Toledo, Ohio, in the US, and afterwards, moved to the capital of the Canadian province of Ontario, London, where extended kin had migrated previously. In 1961, he traveled to and ended up settling with family in Foz do Iguaçu, just as the signature arcs at the base of the Friendship Bridge were put into place and when, in his words, the few town roads had "not even a meter of asphalt." In the following decades, tens of thousands of Middle Easterners repeated this journey. Some set out from Palestinian and Syrian metropoli as early as 1960, but the vast majority stemmed from Lebanon, from not only Baaloul but also Lela, Qillaya-Darafa, and elsewhere in the Beqaa Valley as well as from Dibbine, Jebbayn, Kabrikha, Khiam, and numerous other villages elsewhere in South Lebanon. They were destined for *Amrika*.

Arabs continue to straddle Luso, Hispano, Anglo, South, Central, Latin, North, and other Americas. In the mid-1990s, a newspaper in

Foz do Iguaçu observed that some Arabs "divide their time between Brazil, where they prefer to live, and Ciudad del Este in Paraguay, where they are storeowners specializing in imports."[74] Introduced earlier, Magrão reiterated that some Arabs reside on the Brazilian side and run businesses on the Paraguayan side. Their daily routines start by leaving homes in Foz do Iguaçu, commuting through the border controls on the congested three-lane Friendship Bridge, arriving at businesses in Ciudad del Este, and after an eight to twelve-hour workday, returning along the same route. Less frequently, some Lebanese at the border visited and received relatives from the Canadian provinces of Alberta and Ontario. In 1999, a member of the Omairi family from Alberta visited his sister in Foz do Iguaçu.[75] As an elected public official, Omairi defended an end to visas between Brazil and Canada.[76] Some others possessed business interests in the free trade zones of not only Colón, Panama, but also south Florida, where they imported goods from. The Hammoud brothers opened the Monalisa shopping center in Ciudad del Este in 1972 and, later on, offices in Miami as well as New York City.[77] Mohamad Jebai likewise established the Galeria Jebai Center, on the Paraguayan side of the border in the 1970s and, afterward, financed the building of a mall in Miami and even a gated community in Fort Meyers.[78] Arabs make, and are made by, this hemispheric America.

Identifying with countries or regions of origin and settlement, Lebanese, Palestinians, Syrians, and other Arabs at the border exercise what Aihwa Ong called "flexible citizenship" in responding "fluidly and opportunistically to political-economic conditions in transformation."[79] Whether born or naturalized in Foz do Iguaçu, those with Brazilian citizenship use the standard state-issued identity document, known as the *RG* (the acronym for "General Registry"), and like other Brazilians, speak Portuguese as well as *portanhol* (a blend of Portuguese and Spanish) with Spanish-speakers. Fewer actually residing in Ciudad del Este, born or naturalized as Paraguayan citizens, use the *cédula de identitidad civil*, and speak Spanish and some Guaraní, the country's two official languages, alongside some Portuguese which is usually learned by Paraguayans of varied origins near the border with Brazil. Recent migrants, mostly from Lebanon, have Paraguayan and/or Brazilian visas on their passports, and speak a mix of Portuguese and Spanish, often residing in Foz do Iguaçu and working in Ciudad del Este. Lebanese migrants and some descendants have the Lebanese ID card, the *bitaqat*, and show varied fluency in Arabic. Nearly everyone has some knowledge of English, as is the norm for middle and upper classes in Brazil, Paraguay, and Lebanon, as well as Palestine and Syria too. Despite varied negotiations of identity and language, non-Arab and non-Muslim interlocutors identified Islam as *a religião dos árabes* ("the religion of Arabs").[80] Equally common are nationally specific labels such as "Lebanese," "Palestinian," or "Syrian," as well as the more generic *turco* (Turk), a Portuguese- and Spanish-language nod to the Ottoman origins of earlier migrants.[81] Since local journalists have grown up alongside them, media in both Foz do Iguaçu and Ciudad del Este generally use the moniker "Arab," not only as a synonym of "Muslim," but also interchangeably with "Brazilian" and "Paraguayan," respectively. As local border media reported in 1993, "the 'Turks,' as they were called until a short time ago, came to the two borders (Brazil and Paraguay) more so in the 1970s. Today, they are part of the daily life of the cities and the 'salamaleicom' (peace be with you) and 'chucran' (thank you) are words taken up by all non-Arab merchants when they do business with 'um brimo'" (an Arab cousin, substituting the letter p in *primo* (cousin) with a b).[82] "Flexible citizenship" was practiced by many at the border.

Attentive to anthropologist Aisha Khan's point that "Islam *becomes* as well as *is*" in a hemispheric America, it must be noted that most Arabs at the border identify as Sunni and Shia Muslims, alongside smaller numbers of Druze, Alawi, and Ismaili, as well as Maronite Christians.[83] The first arrivals were mostly Sunni. Since the 1970s, Shia migrated in increasing numbers and became a slight majority by the mid-1990s.[84] Relatively few attend mosques or prayer halls on a regular basis, so *shuyukh* (religious leaders, in Arabic) emphasize not *dawa* (proselytization, in Arabic), but rather the maintenance of descendants in the religion of migrant forebears.[85] The long-distance religious practices of Sunni and Shia, Druze and Alawi, "converge" in the *hajj* to Mecca, as well as differ in pilgrimages to holy cities in Iraq, which for Shia Lebanese are "the focal center" during *'Ashura* and *Arba'iyyn*.[86] In Foz do Iguaçu and Ciudad del Este, Arabs integrate Islamic holy days into Catholic-dominant Brazilian and Paraguayan calendars. In Foz do Iguaçu, in 1983, Muslims, Christians, and others laid the cornerstone of the first mosque, Omar Ibn al-Khattab, supported by Brazilian reformists under the surveillance of a fading authoritarian apparatus. A decade later, a second mosque, the Mezquita Profeta Mohamed, was inaugurated in Ciudad del Este, where Shia Lebanese tend to pray under the watch of counterterrorist authorities from Paraguay, Argentina, Brazil, and the US. Most recently, in 2015, Sunni Lebanese led the founding of a third mosque, also in Ciudad del Este: the Mezquita Alkhaulafa Al-Rashdeen, nicknamed the "Mezquita del Este" (Mosque of the East, in Spanish). Amid such institution building, one religious leader noted his exasperation when asked if there is "terrorist activity" at the border. When intelligence or police officers question him, he quips, "I know terrorism," relating the kidnappings, muggings, and akin everyday violence which is "neither Arab nor Islamic" but rather stem from growing social inequalities under hemispheric-wide market reforms since the 1990s. Under circumstances not of their own choosing, Muslim Arabs draw and are drawn into many Americas from authoritarian to counterterrorist times.

## Familiar and Strange Fields

My anthropological view of hemispheric history brings together what are usually taken for granted as a separate past and present. Fittingly, I take as my guide Eric Wolf, who first undertook an anthropological approach to history in *Europe and the People without History*.[87] Wolf's "unfinished" aim to rectify "large gaps in anthropological knowledge" not only vindicates so-named "people" but also scrutinizes the states that tried to incorporate or erase their history, as anthropologist Engseng Ho more recently gathered.[88] Working this field, I repurpose an old ethnographic guidepost to make "the strange familiar, and the familiar strange." In the first part of this book, I make "familiar" the "strange" exceptions of past authoritarian regimes, which Arabs accommodated at the border. In the second part of the book, I make "strange" the "familiar"

counterterrorist interruptions of the present-day democratic status quo, which Arabs at the border also grew accustomed to. This
framework not only redeems the decades-long Arab presence at the
border that was under erasure but also redresses the still ongoing
broader hemispheric epoch of exceptional rule.

Disrupting the binaries between "home" and "field" critiqued
by anthropologists Akhil Gupta and James Ferguson, I studied not
only in the border cities of Foz do Iguaçu and Ciudad del Este, and
to a lesser extent in Puerto Iguazú, but also in Asunción, Brasília,
Buenos Aires, Curitiba, Rio de Janeiro, São Paulo, and Washington,
DC.[89] I did archival and ethnographic research with business and
civic organizations as well as news and government agencies for
some fifteen months between 2007 and 2011, and for two months in
2019. At the border, I carried out some four dozen informal conversa-
tions or interviews, and I took notes on nearly eighty Brazilians
and Paraguayans who were overwhelmingly of Lebanese origin, as
well as some with Palestinian and Syrian backgrounds. Early in the
research, interlocutors were hesitant to speak with me because of
corporate media that demonized the border as a "terrorist haven."
As a result, I turned to local border newspapers and government
reports where Arabs frequently appeared as civic and business
protagonists. The materials I collected became useful resources
methodologically; reviewing documents with interlocutors elicited greater details about their far-flung connections and compro-
mises at the border. From private and public archives, these written
sources also provoked unease among Arabs themselves. "Karam
está investigando todo mundo" (Karam is investigating everybody),
once joked a colleague, likening my academic research to journalistic or even police "investigations." However, the vast majority of
my interlocutors were men, due to their preponderance in Arab-led
business and civic associations at the border as well as in Brazilian,
Paraguayan, Argentine, and US states. That is, male dominance was
both Arab and American. But I chose not to prioritize gender and
sexuality as my research had done elsewhere.[90] Accordingly, this
study addresses Arab trade and activism in the authoritarian ascen-
sion of Brazil over once Argentina- and US-dominated Paraguay as
well as the counterterrorist emergence of Mercosur and US-led war.

Metamorphosing across academic fields, I initiated this research as an anthropologist and specialist in Brazil, but I came to see myself and this book in area and ethnic studies about the hemisphere. I studied anthropology in my undergraduate and graduate years, when I first became interested in what George Marcus called "multi-sited ethnography."[91] With an excessively literal understanding of what Marcus meant, I intended to live on each side of the trinational border during a short two-month project in 2007. Upon speaking with colleagues and working in archives during the first month, I realized that I needed to focus on the Brazilian and Paraguayan cities linked by the Friendship Bridge, Foz do Iguaçu and Ciudad del Este, respectively. As noted earlier, some Arabs live and work on the Brazilian side while others only reside there and commute daily to stores on the Paraguayan side. Fewer both live and work on the Paraguayan side. On whichever side of the Friendship Bridge they spend more time, Arabs would venture onto the Argentine side of the border only on an occasional weekend or intermittent holiday. So, during an eleven-month stay in 2008–9, I first resided in Foz do Iguaçu, mostly out of habit. With fluency in Portuguese and *portanhol* (a mix of Portuguese and Spanish), it occurred to me that my place of residence and language ability drew upon and reflected Brazilian hegemony over Paraguay. I took measures to guard against my Brazilian-centrism by investing a good deal of energy not only in Ciudad del Este but also Asunción, the capital of Paraguay a few hours westward, where I studied the border in state archives. Unexpectedly, colleagues on the Paraguayan side of the border were more open when I arrived from Asunción rather than the closer Brazilian border town. After this research stint ended in August 2009, it became evident to me that I needed to better grasp Puerto Iguazú on the Argentine side. As was mentioned, hardly any Arabs have ever lived on that side, but Argentine government and military responses to the still unresolved 1992 and 1994 bombings in Buenos Aires carried lasting effects for Arabs and America. Between June and August 2010, I undertook mostly archival work in Buenos Aires on Argentine state and media reports about the border. In 2011, I carried out analogous work on US government and media reports, which nearly always refer to "the tri-border area," and even used the acronym TBA, as if this border was some sort of self-contained zone. As I put the archival and ethnographic pieces together from Brazil, Paraguay, Argentina, and the US, I became conscious of my own folding of anthropology into area and ethnic studies, and Brazil into the Americas. As is seen in the scholarship that I draw upon, these fields possess common substrates and porous boundaries.

The multi-sited hemispheric field of this study took shape in a dozen places, some twenty newspapers, four governments, and more than six decades. It all began by reading and taking notes from the bi-monthly magazine *Revista Painel* (1973 to present), the weekly newspaper *Nosso Tempo* (1980 to 1989), and the daily *A Gazeta do Iguaçu* (1989 to 2016),[92] each written in Portuguese and published in Foz do Iguaçu, on the Brazilian side of the border. The respective editors-in-chief of the latter two publications, Juvêncio Mazzarollo and Rogério Bonato, emphasized to me that local journalists already knew "since childhood" Arab families, and vice-versa, a point reiterated by Magrão, introduced earlier. In each newspaper, Arabs appeared as traders, neighbors, activists, and acquaintances, not one-dimensional suspects as portrayed in corporate media since the 1990s. As the longest running periodicals that covered Brazilian, Paraguayan, and Argentine sides of the border, *Revista Painel, Nosso Tempo,* and *A Gazeta do Iguaçu* provided me with a timeline and a roll call of key players that I used when I spoke with colleagues on each side of the Friendship Bridge and when I worked in archives there and elsewhere. With a list of dates and names from each periodical, I worked with several Asunción-based Paraguayan newspapers, including *ABC Color* (1965 to present) and *Ultima Hora* (1973 to present), which maintained branches in Ciudad Presidente Stroessner / Ciudad del Este in the absence of a local Paraguayan press at the border. In the final leg of research, I used the dates and names from Brazilian and Paraguayan sources to examine major newspapers in Buenos Aires, including *Clarín* (1945 to present) and *La Nación* (1870 to present), neither of which maintained a branch office in Puerto Iguazú. To ensure a broader understanding of the Argentine side, I also worked with *El Territorio*, a newspaper in Posadas, the capital of Misiones, an Argentine *provincia* (equivalent to a state in the US), where the border town of

Puerto Iguazú is located. I also collected media reports from the US and cross-checked the moments that entangled Arabs across the hemisphere. With this range of sources, I use oral histories and archival materials in the first half of the book that culminates in the 1990s while I integrate some ethnography in the second half of the book that ends in the 2010s.

In what anthropologist Michael Kearney called the "changing fields of anthropology," my first book on a national scale, *Another Arabesque*, led to this second book project with hemispheric scope, but not the way I had initially planned.[93] The first book addressed ethnic politics in Brazil's neoliberal turn and this second book turns to transnational dynamics in a hemispheric America. As each work spotlights Middle Eastern migrants and descendants, the doubts that *Another Arabesque* raised about whether post-9/11 US politics would gain traction in Brazil came to serve as the springboard for *Manifold Destiny*'s new hemispheric understanding of exceptional rule from authoritarian to counterterrorist times. This change of course occurred after I fielded unexpected responses to my first book and its Brazilian edition, *Um outro arabesco*, at the border. When I gave the paperback to one interviewee on the Paraguayan side in efforts to gain rapport, I was given a fifty-dollar bill as a gesture of goodwill. After promptly returning the money, I joked that I was not selling my work but instead trying to give an idea of what the outcome of my research at the border would look like. Other Arabs at the border were also unsure or hesitant to accept the book because, I suspect, they too had grown accustomed to bearing some cost from akin interactions with media reporters and government officials. Far from earning credibility and the confidence of interlocutors, my distribution of *Another Arabesque / Um outro arabesco* succumbed to the political conjuncture whose impact I had raised doubts about in the first book. Destiny did not go the way I expected.

So I have been grappling with the "ethics of connectivity" that involve me, the scale of analysis in this book, and my interlocutors at the border in "fieldwork that is not what it used to be," to borrow insights from anthropologists George Marcus and James Faubion.[94] My interest in the subject matter of this book originally stemmed from a diasporic family history marked by my grandmother of

Lebanese origin who was born and raised on the Brazilian side of the border with Bolívia.[95] At the same time, the hemispheric angle I adopt here subsumes, but refrains from centering on, the US where I myself was born and brought up, and now live and work. Without the relatives and friends in São Paulo and Rio de Janeiro who were key to *Another Arabesque*, I nearly abandoned the idea for this book after the aforementioned two-month research stint in Foz do Iguaçu and Ciudad del Este in 2007. Many Arabs found it too difficult to disassociate the US part of my background from claims regarding terrorism at the border that they viewed as being most vociferously made in the US. A colleague on the Brazilian side of the border clarified that most could not "figure me out," despite sharing akin diasporic family histories across the hemisphere. My first name disclosed US Americanness, but my last name and appearance showed Arabness, and my speaking ability in Portuguese implied a claim to Brazilianness as well. I remembered the advice that a US-based Brazilian anthropologist gave me a decade earlier, that it would be difficult to cultivate the rapport necessary to study this border amid the "surveillance and militarization" that anthropologist Carmen Ferradas had noted from Posadas on the Argentine side.[96] But the border kept popping up in the US when I made presentations from my earlier research. At one talk I gave in California, an audience member asked about Muslim Arabs at the "Iguazu" falls in relation to the bombings in Buenos Aires. I replied that such violence remained unresolved and years of investigation failed to produce evidence incriminating the so-called tri-border. But the lack of research precluded saying much else. So, as much as the ties I claimed with Arabness and Brazilianness, it was what cultural critics Ella Shohat and Robert Stam might characterize as an *"anti-US-policy"* stance that kept me going in the research that resulted in this book.[97] That is, I take my place alongside Arabs at the border and other circumstantial protagonists on a hemispheric field of exceptional rule.

# PART I

# AUTHORITARIAN LEGACIES

(1960S–1990S)

## CHAPTER 1

# Semiperipheral Marches

**Lebanese, Palestinians, and Syrians** traded westward and eastward, hardly upsetting the north-south asymmetry of this hemisphere. On the Brazilian side of the border, their exportation of Brazilian manufactures to Paraguay converged with Brazilian military heads of state who renewed the westward expansion previously known as the *marcha para o oeste* (march toward the west, in Portuguese).[1] Likewise, Arabs in the Paraguayan border town imported consumer goods from Panama that were then sold to a mostly Brazilian clientele, fitting into the Paraguayan military head of state's own geopolitical agenda, denominated as the *marcha hacia el este* (march toward the east, in Spanish).[2]

In step with state-led marches, Arabs helped draw Paraguay, theretofore dominated by Argentina and the US, into Brazil's expansive manufacturer and consumer markets from 1960s to the 1980s. Arabs led transnational trade and presided over business associations on each side of the Friendship Bridge between Foz do Iguaçu and what was then called Ciudad Presidente Stroessner (named after the Paraguayan military head of state, Alfredo Stroessner). Attracting attention in neither Argentina nor the US, Arabs at the border were investigated and absolved by the Brazilian military government after the 1970 attack on the Israeli embassy in the Paraguayan capital of Asunción. On the Brazilian side of the border, Arabs exported Brazilian-made manufactures to Paraguayan traders.

On the Paraguayan side of the border, they imported consumer goods from Panama's free trade zone for sale to mostly Brazilian clients. Through liberal trade exceptions in illiberal regimes, Arabs animated a semiperipheral America that neither simply led to nor derived from US sway in the hemisphere.

This chapter engages with Paul Amar's emphasis on the autonomy of the semiperiphery.[3] World systems theorists in the 1960s viewed semiperipheral countries like Brazil and Argentina as mitigating between an economic core or center, namely the US, and a periphery, such as Paraguay. Building on Amar's rethinking of the semiperiphery as "generative," instead of primarily derivative, this chapter looks at economic hierarchies that cannot be reduced to or explained by US influence in Latin America during the Cold War.[4] On the Brazilian side, Arabs extended Brazilian manufacturing over Paraguay. On the Paraguayan side, Arabs expanded Brazilian consumption with imports from the Colón Free Zone (CFZ), which the Panamanian government opened to wrest some economic benefit from US control of the Canal Zone.[5] In helping Brazil "replace Argentina and the United States as Paraguay's principal source of capital and technology,"[6] Arabs folded into this semiperipheral America that can "neither fully escape . . . nor be reduced" to America's so-called core.[7]

Arabs provide a refreshing approach to well-studied liberal economic agendas under authoritarian rule.[8] Turning from state capitals to frontiers, this chapter asks how migrant traders negotiated liberal economic policies of otherwise illiberal, inward-oriented regimes during the construction of the Itaipu hydroelectric dam between Brazil and Paraguay.[9] On the Brazilian side, Arabs used the military regime's tax exemptions in order to export Brazilian-made manufactures to Paraguayan clients across the Friendship Bridge. On the Paraguayan side, Arabs used the dictatorship's "special" import taxes to bring in consumer items that were sold to Brazilian "shoppers" (called *compristas* or *sacoleiros*, in Spanish and Portuguese) who crisscrossed the same bridge. These state fiscal exceptions begun by illiberal authorities were continued by liberal successors, who became increasingly suspicious of Arab traders due not to perceived political subversion but rather presumed tax evasion and other speculations about economic duplicity. In authoritarian and post-authoritarian times, Arabs came to terms with exceptional rule in ways that undermined their fuller enfranchisement later on.

## Redrawing Borders Westward and Eastward

Early Arab migrants helped expand the manufacturing center of São Paulo westward into one of Brazil's economic fringes, then called *a região das três fronteiras* (the region of the three borders, in Portuguese) or *tres fronteras* (three borders, in Spanish). As mentioned in the introduction, in 1951, a sojourner from Baaloul, Ibrahim Barakat, headed to Brazil while his brothers and co-villagers went to Canada and the US. After "peddling with some friends" in the state of São Paulo, Ibrahim's sales routes led him southwestward into the state of Paraná. Eventually, he reached Foz do Iguaçu on the western edge of Paraná that borders with Paraguay. His son recalled: "My father said that at the time, there was not any cloth or clothing. In two or three weeks, he sold everything and, like this, he kept traveling between São Paulo and Foz do Iguaçu."[10] Supplied from São Paulo, Ibrahim set up a shop of clothing and accessories on Avenida Brasil (Brazil Avenue), the main street of the then small town of Foz do Iguaçu.[11]

Ahmed Hamad Rahal extended the influence of São Paulo even further. In 1951, with empty pockets, he departed the same village of Baaloul for São Paulo. As his sales routes led him into the state of Paraná, this Rahal continued westward until he reached Foz do Iguaçu, encountering a few other Arab families, including the Barakat's. Rahal sold clothing and accessories by boat on the Paraná River between Brazil and Paraguay, a decade and a half before the building of the Friendship Bridge. In 1953, his brother, Mohamad, arrived in Foz do Iguaçu. Ahmed's wife followed three years later. By 1958, with start-up capital saved by commercializing goods from São Paulo and other coastal industries, the Rahal brothers opened A Casa das Fábricas (The Factory Outlet, fig., in Portuguese) on

Avenida Brasil. Later, the brothers founded an export firm on the Brazilian side of the Friendship Bridge, catering to clients from Paraguay's then underdeveloped *este* (East, in Spanish).[12]

Likewise drawing upon, and being drawn into, the expansion of São Paulo into Brazil's west and Paraguay's east, Mohamed Ali Osman traded amid the São Paulo coffee boom overflowing into the northern part of the Paraná state where he settled with his brother.[13] In the early 1950s, Osman was given a trunk full of clothes, and as he recalled, "I went off peddling. . . . I would sell on the farms, plantations, and in the coffee fields of the region." This Osman soon started a business buying and selling coffee beans and other grains. In 1959, his younger brother Mustafa arrived and also peddled in northern Paraná, still dependent upon São Paulo's coffee boom. With their savings, the brothers headed westward to Foz do Iguaçu and opened a *lojinha* (little store) of clothing and knick-knacks (*armarinhos*) on Avenida Brasil, with suppliers based in São Paulo and elsewhere. As examined later, these and other Osman brothers went on to establish an export firm, Têxtil Osman Ltda., with mostly Paraguayan customers.

At the time, these continental marches were led by migrants from villages in Lebanon's Beqaa Valley. Originally from Baaloul, the aforementioned Ibrahim Barakat, and his wife, Amine, sponsored the migration of the Omairi family from the neighboring village of Lela where Amine was born. In 1967, Akra Omairi arrived from Lela and was later joined by his brother, Mohamad. Together they set up shop on the Brazilian side of the border. Years later another Omairi family from Lela opened an import/export tire company, Ferrari Cubiertas S.R.L. (Ferrari Tires), on the Paraguayan side. Migrants from the Ghotme, Mannah, Tarabain, and other families repeated such trajectories from Lela and equaled in number their counterparts from Baaloul who ran businesses on the Brazilian and Paraguayan sides of the border. Others departed from elsewhere in the Beqaa Valley and South Lebanon, but the largest portion of migrants in the 1950s, 1960s, and 1970s stemmed from Baaloul and Lela.

These and other Arabs helped redraw a hemispheric border between west and east without upsetting the north-south order of the US Alliance for Progress in Latin America.[14] Mohamad Rahal stated that he and other migrants chose Foz do Iguaçu because "bordering with two other countries was really important. We knew that Paraguay wasn't industrialized . . . so we were certain that Paraguay would be a great market for industrialized goods" (from Brazil).[15] As noted, he and others peddled manufactures from mostly São Paulo on the Brazilian and Paraguayan sides of the border. Abdul Rahal, another member of *beyt Rahal* (Rahal "house," lit., or "lineage," fig., in Arabic) who arrived on the Brazilian side at midcentury, remembered the "cold" nights he spent on his sales routes that brought Brazilian goods into the "East of Paraguay." Rahal continued, "at that time, around 1959, Argentina was the power over Paraguay. Only Argentine products were allowed." So when he straddled the river by boat selling Brazilian-made wares to Paraguayans, Rahal laughed, "it was if they had seen a snake with two heads."[16] Indeed, in 1960, Argentina and the US were the largest sources of imports into Paraguay, while Brazil accounted for less than 1 percent.[17] Arab traders helped strengthen Brazil's economic expansion over Paraguay with continental ramifications.[18]

In sidestepping the town of Puerto Iguazú on the Argentine side of the border, Arabs signaled the end of Argentina's "long-run advantage" over Paraguay, to borrow a phrase from historian Harris Gaylord Warren.[19] In 1969, the Argentine official, Isaac Rojas, warned of Argentina's loss of influence to Brazil in the River Plate Basin (*Bacia do Prata*, in Portuguese, and *Cuenca del Plata*, in Spanish), a watershed basin of three million kilometers whose center is the border where Brazil, Paraguay, and Argentina meet.[20] At the time, Argentina's largest newspaper, *Clarín*, bemoaned this geopolitical loss in a series of reports on "Puerto Iguazú," located in the Argentine province of "Misiones," named after the ruins of Jesuit missions, flanked by Paraguay to the west and Brazil to the east. Though mentioning the *cataratas* (waterfalls) as a "Giant of America," *Clarín* bemoaned Puerto Iguazú's lack of "progress" in relation to not only other parts of Argentina but also the "booming" Brazilian and Paraguayan sides of the border.[21] "Argentina is losing the battle against Brazil and Paraguay," decried *Clarín,* expressing envy of the "developed infrastructure" along "the Friendship Bridge, over the Paraná River." The Argentine daily called to connect the Argentine side of

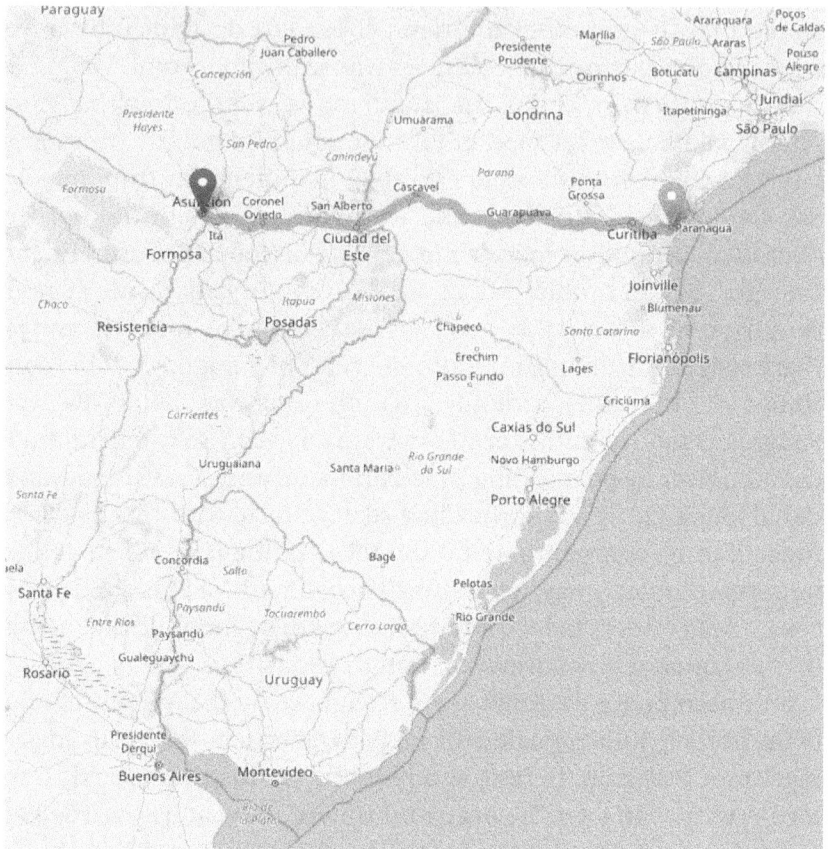

**Figure 1.1.** Transcontinental view of the Brazilian federal highway BR-277, from the Brazilian port of Paranaguá on the Atlantic coast that turns into the Paraguayan Ruta 7 after the Friendship Bridge and ends in the Paraguayan capital of Asunción. © OpenStreetMap contributors

the border to the Brazilian side as well as a paved roadway to Posadas, the provincial capital of Misiones.[22] Arabs generally avoided the Argentine side that was relatively detached from the wider border.

Trading across the Friendship Bridge between Brazil and Paraguay, Arabs helped to displace Argentina without drawing attention from the US.[23] On the Brazilian and Paraguayan sides of the border, Arabs brought in goods on Paraná's federal highway, the BR-277, which led from and to the Atlantic Ocean port of Paranaguá where the Brazilian government had conceded a duty-free zone for Paraguay.[24] The infrastructure enabled the transportation

**Figure 1.2.** Border view of the connection between the Brazilian federal highway BR-277 and the Friendship Bridge that leads to/from the Paraguayan Ruta 7. © OpenStreetMap contributors

of manufactures westward from Brazil to Paraguay, and in return, agricultural goods eastward from Paraguay to Brazil.[25] The Paraguayan military head of state characterized this link to the Brazilian coast as a "second lung," in addition to the port of Buenos Aires in Argentina that had theretofore been landlocked Paraguay's primary maritime access.[26] Not jeopardizing relations with the US, Paraguay's turn from Argentina toward Brazil gained momentum after the founding of "Ciudad Presidente Stroessner" (as noted, later renamed "Ciudad del Este") at the border in 1957.[27] At the Friendship Bridge, Arab importers and exporters embarked upon a new west-east passage in a hemispheric America generally imagined on a north-south grid.

Paraguay's eastward turn toward Brazil materialized in the new Paraguayan border town where Arabs increasingly led much of the trade and finance. Initially, Christian Syrians from the Paraguayan capital of Asunción acquired real estate in what became the town's "microcenter." Known by his initials, HDD, Humberto Domínguez Dibb obtained sizeable properties and was said to have owned shares in the Paraguayan border town's *Acaray Casino*.[28] HDD was born to Syrian-Lebanese parents in Asunción in 1943. His marriage to Stroessner's daughter, Graciela, magnified his sway.[29] Known for imported cloth in Asunción, Elias Saba constructed one of the first buildings in the Paraguayan border town in 1973, and Saba's own son married the daughter of General Andrés Rodríguez before the latter led an internal coup that toppled Stroessner, discussed later.[30] With such high-profile marriages, Arabs' image transformed from that of lowly peddlers to high rollers.[31] On his own path of upward mobility, Mihail Bazas hailed from the same Syrian village as HDD's parents, Mharde (Muharda), near Hama. Bazas was based in his uncle's wholesale business in Asunción and followed a sales route that ended in the Paraguayan border town.[32] Having arrived in 1967, Bazas recalled that his uncle's store specialized in imports from Germany and Japan, such as personal care accessories, like nail clippers, as well as gift items including stainless-steel cutlery sets and ceramic or crystal decorations. His uncle placed the orders through a German importer in Asunción, and Bazas served as the distributor to predominantly Muslim Lebanese retailers based in Ciudad Presidente Stroessner, who in turn sold such products to mostly Brazilian customers temporarily crossing over the bridge.

Catering to these Brazilian clients, Muslim Lebanese from Baaloul and Lela established brick and mortar stores in the Paraguayan border town while their Christian counterparts, with the exception of Bazas, generally remained in the Paraguayan capital. In the mid-1960s, Ali Said Rahal from Lela opened the Casa de la Amistad (Friendship Outlet, fig., in Spanish) named after the bridge. Located on Avenida San Blás, the main thoroughfare of the Paraguayan border town, this Rahal catered to Brazilian consumers in search of name-brand imports without the high taxes of Brazil's then protectionist economy. According to his son, Fawas, the father "would sell whiskey, imported spirits that you didn't have here, as well as Lee jeans."[33] Hussein Taijen from Baaloul, who soon sponsored the migration of his brother, Said, opened the Casa Colombia (Colombia Outlet, fig., in Spanish). According to Said, the brothers set up their shop "next to Rahal's store."[34] The name of the store derived from Hussein's migration route from Lebanon to Colombia, around 1963.[35] Moving from Barranquilla to Maicao on the

Colombian-Venezuelan border, this Taijen subsequently headed to Foz do Iguaçu until permanently settling in the Paraguayan border town in 1969.[36] His Casa Colombia sold clothing, perfume, liquor, electronics, and other items for Brazilian and Argentine customers. As explored later, in the 1970s and 1980s, Rahal, Taijen, and other Arabs in the Paraguayan border town imported consumer goods from Panama for sale to consumers based on the other sides of the border.

Arabs at the border became subjects of interest of the Brazilian state after an unrelated shooting occurred at the Israeli embassy in Asunción on May 4, 1970.[37] Brazilian, and not Paraguayan,[38] media directed suspicion toward Arabs at the border, citing the Paraguayan police as a source in questioning whether "the guns used by two Palestinians in the attack against the embassy of Israel in Asunción could have been bought in Brazil." By September 1970, the Department of Political and Social Order (DOPS) of Brazil's Federal Police in Curitiba solicited the police commissioner in Foz do Iguaçu to investigate several allegations.[39] On a mimeograph entitled "Activities of Arab Terrorist Organizations in Brazil," DOPS asked whether Arabs at the border were involved in Palestinian causes and helped plan the embassy attack in Asunción. Three Lebanese in Foz do Iguaçu and Ciudad Presidente Stroessner were named as suspects and alleged *contrabandistas* (tax-evasive "smugglers"). After a month, however, the officer responded that no evidence linked the shooting in Paraguay's capital to this border. His report, however, provided details about mostly Lebanese and Palestinians who lived in Foz do Iguaçu and operated businesses in Ciudad Presidente Stroessner, including passport or ID information as well as home and business addresses. The Brazilian state used the incident in the Paraguayan capital to surveil Arabs at a border of increasing significance.

Gaining institutional influence the same year in Paraguay's east, Hussein and Said Taijen co-founded what was called the Centro de Comerciantes de Ciudad Presidente Stroessner (Center for Traders of Ciudad Presidente Stroessner).[40] In 1972, it was renamed the Cámara de Comercio (Chamber of Commerce) of Ciudad Presidente Stroessner "by a decree made by Stroessner."[41] Said explained that the chamber of commerce was established with the intention to "help the city's commerce progress" and "represent the interests of traders before the government." Although the first president was a "paraguayo" (Paraguayan), Said pointed out that mostly Arabs and Asians were founding members since they controlled much of the border town's trade. By the early 1980s, Hussein became president of the chamber of commerce and held the post for the next two decades. In interacting with other chambers of commerce as well as governments and businesses, Taijen's presidency put him in a key position to arbitrate disputes among importers in the Paraguayan border town and suppliers abroad.

Likewise gaining influence in Brazil's west, Fouad Mohamed Fakih was invited to become president of the Commercial and Industrial Association of Foz do Iguaçu, known by its acronym, Acifi, mentioned in the introduction. Founded by lumber traders decades before,[42] Acifi expanded into commercial affairs under Fakih's two mandates from 1974 to 1980. Born in Baaloul, Fakih migrated to Brazil as a young boy after his father, Mohamed (nicknamed sr. Júlio), returned to Lebanon after a short stint in Colombia.[43] With his parents and five siblings, Fakih studied in schools on the outskirts of Foz do Iguaçu. Attentive to news reports about the Itaipu dam project, Fakih decided to settle in the city because, as he later recalled, Foz do Iguaçu had "a very promising perspective" since "it bordered on two countries."[44] Initially, Fakih opened "uma lojinha de roupas" (a small clothing store) on Avenida Brasil.[45] His subsequent appointment as Acifi president put him in a position of influence in relation to Foz do Iguaçu's military-appointed mayor, Coronel Clóvis Viana, who Fakih lobbied to ensure the donation of a public plot of land where Acifi's headquarters were built.[46] This Arab-led trade took shape as Brazilian and Paraguayan states signed the Itaipu Treaty in 1973, flowing alongside the "pharaonic" construction of the world's then largest hydroelectric dam.[47]

## Centering Brazil on the Continent

Arabs' exportation of Brazilian manufactures to Paraguay sidestepped Argentina and avoided taking on the US. From Avenida

Brasil in the city center of Foz do Iguaçu, most Arabs opened export-trading firms (*exportadoras*) in the neighborhoods of Jardim Jupira and Vila Portes next to the Friendship Bridge. Introduced earlier, Ahmed and Mohamed Rahal used profits from their shop to open Exportadora Tupy (Tupy Export) in 1968, selling several lines of Brazilian-made manufactures to Paraguayan clients.[48] Abdul Rahal established the Exportadora Líder (Leader Export) that earned "12 million cruzados a month selling processed foods and cleaning supplies to Paraguay." According to this Rahal, "Early on, we would sell only to buyers in the Paraguayan capital of Asunción . . . [but] Itaipu brought the clientele almost to within our stores."[49] Akra and Mohammad Omeiri opened the Exportadora Real (Royal Export), which a Brazilian newspaper later characterized as "an example of immigrants [in Brazil] taking initiative with Paraguayans in commercial affairs."[50]

Arabs applied for Brazilian state fiscal exceptions and avoided questioning the National Security Doctrine that suspended constitutional processes, more fully addressed in the next chapter. The bureaucratic state's first Minister of Finance, Roberto Campos (1964–1967), and his successor, Antônio Delfim Netto (1967–1974), expanded an "export incentive program" for "the rapid growth and diversification of exports," prioritizing the creation rather than distribution of wealth.[51] Passed in 1969, "Law-Decree Number 491" provided "fiscal incentives," mostly tax exemptions, for the "exportation of Brazilian manufactures."[52] Arabs and others at the border used this law and avoided questioning "Law Number 5449" that gave federal authorities the right to appoint mayors in "Áreas de Interesse da Segurança Nacional" (Areas of National Security Interest), including Foz do Iguaçu. In 1974, Brazil's National Security Council appointed the former army colonel, Clóvis Cunha Viana, as mayor of Foz do Iguaçu, just before Itaipu damn construction began.[53] Viana remained in that position for the next decade while nominal elections with a censured list of candidates took place elsewhere.[54] Arabs, like other merchants, applied for tax rebates and avoided challenging the military government.[55]

In what came to be called the *comércio de exportação* (commercial exportation) in Foz do Iguaçu, Arabs leveraged the liberal exceptions of illiberal government. Ibrahim Barakat and his son, for instance, cultivated long-lasting friendships with Brazilian state tax inspectors and high-level authorities through their businesses in Foz do Iguaçu which served clientele across the border. Although they were unduly investigated by intelligence and police forces after the unrelated May 1970 shooting at an Israeli diplomatic office in Asunción, mentioned above, the son, Mohamad, today emphasized not this repression but rather the policy that enabled exporters in Foz do Iguaçu to cut nearly in half their taxable income by selling Brazilian-made goods to Paraguayans.[56] In an "area of national security," on Brazil's side of the border, Arabs' most common experience with the military government was filling out a carbon-copy application form for exportation, the "guia de exportação" (Export Delivery Note) attached to the sales receipt of the exported goods and filed in the office of the Carteira de Comércio Exterior (Foreign Trade Portfolio, known by the acronym in Portuguese, *Cacex*) of the *Banco do Brasil* (Bank of Brazil). The Cacex branch in Foz do Iguaçu "was the agency that emitted the largest number of *guias de exportação* in Brazil." When this paperwork procedure was digitalized years later, it was reported that the city of Foz do Iguaçu alone was annually generating 300,000 delivery notes, "the largest in volume" in Brazil.[57] Rather than the intelligence and surveillance forces, Arabs emphasized greater contact with fiscal exceptional rule in authoritarian times.

Arab-run export businesses gained renown among financial and governmental officials in authoritarian times. The respective export firms of the Rahal and Osman brothers that sold "cloth and food staples to Paraguay" were etched into the memory of Tibiriçá Botto Guimarães, a Brazilian of Portuguese origin born in the city of Join-ville in the neighboring state of Santa Catarina. Guimarães recalled that, when he arrived in Foz do Iguaçu as a branch manager of the *Banco Nacional do Comércio* in 1967, "I would pick up the cash from these export firms in sacks. A lot of money was being made and the export firms were really growing."[58] In 1974, so many Arabs ran businesses in the aforementioned neighborhood of Jardim Jupira that a bill was proposed to rename one of the streets Rua República Árabe Unida (United Arab Republic Street), after the short-lived

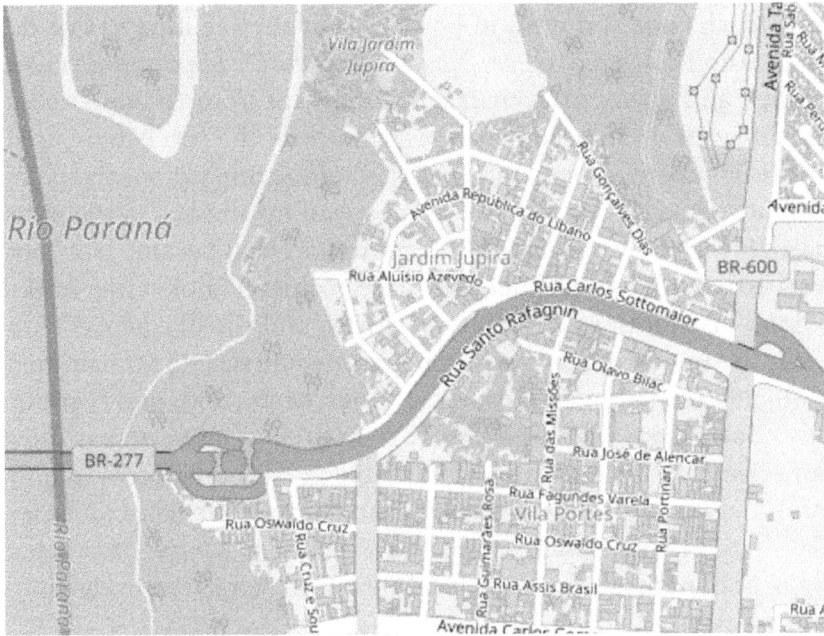

**Figure 1.3.** Map of the location of the Avenida República do Líbano in the neighborhood of Jardim Jupira in Foz do Iguaçu, just north of the BR-277 and minutes from the Friendship Bridge. © OpenStreetMap contributors

polity that brought together Egypt and Syria.[59] Although that legislation never passed, two years later city councilor Aguinello Favero Haus proposed another bill that successfully renamed another thoroughfare in the same neighborhood Avenida República do Líbano (Republic of Lebanon Avenue).[60] With the support of the military government's political party (ARENA) that Haus belonged to, the bill related that, "one finds innumerable Lebanese there, constructing new buildings" and "they came here when the city still did not offer the best conditions of prosperity, helping our development." The military-appointed mayor signed the bill into law the same year. For authoritarian-era bank employees and government officials, Arabs helped give rise to Brazil at this crossroads.

Arabs in Foz do Iguaçu utilized their networks with São Paulo in expanding Brazilian industrial influence westward into Paraguay's east. In the mid-1970s, the Rahal brothers' Exportadora Tupy became a beer and soft-drink distributor for Brazilian and multi-national companies based in São Paulo, starting out "with two trucks and a thousand bottles" that they refilled in Foz do Iguaçu and delivered to Paraguayan customers.[61] Exportadora Líder, owned and operated by their fellow migrant from Baaloul, Abdul Rahal, went on to become the distributor of the São Paulo-based textile company, Alpargatas, allegedly selling thirty thousand pairs of blue jeans every month to Paraguayan businesses in the early 1980s.[62] Similarly, the Omeiri's Exportadora Real became "the largest reseller of Cônsul," a household electronics manufacturer in São Paulo, distributing refrigerators, stoves, and the like across Paraguay as well as other "Latin American countries."[63] Mohammed Osman's Têxtil Osman Ltda. represented Kraft Foods and "various Brazilian brands with the exclusive right to exportation across Latin America."[64] The non- and semi-durable goods commercialized by Arab-owned *exportadoras* arrived from coastal Brazilian industries for storage in warehouses next to the Friendship Bridge. After being sold, shipments were transported westward across the bridge into Paraguay.

Arabs in Foz do Iguaçu specialized in Brazilian-based industrialized goods that were purchased by everyday Paraguayans. On the Brazilian side of the border, Arabs led commercial establishments that annually doubled in number "to attend to the neighboring country [Paraguay]."[65] The "system of commerce" in Foz do Iguaçu, observed *Nosso Tempo* in 1983, included "supermarkets" and "stores that sell electrodomestic appliances and heavy machinery."[66] In 1986, the estimated three hundred "export businesses" in Foz do Iguaçu transacted an estimated one-hundred million dollars of external sales to Paraguay.[67] From the neighborhoods of Jardim Jupira and Vila Portes, Arab-run firms commercialized canned foods, grains, textiles, household appliances, and some heavier machinery.[68] In 1987, the former president of Acifi, Fouad Fakih, noted that "Paraguayans are responsible for 75 percent of all this [commercial] movement."[69] He continued: "Paraguay doesn't produce practically anything and its population can't afford to buy what is sold in Ciudad Presidente Stroessner, expensive products directed toward [Brazilian] tourists." As a result, Fakih concluded, everyday Paraguayans shopped for clothing and foodstuffs as well as home appliances in Foz do Iguaçu. The familiarity of Arab-driven border trade was evident when a Paraguayan client gave a blank check to Mohamed Osman and asked him to fill in the cost of her purchase. "It's trust," Osman remarked.[70] Another Paraguayan farm owner purchasing supplies in Foz do Iguaçu noted, "we came by car to get supplies and other necessary products for the start of the harvest."[71]

But Arabs in Foz do Iguaçu avoided criticism of authoritarian Paraguay and Brazil's support of it, despite exercising a range of political affiliations after the most repressive years of Brazilian military rule under Emílio Garrastazu Médici (1969–1974). In 1975, Mohamad Barakat became a naturalized Brazilian citizen.[72] He and his father ran Novo Mundo Eletrodomésticos Ltda (New World Appliances), which the progressive newspaper *Nosso Tempo* called "one of the largest commercial businesses in Foz do Iguaçu." Barakat later opened Barakat Free Shop, which specialized in domestic home supplies. Having studied in Canada and the US, Barakat cultivated this business savvy as he drifted toward the Partido Movimento Democrático Brasileiro (Party of the Brazilian Democratic Movement, known by the acronym in Portuguese, PMDB), after the legalization of a plural political party system in 1979. In contrast, Kamal Osman distanced himself from *Nosso Tempo* when the progressive newspaper drew the ire of the military-appointed mayor, who Osman welcomed at the grand opening of his store, Kamalito Magazine, on Avenida Brasil.[73] This Osman had previously settled in the town of Assaí in northern Paraná and earned his degree in economics at the Universidade Estadual de Londrina before establishing his store that specialized in women's, men's, and children's clothing, sports accessories, toys, house utensils, and kindred goods.[74] Later, this Osman founded the mosque and inaugurated Kamal Osman Exportação to export Brazilian textiles and clothing to Paraguay.[75] Discussed more in detail next chapter, Arabs on the liberalizing Brazilian side of the border did business with but avoided criticizing illiberal Paraguay.

Centering Brazil on the continent, Arabs and others in Foz do Iguaçu lobbied to export goods in Brazilian currency, the cruzeiro (Cr$, 1970–1986, 1990–1993) and the cruzado (Cz$, 1986–1990). According to Fakih, in 1975 Brazil's Federal Revenue Secretariat passed a normative resolution to "do away with exportation" in Brazilian currency and attempted to standardize Brazilian exportation in US dollars. Fakih recalled, "we had a fight of two years to maintain the system" in Brazil's currency.[76] At the end of his second term, in 1980, this "Homeric struggle" was continued by incoming Acifi president Wádis Benvenutti, a Brazilian of Italian origins, born and raised in Rio Grande do Sul. Benvenutti explained that Brazil's exportation to Paraguay had the advantage over neighboring Argentina, whose exported goods in US dollars were more expensive. In Foz do Iguaçu, commercial exporters' preference for Brazilian currency was also probably due to the practice of "profiting through stockpiling" ("ganhar em cima do estoque"), when they purchased large amounts of manufactures from Brazilian industries at a set price (in Brazil's currency) and placed them in storage.[77] With time, these stockpiles were worth several times their original value, as price indexes rose with skyrocketing Brazilian interest rates.[78] Exporting in the US dollar would have curbed this lucrative tactic. Whichever was the key motivating factor, Arabs and other exporters successfully sought to export merchandise in Brazilian currency by repeatedly meeting with Cacex and other Brazilian government officials. Even in 1988, "Arab community leaders who commercially export via Foz do Iguaçu to Paraguay asked authorities to pressure Cacex in order to safeguard their (Arabs') ability to make transactions in cruzados for all merchandise."[79] In a semiperipheral America, Arabs and others in Foz do Iguaçu secured "a freer exchange between the three countries (Brazil, Paraguay, and Argentina), since no one had US dollars."[80]

Not taking on but unable to escape from the US, Arabs paid attention to Paraguayan purchase power that was tied to Brazilian exchange rates relative to the US dollar. When Brazil's currency lost value relative to the US dollar, Paraguayans could afford to buy greater quantities of goods in Foz do Iguaçu, whether or not paying in Paraguayan currency, the Guaraní (₲). In 1980, a Brazilian reporter took note of the devalued cruzeiro that made Foz do Iguaçu into a "center for shopping . . . with the prices of foodstuffs and clothing cheaper than in Paraguay. . . . All kinds of goods are acquired in Foz and it's obvious that there was a daily increase of Paraguayan . . . shoppers in Foz do Iguaçu, in order to obtain supplies of canned goods, cereals, meats, and fruits and vegetables."[81] Contrastively, when Paraguay's Guaraní lost value in relation to the US dollar, Paraguayans curtailed shopping on Brazil's side of the border. In 1985, commerce in Foz do Iguaçu nearly ground to a halt when the Guaraní was devalued, losing more than half its value in relation to the US dollar.[82] Accordingly, Arabs in Foz do Iguaçu priced exports in Brazilian currency and kept an eye on the value of the US dollar because the purchase power of their Paraguayan customers was tied to it. Arabs strengthened trade on the semiperiphery, neither escaping nor adopting the US currency in a hemispheric America. Moving aside but not removing so-called "manifest destiny," Arabs folded into and took ownership of this semiperipheral America.

## Paraguay's "Port" Linking Central and South America

Meanwhile, Arabs on the Paraguayan side of the border helped transform Ciudad Presidente Stroessner into a kind of "port" on land (*puerto*, in Spanish, or *porto*, in Portuguese). In Paraguay's *este*, they opened stores on or near Avenida San Blás and Avenida Monseñor Rodríguez, parallel to the Ruta 7 highway that leads to and from the Friendship Bridge. In 1972, Faisal Hammoud, alongside his brothers Sadek and Sharif, established the Monalisa store that specializes in imported spirits, perfumes, cosmetics, and electronics. Faisal had departed Baaloul for São Paulo and eventually landed in Paraguay with the equivalent of five dollars in his pocket.[83] After some success, the Hammoud brothers constructed their six-story complex, and a decade and a half later, Faisal became the president of the Paraguayan border town's branch of the US-sponsored Cámara de Comercio Paraguayo Americano (further discussed in Chapter 4).[84] Arriving in 1972, the Mannah brothers, Mohamed (nicknamed Alexandre) and Atef, opened La Petisquera (On a Silver Platter, fig.), which came to specialize in imported spirits, highbrow foods, perfumes, and cosmetics.[85] Alexandre co-founded the Cámara de Comercio de Ciudad Presidente Stroessner and much later headed the local branch of Paraguay's Federation of Production, Industry, and Commerce (whose acronym, in Spanish, is FEPRINCO).[86] Five Hijazi brothers likewise departed Kabrikha in

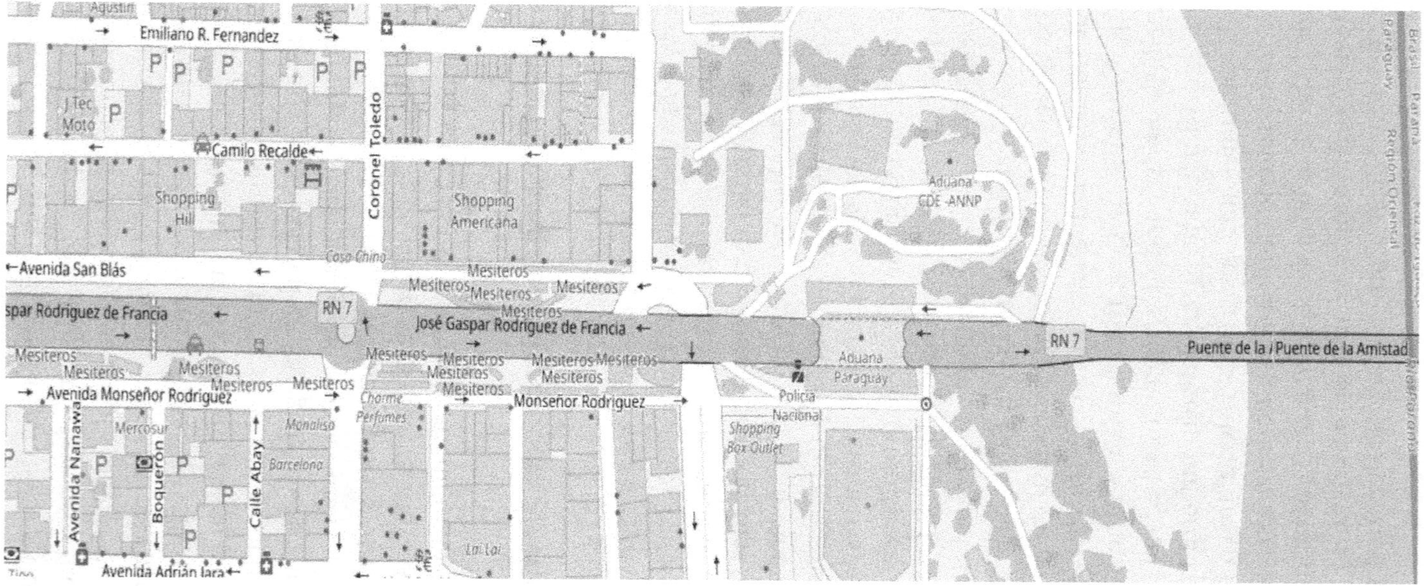

**Figure 1.4.** Partial view of the Paraguayan national highway Ruta 7, in Ciudad Presidente Stroessner (which became Ciudad del Este after 1989). Avenida San Blás is just to the north and Avenida Monseñor Rodríguez is just to the south of Ruta 7. © OpenStreetMap contributors

South Lebanon in the 1970s and opened Mundo Electronico (Electronic World). Led by Adnan and Hassan, their business was called "one of stores that has the largest commercial movement of this city," specializing in electronic goods of "North-American, Japanese, German, and Panamanian origins."[87] In the 1980s, "Arab, Chinese, and Korean immigrants"[88] made up most of seven-hundred or so shops in the Paraguayan border town that was often called "Puerto" or "Porto" Presidente Stroessner.

On this Paraguayan side of the border, Arabs served Brazilian consumers amid the relative suspension of authoritarian-era border controls and tariffs. Bazas, Rahal, and Taijen explained that stores on the Paraguayan side of the border "always" catered to "Brazilian buyers" (*compristas brasileños*, in Spanish). Their clients were formally called "tourist-shoppers" (*turista-compristas*, in Portuguese and Spanish), but were also known by the pejorative label *sacoleiro* (bagger, lit., shopper fig., in Portuguese). At least since the 1960s, everyday Brazilians traveled to Foz do Iguaçu, crossed the Friendship Bridge to shop for the day in Ciudad Presidente Stroessner, and later returned to their homes elsewhere in Brazil. These tens of thousands of Brazilian shoppers could meet formal border-crossing requirements such as a police exit visa (*visto policial de saída*) from Brazil's Federal Police or a provisionary tourist card (*tarjeta de facilitación turistica*) from Paraguayan police.[89] With exceptional ease in crisscrossing this policed border, Brazilian shoppers headed to mostly Arab-owned shopping complexes in Ciudad Presidente Stroessner, including the Jebai Center, the Galeria Rahal, and the Hijazi Shopping Center.[90] Arab-owned stores carried everything from "sophisticated electronics" to the "famous Chinese ointment" (tiger-balm).[91] Brazilian shoppers sought out Sony video-cassette recorders, Olympus cameras, Toshiba or Brother word-processors, and to a lesser extent, carpets from Iran, perfumes from France, and spirits from Scotland, or cheaper imitations.[92] This merchandise was prohibitively expensive in Brazil due to authoritarian and post-authoritarian government tariffs of "up to 300 percent of the imported item's value."[93] Between the 1960s and 1980s, so many Brazilian "housewives, senior citizens, students, liberal professionals, and idle folks" crossed the Friendship Bridge to buy lower-priced consumer goods that it was like "a Brazilian party in Ciudad Presidente Stroessner."[94]

Arab trade on the Paraguayan side of the border developed in tandem with Brazil's growing influence.[95] In 1973, a Paraguayan border trader, Luis O'Hara, associated each "foreign" presence with one another at an event in the Asunción headquarters of FEPRINCO. O'Hara bemoaned not only that "60 percent of commerce" was "in the hands of Syrian-Lebanese" (*sirio-libaneses*) but also that 70 percent of agricultural production was dominated by "ciudadanos extranjeros de otras nacionalidades" (foreign citizens of other nationalities), in reference to (non-Arab) Brazilians who owned large plots of land on the Paraguayan side of the border.[96] Hailing from the state of Paraná where Foz do Iguaçu is located, the state of Rio Grande do Sul to the south, and later, elsewhere, (non-Arab) Brazilian migrants settled in Paraguay's east,[97] namely in the Paraguayan *departamento* (department, or state) of Alto Parana, tripling the percentage of foreign-born residents between the early 1970s and early 1990s.[98] Thanks to the Paraguayan dictator's repeal of the law that forbid foreigners from buying land, (non-Arab) Brazilian citizens owned agricultural fields around the Paraguayan border town, fitting into the Brazilian state's goal for sway over the one-time Argentine- and US-dominated Paraguay.[99] Though the grandson of migrants from Ireland, O'Hara claimed that he and other Paraguayans defended "national sovereignty," and he called upon the Paraguayan state capital to "rescue" the borderland. His position rallied no support. "Syrian-Lebanese" commercial puissance had transformed Ciudad Presidente Stroessner into the second largest city of Paraguay, which now breathed through what the military head of state called a "second lung" in Brazil.

Arabs imported goods into the Paraguayan border town that were then sold to Brazilian consumers thanks to the "complementary" liberal economic exceptions of illiberal regimes.[100] In 1971, the Paraguayan dictatorship simplified customs procedures and lowered import tariffs for businesses specifically in Ciudad Presidente Stroessner.[101] Dubbed the Régimen de Turismo or Régimen Especial, this "tourism duty regime" or "special tax regime" levied a one-time tax on imports upon entrance to the country, based on the expectation that the government inspector would verify the value of merchandise declared by importers and their suppliers.[102] Hussein Taijen later recalled that the tax ranged between 7 and 10 percent for non- and semi-durable merchandise.[103] Paraguayan customs officers next to the Friendship Bridge determined the tax amount after inspecting shipments to verify the country of origin and weighing the container.[104] These procedures took place under the jurisdiction of the appointed mayor (*intendente*) of Ciudad Presidente Stroessner, Carlos Barreto Sarubbi, and his uncle Antonio Oddone Sarubbi, the administrative and police head of the Alto Paraná department. Appointed in 1975, the imperious Sarubbi family was said to "boost trade and traders, with the intention of collecting more for the municipal treasury" and allegedly for themselves too.[105]

Arab trade in Ciudad Presidente Stroessner drew upon and was drawn into this authoritarian Paraguayan apparatus as well as its newfound rapprochement toward Brazil. Take for instance Mohamed Jebai, who I introduce here and more fully explore in the next chapter. Having migrated from Jebba in South Lebanon to South America in the 1960s, Jebai claimed that Paraguay's dictator urged him to go into business because of the so-called "free trade policy" of the border town.[106] Others opined that Jebai got his start in commerce only after accepting Stroessner's wife as his business partner. Temporarily heading the Cámara de Comercio de Ciudad Presidente Stroessner in the 1970s, Jebai imported JVC, Roadstar, and other electronics from Southeast Asia.[107] He and other importers benefited from the Paraguayan Central Bank's policy that suspended the requirement to deposit 100 percent of the value of the imported goods, allowing importers to reimburse the bank after full payment was transferred to creditors abroad.[108] With dizzying sales to a mostly Brazilian clientele through such Paraguayan governmental exceptions, Jebai used his profits to build Ciudad Presidente Stroessner's largest shopping and residential complex in the 1970s. The Galeria Jebai Center, explained a manager later on, had around four hundred store spaces, roughly 40 percent run by Arabs.[109] Arabs reaped the rewards of being "on good terms with the regime" in authoritarian times.

Arabs' transnational trade highlights the heretofore unacknowledged economic flows between Central and South America. In the

1970s and 1980s, Bazas explained, Arabs in Paraguay used the *zona franca* in the Panamanian city of Colón, which attracted businesses with tax benefits and exemptions, strategically located near the then US-dominated Canal Zone.[110] His uncle's store telexed orders for cutlery sets and other merchandise to French, German, and akin companies, which arranged for deposits in Panama to ship the cargo to Paraguay. Jebai and the Hijazi brothers, mentioned earlier, likewise used this shipping entrepôt in requisitioning electronic goods from Japan and other parts of East Asia. In the 1970s, the Taijen brothers also brought many goods—at the time, spirits, jeans, and cigarettes—from Panama. Bazas even wondered whether the commercial tie between Panama and Paraguay had been initiated by Hussein Taijen, or another *paisano* (countryman, lit., Arab countryman, fig., in Spanish) with relatives along the Panamanian and Colombian coasts. Taijen, or another Baaloul villager, was allegedly asked to *llevar en su mala* (to carry in his luggage) some items *para vender* (to sell) in Paraguay. As mentioned, Lebanese from Baaloul were listed as merchants in small towns near and on the Colombian coast just before the mid-twentieth century.[111] Said Taijen, Hussein's brother, shrugged off this possibility and noted that Panama's zona franca was common knowledge and had competitive shipping rates and times.[112] Regardless, Arabs traded through liberal economic exceptions among illiberal states in a Central-South America.

From Panama to Brazil and then to Paraguay, Arabs fashioned a supply chain for the Brazilian consumer market. Varied water and land routes connected Panama's free trade zone to landlocked Paraguay. Before the 1960s, shipments from Colón would first pass through the canal, still under US "stewardship," and then southward to the port in Buenos Aires, whence they were transported north to Asunción. After the aforementioned interstate and infrastructural developments in Brazil, cargo was also shipped to Paraguay's duty-free zone in the Brazilian port of Paranaguá where the BR-277 begins. From there, shipments on trucks headed westward and crossed the Friendship Bridge into Paraguay's east. In the ever-growing customs inspection offices in Ciudad Presidente Stroessner,[113] cargo containers were weighed, and customs officials calculated the tax to be paid by the importers, based on weight and the country of origin. Arab and other importers on the Paraguayan side of the border had cargo shipped from Colón to Paranaguá, and then transported across the BR-277 highway. After transiting through the Paraguayan customs terminal beside the Friendship Bridge, the merchandise in Arab stores was finally sold to consumers mostly stemming from Brazil.

Arabs in Ciudad Presidente Stroessner linked Central and South America in ways that distanced but did not escape North America. On the Paraguayan side of the border, Arabs bought goods from Panama priced in US dollars for sale to Brazilian customers. So, a more expensive US dollar decreased Brazilian purchase power in Paraguay. In 1982, for instance, Arabs and other traders in Ciudad Presidente Stroessner complained that the expensive US dollar after the "devaluation of the cruzeiro" had "completely stopped Brazilian shoppers from coming."[114] But when the US dollar later lost value, according to Brazil's finance minister, Brazilian shoppers made a "large volume of purchases in Puerto Stroessner."[115] In Hassim Mahmoud's Casa Astor in the Paraguayan border town, for instance, the price of a Panasonic videocassette recorder with remote control dropped from $400 to $300, and then to $250.[116] A year later, however, the Brazilian Central Bank's intervention strengthened the US dollar and reduced Brazilians' purchasing power in Ciudad Presidente Stroessner. At the time, Hussein Taijen observed that most shoppers "enter, ask the price and dollar quote, and leave without buying anything."[117] Arab businesses on the Paraguayan side of the border kept on eye on the US dollar in order to gauge Brazilian purchase power. Arabs bolstered trade in a semiperipheral America that could "neither fully escape . . . nor be reduced" to the US.[118]

## A Semiperipheral "Economy of Appearances"

On the semiperiphery, Arabs played leading roles in what anthropologist Anna Tsing called an "economy of appearances."[119] As the "economic structure of Paraguay" became "directly linked" to the "large economic growth" in Brazil, according to a UN report in 1987, Arabs appeared to be profiting as well as profiteering at the border.[120]

On the Brazilian side, Arabs attracted most Paraguayan clients in March, April, and May, the start and high-point of soy, cotton, and other harvests. Meanwhile on the Paraguayan side, Arab stores drew Brazilian consumers year-round, except for January and February, summer vacation months in the southern hemisphere when most people traveled elsewhere. A mélange of authoritarian and post-authoritarian state officials kept close watch over the resultant daily "traffic jams" with "heavy shipments" and "hundreds of vehicles," as well as "antlike" lines of pedestrians and porters crisscrossing the Friendship Bridge.[121] Whether trading westward or eastward across this semiperipheral America, Arabs appeared to consumers, suppliers, state authorities, and even one another as agents of development as well as suspects of double-dealing.

Arabs gained visibility and notoriety in their economic roles. In 1981, the *Diário do Paraná* noted that the members of "the Arab community of Foz do Iguaçu" are "persons with an elevated sensibility" through "their active participation, especially in commerce."[122] Indeed, Mohamad Barakat characterized Arab commercial exportation to Paraguay as "the Arab contribution to Brazilian development."[123] But Humberto Domínguez Dibb, mentioned earlier, accused Arabs on the Brazilian side of the border of economic duplicity. In the *HOY* newspaper he owned in Asunción, Dibb endeavored to show that between 1977 and 1982, not even half of the exports from Brazil were disclosed to Paraguay's Central Bank, relative to the data in Brazil's government export agency, Cacex.[124] Moreover, Paraguayan garment industrialists complained of being undersold by "export firms in Foz do Iguaçu" that had "large warehouses near the bridge," which shipped Brazilian-made clothing to Paraguay each day "without paying any taxes" in Paraguay itself.[125] They pointed fingers at Abdul Rahal's Exportadora Líder in Foz do Iguaçu, which according to the São Paulo-based Alpargatas jeans factory, "sold to the Paraguayan market more jeans than all the jeans factories of Paraguay put together."[126]

Suspicions of double-dealing came to overshadow Arab exporters on the Brazilian side of the border. Their "exported" manufactures that qualified for Brazilian tax breaks were allegedly sold to domestic Brazilian customers. As early as 1973, *ABC Color* took note of "exporters" manipulating "Brazilian policies of stimulation and promotion of exportation" in order to earn a "financial return on top of the value of their exportation that would reach around 40 percent."[127] *ABC Color* found that "one would obtain a delivery or return note in Foz do Iguaçu to export to Paraguay" but the goods never reached "Paraguayan territory."[128] A Brazilian tax inspector much later observed, "at least three hundred businesses from Foz do Iguaçu" filed for tax breaks but the "Brazilian merchandise marked for exportation" came to be "sold to domestic customers" in order "to generate larger profits."[129] According to an Acifi employee, exporters near the Friendship Bridge commonly undertook this practice.[130] He explained that household appliances, foodstuffs, textiles, or other goods marked for exportation to Paraguay were sold domestically in Brazil. He gave the example of Brazilian-made air-conditioners built to work on 120 volts, the electric current in Paraguay. But since 110 voltage is more common in Brazil, exporters sold both the air-conditioner and an "electronic converter box," presumably to use in Brazil. Without Paraguayan verification, the Brazilian government's export agency, Cacex, granted the fiscal exemption when export firms in Foz do Iguaçu filed tax rebate forms with the receipts from ostensible "export" sales. Arab profit-earning could be imagined as profiteering too.

Such suspicions of Arabs distracted attention from authoritarian Brazilian state officials who capitalized on what was still idealized as an "ordered march" of development.[131] In 1980, Foz do Iguaçu's military-appointed mayor "defended" a new "customs office" and undertook infrastructural projects such as the widening of traffic lanes near the bridge to facilitate "export commerce with Paraguay."[132] Located next to the bridge, businesses exporting merchandise to Paraguay did not comment on the fiscal controls but "felt the benefits" of improved roadways.[133] With greater state controls, Brazilian Federal Revenue took charge of inspecting goods and Brazilian Federal Police had jurisdiction over persons, which led to a "war on the backstage." [134] In one instance in 1983, a shipment of goods approved by revenue authorities was stopped by Brazilian police officers ostensibly intending to verify the papers of the individuals transporting the merchandise. "The constant tensions" were not only "disputes over dominion" but also "who got a slice of the lucrative business of *acertos*" (kickbacks, fig.).[135] Not only Arabs and other merchants, but also border government officials could appear as suspects of profiteering if a free press were permitted to more fully undertake investigative reporting.

Similar dynamics took shape on the Paraguayan side of the border, once considered a beacon of "development."[136] In 1982, *ABC Color* noted that "Arabs and Chinese (*arabes y chinos*) were "vying for supremacy in business," with "up-to-date" businesses that sold "valuable, imported products."[137] Their "commercial outlets" (*casas comerciales*) stocked and sold "Scotch whiskies, Japanese electronic equipment, French perfume, Chinese and Japanese silks" and other "foreign products" (*productos extranjeros*). A storeowner in Ciudad Presidente Stroessner related that such goods were "predominantly" sold to "Brazilians," said to be arriving daily in some ten thousand vehicles from Foz do Iguaçu.[138] Another storeowner emphasized that he and others contributed to the development of the zone not by "creating" agricultural or industrial wealth, but rather by "paying for patent rights and other import taxes to the local government" as well as employing local Paraguayan residents. Meanwhile, Brazilian media occasionally lauded some businesses for importing "legitimate" name-brand products, namely the Mannah brothers' La Petisquera and the Hammoud brothers' Monalisa.[139]

But Arabs and the Paraguayan border city also drew suspicions of dealing in *contrabando*, or the tax-evasive smuggling of goods. Early on, *ABC Color* warned of the Paraguayan border city being connected to Panama's Free Trade Zone, which served as "the center of contraband for South America."[140] An Asunción-based business association likewise alleged that the dictatorship's "Special (Tax) Regime" at the border facilitated the clandestine entry of whiskey, cigarettes, and other merchandise that skirted the tariffs stipulated in Paraguayan legislation.[141] Humberto Domínguez Dibb claimed to expose a tax-evasive practice that took advantage of the customs procedure for cargo containers arriving in Ciudad Presidente Stroessner. According to Dibb, importers and state customs officials colluded to reduce the estimated worth of the merchandise, so importers would be charged less tax and state authorities could take their *mordidas* (bites).[142] This *subfaturamento* (under-billing), wrote Dibb, was the "most important economic crime ever committed in the history of our country" of Paraguay.[143] State fiscal exceptions not only underwrote but could also undermine the Paraguayan side of the border, including Arab-led business there.

Authoritarian Paraguayan state officials gained notoriety for lining their own pockets.[144] The mayor of Ciudad Presidente Stroessner, Barreto Sarubbi, allegedly charged importers to use his family's clandestine airstrip to avoid taxes by flying in merchandise, from Panama or elsewhere, splitting the pay-offs with "authorities from Asunción."[145] Juan Pereira, the president of both the city council and the local branch of the regime's political party, started smuggling not long after the founding of Ciudad Presidente Stroessner. In 1983, Sarubbi and Pereira, alongside the aforementioned administrator, Coronel Antonio Sarubbi, attempted to distract attention from their own defrauding of the state by associating "the grave evil of contraband" with *paseros* (porters, fig.), everyday Paraguayans who transported goods from Paraguay to Brazil. Subsequently targeted by state border officials, *paseros* complained that the "authors of the repressive measures 'are the biggest smugglers of the country.'" Paraguayan state-sponsored profiteering expanded by alleging to crackdown on small-time tax-evasive smuggling. Border authorities began "demanding" double the regular amount of kickbacks for each time they "looked the other way" to allow porters to pass across the bridge. These lower-level officials likewise complained of being shaken down by even higher-level authorities who reported to Paraguay's dreaded Interior Minister and Stroessner's own private secretary, Abdo Benitez, addressed more fully next chapter.[146] The regime's leaders drew attention away from their own systematic profiteering by targeting the small-scale "smuggling" of goods, which were purchased from Arab-owned and other stores in Ciudad Presidente Stroessner.

Not speaking of profiteering, Hussein Taijen pointed to the profits on the Paraguayan side of the border. With a nod to liberal exceptions in an otherwise illiberal state, Taijen later stated that the Paraguayan border city is "privileged by certain government concepts. Here we buy merchandise from the world and sell it to Latin

America."[147] With a transcontinental vision, he continued that the Paraguayan side of the border was home to "hundreds of distributors and resellers of products from five continents" that contribute to the "relations between the three countries," Brazil, Paraguay, and Argentina. Taijen affirmed that this "commercial exchange" brought "benefits . . . effectively shared" by Foz do Iguaçu, Ciudad Presidente Stroessner, and Puerto Iguazú. In the Paraguayan border city, he and others "sell imported products from five continents for Brazilians" and the cash they collect "is deposited in bank establishments in Foz do Iguaçu or used to acquire Brazilian merchandise for consumption or commercialization within Paraguay."[148] More fully explored in the sixth chapter, Taijen was referring to a type of bank account in Foz do Iguaçu used by businesses from the Paraguayan side of the border.

Regardless, in a semiperipheral "economy of appearances," any sales transactions on the Paraguayan side, often quoted in the Brazilian currency, could appear as either bolstering or undermining the Brazilian side of the border. Similar to Taijen, Brazilian federal deputy Sergio Spada surmised "a certain balance at the border" since "the Brazilian spends cruzados in Paraguay [and] Paraguay uses these same cruzados to buy foodstuffs, clothing, electronic appliances, and thousands of other products in Foz do Iguaçu, in Brazil."[149] Another Acifi director likewise stated, "The Brazilian tourists leaves many cruzados in Paraguay, but this money, in large part, ends up re-entering Brazil through Paraguayans who buy in Foz do Iguaçu."[150] But Arab and other storeowners in Foz do Iguaçu, like everyday Brazilians traveling to Ciudad Presidente Stroessner, tended to deride Paraguay as synonymous with "counterfeit" goods and "low-brow" tastes.[151] Kamal Osman complained that "the millions of [US] dollars that enter Paraguay could stay in Foz do Iguaçu."[152] Hassan Wahab, a commercial exporter in Foz do Iguaçu, protested that his own Paraguayan clients could not find parking because of Brazilians who "leave their vehicles here and go shopping in Paraguay."[153] Likewise on the Brazilian side of the border, Nagib Assaf observed that "Paraguayans, our biggest clients" could not "even see (our) stores" because of so many Brazilian shoppers parking and heading to the Paraguayan side. The conflicting ways that Arabs and others saw their economic role in this semiperiphery would inform what would become their destiny in subsequent South American state accords for free trade, addressed in Chapter 4, as well as more recent US-led pursuits of allegedly terrorist monies, explored in Chapter 6. Suffice it to say now that on western and eastern sides of the border, as well as of the hemisphere, Arabs served as agents of development as well as suspects of double-dealing during and after authoritarian rule.

From the 1960s to the late 1980s, Arab transnational traders connected and were connected by continental marches: Brazil's "march to the west" and Paraguay's "march to the east." Through commercial networks that reached across the Brazilian coast, landlocked Paraguay, the Panamanian free trade zone of Colón, and beyond, migrants from mostly Lebanon, as well as Palestine and Syria, on both sides of the Friendship Bridge helped link and were linked by this hemisphere. They exported Brazilian-made manufactures to Paraguay and imported goods from Panama into Paraguay for resale to Brazilian consumers. Arabs' respective supply chains and customer bases drew Paraguay away from Argentina and the US and toward Brazil. Neither beginning nor ending in the US, their transnational trading networks folded into this semiperipheral America. But Arabs' accommodation of liberal economic exceptions in authoritarian times made them into easy targets for allegations of economic duplicity, which would come to work against their full enfranchisement in seemingly post-authoritarian transitions.

## CHAPTER 2

# Third World Limits

**Lebanese, Palestinian, and Syrian** migrants on both sides of the Friendship Bridge mobilized in what Vijay Prashad called a "Third World project."[1] Though historically aligned with South American and Middle Eastern governments, their activism was twisted after the Israeli embassy bombing in the Argentine capital of Buenos Aires in 1992. Authorities in Argentina, backed by the US, unduly laid blame with Arabs at the border following governmental failures to bring to trial the authors of the still unresolved attack.[2] Speaking out on the Brazilian side but more openly targeted on the Paraguayan side, Arabs at the border came to embody the "dramatic decline" of Third Worldism.[3]

Arabs experienced this historic arc of the Third World (*terceiro-mundo*, in Portuguese, or *tercer mundo*, in Spanish). Under military- and civilian-led governments at the border, many Lebanese, and some Palestinians and Syrians, called for solidarity with Palestine, as well as Libya or Iran, respectively. On the Brazilian side of the border, Arabs' activism shifted from the military to civilian successors that eventually took over the state. Meanwhile, on the Paraguayan side of the border, Arabs' activism complied with an internal military coup that ousted the dictator but retained the political party of the old regime that won nominally liberal democratic elections. After the unresolved 1992 Israeli embassy attack in Buenos Aires, Arabs on the Brazilian side of the border continued mobilizing, but not in solidarity with counterparts on the Paraguayan side who were targeted by Paraguayan state authorities in collaboration with Argentina and the US. Arabs' activism came to terms with illiberal states that made liberal exceptions as well as liberal states that made illiberal exceptions across the hemisphere.

Set between the 1960s and early 1990s, this chapter intervenes in scholarship on the "Third World" and "Global South" by exploring not only the possibilities but also the limitations of such visions during and after the Cold War.[4] On the Brazilian and Paraguayan sides of the border, migrants mobilized for Palestinian self-determination, as well as Libya's self-declared revolutionary regime or Iran's self-styled Islamic Revolution. Drawing on the work of Pamila Gupta, Christopher Lee, Marissa Moorman, and Sandhya Shukla, this chapter considers the "texture of interpersonal exchanges" in mobilization efforts that "challenge(d) the geopolitical frameworks of the United States and Europe."[5] I locate Arabs at the border in "more vertically oriented South-South engagements," reinforcing the military- and civilian-led Brazilian administrations that "sustained" Paraguay's dictatorship and its political party that held onto power and became increasingly at odds with Argentina and the US.[6] In the authoritarian and post-authoritarian rise of Brazil over the historically Argentine- and US-dominated Paraguay, Arab transnational activism folded into this Third World America.

Arabs at the border accommodated US-backed South American state exceptions toward a transnational Middle East.[7] In the 1970s and 1980s, Arabs mobilized through Third Worldist deviations in what sociologists Cecilia Menjívar and Néstor Rodríguez called the "US-Latin American interstate regime," infamous for the state terror network Operation Condor (1968–1989).[8] But after the 1992 Israeli embassy bombing in Buenos Aires, the Argentine state, with US support, put pressure on Brazilian and especially Paraguayan counterparts to take exceptional measures against Arabs, effectively suspending their enfranchisement after the formal end of authoritarian rule. At this time, transnational activism for Middle Eastern causes became overshadowed by multiple government investigations that neither clarified the still unresolved bombing in the

Argentine capital nor found evidence implicating Arabs at the border. Once animating authoritarian state exceptions that sought rapprochement across the Third World, Arabs at the border later abided by post-authoritarian US and South American states' revanchism toward a transnational Middle East.

## Arab and Islamic Associations in US-South American State Exceptions

Arabs at the border mobilized under states of exception. The first civic association, the Clube União Árabe (Arab Unity Club), was inaugurated in Foz do Iguaçu's downtown in 1962 and was later relocated to larger facilities on the main highway near the airport.[9] Through the following decades, the club was monitored by Brazil's Serviço Nacional de Informações (SNI, National Intelligence Service).[10] Repeatedly reporting that the club served "cultural and recreational ends," SNI reports expressed not alarm but rather routine information-gathering, containing details that suggest Arabs might have reported on their own community organizing, if only to remain on good terms with the status quo.[11] The club's founding members, with businesses on Brazilian and Paraguayan sides of the border, "modeled" the organization as a "country club," with "social, cultural and sporting" activities for some 150 families, most of whom were Lebanese but also included some Palestinians, Syrians, and others.[12] The club's name evokes the Arab nationalism of Egyptian president Gamal Abd el Nasr (1956–1970), captivating not only Barakat, Rahal, and others mentioned in the first chapter, but also Brazilian and Paraguayan heads of state. At the time of the club's founding, the civilian Brazilian president hung a photograph of Nasr on the walls of the presidential office, and in the following decade, military successors began "advocating closer relations with Arab nations."[13] Meanwhile, the Paraguayan military head of state Alfredo Stroessner bestowed upon Nasr the highest national honor, the Mariscal Francisco Solano López medallion, and Stroessner declared three days of official mourning upon the Arab nationalist leader's death in 1970.[14]

Arabs registered this and other civic organizations in what anthropologist Matthew Hull called a "regime of paper documents," including facsimiles and photocopies, adhering and adapting to an authoritarian bureaucracy.[15] In 1978, in order to formulate a "charter" for another civic organization, the Sociedade Beneficente Islâmica (Islamic Benevolent Society), Barakat, Rahal, and others in Foz do Iguaçu consulted with the Sociedade Beneficente Muçulmana (Muslim Benevolent Society) in São Paulo, founded by Syrians, Lebanese, and Palestinians decades previously. Barakat received a faxed copy of the former's charter sent from São Paulo and asked one of his Brazilian employees to "retype the charter, switching 'São Paulo' to 'Foz do Iguaçu,'" in order to officially obtain civic, not-for-profit status from the military government. Mohamad Barakat convinced the then president of the Clube União Árabe, Mohamad Rahal, to found this Islamic charity organization. Rahal, whose export firm distributed a well-known beer, Skol, initially expressed reservations about compromising support for the country club. But Barakat reasoned that the duly-registered "Islamic" civic association would attract donations from Muslim-majority Arab member states of OPEC (Organization for Petroleum Exporting Countries). At that time, South American military regimes redoubled diplomatic efforts toward Middle Eastern and Islamic states.[16]

As authoritarian Brazil sought rapprochement with Tehran after the 1979 Iranian Revolution, despite its demonization by Washington, DC, Shia Lebanese coalesced around the Islamic Benevolent Society.[17] In 1984, their Islamic Benevolent Society hosted Shahmard Kanani Moghaddam, the Iranian ambassador, then posted to Brasília, as well as the Mullah Mohammed Tabatabai from Curitiba, who "enjoyed prestige and respect among Shia Muslims spread across the Three Borders."[18] Kanani and Tabatabai prayed with Shia Lebanese "at a location on the Rua da República do Líbano" (*sic*) in the neighborhood next to the Friendship Bridge. Kanani and Tabatabai later spoke about Islam and Iran to a "packed" audience in the "Diamond Salon" at the Hotel Salvatti in downtown Foz do Iguaçu. "A Muslim Shia from Ciudad Presidente Stroessner" in attendance declared: "he (the Iranian diplomat, Kanani) came here because we

**Figure 2.1.** Picture of Mohammed Tabatabai speaking at an event. Note the Lebanese flag in front of the table. © *Nosso Tempo*

asked" and "with the Mullah (Tabatabai), we are more united, following the teachings of Islam in all senses and praying five times a day."[19] Tabatabai was born in Najaf, Iraq, and recounted to the newsweekly *Veja* that he was "sent to Brazil by the Ayatollah Khomeini" to ensure Islamic precepts of *halal* in Brazilian meat exports as well as to "publicize the basics of Islam."[20] Though the Brazilian foreign ministry asked its Iranian counterpart for a replacement, the Shia Lebanese public embrace of Iran at the border dovetailed with Brazil's "institutionalized" diplomatic relations with and increased exports to Iran.[21] These ties with Tehran cultivated on Brazil's side of the border and the capital of Brasília hardly drew any concern in Washington, DC, even at the time of the US Iran-Contra scandal.

The fact that Brazil's authoritarian bureaucracy maintained relations with Middle Eastern and Muslim states that were sanctioned by the US is key to grasp another important association founded in 1981, the Centro Cultural Árabe-Brasileiro (Arab-Brazilian Cultural Center).[22] Located on the Brazilian side of the border, this center championed Muammar Qaddafi's Libya with an explicitly "Third Worldist" (*terceiro-mundista*) ethos. At the time, the Brazilian

**Figure 2.2.** Picture of the Centro Cultural Árabe-Brasileiro (Arab-Brazilian Cultural Center). © *Nosso Tempo*

military regime ran up a chronic trade deficit with the oil-rich Libyan state yet distanced itself from Qaddafi's self-declared revolutionary rhetoric.[23] Walking this fine line, the Arab-Brazilian Cultural Center offered Arabic language courses, sponsored folkloric and commemorative events, ran food distribution drives during Ramadan, and hosted speakers and diplomats from the Arab world.[24] In the center's marches and statements, two key founders, Mohamad Barakat and Ali Mohamad Sleiman, represented Qaddafi as standing up to US interventionism in Central America, expressing solidarity with Sandinistas in Nicaragua as well as supporting the people's struggle in El Salvador.[25] The Arab-Brazilian Cultural Center also distributed the Portuguese translation of Qaddafi's *The Green Book*, which claimed a "third way" beyond capitalism and communism, and hosted commemorations of the 1969 defeat of the US in Libya as well as Qaddafi's victory.[26] Such events often included the military-appointed mayor of Foz do Iguaçu Clóvis Viana, mentioned last chapter, among other authoritarian officials at the border.

Shortly after its founding, the Arab-Brazilian Cultural Center welcomed the Libyan ambassador then posted to Brasília. *Nosso Tempo* covered the event and clarified: "Arab immigrants in Foz do Iguaçu and in Ciudad Presidente Stroessner are not from Libya but rather nearly all stem from Lebanon and Syria."[27] Lebanese speakers condemned "capitalist exploitation" and praised Qaddafi's Libya, rebuked "North American imperialism" and Zionism, and exalted liberation struggles in El Salvador, Nicaragua, and Palestine. What aroused the consternation of *Nosso Tempo*, however, was not the some three hundred attendees of predominantly Lebanese origin from the Brazilian and Paraguayan sides of the border. Rather, it was the presence of authorities "committed to the rightist, reactionary ideology of the three countries," including Foz do Iguaçu's army commander and Federal Police chief, Ciudad Presidente Stroessner's appointed mayor, and the Argentine consul in Foz do Iguaçu, about whom Arabs were "reluctant to speak."[28] In 1982 and 1983, the center again hosted the Libyan ambassador at events that brought together Foz do Iguaçu's military-appointed mayor and the municipal council opposition leader Arialba Freire, in addition to others who ostensibly reported on such events to the SNI.[29] At the start of what, in Spanish, is called *la guerra de las Malvinas* (Malvinas War), or, in English, the Falkland's War (1982), the ambassador declared that "Libya supports Argentina on the issue of the Malvinas Islands and we are certain that . . . just as the territories occupied by Israel will soon be Arab, the Malvinas Islands will be Argentine." Tacitly approved and monitored by military governments at the border, Qaddafi's Libya tried to appeal to South American sentiments against Euro-American imperialism.

# COM EMBAIXADORES E SHEIKS É INICIADA CONSTRUÇÃO DA MESQUITA

**Figure 2.3.** News article: "With ambassadors and sheiks, mosque construction begins." Arialba Freire is pictured near the center of the photograph on the right. © *Nosso Tempo*

Also accommodated in an authoritarian regime, the Centro Cultural Beneficente Islâmico (Islamic Benevolent Cultural Center) was organized by Ali Said Rahal and Ahmad Ali Osman. They and others convened a meeting on the Avenida República do Líbano in 1982 that outlined the not-for-profit charter of this "charity, cultural, and social-service" center and fundraised among fifteen founding members with businesses in Foz do Iguaçu and Ciudad Presidente Stroessner.[30] Months later, this center sponsored page-long articles about "Islamic culture" in *Nosso Tempo*.[31] The articles stressed Islam as a "universal brotherhood" and cited verses of the Quran as well as ideas from Pakistani theologian Sayyed Abul Ala Mawdudi alongside British convert Marmaduke Pickthall. Noted in the first chapter, *Kamalito Magazine* advertised on the same page but stopped doing so because the Federal Revenue Service sought retribution on "the businesses that advertised in the newspaper," according to *Nosso Tempo* editor Juvêncio Mazzarollo. Subsequently, the founding members of the Islamic Benevolent Cultural Center requested that the Foz do Iguaçu military government donate land in order to build a mosque and community center for families with "school-aged children."[32] Approved by the city council and signed by the military-appointed mayor, the municipal law "authorize[d] the Head of the Executive Branch of the Municipal Government to donate a plot of land to the Centro Cultural Beneficente Islâmico of Foz do Iguaçu."[33]

Arabs accommodated both military rulers and civilian aspirants at the Islamic Benevolent Cultural Center's ceremony that laid the cornerstone of the future "Mosque of Foz do Iguaçu."[34] After the official welcoming that presented the goals of the mosque and community center, the president of the Foz do Iguaçu city council Arialba Freire took the podium. As a member of the permitted political opposition, and married to a career military man opposing the 1964 coup, Freire spoke "in the name of Foz do Iguaçu," and emphasized "the participation of the Arab community in the development" of the border. Her mention of Arabs as agents of development accommodated the board members present, including Ali Said Rahal as president; Mohamad Ali Omairi, vice-president; Kamal Oman, secretary; Ahmad Ali Osman, treasurer; and others from the Barakat, Rahal, Safa, and Safadi families. This cornerstone-laying ceremony also welcomed diplomats from the Arab League of States, Iraq, Kuwait, Lebanon, Libya, and Saudi Arabia; and a half-dozen religious leaders from Curitiba, São Paulo, and Rio de Janeiro; as well as officials of the Foz do Iguaçu city and Paraná state governments. The MC was Mohamad Abouferes, a representative of the Islamic Conference of South America and the Caribbean, part of the Saudi-supported Muslim World League.[35] More fully explored in the next chapter, hundreds of onlookers celebrated what was called the *comunidade islâmica fronteiriça* (Islamic border community, in Portuguese).

Palestinians also mobilized at the border, soon after Brazilian military and civilian leaders permitted representation of the Palestinian Liberation Organization (PLO) in Brasília.[36] Wafa Abdel was co-founder and president of the Associação Cultural Sanaúd, the "We Shall Return [in Arabic] Cultural Association [in Portuguese]."[37] She and her brother, Arafat, arrived with their Palestinian family in Foz do Iguaçu when she was six years old. In front of Barakat's

Novo Mundo (New World) store in 1984, Sanaúd exhibited panels with images of "the massacre perpetrated by Israel in the refugee camps of Sabra [and] Chatila, killing thousands of Palestinians."[38] In 1986, months after the Clube União Árabe welcomed the PLO representative from Brasília, another Palestinian-led association, the Sociedade Árabe Palestino Brasileira (Arab Palestinian Brazilian Society), organized the commemoration of the International Day of Solidarity with the Palestinian People.[39] According to *Nosso Tempo*, the commemoration included "innumerable Brazilian authorities" from centrist and leftist political parties, Brazilian student union leaders, and newly democratically elected Foz do Iguaçu city government officials.[40] In 1988, members of these Palestinian organizations were flanked by mostly Lebanese counterparts in a march of more than seven hundred people that celebrated the precocious declaration of a Palestinian state.[41] "The march was an expression of joy for the declaration," reflected the Lebanese trader Ali Osman, who called for Palestine to be "officially recognized" by "the world's governments and the UN." Wafa Abdel added, "We, Palestinians and Arabs of all states, want the wider acceptance of the UN resolutions that recognized the right of Israel and Palestine to constitute themselves as sovereign and independent states."

Neither openly condoning nor condemning US-backed South American authoritarian rule and the post-authoritarian transition, Arabs felt far more ease in voicing criticism of US policy toward the Middle East as well as related Israeli incursions there. In June 1982, the Lebanese-led Islamic Benevolent Society and the Arab-Brazilian Cultural Center co-organized "one of the most stirring acts of life of the municipality" against the Israeli occupation of Lebanon that would last for nearly two decades. Advocates "took to the streets of the city in a protest march condemning Israeli aggression."[42] After the Sabra and Shatila massacres the same year, they and others again collaborated in a declaration of "Solidarity with the Palestinian People," not mentioning Lebanese complicity in the killing of Palestinians. In *Revista Painel*, a collective statement denounced the "massacre of the Palestinian and Lebanese peoples" at the hands of Israel with the "active complicity of the US American administration" and the "indifference of most governments."[43]

**Figure 2.4.** Picture of a street march in favor of Palestinian self-determination led by Arabs on Avenida Brasil in Foz do Iguaçu. © *Nosso Tempo*

Best understood as "new social movements" that "recreated civil society" in a hemispheric borderland, to borrow from the work of sociologist Howard Winant, Lebanese shored up events for Palestinian self-determination, Sunnis frequented what became the Shia-led Islamic Benevolent Society, and Christians and Jews, as well as Muslims, contributed to the construction of the mosque.[44]

Arab and Islamic civic associations negotiated their own boundaries of national and religious difference, as more fully explored in the following chapter, but they were nonetheless monitored through a sectarian lens by authoritarian Brazilian intelligence. In 1984, the SNI identified a disconnect between "a Sociedade Islâmica de Foz do Iguaçu, whose members are Shia and support Iran" and "the Centro Cultural Beneficente Islâmico de Foz do Iguaçu, formed by Sunnis that are attached to Iraq."[45] Indeed, Shia members of the Islamic Benevolent Society tended to empathize with the ideals of the self-declared Islamic revolution in Iran, in addition to defending Palestinian self-determination.[46] In 1984, during the visit of the Iranian ambassador and religious leader mentioned above, *Nosso Tempo* featured a photograph of some one hundred *muçulmanos xiitas* (Shia Muslims) marching on Avenida Brasil in Foz do Iguaçu with images of Ayatollah Khomenei, banners calling for the return of

"Jerusalem," and pictures of the Dome of the Rock.[47] Meanwhile, the mostly Sunni founders of the Centro Cultural Beneficente Islâmico "didn't want anything to do with Shia" and leaned toward Sadaam Hussein's brand of Arab nationalism, explored later.[48] Mohamed Barakat reflected that the Arab-Brazilian Cultural Center that championed Muammar Qaddafi also tended to alienate Shia Lebanese at the border, due to Qaddafi's presumed role in the disappearance of Musa al-Sadr, a popular Shia leader in Lebanon. Occasionally conflicting with each other, these Third World projects were based on the Brazilian, not Paraguayan, side of the border, though both states shared surveillance in a rapprochement that outlasted formal authoritarian rule itself.

## Transnational Middle East in Brazil's Authoritarian *Abertura*

A transnational Middle East gained visibility on the Brazilian side of the border during a time of *distensão*, a top-down political liberalization process controlled by the military regime's last two heads of state, Ernesto Geisel (1974–1979) and João Batista Figueiredo (1979–1985). The ascendancy of Geisel and what later became the *abertura política* (political opening) shifted course from the 1964 military coup and the "hard-liners" that enforced the "National Security Doctrine," a Cold War-era state policy "constantly looking for new targets, and etching its violence ever deeper into society," according to historian Jerry Dávila.[49] President Geisel, and later President Figueiredo, worked to "diminish" the autonomy of military forces that hard-liners enabled previously in what was envisioned to be a controlled and incremental transition.[50] As a result, the politically liberalizing Brazilian regime continued surveillance over Arabs and others at the border but began to reign in repressive "enforcement."

As easy targets of retribution, Arabs tended to steer clear of any opposition to the Brazilian state, whether in authoritarian or post-authoritarian times. Antônio Vanderli Moreira, a one-time activist of the Movimento Democrático Brasileiro (MDB) in Foz do Iguaçu, stated that no Arabs at the border dared join before the 1979 legalization of political parties at which time the MDB added a *P* for *Partido* (Party), becoming the Party of the Brazilian Democratic

Movement (PMDB).[51] PMDB members grew increasingly critical of the military government's classification of Foz do Iguaçu and other municipalities as "Áreas de Interesse da Segurança Nacional" (Areas of National Security Interest), which enabled federal authorities to appoint the mayor, briefly mentioned last chapter. In 1983, Arabs were generally absent in a series of protests and strikes for *eleições diretas* (direct elections) in Foz do Iguaçu.[52] At one of the *comícios* (rallies), the city council president Arialba Freire called for the departure of Clóvis Viana and the return of the people's right to elect their own representatives, emboldened by the democratic victory of the Paraná state governor José Richa, born in Rio de Janeiro to Lebanese migrant parents. Mentioned earlier, Arialba Freire had spoken at the mosque's cornerstone laying ceremony, and officially represented PMDB at a congress in Tripoli, Libya. In 1984, Arabs at the border did not publicly appear with these or other pro-democracy forces that demanded the return of "direct elections."[53] Arabs tended to avoid outright political stands for and especially against authoritarian or post-authoritarian regimes.

But Brazilian intelligence continued to monitor Arabs at this crossroads. In 1983, in the middle of the protests for direct elections, the SNI requested information about Mohamad Barakat, for "spreading the ideology of Qaddafi" among "certain segments of PMDB of Foz do Iguaçu" and "more radical factions of the party."[54] The report gave details about Barakat and other "Arab organizations," but no repressive measures were taken against him or the Arab-Brazilian Cultural Center, reflecting the aforementioned detachment of intelligence gathering from repressive measures. Barakat himself recalled that he tended not to fear reprisals from Brazil's authoritarian regime because the *militares* (military men) in command of both Brazilian and Arab states were similarly anti-communist and cultivated trade as well as diplomatic ties with one another.[55] Moreover, he pointed out, Arab-Brazilian Cultural Center events were attended by none other than Foz do Iguaçu's appointed mayor before his departure with civilian rule. What is striking about state intelligence, however, is not that the SNI took note of Barakat's rapprochement toward progressive political parties, but rather that such surveillance continued through 1990, after the return of liberal democracy.[56] Though

**Figure 2.5.** Advertisement of the Centro Cultural Árabe-Brasileiro (Arab-Brazilian Cultural Center) expressing solidarity with journalist and activist Juvêncio Mazzarollo. © *Nosso Tempo*

Barakat's stances did not change all that much, continuing to champion Palestinian self-determination and Libyan revolutionary pretensions, it was Brazilian democratic forces that had taken over the state that still collected information about him. Neither targeted for repression nor taken into custody, Barakat bore witness to surveillance after the formal eclipse of an authoritarian order.

In a Third World project, Barakat supported *Nosso Tempo*, the newspaper with a "critical editorial line" founded in 1980 and harassed by military rulers, mentioned in the introduction.[57] Its co-founder

Juvêncio Mazzarollo remembered that Arabs tended to avoid local politics because they settled in Foz do Iguaçu to *ganhar a vida* (earn a living), and their status as migrants made them easy targets.[58] Mazzarollo knew the security state apparatus first-hand. He was the last journalist imprisoned by the National Security Law that Brazil's Minister of Justice was allegedly "rethinking" in 1983, at the very twilight of military rule.[59] Targeted and imprisoned by the authoritarian regime, Mazzarollo emphasized the role of Mohamad Barakat, who "opened my eyes to the Palestinian cause."[60] Mazzarollo stated, "Barakat was, ideologically speaking, of the same political stripe as us." He concluded, "In making solidarity with us, he [Barakat] naturalized as Brazilian and entered into the struggle for freedom."[61] Indeed, when Mazzarollo was still in jail during Christmas time in 1983, the Arab-Brazilian Cultural Center that Barakat founded took out a quarter-page advertisement, stating: "The best gift for this newspaper . . . would be the liberation of its director, Juvêncio Mazzarollo."[62]

In another distinct Third World project, one of *Nosso Tempo*'s co-founders, Aluízio Palmar, was invited to Tehran in order to observe a "week of war" with Iraq, arranged after Shia Lebanese at the border hosted the aforementioned Iranian ambassador in 1984.[63] Palmar had been in the Brazilian armed resistance group MR8, imprisoned and tortured by the Brazilian dictatorship, hunted by the covert Operation Condor state network, and had just returned from living in exile.[64] In concluding a lengthy article about his visit to "the land of the Ayatollahs," the resistance-fighter-turned-journalist criticized Iran as "just one more country of the Third World serving the interests of imperialism that needs wars in order to sell people-killing machines," especially in the Iraq-Iran war from 1980 to 1988.[65] Having taken up arms and endured state violence himself, Palmar criticized the war that the Iranian state waged, but he concluded that the "Iranian people will bring front and center their popular and national revolution." Critical of the continued subjugation of the Third World to the arms industry based in the First World, this former Brazilian insurgent upheld the broader ideals of the self-styled Islamic revolution that appealed to many Shia Lebanese at the border.

In yet another Third World project, Barakat and the Arab-Brazilian Cultural Center arranged for *Nosso Tempo* and other pro-democracy

activists to participate in the "International Congress of Solidarity," held in the Libyan capital of Tripoli, in 1984.[66] Fourteen people
made up the Brazilian delegation. Mazzarollo had been invited by
the Libyan ambassador in Brazil "out of recognition of the revolutionary mission of the newspaper *Nosso Tempo* and the attention
it always sought to give to the advances of the Libyan revolution."[67]
In retrospect, Mazzarollo reflected that he saw in Qaddafi a critic
of the US, and in Libya, a way to see "our own" lack of "egalitarian"
prospects in Brazil.[68] Arialba Freire was the only woman in the delegation, officially backed by her party, PMDB. The Foz do Iguaçu
City Council "conceded permission to the City Councilor Arialba do
Rocio Cordeiro Freire . . . to undertake an official trip in interest of
the municipal government . . . in the International Congress in Solidarity with the Arab Libyan People."[69] Freire, for her part, prepared
a speech that she delivered at the congress about the adherence of
PMDB and a liberalizing Brazil that returned to civilian rule the following year.[70] As Barakat helped make the travel arrangements (but
did not accompany the delegation),[71] Brazilian reformists joined
with Arab self-styled revolutionaries in what they considered to be
a Third World project with democratic aspirations.

But activists in the Arab-Brazilian Cultural Center and akin
Lebanese-led associations refrained from transgressing the limits of state-led Third Worldism. Such activists were absent from
the Jornada de Solidariedade ao Povo Paraguaio (March in Support
of the Paraguayan People) that criticized the Paraguayan dictator
Alfredo Stroessner and his alliance with Brazil.[72] In 1984 and 1985,
*Nosso Tempo* organized Paraguayan solidarity campaigns. But Lebanese, Palestinians, Syrians, and other Arabs steered clear of any protest against Stroessner, which would have brought the Paraguayan
state's retribution on their businesses and clients at the border.
In 1984 and 1985, Paraguayan forces gathered intelligence at Paraguayan pro-democracy events held on the Brazilian side of the border, recording the names of the organizers and speakers.[73] Indeed,
the last two Brazilian military heads of state that led the "political opening" process, Geisel and Figueiredo, renewed ties with the
Paraguayan dictatorship and its security apparatus, headed by Pastor Coronel in the Departamento de Investigaciones (Department

of Investigations), which engaged in the "torture, exile, and execution" of Paraguayan citizens.[74] In Third World projects, Arabs at the border remained silent about Brazilian state complicity in authoritarian Paraguay.

Arabs accommodated the exceptional alliance between a liberal democratic Brazilian government and illiberal Paraguay. In 1985, Arabs attended the campaign rally that the aforementioned Governor José Richa headlined for PMDB candidates in the Foz do Iguaçu municipal elections that concurrently hosted Antonio Sarubbi, the military-appointed governor of the neighboring Paraguayan state, Alto Paraná.[75] Accompanying the Brazilian democrat and Paraguayan autocrat were three Arab traders: Abdo Rahal whose Exportadora Líder in Foz do Iguaçu sold significant quantities of merchandise to Paraguay; Hussein Taijen, president of the Cámara de Comércio de Ciudad Presidente Stroessner, whose Casa Colombia sold consumer imports from Panama; and Mohamad Barakat of the Arab-Brazilian Cultural Center.[76] A month later, Arabs and others at the border overlooked the embrace between Brazil's first civilian president, José Sarney, and the Paraguayan military dictator at the border, but praised Sarney's censure of an Israeli offensive against Palestinians.[77] After the formal end of the authoritarian Brazilian regime, Arabs at the border accommodated PMDB's post-authoritarian rapprochement toward the Paraguayan dictatorship in what heads of state declared to be "continental unity."[78]

Authoritarian oversight persisted in a civilian-ruled Foz do Iguaçu, evident in the inauguration of the mosque and adjacent school in 1988. The mosque's cornerstone had been laid five years previously and the final stages of construction were publicly celebrated by the first democratically elected civilian mayor, Dobrandino da Silva (PMDB).[79] Arialba Freire, president of the city council at the time, was also in attendance. Impromptu, she was called upon to give a speech, thanking local leaders but forgetting to mention the "director of the Receita Federal" (Revenue Secretariat, equivalent to the IRS), who was at the time one of the SNI's *cachorros* (dogs), public servants who provided intelligence in exchange for favors from government authorities.[80] The particular official was offended and threatened to use his sundry connections to enact retribution.

Days after the inauguration, the offended official sent an emissary to Freire's office who threatened to provoke "an even bigger misunderstanding." Freire shrugged her shoulders and explained that she was surprised to have been asked to speak and forgot to acknowledge his presence.[81] Her self-assured response perhaps presumed that the offended official could not make good on his threat because the SNI's new director was General Ivan de Souza Mendes, who historian Thomas Skidmore characterized as a "moderate" in favor of "democratic government" with little prior experience.[82] The mosque inauguration ceremony in 1988 throws into relief the residual influence of military-controlled intelligence in post-authoritarian Brazilian rule over Arabs and others at the border.

Arabs on the Brazilian side of the border, instead of being enfranchised, were audited by the one-time democratic opposition that took over the reins of the state. In 1988, Brazilian state tax inspectors targeted Arab businesses near the Friendship Bridge after PMDB victories in municipal, and mayoral, and gubernatorial contests.[83] Arabs and other traders in Foz do Iguaçu supported PMDB in the lead-up to elections partly because the slate of candidates promised "to not do the feared 'operation fine-comb'" that would audit state tax returns. According to *A Gazeta do Iguaçu*, "it was public and notorious that a large number of state tax inspectors from ICM [Imposto Sobre Circulação de Mercadorias, akin to a state sales tax in the US], intended to audit at the border, especially in the area of exportation" in the Vila Portes and Jardim Jupira neighborhoods near the Friendship Bridge.[84] Having been suspected of economic duplicity, mentioned last chapter, Arab and other commercial exporters ended up being targeted by some sixty-six state tax inspectors after having declared their support of the victorious PMDB. Many exporters received steep fines for not paying the state tax or not declaring their entire stocks. One disillusioned trader complained that "it's lamentable that this takes place soon after the election."[85]

## *Paisanos* in Paraguay's Authoritarian Legacies

Arabs working and/or living on the Paraguayan side of the border faced the *stronato*, the moniker for the "personalist-authoritarian regime" of General Alfredo Stroessner (1954–1989).[86] According to political scientists Frank Mora and Jerry Cooney, as well as Marcial Antonio Riquelme, the Paraguayan dictator tried to appear "reserved and mild-mannered,"[87] presiding over the regime's political party, the Asociación Nacional Republicana (ANR), usually called the Partido Colorado (Colorado Party), which far outlived the dictator himself. Early on, Stroessner quelled divisions among party members through a "patrimonial" style with "personal, reciprocal ties of faithfulness and obligation" that political scientist Paul Sondrol assessed.[88] With the support of the Colorado Party, Stroessner had unchecked control over "the functioning of the state's institutions," enshrined by Paraguay's 1967 Constitution.[89] The most "dreaded" entity of this rule was the aforementioned Department of Investigations, under the Ministry of Interior, led by Sabino Augusto Montanaro and "shielded from controversy" in intelligence and enforcement.[90] This authoritarian power remains a living legacy in Paraguay.

Arabs accommodated and were accommodated by this exceptional rule. Mentioned earlier, HDD was likely granted ample discretion by his father-in-law, the dictator, to found the Paraguayan branch of the Federación de Entidades Árabes (Federation of Arab Entities, or FEARAB).[91] Life-long Colorado Party member of Syrian-Lebanese origin, Bader Rachid Lichi, likewise wrote about Palestine for the anti-Stroessner newspaper, *Nosso Tempo* in Foz do Iguaçu, without retribution.[92] Though enabling this freedom of expression for Arab liberationist causes, the *stronato* could also make or break any business by granting or revoking importation licenses and trademark rights for whiskey, tobacco products, jeans, and other high-brow consumables from abroad.[93] For this reason, "todos los árabes eran *stronistas*" (all Arabs were Stroessner supporters), quipped a long-time resident and journalist on the Paraguayan side of the border.[94] He explained that Mohamad Jebai, Ali Said Rahal, and others previously mentioned made sure "para estar bien con el régimen" (to be on good terms with the regime). Introduced last chapter, Jebai was said to have struck a business partnership with Stroessner's wife, Eligia Mora Delgado, in the Galeria Jebai Center. He also hosted Stroessner at the shopping center's official inauguration in 1977. Other storeowners likewise financed Colorado Party candidates who consistently won in the skewed municipal, departmental, and national elections.

Arabs' accommodation of Colorado rule continued during the party's infighting in the 1980s. Arabs got used to the polarization between so-named *militantes* (militants) and *tradicionalistas* (traditionalists). The key point of contention regarded Stroessner's successor. Militants readied Stroessner's son while traditionalists looked to the party's ranks. As the reigns of the dictatorship were pushed and pulled, the mayorship of Ciudad Presidente Stroessner changed hands from Carlos Barreto Sarubbi to Hugo Martínez Cárdenas in 1986.[95] As the dictator tried to ensure the ascendancy of his son and everyday civilians increasingly questioned the regime, the armed forces general, Andrés Rodríguez, led an internal military coup in early 1989. Three months after deposing Stroessner, General Rodríguez, with the support of the military and the Colorado Party, ran for and won the presidency, having "co-opted the rhetoric of the opposition–concern for democracy, social justice and human rights."[96] For the Paraguayan border town, Rodríguez changed the name to Ciudad del Este (City of the East) and replaced the Stroessner-era-associated mayor with Óscar Ovelar Rojas.[97] Marking continuity, and not rupture, this so-called "democracy" allegedly "audited" and "approved" the ledgers of its predecessor, the dictatorship-appointed mayoral administration.[98] As the military and the Colorado Party retained power in Paraguay, most Arabs continued to be on good terms with an illiberal state apparatus that outlived authoritarian rule itself.

Having grown accustomed to this sort of power, Arabs shifted allegiances from the deposed dictator to the military coup leader, General Rodríguez. In 1989, Mohamad Jebai allegedly invited the general-cum-president Rodríguez to become his new business partner, cutting out his original associate, Elígia, the wife of the overthrown dictator.[99] The once influential "ña Eligia" (Mrs. Eligia, in Guaraní) allegedly took revenge and denounced Jebai for tax evasion. The battle was said to have ended up in the courts. In this or some other mishap with an illiberal Paraguayan state, Jebai was said to have placed some of his property in the name of his nephew. Some of the lucrative real estate consisted of a vacant lot behind the mayoral building (*Intendencia*). The nephew allegedly never returned it. Though not unscathed, Mohamad Jebai was said to have won the judicial case put forth by Stroessner's wife, undoubtedly with the support of his novel business associate, President Rodríguez, the newly elected president in an illiberal democratic Paraguay.

At the dusk of Third World solidarity, Arabs came to terms with this alliance between an illiberal Paraguay and a liberalizing Brazil, symbolized by the close ties between (former general) President Rodríguez and Fernando Collor de Mello, the democratically elected civilian president of Brazil in 1989. Since Paraguay's largest creditor and trading partner was Brazil, Rodríguez met twice with Collor, who characterized Paraguay and Brazil as "brotherly peoples," in an embrace at the border.[100] Arabs at the border led a sizeable protest not against this illiberal exception to liberal democratic rule but rather against Collor's unsuccessful intention to close the PLO office in Brasília. Covered by *Nosso Tempo*, Arab activists at the border were said to defend Palestinian "self-determination" because "we are Brazilians" and "we want a Brazil that is progressive, democratic, and that stands in solidarity with the oppressed."[101] Collor ended up canceling his trip to Foz do Iguaçu, alleging a busy schedule, but for protestors, primarily of Lebanese origins, his absence was due to the "stupendous demonstration of repugnance."[102] As one of many acts of solidarity with Palestine in the second half of the 1980s,[103] this protest accommodated liberal Brazilian democrats' renewed alliance with the illiberal Paraguayan old guard at the end of state-led Third Worldism.

Arabs and others at the border expressed solidarity with Palestine but kept silent about the illiberal status quo in Paraguay that was itself supported by the Brazilian state. In 1989, just after the internal military coup in Paraguay that led Stroessner to seek exile in Brasília, "the Arab community of Foz do Iguaçu and Ciudade Presidente Stroessner hosted one of the leaders of the Palestine Liberation Organization (PLO) in Lebanon."[104] Not mentioning the illiberal status quo that continued at the border, the PLO leader urged the "local Arab community . . . to remain committed to the struggle for liberation" and the "popular Palestinian uprising known as

**Figure 2.6.** From left to right, Hussein Taijen, Sra. Hussein Taijen, Tércio Albuquerque, and Mohamad Barakat, at an Arab community event. © *Nosso Tempo*

'Intifada.'" Later the same year, after the Paraguayan border city changed its name to Ciudad del Este, the "Arab community of Foz do Iguaçu and Cidade del Leste [*sic*]" celebrated the second anniversary of the Intifada, the International Day of Solidarity with the Palestinian People, as well as the first anniversary of the proclamation of the Palestinian State.[105] Arabs at the border publicly mobilized for Palestine and avoided taking a stand on the authoritarian legacies of the Paraguayan state underwritten by post-authoritarian Brazil.

Arabs came to terms with Paraguay's illiberal regime. Less beholden to the Colorado Party, Hussein Taijen exercised some leverage through his presidency of the Paraguayan border town's Chamber of Commerce that mitigated relations between local businesses and suppliers abroad. Indeed, a day after the internal military coup, Taijen publicly lashed out at the Colorado Party–dominated Chamber of Deputies and Senate of the Paraguayan government, which had raised the import taxes on a range of products that jeopardized business in the Paraguayan border town. Taijen complained that higher taxes "only came to hurt trade and the government, because the traders imported less, sold less, and consequently, generated less taxes."[106] A year later, Andrés Rodríguez vetoed the measure and reinstated the old system of 7 to 10 percent tax depending on the country of origin of the imported merchandise. Business as usual returned. After Rodríguez changed the name of the Paraguayan border town that had referenced the deposed Paraguayan dictator, Taijen likewise renamed the chamber of commerce as the Cámara de Comercio de Ciudad del Este (Chamber of Commerce of Ciudad del Este). Neither condemning nor condoning illiberal government, Arabs on the Paraguayan side of the border defended business interests and generally accommodated the status quo.

But Third Worldist sentiments outlived the demise of the states that claimed to be the vanguard. It was mostly Lebanese who still found a place for long-distance Arab nationalism in Paraguay. Hussein Taijen and his brother, Said, broadly identified with Arab nationalism. Having migrated from Lebanon to the Paraguayan side of the border, Said Taijen stated that he and his brother considered themselves Arabs, because Lebanon was part of Syria, and Greater Syria was linked to Iraq and Palestine before British and French colonialism.[107] Indeed, Hussein Taijen participated in the street protests that condemned Israeli violence in Lebanon and Palestine as well as in the welcoming parties for Libyan diplomats and visitors at the Arab Brazilian Cultural Center and the mosque.[108] With righteous convictions, Hussein Taijen attracted members of the Partido Revolucionario Febrerista (PRF, or Februayan Revolutionary Party), a socialist party banned by Stroessner and allowed to return after the coup. Ricardo Jimenez, a PRF activist who had lived in the Paraguayan border town since 1980, stated that he "brought Taijen along with other Arabs to join the party."[109] Jimenez broached the topic of "febrerismo" (Febrero ideology that mixed Third World nationalism and socialism) with Hussein Taijen after the fall of Stroessner. Jimenez remembered that Taijen initially retorted, "soy colorado" (I am of the Colorado Party). Nonetheless, when Jimenez explained the history of the party, and its leanings toward social justice, Taijen allegedly responded, "quiero apoyar este partido, porque soy socialista en mi país" (I want to support this party, because I'm a socialist back in my country, in Spanish). In connecting the PRF to Arab nationalism, Taijen was said to have "economically supported" the party, "providing transportation and funding" according to Jimenez. For another PRF activist, most Arabs in the Paraguayan border town needed to be Colorado Party members in order to do business, but "ideologically . . . they don't get along . . . they are anti-imperialists," because "Arabs" experienced US imperialism in the lands they departed and settled.[110] Third Worldist sentiments survived the "dramatic decline" of state-led visions.[111]

Like most Arabs at the border, Hussein Taijen maintained a measured distance from Paraguay's illiberal democratic government, which still looked similar to the deposed military regime. Taijen recurrently stated, "Soy comerciante, no mercachifle" (I am a businessman, not a huckster, in Spanish), especially meaningful amid mounting accusations of state-led profiteering after the internal military coup.[112] In the 1991 elections, Paraguayan voters could choose new representatives for the Paraguayan national constituent assembly as well as municipal governments. Colorado Party candidates from rival factions accused one another of corruption while drawing the same indictments from candidates in previously banned oppositional parties. Many front-runners for a constituent assembly seat or municipal office were suspected of smuggling merchandise, especially through the department, or state, of Alto Paraná, whose capital is Ciudad del Este. With less popularity than when he assumed the presidency two years previously, General Rodríguez vowed to put an end to this corruption and claimed to investigate the department's alleged four hundred clandestine air strips, especially those associated with his political competitors.[113] In the mayoral election of the newly renamed Ciudad del Este, a former university rector, Amado Benitez Gamarra, became the official candidate of the Colorado Party. Promising to remove street vendors from the city streets and "increase the integration between Ciudad del Este and Foz do Iguaçu," the Colorados prevailed by a narrow margin.[114] The same political party of the overthrown Paraguayan dictatorship won electoral victories, maintaining the illiberal status quo in post-authoritarian times.

In this authoritarian legacy, Arabs found their businesses under greater scrutiny, especially by the Dirección General de Aduanas

(Directorate General of Customs). Federal Paraguayan government officials removed thirty border customs employees from the office in newly designated Ciudad del Este. They also publicly announced a list of merchants suspected of paying off those employees. As stated in *A Gazeta do Iguaçu* from the Brazilian side of the border, "The majority of the names on the list are Arab . . . all having stores and import businesses in Paraguay."[115] The article listed several names, including Hassan Assad, Imadi Assim, Hassan Diab, Hussan Nasser, Ali Narakat, Mohamed Mabousi, Abou Ltaif, and Abas Mossem. By actually naming and placing blame on Arab traders, the illiberal democratic Paraguayan government drew attention away from its own systemic profiteering that had for decades underestimated the value of requisitioned cargo in exchange for payoffs from importers, explored in the last chapter. Illiberal democratic state powers, rather than enfranchise, audited Arabs with greater fiscal surveillance at the limits of the Third World.

## Disenfranchisement in a Post-Authoritarian America

Unresolved violence in Argentina further limited enfranchisement after the formal end of authoritarian rule. On March 17th, 1992, a vehicle loaded with explosives blew apart the five-story Israeli Embassy in Buenos Aires.[116] Thirty persons were killed and over 250 were wounded. The force from the explosion shattered windows for a half-dozen city blocks, blew apart trees, and covered the sky with smoke. After an emergency cabinet meeting convened by Argentina's democratically elected president, the intelligence director characterized the attack "as a derivation of the conflict in the Middle East inside Argentina and with the participation of Argentines."[117] Media coverage focused on a statement issued by the amorphous "Islamic Jihad" in Beirut, taking at face value the claim that it authored the attack in retribution for Israel's killing of Sheikh Abbas Musawi, then Hizbullah's Secretary-General, and much of his family, in Lebanon.[118] In the same press, Hizbullah disavowed the attack and the Islamic Jihad in Beirut was said to have confirmed that an Argentine convert to Islam carried out the bombing. Despite domestic suspects, the Argentine president "asked both Israel's Mossad secret service and the United States Central Intelligence Agency [CIA] to help in the investigation."[119] In framing the violence as a "derivation" from the "Middle East," and reaching out to the US, the nominally liberal democratic Argentine state took steps to disavow its own accountability in the still unresolved 1992 Israeli embassy bombing.

Liberal governments now made illiberal exceptions toward a transnational Middle East, obfuscating hemispheric America's own past of state-sponsored terrorism. The US Department of State's *Patterns of Global Terrorism 1992*, declared that, "The bombing of Israel's Embassy in Buenos Aires" bore not a resemblance to authoritarian-era state terrorism that it had supported in South America, but rather served as an example of specifically "Middle Eastern violence and the single most lethal terrorist event of the year." Without evidence, the US State Department conjectured that, "communities of recent Shiite Muslim émigrés in the remote border areas of Argentina, Brazil, and Paraguay could provide cover for international terrorists," and in particular "Hizballah activity in Latin America."[120] Just days after the bombing, the State Department admitted lacking "information to confirm this reported claim" regarding Islamic Jihad or other suspects that carried out the bombing.[121] As explored more fully in the next chapters, the US did not disclose evidence but nonetheless associated the still unresolved violence in Argentina with Arabs and Muslims on the Brazilian and Paraguayan sides of the border.

Backed by the US, the Argentine state pressured the Paraguayan National Police to search for "two Arab citizens" (*dos ciudadanos árabes*) in Ciudad del Este suspected of holding sympathies for the Islamic Jihad.[122] Claiming their names were withheld due to the secret nature of the investigation, *ABC Color* stated that, "the Arabs who are wanted may be sympathizers of the Islamic Jihad, the pro-Irani terrorist group that claimed authorship of the explosive attack in a statement released in Beirut, according to information compiled by the police forces of Argentina, Paraguay, and Israel."[123] The chief of the Paraguayan National Police was cited as saying: "In Ciudad del Este, there are people of Arab and Lebanese nationality, and for this reason, we are doing secret intelligence work, if by chance there's a relation. But for now, there doesn't exist any suspicions." In the same breath, he added, "work is in progress to track Arab and Lebanese citizens [*ciudadanos árabes y libaneses*] in Ciudad del Este." Such tracking was ostensibly undertaken by military commanders in Paraguay's National Police since Paraguay's 1992 constitution reserved domestic security matters for the armed forces.[124] Embodying the continued influence of the armed forces in civilian governance, the military-led Paraguayan National Police set its sights on Arabs at the border.

Arabs on the Paraguayan side of the border pointed out not continued surveillance in post-authoritarian times, but rather migrant suffrage and migrants' right to vote in elections for city councils and mayorships. The 1992 Paraguayan constitution ensured that "foreigners with permanent settlement will have the same rights in municipal elections."[125] This migrant suffrage was reinforced by Paraguay's Electoral Code, which obliged "foreigners with permanent residence" to enroll in a Civic Registry of Foreigners that was used to ensure voting rights.[126] Said Taijen explained that, since the new constitution, "anyone who settles in Ciudad del Este," or any other city in Paraguay for that matter, has the right to elect the mayor (*intendente*) and the city councilors (*concejales*). He surmised: "This is probably the only country in the world that gives the right to vote to migrants who are neither native nor naturalized." Overstating the influence of the Arab electoral bloc, Said added that, "here in Ciudad del Este, we [Arabs] number seven thousand voters. If we wanted to elect the city government, we could, but we are not zealots."[127] Despite migrant suffrage, the backlash from the unresolved 1992 bombing in Buenos Aires limited substantive enfranchisement.

Especially evident on the Paraguayan side of the border, Arab transnational ties could no longer be articulated on their own terms, a civic and collective right otherwise expected after the formal end of authoritarian rule. Though most Arab civic organizing historically took place on the Brazilian side, Lebanese, Palestinians, and Syrians had begun to debate the forms their advocacy took. A month before the bombing in Buenos Aires, in early 1992, "commercial establishments of Ciudad del Este in Paraguay and Foz do Iguaçu" closed their doors "in protest" of Israel's assassination of Hizbullah's Secretary General Abbas Musawi and his family in Lebanon.[128] Some participated in this protest while Hussein Taijen, as president of the Chamber of Commerce of Ciudad del Este, criticized the work stoppage for "diminishing the flow of merchandise at a difficult time for storeowners."[129] But Argentine- and US-derived suspicions cast a shadow over this and any other form of Arab or Muslim civic engagement as allegedly precipitating the bombing of the Israeli embassy in Buenos Aires.

After the formal end of the authoritarian-era covert Operation Condor network, the scrutiny over Arabs' presence at the border legitimated exceptional surveillance and intelligence-sharing among multiple government authorities. Paraguay's National Police chief specified that "we are in permanent contact with Argentina's Interior Minister, Jose Luis Manzano, and we are exchanging information."[130] This police chief and Paraguay's "Commander in Chief," General Rodríguez, separately met with "Brigadier General Yehuda Duvdevani," who was an attaché in the Israeli embassy in Buenos Aires.[131] But Brazilian intelligence officials, not mentioned in contemporaneous Paraguayan, Argentine, or Brazilian news coverage, later affirmed that "those actions that occurred in Buenos (Aires) had a very different origin from that which was claimed," which led the Brazilian state to adopt the position that "there was not . . . planning or logistical support or people for those attacks from our territory."[132] At the time, Brazilian officials did not express concern about the border but rather shored up the security of the Israeli embassy in Brasília and Jewish associations in Rio de Janeiro and São Paulo.[133] The state increased security but eschewed charging Arabs at the border with any infringement of the law.

Arabs spoke out on the Brazilian side, but remained silent about the Paraguayan side in limited Third World solidarity at the border. In Foz do Iguaçu, Mohamad Barakat criticized democratically elected governors of three Brazilian states bordering on Argentina who released a collective statement in condemnation of the bombing in Buenos Aires. The governors of Paraná, Rio Grande do Sul, and Santa Catarina condemned "the barbarity and political impositions apparent in the terrorism recently practiced against the embassy of Israel." Roberto Requião, the governor of the state of Paraná who will be mentioned again in later chapters, added that "Arabs, Palestinians, and Israelis should take Brazil as an example, where the three peoples live in peace."[134] In his open rebuke, Barakat criticized the Brazilian governors who "never took a stand against the acts of barbarism practiced by Zionists. If in some moment they had done so, we could accept the collective statement signed by these governors. But no, when massacres happened to the Palestinian people, they were silent."[135] Barakat went on to characterize Israel as "anti-human" and "racist," and condemned the violence that it has enacted on Palestine for some fifty years.[136] Rather than express empathy for those who suffered from the bombing in Buenos Aires, Barakat emphasized Israel's victimization of Palestinians and Lebanese. Barakat explained that Israel had just unilaterally assassinated the aforementioned Abbas Musawi and his family in Lebanon. Barakat spoke out against Israel and Brazilian governors but said nothing of the state surveillance targeting Arabs in Ciudad del Este.

Indeed, on the Brazilian side of the border, Arabs accommodated greater governmental power with the ascendancy of PMDB, despite the tax audits undertaken years previously, as discussed last chapter. Electorally, "Arabs conceded their unlimited support to then candidate Dobrandino Gustavo da Silva" of PMDB in the 1993 municipal elections.[137] Having already served as mayor with the return of democracy, Dobrandino thanked his Arab supporters by improving the infrastructure in the neighborhoods of Vila Portes and Jardim Jupira, next to the Friendship Bridge. Ali Osman thanked the mayor by stating that "the restoration of the streets of Vila Portes was an old demand of the Arab community and it positively resonated among community members."[138] Dobrandino's administration included Arabs: Ahmad Nagib Al Ghazaqui headed the department of human resources, Geber Nasser ran the department of commercial and industrial development, and Hichen Mohamad Hachan became the director of public works. Hachan stated that "All public works undertaken . . . are determined by the mayor, who has answered most of the demands of the Arab community." Arabs joined the political party that once opposed the Brazilian authoritarian regime but accommodated the illiberal Paraguayan status quo that continued to limit the fuller enfranchisement of the border.

Arabs and their liberationist causes took center stage in the PMDB-led Foz do Iguaçu government. One telling moment was the issuing of a municipal decree that instituted Foz do Iguaçu's annual observance of the International Day of Solidarity with the Palestinian People on November 29, proclaimed by the UN some fifteen years previously.[139] Álvaro Neumann, the successor of the first democratically elected mayor, signed it into law. At the ceremony at a luxury hotel, he stated, "November 29 is a date of deep importance for the Arab-Palestinian people because it's in tune with the love of all peoples for their cause." The aforementioned Sanaúd Cultural Association, as well as the Arab Palestinian Brazilian Society among others, helped coordinate the festivities. Lebanese, Palestinians, Syrians, and others spoke out for Palestine and against Israel in Foz do Iguaçu, and not Ciudad del Este. Having avoided public stands on the Colorado-dominated Paraguayan side of the border, the event they organized again came under surveillance by Brazilian state intelligence in liberal democratic times.[140]

From the 1960s to the early 1990s, Lebanese, Palestinians, and Syrians experienced the clarion and decline of state-led visions for the Third World. At the border, they mobilized under the liberal exceptions of authoritarian leaders and the illiberal exceptions of post-authoritarian successors. In advocating for Middle Eastern and Islamic causes alongside South American civilian and military authorities, they accommodated forms of exceptional rule, engaging reformists and reactionaries in Brazil and Paraguay, maintaining some distance from Argentina, and occasionally criticizing US interventionism. Their support of Middle Eastern and Islamic liberationist movements, however, precluded criticizing the illiberal status quo in Paraguay, which depended on Brazilian military- and civilian-led governments. At the border, Arabs folded into these Third World possibilities and limits. Nonetheless, their enfranchisement after the formal end of authoritarianism was interrupted by the 1992 bombing of the Israeli embassy in Buenos Aires. Following another attack in the capital of Argentina two years later, their faith in the rule of law would be again tested on the Brazilian and Paraguayan sides of the border.

## CHAPTER 3

# Test of Faith

**Arabs led mosques and** prayer halls as well as commemorated *'eidun* (holy days, in Arabic) at the border under a fading authoritarian apparatus. But in 1994, their faith was questioned after the post-authoritarian Argentine state neither deterred nor detained the perpetrators of an attack in Buenos Aires which leveled a historic building home to Jewish Argentine associations, referred to as AMIA (Asociación Mutual Israelita Argentina, or Jewish Argentine Mutual Association, in Spanish).[1] Arabs on the Brazilian and Paraguayan sides of the border found themselves being accused of complicity in the still unresolved violence.

Having mobilized around Sunni and Shia markers of difference at the border during and after authoritarian rule, Lebanese, Palestinians, and Syrians came to collectively see themselves as foils for the AMIA attack that remains without resolution. In the immediate aftermath and since that time, Argentine and US authorities perceived Arabs at the border as suspects who would or could kill Jews, and expected Brazilian and Paraguayan officials to do likewise. Argentine security forces detained and released Arabs venturing onto the Argentine side of the border, while Argentine and US government officials put pressure on Brazilian and Paraguayan counterparts to scrutinize Arab religious leaders who were apprehended, investigated, and released as well. Without evidence against them in the still unresolved bombing, Arabs rebutted Argentine, US, and other powers that they felt scapegoated them. In this Ummah America, Arabs shaped and were shaped by the ideal of a universal Islamic camaraderie, condemning the anti-Jewish violence in Argentina that had been similarly denounced in the US and further consolidating Islam on the Brazilian and Paraguayan sides of the border.

This chapter explores what political scientist Olivier Roy called "the new frontier of the imagined ummah" in this hemisphere's unresolved anti-Semitism.[2] Since arriving at the border, Arabs began to institutionalize an Ummah by accommodating state power and steering clear of its violence, including Argentina's "Dirty War" (1976–1983). After the bombing of AMIA in Buenos Aires, however, Arabs at the border felt "compelled . . . to apologize for acts they did not commit [and] to condemn acts they never condoned," to paraphrase anthropologists Sally Howell and Andrew Shryock in their critique of post-9/11 backlash in the US.[3] In consonance with the considerable scholarship on Jewish suffering after the AMIA bombing, this chapter shifts focus from ground zero in Buenos Aires to the subsequent backlash at the border.[4] Argentine and US officials, having failed to redress attacks against Jews in the Argentine capital, pressured Brazilian and Paraguayan counterparts to profile and pick up "Muslims" or "Arabs" at the border, who were later discharged. Folding into an Ummah America, Arabs mobilized on the Brazilian and Paraguayan sides of the border in response to accusations that they perceived to be emanating from Argentina and the US.

This chapter contributes to scholarship on military power in Latin American political transitions by directing attention to a seldom acknowledged shift after authoritarian rule.[5] In historically US-backed Argentine, Brazilian, and Paraguayan authoritarian regimes, the military was deployed on domestic territory by alleging to combat *terroristas* (terrorists), who were construed as neither Arabs nor Muslims but rather communists, dissidents, or anyone perceived as such. With the formal end of authoritarian rule, civilian-led administrations attempted to limit the military in domestic affairs, but the Argentine state suspended such norms in order to search for suspects in the unresolved bombings in Buenos Aires, pressuring

Brazilian and Paraguayan counterparts to do likewise under US scrutiny.[6] Consequently, an array of civilian and militarized security forces helped carry out exceptional domestic operations that targeted Muslim Arabs at the border in the name of so-called *antiterrorismo* (counterterrorism, in Portuguese and Spanish), an authoritarian legacy in the transition toward civilian rule. Arabs' faith was tested as a target proxy in post-authoritarian times.

## Crossing, Redrawing, and Debating Borders

Arabs "crossed and reinforced" borders.[7] Ali Said Rahal stated that the mosque and school, introduced last chapter, fostered "community union, integration into Foz do Iguaçu society, and the . . . development of Arab cultural values in the region of the Three Borders."[8] But in naming the mosque, Rahal and other Sunni chose Omar Ibn Al-Khattab, a figure they claimed was "considered by Muslims as the 'prince of believers.'"[9] This naming estranged Shia for whom Omar Ibn Al-Khattab usurped power from 'Ali, who they theologically imagined as the true heir to lead the Ummah. "Wealthy Sunnis," it was said, chose the designation so that "no Shia would want to go" to the mosque. Meanwhile, the adjacent school was named 'Ali Ben Abi Taleb, because this caliph was a "gateway to knowledge" according to Kamal Osman, not the wronged Muslim leader as Shia believe.[10] As a result, Shia tended to coalesce around the Islamic Benevolent Society in a nearby building they named after Iran's religious leader, Imam Al-Khomeini, and frequented its prayer space (*mussalah*, in Arabic) that they called the *huseiniya* (in Arabic), after Husein, the martyred son of 'Ali. Arabs traversed the borders of the Ummah but also redrew "Sunni" and "Shia" boundaries within it.

Sunni and Shia at the border also debated the 1991 Gulf War that Washington, DC, initiated, Brasília kept watch over, Asunción sat out, and Buenos Aires sent troops for.[11] "Impassioned Sunnis . . . backed Saddam Hussein" and ignored his brutality toward Shia, remembered a Shia shaykh in the *huseiniya*.[12] Indeed, Sunni Lebanese and Palestinians called for renewed support of the Iraqi leader as "the gateway of the Arab world to the east." Both Mohamad

# MESQUITA PODERÁ SER INAUGURADA EM ABRIL

Uma das mais belas construções de Foz da Iguaçu é a mesquita situada atrás do INSS no Jardim Porto Belo. A beleza arquitetônica, com suas linhas sublimes tem sido motivo de admiração não só dos iguaçuenses, mas um bom de todos que não visitaram. Logo desde a avenida, Paraná a mesquita tem como fundo o Paraguai.

Sua construção começou em 1983 e já se em fase de terminação se terá inaugurada no mês de abril. Em Foz do Iguaçu Cruttef Presidente Stroessner vivem harmoniosamente dois

mil iguaçuenses, muitos com maioria vindo anos de residência na região. Todas as certas lojas são renovados encontros de comunhão no preditermos. Além de ser um local de oração a mesquita será um local de pesquisas, escola e guarda dos costumes. A altura de sua cúpula é de 40 metros, com um minarete de 32 metros, tendo a mesquita 1200 metros quadrados em total. É um símbolo da universalidade de Foz do Iguaçu, estado que agora comunicados de todas as raças e religiões.

Armação pranta...

A mesquita será um local para cultivar a fé e os costumes

Começo da construção

São colocados os primeiros tijolos

Sua inauguração está prevista para abril

**Figure 3.1.** Article on the upcoming inauguration of the Omar Ibn Al-Khattab mosque. © *Nosso Tempo*

**Figure 3.2.** Front page of a special supplement of *Nosso Tempo* commemorating the official inauguration of the Omar Ibn Al-Khattab mosque. © *Nosso Tempo*

Barakat and Kamal Osman euphemized Iraq's invasion of Kuwait as "the Iraqi state's recuperation of an area that belonged to it," which in fact precipitated the US declaration of war.[13] Wafa Abdel, president of Sanaúd, likewise considered "that Iraq has historical rights in the region." In contrast, a Shia Lebanese, Ali Farhat, "expressed his opinion" that "Iraq's invasion of Kuwait is unjust and Iraq's president is a true war criminal." Another Shia Lebanese, Hussein Abbas, then director of the Islamic Benevolent Society, pointed to the US equivocation of having previously supported Iraq against Iran. The then shaykh of the *huseiniya*, Ibrahim Kassir, echoed that the US had been aligned with Iraq against Iran. Having gained salience during the Iraq-Iran War mentioned last chapter, Sunni

**UM CENTRO PARA PRESERVAR A CULTURA ÁRABE**

Mesquita Omar Ben Elkhatab

Desde que foi fundado em 1981, com fins filantrópicos e religiosos, o Centro Cultural Benficente Islâmico de Foz do

**Figure 3.3.** Article on the Arab cultural center and school attached to the mosque. © *Nosso Tempo*

and Shia boundaries at the border became further entrenched by US-led war in the Middle East.

At the border, as well as across and beyond the hemisphere, liberal progressives and Sunni counterparts coalesced in the "demonization" of Shia and Iran.[14] Having collaborated with Sunni Lebanese, the *Nosso Tempo* editor Juvêncio Mazzarollo criticized the "religious fanaticism" of Khomeini, in particular.[15] Mazzarollo expressed concern over the "silencing" of the press after Khomenei issued the edict against Salman Rushdie.[16] But Mazzarollo's stand against censorship drew on standard orientalism in labeling Iranian mourners as "the largest manifestations of fanaticism in human history" after "the death of Ayatollah Khomeini."[17]Ali Said Rahal in

the Islamic Benevolent Cultural Center shared this stance by calling Iran's Ayatollah Ruhollah Khomeini "a fascist" in response to a
reporter's question about the decree issued against Salman Rushdie after the publication of *The Satanic Verses*.[18] After his statement
caused a "controversy" at the border about Khomeini's "application
of Islamic principles," the new president of the Islamic Benevolent
Cultural Center, Ahmad Hamad Rahal, "clarified" that "Khomeini
simply leads one faction of Muslims."[19]

Exercising a short-lived enfranchisement after the ostensible
end of authoritarian rule at the border, Shia reasserted themselves
not as a "minority" or "faction" but rather as defining a global
Ummah. The Shia-led Islamic Benevolent Society characterized
Khomenei as the "maximum leader" of not only "Muslims" but
also "the oppressed of the world."[20] In 1989, the Islamic Benevolent Society took out a quarter-page announcement in *Nosso Tempo*
to "express its grief and consternation at the death of Ayatollah
Ruhollah Al-Khomeini."[21] Verse 156 of the Surat Al-Baqarah of the
Quran was recited: "when sadness befalls, state, we are of God and
to him we will return." The piece reminded the public that Khomeini, before his death, called upon "Muslims of the entire world
to defend the Islamic Republic of Iran as a 'present of God.'" The
Islamic Benevolent Society expressed "sincere condolences" to "the
entire Islamic community" at the border and extended an invitation
to "religious worship in praise of his (Khomeini's) soul that will be
celebrated . . . at the community center."[22]

Having migrated predominantly from Lebanon, Shia at the border advocated for Iran against the backdrop of the Brazilian state's
own rapprochement with the self-declared Islamic republic, as
explored last chapter.[23] Accordingly, in 1990, on the one-year anniversary of Khomenei's death, Shia Lebanese in the Islamic Benevolent Society invited "the general public" to a religious observance and an "ideological symposium" about the "persona of the
deceased Imam Khomeini and his generous and blessed revolution."[24] Instead of being held in the Omar Ibn Al-Khattab mosque,
the Shia religious observance was carried out at the society's own
building and the political symposium in an upscale hotel. The new
sheikh, Khaled Atai, led the events as well as the distribution of

two hundred food baskets to the needy who formed lines in front of the society's building. Based in the state capital of Curitiba, Atai was called the "spiritual leader of the Colônia Islâmica [Islamic Community] of Foz do Iguaçu." Atai clarified that the symposium intended to explore "the different sides of the Imam's personality . . . and to clarify some subjects that the audience can ask in regards to him and the Islamic Republic." With Iranian diplomats visiting from Brasília, Atai expressed his goal to break "the barriers of con-tradictory and confusing propaganda . . . against the personality of Khomeini and the Islamic revolution." Shia Lebanese put their historic disenfranchisement in perspective, articulating a "politics based on Islamic principles."[25] Brazilian state intelligence, mean-while, characterized them as "defend[ing]" not an Ummah, but rather "the regime of the government of Iran."[26]

At this time, Shia Lebanese made up a slight majority of migrants, though greater numbers of Sunni counterparts began settling ear-lier. Overwhelmingly stemming from the Beqaa Valley and South Lebanon, Shia came in hopes to make a better life and "because of constant Israeli attacks on the region," according to *A Gazeta do Iguaçu*.[27] Take for instance a migrant who left the village of Khiara in the Beqaa Valley in 1980, sometimes referred to by the initials of his full name, MYA, Muhammad Yusef Abdallah. MYA initially joined his brother who had settled on the outskirts of Uberlândia in the Brazilian state of Minas Gerais, just before their ancestral vil-lage and much of South Lebanon was invaded by the Israeli Defense Forces (IDF). Deciding to try his luck at the then booming border, MYA reached Foz do Iguaçu, and after some tepid business ventures, he and his family crossed the bridge from Brazil to Paraguay and opened a store in the Jebai Center. Just as Israel occupied their vil-lages, Shia Lebanese migrated and equaled in number their Sunni counterparts at the border.

MYA mobilized an Ummah at what seemed to be the twilight of authoritarian rule. Before Stroessner was ousted in 1989, MYA helped establish the Centro Árabe Islámico Paraguayo (Arab Islamic Paraguayan Center).[28] MYA recalled that he never experienced a brush with the *stronato* or the successive regime because he steered clear of criticizing "military men." In that transition, MYA idealized a nineteen-story residential building whose forefront houses the green-domed Mezquita del Profeta Mohammed (*sic*, Mosque of the Prophet Mohammed). At the time, Andrés Rodríguez (1989–1993) led the internal military coup and became Paraguay's first elected president,[29] integrating the military into the new police force, the *Policia Nacional*.[30] Although this police force harassed Arab store-owners, mentioned earlier and more fully explored later, MYA did not express fear of reprisals from this illiberal democratic Paraguay. Located in downtown Ciudad del Este, the mosque began to be built in 1993 and opened in 1994. After the mosque, the adjacent nineteen-story building was constructed floor by floor. As Sunni continued to congregate in the mosque in Foz do Iguaçu, Shia frequented MYA's mosque in Ciudad del Este. An Ummah became institutionalized at the post-authoritarian border.

In gaining greater visibility, Shia Lebanese at the border, like Brazilian and Paraguayan state authorities, expressed empathy as well as indifference toward Hizbullah and AMAL, self-styled resistance movements that took shape during Israel's nineteen-year occupation of Lebanon that started in 1982, briefly mentioned last chapter. Respectively identified with each movement, the son of Fadlalla, from Beirut, and the shaykh of the Shia mosque in São Paulo, Mohsen Bilal Wehbi, came for the inauguration of the Mezquita del Profeta Mohammed in Ciudad del Este.[31] Yet the idealizer, MYA, emphasized that he built the mosque for the "Muslim community," the Ummah, of the border, not for any political party or movement. MYA's father, for instance, arrived in the Paraguayan border town shortly after Israeli incursions in their Lebanese hometown of Khiara, in 1983 and 1984. When the Israeli military invaded their house to detain the father, the latter fled and found shelter with his son and daughter-in-law who had just settled at the border. Not only in the case of MYA, unfounded suspicions that Shia Lebanese could be formally organizing or fundraising for Hizbullah or any armed resistance had to do with their forced departure from then Israeli-occupied Lebanon.

Hardly conspiring between war-torn Lebanon and post-authoritarian Paraguay, Shia and other Lebanese in Ciudad del Este established the Centro Educacional Libanés (Lebanese Educational

Center), often called the Colégio Libanés (Lebanese School). According to anthropologists Paulo G. Pinto and Silvia Montenegro, the school began to be organized in 1992 when a Catholic priest from Qabrikha secured "the donation of land and afterwards the economic collaboration of some Arab merchants."[32] Eventually, the school was linked to the Asociación Beneficente Islámica del Alto Paraná (Islamic Benevolent Association of Alto Paraná), integrating educational materials approved by the Supreme Islamic Shia Council in Lebanon. A key figure in the school's development was Ziad Fahs, born in Qabrikha and educated in Lebanon, Iraq, and Iran. In 1992, Fahs arrived on the Paraguayan side of the border, working with Lebanese and Paraguayan officials for an accredited curriculum.[33] With official recognition from Paraguayan and Lebanese government education ministries, the Colégio Libanés is now authorized to transfer credits and coursework between Paraguay and Lebanon.[34] Such institutional ties were likely mitigated by the AMAL movement that drew the sympathies of "various Shia leaders of Foz do Iguaçu and Ciudad Presidente Stroessner" since Nabih Berri first came to the border in 1986 (and returned a decade later, discussed shortly).[35]

In post-authoritarian times, Islamic institutions at the border bifurcated into, on the one hand, Sunni partial to pan-Arab nationalism, and, on the other, Shia sympathetic to the Iranian revolution as well as the Lebanese movements of Hizbullah and AMAL.[36] Mentioned earlier, Said Taijen, nominally Sunni, opened a musallah on an upper floor of the building that he and his brother owned, ostensibly avoiding the Shia-led mosque that MYA established down the street on the Paraguayan side of the border. Initiated in 2012 and inaugurated in 2015, Said Taijen also led the construction of a new, ostensibly Sunni mosque in Ciudad del Este, discussed in the sixth chapter. Nonetheless, Said Taijen stressed to the Paraguayan statesman and writer, Alejandro Hamed Franco, "our religion makes no distinction of nationality, neither culture nor ethnicity. Every Muslim is a brother in religion, equal in rights, in all aspects."[37] Though praying in separate spaces, Sunni and Shia alike abided by the ideal of a universal Islamic camaraderie, an Ummah, unexpectedly interrupted by violence in Argentina.

## Aftershocks of Anti-Semitic Violence in
## Post-Authoritarian Argentina

The bombing of AMIA on July 18, 1994, made the legacy of authoritarian-era violence and impunity all too real in post-authoritarian Argentina. President Carlos Menem (1989–1999) declared a state of emergency and the *gendarmería* (gendarmerie) closed the country's borders, including in Puerto Iguazú.[38] The still unresolved 1992 Israeli embassy attack was etched in the minds of victims. First-responders and reporters in Buenos Aires called the bombed-out *AMIA* building *la embajada* (the embassy [of Israel]) in a "verbal lapse" that made the two places "synonymous with one another."[39] *Clarín*'s caption over news articles about the AMIA bombing put the watchwords in caps, OTRA VEZ (AGAIN). As the public perceived a repetition of violence similar to the state-sponsored terror that was then on trial, Argentina's Interior Ministry proposed National Decree Number 2023, reserving "permanent funds" in order to "clarify the international terrorist attacks perpetrated against the EMBASSY OF THE STATE OF ISRAEL in our country and the headquarters of the ASOCIACIÓN MUTUAL ISRAELITA ARGENTINA, on March 17, 1992, and July 18, 1994."[40] Argentina's "deferential" Supreme Court, having reversed censures of former military heads of state, took charge of formal investigations into both the 1992 Israeli embassy bombing and the 1994 AMIA bombing. In a larger systemic "operation of 'forgetting'" that critic Beatriz Sarlo observed, militarized power benefited and redefined its targets elsewhere.[41]

Accordingly, US-backed Argentine intelligence bureaus profiled Muslim Arabs at the border as terrorists who would or could kill Israelis and Jews in Buenos Aires. *Clarín* related that "the CIA" gave "the Argentine government a map . . . where it detected the presence of Hizbullah. . . . One of the marked zones is the tri-border between Argentina, Brazil, and Paraguay."[42] Though not stated, the CIA's map would have likely reached Argentina's "civilian intelligence agencies" then dominated by "military officers," namely the Central Nacional de Inteligencia (CNI, or National Center of Intelligence) that directly answered to the Argentine president, and the more independent Secretaría de Inteligencia del Estado (SIDE, or Intelligence State Secretariat).[43] Indeed, such agencies claimed a "terrorist structure" at the border "would provide logistical assistance for the attack against Jewish targets [*objetivos israelitas*]." A day after the bombing, the CNI "dusted off a report . . . about the supposed existence of a 'support base' of the pro-Irani organization, Hizbullah, . . . in the Brazilian south and in Paraguay, in Ciudad del Este."[44] Arabs and Muslims on the Brazilian and Paraguayan sides of the border became undue foils of the lack of justice in post-authoritarian Argentina.

Under pressure from Argentina and elsewhere, Paraguay's National Police and Interior Ministry were strong-armed into targeting "Muslims" and "Arabs" at the border. Initially, Enrique Martinetti, the Paraguayan National Police chief, dismissed as "exaggerated" the Argentine claim that Hizbullah established a base among "Lebanese or other Arab residents in Ciudad del Este" whose political sympathy for resistance against Israel did not indicate any institutional link, let alone complicity in violence against innocent civilians.[45] However, Paraguay's Interior Minister, Miguel Ramírez, reproached Martinetti, relating that the police failed to assist "the Israelis" in locating a suspect who "would be protected by the numerous foreign colony (presumably Lebanese Arab [*sic*]) settled in the Ciudad del Este border city."[46] As a result, Martinetti toughened his position, stating that "Paraguayan, Argentine, Israeli, and Brazilian special agents continue to question Arabs at the tri-border."[47] A year later, Martinetti went so far as to say that Ciudad del Este was "a sanctuary of sleeper cells of Hizbullah."[48]

The post-authoritarian Brazilian state rejected Argentine allegations of terrorism at the border but also increased security and "update(d)" police "files" on "Arab communities."[49] Brazil's Federal Police as well as the Strategic Affairs Secretariat of the Presidency of the Republic reported "no signs" that "the terrorist acts . . . in Argentina" were "planned from Brazil, as the Argentine government has come to suspect."[50] Later on, the Brazilian consulate in Buenos Aires wrote that "investigations pointed to the involvement of police officials of the province of Buenos Aires," despite the Argentine government "discreetly insinuating that the blame lies with neighboring countries," Brazil and Paraguay.[51] Having discovered "small traders, some having been there" for some time, "the Brazilian government maintained that there are no signs of the presence or even passage of terrorists on Brazilian territory," repeated the Agência Brasileira de Inteligência (ABIN, Brazilian Agency of Intelligence), founded in 1999 and headed by career military men after the dissolution of the aforementioned Serviço Nacional de Informações (SNI, National Service of Information) of the "old authoritarian regime."[52] Though dismissing Argentine suspicions that the AMIA attack was planned from Brazil, in 1995, Brazilian foreign minister, Luiz Felipe Lampreia "ended up bending toward" an Argentine proposal for a security accord between the three states of the border "in the fight against terrorism, drug-trafficking, and smuggling," explored later in this chapter.[53]

Arabs and others on the Brazilian side of the border spoke with Argentine media in order to denounce anti-Semitic violence in Buenos Aires as well as to represent themselves as scapegoats. The Imam of the Omar Ibn Al-Khattab mosque dedicated his sermon to condemning violence and expressing solidarity with "the victims of the brutal attack on the AMIA headquarters."[54] Kamal Osman stated that there is no place for terrorists at the border because "I would be the first to turn them in."[55] Hussein Taijen specified to *La Prensa*, "the press wants to put all the blame on us."[56] Mohamad Barakat echoed that "they always throw blame on Arabs."[57] Mayor Dobrandino da Silva, having ushered in the return of civilian rule and inaugurating the mosque six years previously, reassured the *Clarín* reporter that "there are no undocumented Arabs" who are "well integrated in our society."[58] However, Argentine media diminished such standpoints by emphasizing the "armed guards" around Arab-owned stores on the Avenida República do Líbano in Foz do Iguaçu and lending more credence to predominantly Argentine and US suspicions of terrorists allegedly lurking at the border.

On Brazilian and Paraguayan sides of the border, Arabs again "condemned violence they never condoned" and portrayed themselves as easy marks.[59] In *A Gazeta do Iguaçu*, they rebuked "the CNI" and Argentina for blaming "the Arab community of Foz do Iguaçu and Ciudad del Este" for "the terrorist attack against Buenos Aires."[60] Mohamad Rahal repeated, "we are against the terrorist attack in Buenos Aires" and no terrorists exist in Foz do Iguaçu and Ciudad del Este because "We all know one another . . . we are relatives, friends, and acquaintances. . . . There are no strangers among us." Kamal Osman warned that "national and international news coverage" about alleged terrorists is "bad for the city, for tourism, for business, and bad for all of us who live here at the border." Osman also repeated his declaration to *Clarín* the day before, "I myself would denounce to the authorities anyone with terrorist or extremist tendencies." Mustafá Jaber, a Palestinian Brazilian, likewise stated, "I will be the first to turn into the police any person who I mistrust may be a terrorist," adding "Islam condemns criminal acts like that which occurred in Buenos Aires where innocents died and hundreds were wounded." On the following day, the Imam of the mosque again condemned the AMIA bombing and "the suppositions of Argentine authorities and the international press in linking the attack . . . to the resident Arab community in Foz do Iguaçu and Ciudad del Este."

Shortly after the bombing, Argentina's gendarmerie took exceptional measures against Arabs. The gendarmerie retained power over the country's infrastructure, including borders, after authoritarian rule, having aided the Argentine military junta's repression and disappearance of tens of thousands of alleged "subversives."[61] With new orders to "minutely examine" the "foreigners" crossing onto the Argentine side of the border, in Puerto Iguazú, the gendarmerie commandeer admitted that: "We don't have either a name or a face. Nothing. We are totally up in the air. . . . The only thing is that one speaks about the Arabs in general, so everything gets directed toward them."[62] Aware of Argentine "prejudice," "Arabs in Foz do Iguaçu" began "avoiding crossing the border to the Argentine side" because the "climate is very tense at the tri-border."[63] Soon after, the gendarmerie in Puerto Iguazú detained six Shia Lebanese as AMIA bombing suspects.[64] Living in Foz do Iguaçu and working in Ciudad del Este, they allegedly entered Argentina in order to pick up friends arriving at the airport in Puerto Iguazú. Argentine media spun conspiracy theories that they were a "sleeper cell of Hizbullah" at the border that planned the bombing.[65] After transferring and holding them incommunicado in Buenos Aires for ten days, the Argentine state released the "suspects" since they "had nothing to do with the AMIA case."[66]

Arabs both appealed to and held the Argentine state responsible for exceptional measures. An Argentine lawyer of Lebanese origins, Alfredo Jalaf, came to the defense of Shia Lebanese migrants being held in extraordinary circumstances in Buenos Aires. Jalaf was the grandson of a distinct wave of Maronite Lebanese migrants from Zahle, growing up in the Argentine cities of Mendoza and Cordoba, before moving to the Misiones province.[67] Called a *misionero* (inhabitant of Misiones) in the press, Jalaf was a member of the post-authoritarian constituent assembly that revised democratic municipal governing legislation in 1994. Jalaf defended the Lebanese citizens after their detention in Puerto Iguazú and while they were held incommunicado in Buenos Aires.[68] Meanwhile, on the Brazilian side of the border, in Foz do Iguaçu, Mohamad Barakat spoke out against "the government of Argentina" for "practicing terrorism in arresting . . . Lebanese who appear in their country. If there are suspects here at the border, then Argentina should release the list. We cannot accept that honest traders, family fathers, be despised by incompetent authorities . . . and kidnapped by the Argentine state."[69]

Argentine scapegoating of Arabs at the border failed to redress the violence in Buenos Aires. In 1995, the Argentine state itself came under fire for hindering the prosecution of both the 1992 Israeli embassy bombing and the 1994 AMIA bombing. The Israeli ambassador complained that "not much has been done" by Argentina's Supreme Court "to clarify the attack."[70] Rubén Beraja, the president of DAIA (Delegation of Jewish Argentine Associations), asked a Supreme Court judge to resign "if he could not advance the case."[71] The AMIA president likewise regretted that "Argentina is still a place where the attacks go unpunished."[72] Meanwhile, Argentine policemen were detained for interfering in the investigation, the Argentine Minister of Justice, Rodolfo Barra, resigned amid alleged Nazi sympathies, and the Argentine Minister of the Economy, Domingo Cavallo, stepped down and denounced not only the new Minister of Justice, Elias Jassan, but also the Minister of the Interior, Carlos Corach, for meddling with judges and prosecutors in each case.[73] Public perceptions of a state cover-up exacerbated orientalist representations of the president Carlos Menem who was the son of Muslim

Syrians, and his ministers of Jewish origins, derogatorily called *los judíos de Menem* (Menem's Jews).[74]

The US likewise faulted the Argentine state for failing to prosecute the violence perpetrated in its own capital. In 1995, the US House of Representatives Foreign Affairs Committee convened a hearing on "international terrorism in Latin America, in particular Argentina and the bombing of the Jewish Community Center (AMIA) in Buenos Aires."[75] Though another hearing on authoritarian Argentina had been held less than a decade and a half previously, there was no substantive engagement with the country's past of state-sponsored violence and human rights abuses that were often justified by allegations of combating terrorism.[76] The nearly two-hundred-page report on the AMIA bombing instead made a few references about Arabs or Muslims at the border and more frequent criticisms of the Argentine state's handling of the two attacks in Buenos Aires. Philip Wilcox, the US Department of State's Coordinator for Counterterrorism, explicitly blamed the unsolved bombings on Hizbullah, and claimed there were Hizbullah "cells" at the "tri-border area of Argentina, Brazil, and Paraguay."[77] However, the majority of Jewish Argentine testimonies, and their answers to US committee members, put greater emphasis on the "failings" of Argentine officials in punishing the perpetrators of the 1992 and 1994 bombings.

Failing to redress anti-Israeli and anti-Jewish violence, the Argentine state continued to point fingers at the border. President Menem took up a suggestion made on Capitol Hill, and proposed a "system of information" for Argentine, Brazilian, and Paraguayan law enforcement agencies to guard against alleged "terrorist cells" at the border.[78] "Menem's proposal," reported *Folha de S. Paulo*, was "linked to recent pressures the Argentine government received from the local Jewish community and the United States."[79] A year later, in 1996, Menem's plan spawned the *comando tripartite* (Tripartite Command), a security network with shared intelligence and rotating leadership between the Argentine and Paraguayan Ministers of the Interior, and Brazil's Minister of Justice, the first of its kind since Operation Condor.[80] Operationalized by Brazil's PF, Paraguay's PN, and Argentina's gendarmerie, the security accord mitigated Argentine and Brazilian states' distinct agendas in relation to Paraguay, more fully explored in the next chapter. Argentine officials were interested in "fighting terrorism" and pushed for the "identification and documentation of foreign citizens who reside in the [border] region, principally those of Arab origin."[81] Brazilian authorities rejected the Argentine idea of IDs for Arabs as "discriminatory," but they welcomed stricter border controls to curb tax-evasive trade and what was called "Paraguay's endogenous banditry."[82] Argentina's Interior Minister still blamed Arabs and "lax" border controls, but Brazil's Foreign Minister retorted that Argentine officials used "conspiracy theories" in order "to excuse themselves" due to "unsuccessful Argentine efforts at finding the culprits" of the attacks in Buenos Aires.[83]

## Making an Ummah America

Without full enfranchisement, Arabs in Foz do Iguaçu and Ciudad del Este nonetheless forged an Ummah that "signified both a common heritage and new modes of Muslim identity, unity, and difference," to borrow from the work of religious studies scholar Jamillah Karim.[84] Sobhi Mohamad Issa, for instance, migrated to Brazil in the 1980s where he met and married his wife, Cabura, born to Lebanese parents in northern Paraná. Settling at the border, this couple participated in the baptism of the son of Catholic Brazilian friends. Their children studied Arabic in the morning, and in the afternoon, they attended "a traditional high school of Foz do Iguaçu." Cabura reflected, "we aren't distorting our culture, but integrating into the society of the country that received us."[85] Likewise, the daughters of Hussein Taijen studied in Paraguayan and Brazilian schools, and after earning degrees, opened law and business offices in their father and uncle's building in Ciudad del Este. The aforementioned prayer space functioned in this same building, typifying what Alejandro Hamed Franco called the "free exercise of Islamic worship in Paraguay."[86] Arabs enmeshed with such everyday dynamics, experiencing no inherent conflict in being Muslim, Brazilian, and/or Paraguayan.

Suspected of complicity in still unresolved violence in Argentina, Muslim Arabs at the border commemorated religious holidays alongside Brazilian and Paraguayan authorities. Year after year in *A Gazeta do Iguaçu* during the 1990s, Sunni members of the Islamic Benevolent Cultural Center and the Omar Ibn al-Khattab mosque explained the meaning of Ramadan, the month of fasting from dawn to sunset, as a time of sacrifice and reflection. The "principal characteristic of Ramadan," explained one adept, is "the integration of Muslims," with the rich and poor coming together at the end of the day as well as a "more just distribution of wealth."[87] Through the 1990s, the mosque invited and hosted local government officials in celebrating Eid al Fitr that marks the end of Ramadan as well as Eid al Adha that commemorates Abraham's willingness to sacrifice his son.[88] Local media even covered children, like twelve-year old Leila who fasted during Ramadan: "The first Sunday was difficult. My mother was cooking and I took a plate to eat three times, but I overcame [the temptation] and learned to practice patience."[89] Thirteen-year old Iman Safa added that "the fasting doesn't count if we have bad thoughts about others." Twelve-year old Hanan concluded, "we come to know the suffering of poor people . . . when we feel hungry during this month." Notwithstanding Argentine and US vitriol that disembodied them as threats, Arabs continued making an Ummah America.

Like their Sunni counterparts, Shia Lebanese publicly collaborated with government, media, and civil society at the border. Shia members of the Islamic Benevolent Society commemorated *Arba'iyyn*, "the fortieth day," after *'Ashura*, which observes "the martyrdom of the Imam Hussein, grandson of the Prophet Mohamed."[90] Instead of the public banquets sponsored by the Omar Ibn al-Khattab mosque, Shia used this and other holy days to organize clothing or food drives, donating two and three "tons of clothing" for "the needy of the city" through a local, non-Arab NGO in 1996 and 1997. Speaking in the name of the Islamic Benevolent Society, Ali Abdallah reflected that "we collect the donations among the members of the Society and we store everything so we can donate to the most needy. The key is to collaborate with people." In the following years, he and his wife, Hayat, continued to oversee the donations. Hayat Abdallah stated, "We are commemorating a very important date, because this is the month of Ramadan, in other words, the month of God when we feel the religious and human obligation to help others. That way, we collaborate to diminish suffering in the world."[91] The Foz do Iguaçu mayor's wife headed the NGO that received Muslim donations and redistributed them in Foz do Iguaçu, calling the Islamic Benevolent Society "an example for other civil society groups. . ."

As Argentine and US authorities unduly associated Arab Muslims at the border with the AMIA and Israeli embassy bombings in Buenos Aires, Brazilian everyday citizens and government officials formalized the mosque in Foz do Iguaçu as an icon. A long-time staple of tourist maps and attracting thousands of visitors every month,[92] the Omar Ibn al-Khattab mosque was formally opened for visitation in 1998, especially for elementary and high school students. The mosque's cultural director, Ale Ahmad Ghazzaoui, reflected, "the last school we received touched us with the creativity of the questions made by the students. Sometimes, Muslims are not even that interested."[93] In the same year, the Brazilian post office branch inaugurated a commemorative stamp in homage to the mosque. Showing the mosque's dome flanked by two minarets and its official title as the "Mesquita Omar Ben Al-Khattab," the stamp was used on "all correspondence of the Islamic Benevolent Cultural Center." Having frequently rebuked associations with lawlessness and violence in Argentina, the mosque's secretary, Kamal Osman, called the Brazilian postage stamp "a historic mark," literally and figuratively.[94]

Arabs even enmeshed Islam with the *Dia de Finados* (All Souls Day, in English), a date in the Catholic religious calendar whereby the souls of the departed are remembered in prayer and through visitation to grave sites, officially recognized by the state in Brazil but not Paraguay. Stores and schools are closed in Foz do Iguaçu, as many head to the city's cemeteries, São João Batista or Jardim São Paulo. Ali Ghazzaoui recounted that "Muslims of Ciudad del Este and Foz" partake in this Brazilian ritual of visiting the deceased "out of respect for the customs of the people who welcomed them." Muslim families headed to the corner of the Jardim São Paulo cemetery, originally purchased in 1981 by and for Muslims to "bury their dead with the feet facing east."[95] Ghazzaoui noted that Muslims generally avoided the use of candles in the cemetery. Many, however, adopted the Catholic practice of bringing flowers and placing them on the tombs. Whereas Catholic counterparts recited the "Hail Mary" and the "Our Father," Muslims read aloud "Yā sīn, 36th surah [chapter] of the Quran" in front of the graves of loved ones whose "faces were turned toward Mecca, toward the sunrise, because on the final day of judgment, when the dead will rise, they'll look toward the holy city."[96]

Amid Argentine and US machinations that vilified their transnational reach, Muslim Lebanese on the Brazilian and Paraguayan sides of the border maintained long-distance ties, including with Lebanon's AMAL party, headed by parliamentary president Nabih Berri. In 1996, Berri and twenty-one Lebanese parliamentarians visited Foz do Iguaçu and Ciudad del Este. Berri stated his intention to "reinforce the ties between the Arab Community and the "Government of Lebanon."[97] Border media explained that "Berri commands the radical political organization, AMAL (Shiite)" and transformed himself from "one of the most feared terrorists of the world" to "an internationally respected persona."[98] Arabs hosted a banquet for a thousand people in the luxurious Hotel Bourbon and accompanied Berri on visits to the Iguaçu waterfalls, the Itaipu damn, and Islamic charity associations. In these venues, Berri referred to the nearly twenty-year Israeli occupation in southern Lebanon and emphasized that "the invaders are them [Israelis]." Lebanese at the border "wanted to show the parliamentary president the development that they brought to the region and reinforce support for the reconstruction of Lebanon."

Arabs at the border imagined themselves as victims, not victimizers, publicly raising the question of whether Israeli incursions in Lebanon could fuel Argentine offensives against the Brazilian and Paraguayan sides of the border. After Berri's visit, in 1996, Israel shelled South Lebanon and the Beqaa Valley. Called "Grapes of Wrath," the Israeli attack allegedly aimed to stomp out Hizbullah bases but it resulted in thousands of civilian casualties that provoked fear on the Brazilian and Paraguayan sides of the border. As Israel attacked Lebanon, a Foz do Iguaçu newspaper reported on "a rumor in the Arab community that the region would be a possible target of Israeli terrorists who would try to strike at Hizbullah and the Lebanese government through their compatriots in Latin America."[99] It was feared that "Israeli terrorists" would enter via Argentina in order to attack Arabs on the Brazilian and Paraguayan sides of the border. A military spokesman in Puerto Iguazú dismissed the rumor, attempting to disassociate Argentine stances toward Brazil and Paraguay from the Israeli attack on Lebanon.

At this hemispheric crossroads of an Ummah, Arab traders from Brazilian and Paraguayan sides organized a street march in protest of Israel's shelling of Lebanon. "Stores run by Arabs in Ciudad del Este," related *A Gazeta do Iguaçu*, "closed their doors . . . in protest and went to Avenida Brasil (in Foz do Iguaçu) where the demonstration began."[100] They joined some three thousand civic demonstrators who condemned the Israeli war on Hizbullah that resulted in thousands of innocent deaths in Lebanon. Although the Israeli offensive targeted Shia-majority areas of Lebanon, the protest's most outspoken critics were Sunni. Kamal Osman, Mohamad Barakat, and others condemned Israel's shelling that resulted in civilian and non-combatant deaths. To commemorate the forty-day anniversary of the war, in tribute to the civilians murdered, the Shia-led Islamic Benevolent Society held a ceremony that included these as well as other Sunni and non-Muslim residents.[101] Together at an Ummah American border, Sunni and Shia Muslims mourned and protested the killing of innocent civilians.

With the unlikely return to villages attacked or occupied by Israel, Shia Lebanese deepened their roots at the border by founding a new school, the "Escola Libanesa Brasileira" (Lebanese Brazilian School). According to Reda Soueid, "this school" would "better connect the Arab community into the Iguaçu community" and "the cultural exchange between them."[102] Mohsen Bilal Wehbi from São Paulo collaborated with the Islamic Benevolent Society, arranging for a Lebanese migrant, Ali Khazan, to become the school principal.[103] Opened in 2000, the school is located on a main highway outside the city center in Foz do Iguaçu. It started offering "elementary education" for some six hundred children on three floors and around twenty-seven classrooms, expanding later on.[104] According to the Brazilian principal, Regina Venâncio, the Escola Libanesa Brasileira and the previously established Colégio Líbano

Brasileiro, "have the goal of attending to the children, descendants of the Islamic community, as well as all the students from other communities."[105] Brazil's Ministry of Education approved the school curriculum with classes in Arabic, English, and Portuguese, as well as Islamic religion and history.[106] "Dona Regina," as she is known, observed that parents would arrange for children enrolled at the Escola Libanesa Brasileira to study abroad in Lebanon, who after a short time, returned to Foz do Iguaçu. Migrant parents wanted their children to renew family ties, improve language skills, and attend Lebanese schools based on a US curriculum, which offered special classes for study abroad students from Brazil and Paraguay.[107]

Arabs folded into this Ummah America in ways that precluded the Argentine side of the border. In 1998, *Veja* stated that "Arab immigrants of Foz do Iguaçu and Ciudad del Este avoided visiting Puerto Iguazú. . . . They know they are not welcome."[108] The newsweekly pointed out that the Argentine state suspected Arabs of providing "shelter to terrorists of Hizbullah" and "it hopes to blame" them "for the two anti-Jewish attacks [*sic*] that killed more than 100 persons in Buenos Aires."[109] A month later, Brazilian diplomats in Asunción made the same observation that Argentine counterparts blamed the border for the violence that the Argentine state failed to prevent and prosecute in Buenos Aires.[110] *Veja*, reflecting Brazilian government policy, explained that "there is no proof" of Argentine accusations against Arabs, but "the immigrants are suspected because the majority come from the south of Lebanon and belong to the Shia branch of Islam." *Veja* qualified that "sympathy for Hizbullah is no secret in the community," but also that Brazilian and Paraguayan states did not consider Hizbullah (or AMAL) "terrorist organizations."[111] *A Gazeta do Iguaçu* more explicitly criticized the Argentine government for having "ceded to the interests of the United States and Israel," which "demanded energetic actions from the Brazilian and Paraguayan governments to undertake surveillance of Arab communities."[112] Having helped in the authoritarian rise of Brazil over Paraguay, Arabs at the border became a target of post-authoritarian Argentina and the US.

## "Muslim First . . ." in America

The "Muslim First . . ." configuration of identity that anthropologist Nadine Naber studied among Arabs in the US was both imputed to and taken up by counterparts on the Brazilian and Paraguayan sides of the border.[113] State authorities in the aforementioned "Tripartite Command" referenced the Muslimness of the border especially in relation to unresolved violence against Jews in Argentina.[114] Just after the command's representatives met in Buenos Aires, the Brazilian Federal Police apprehended a Shia shaykh, Seyed Mohsen Tabatabai, for allegedly conspiring in the AMIA bombing.[115] Usually characterized as "Islamic," Tabatabai's Iranian passport had a Paraguayan residency stamp that apparently dated back to 1984, which had been just renewed. For some two years previously, Tabatabai used legitimate credentials as the religious leader in the Shia-led Islamic Benevolent Society in Foz do Iguaçu and in the Mezquita del Profeta Mohamad in Ciudad del Este. Without this backdrop, *ABC Color* reported that Tabatabai was one of the "kingpins" of Hizbullah, protecting other "Arab terrorists who participated in the attack" on AMIA, though Brazil's Federal Police maintained that Tabatabai had not infringed upon any law.[116] Tabatabai's Iranian passport with the necessary visas was confiscated in Foz do Iguaçu and forwarded to Interpol. After a week, Brazil's Federal Police declared that Tabatabai was innocent. Years later, upon verification from the embassy in Tehran, the Brazilian state extended official Brazilian visas for Tabatabai and his family.[117] State authorities detained, defamed, and absolved a Shia religious leader at the border.

Without reference to Arab, Iranian, or other Middle Eastern categories of difference in this Ummah, Muslims came together to represent Shia identity on its own terms. After Tabatabai explained to a journalist that Shia uphold a "more democratic" form of governing, his Sunni counterpart, Mohamad Barakat, then Secretary of Industry and Commerce of the Foz do Iguaçu government, added, "in this system, the way of governing among us is by consultative means, through popular councils, where the members are chosen by the people." Tabatabai and Barakat stressed that Muslims at the border were "blamed" for the AMIA bombing in Buenos Aires.[118]

With overwhelmingly Sunni and Shia Lebanese by his side, Tabatabai explained, "the first thing that I learned was tolerance amid any
false accusation. We always hope that the accuser apologizes. That
way, we are obliged to forgive, especially when we are in a position of
power." Indeed, Tabatabai had authority, bearing a distant relation
to the prominent scholar of Shia Islam, Muhammad Husayn Tabatabai. He concluded that "false news reports" about alleged ties to
the AMIA bombing "committed violence against truth, democracy,
humanity, and above all, the security of the peoples of the *três fronteiras* (three borders)."[119]

Shia Lebanese in Ciudad del Este likewise supported Tabatabai.
Ibrahim Hijazi conceded an interview to *ABC Color* as "the official
representative of Lebanon's AMAL party," explaining that AMAL
was "against violence" and guaranteed that Tabatabai was "guid-
ing, helping, and encouraging the religious customs of his community and has no connection with terrorism."[120] Without referencing
Tabatabai's Iranian background, or his scholarly pedigree, Hijazi
explained that the title of Tabatabai as *shaykh* meant that he was
a "religious" leader in Islam, "respected for his charity work." Likewise, not commenting on the shaykh's undeserved association
with the unresolved violence perpetrated against Israeli and Jewish institutions in Buenos Aires, Hijazi emphasized that Muslims
are against terrorism because the "founder of the AMAL party,"
Musa al-Sadr, was kidnapped and killed by terrorists. As a Muslim and self-identified AMAL representative, Hijazi declared that
fellow "Lebanese merchants living in Ciudad del Este" sought to
escape, not spread, conflict. Lebanese Shia defended Tabatabai and
portrayed Muslims not as the perpetrators but rather as victims of
violence.

Post-authoritarian Brazilian authorities defended Tabatabai and
associated him with the Muslim-majority "Arab community." The
Workers' Party (PT), the Party of the Brazilian Democratic Movement (PMDB), the Party of Brazilian Social Democracy (PSDB), and
the Communist Party of Brazil (PC do B), among others, wrote an
open "Statement of Support to the Arab Community of the *Tríplice
Fronteira*."[121] The letter began, "Political parties in Foz do Iguaçu
publicly denounce the existence" of a "biased and smear campaign"

levied "against the region of the Three Borders and principally against the Arab Community that has lived and worked here for dozens of years." It continued that "since the attack against AMIA," mainstream media portrayed the border as a "central base of operations for Arab Terrorists who control all terror in Latin America." The letter explained that Tabatabai's ordeal began when an unspecified "Paraguayan newspaper from Asunción" claimed "the Muslim priest and missionary [*sic*]" was "the leader of a terrorist group in charge of spreading terror in Latin America." However, "after an investigation through Interpol, the untrue allegations led the local Federal Police chief to challenge the news." The letter concluded that Muslims and Arabs "always contributed to the construction and development of the *tríplice fronteira*," and thus, "should be respected in their dignity and citizenship." Without taking note of the difference between Tabatabai and the predominantly Arab public at the border, the Foz do Iguaçu city government defended a wrongly detained Islamic religious leader.

Shortly after Tabatabai's vindication, the Shia-led Islamic Benevolent Society celebrated the end of Ramadan by donating food, toys, and clothing for the needy. In subtle reference to the conspiracy theory spun by big media, Ali Abdallar stated, "it's important that the press covers this kind of action, so this example can be followed by other persons, independently of nationality or belief."[122] Abdallar made a "call to fraternity. This border is so rich. If each of us gives a little, we wouldn't have poor people." He paraphrased the Quran, "Never will one arrive at the altar of fraternity or goodness, if they don't give away a little of what they enjoy." Repeating the gesture in subsequent years, another member, Ali Abdala, made it clear that "Our goal in making donations is to fulfill a religious and humanitarian obligation to help who is near."[123] Their donations went to the local NGO known by the acronym Provopar (Programa do Voluntariado Paranaense, or Paraná State Volunteer Program). After a Shia shaykh was wrongly detained by law enforcement, the Islamic Benevolent Society where he led prayer carried out an annual donation event for the needy.

Nonetheless, the Argentine state strong-armed its Paraguayan counterpart to produce any Muslim Arab suspect for still unresolved anti-Semitic violence in Buenos Aires. In 1998, "Paraguayan and Argentine police forces" together issued "an international arrest warrant" for Khaled Taki Eldin, a Sunni religious leader allegedly wanted "in the AMIA case."[124] The case began when Argentina's SIDE, navy, and gendarmerie published a report that *grupos chiitas* (Shia groups) in Ciudad del Este "benefited from the backwardness of the Paraguayan government in the implementation of security measures."[125] At first, Paraguay's Foreign Relations Ministry rebuked this Argentine report as an excuse for "failing to investigate the attacks."[126] Even the *stronista* strongman of Alto-Paraná, Carlos Barreto Sarubbi, expressed disbelief at the accusations levied against "the Islamic population" because "they are people who all of us know."[127] His son, just elected as mayor of Ciudad del Este, echoed, "Here, we never had any attacks and never detected terrorist cells."[128] In the following months, however, Paraguayan authorities carried out what *Clarín* called an "anti-terrorist dragnet" in Paraguay, detaining Lebanese Muslims with purported "connections" to "the massacres of the Embassy of Israel in 1992 and AMIA in 1994 in Buenos Aires."[129] When this roundup failed to produce evidence, Argentina's Interior Minister, Carlos Corach asked for better results from his Paraguayan counterpart,[130] and on the same day, Paraguay's National Police received a judicial order to search and detain the Egyptian-born Eldin in Ciudad del Este.

But the post-authoritarian Brazilian state pushed back against Paraguay in spite of Argentine pressure. After all, Eldin was a naturalized Brazilian citizen living in Foz do Iguaçu for twelve years with his wife and four Brazilian-born children.[131] Brazilian officials asked Eldin to wait for Paraguayan authorities to follow diplomatic protocol and request Eldin's testimony at the Brazilian embassy in Asunción, which then would be forwarded to Brazil's Foreign Ministry.[132] "If the request was approved," *A Gazeta do Iguaçu* explained, "Eldin would have the right to be heard in Brazil by a Brazilian judge."[133] Eldin spoke of his religious duties under Brazilian sovereignty, "I exercise my religious responsibilities in strict obedience to Brazilian law and supported by the constitution, which guarantees freedom of consciousness and religious worship."[134] Eldin likewise spoke of neither Sunni nor Shia but rather of the "comunidade árabe-islâmica."[135] Although Eldin expressed his willingness to meet with Paraguayan authorities alongside Mohamad Barakat, Said Taijen, Atef Manah, and others in the Centro Cultural Beneficente Islâmico, the Brazilian state intervened against Argentine-influenced Paraguay.[136]

Sunni and Shia came together against post-authoritarian Argentina's "diplomatic offensive" that vilified the Ummah as being "responsible for two major anti-Jewish attacks in the country's capital."[137] After *ABC Color* alleged that Eldin had "supposed ties with the terrorist arm of Hizbullah,"[138] Reda Soueid, a Shia from Khiam in South Lebanon, replied that "Khaled Eldin is Sunni, which shows the wrong-headedness of the accusations" that associated him with "Hizbullah and Iran" that are of "the Shia line of Islam."[139] Soueid lobbied against anti-migrant "dragnets" in Brazil, discussed in the next chapter, delivering to Brazil's Minister of Justice a report about the "persecution of Arabs" that was exacerbated by baseless accusations of "Islamic terrorist cells in the region."[140] A one-time member of the Lebanese communist party, Soueid lived in Foz do Iguaçu since 1978, presided over a local branch of the Worker's Party (PT), and ran a store in the Paraguayan border town. Around this time, Soueid noted, "We have a hidden war here, and we Arabs are on the defensive."[141] Indeed, Muslim Arabs' sense of being under collective attack heightened after Paraguay's National Police claimed that Eldin used the "Sunni mosque of Foz do Iguaçu" as a cover for ties to "Hamas and Al Gamat al Islamiya" [*sic*].[142]

Arabs again pointed fingers not at Paraguay but rather at Argentina for the anti-Israeli and anti-Jewish violence that the state failed to prevent and prosecute. In Ciudad del Este, Hussein Taijen stated to *Clarín* that "AMIA is an internal problem of your own" in Argentina. Argentine authorities, he counter-accused, sought "to transfer the problem to the *triple frontera* because they couldn't clarify the attack and because there's a lot of cash moving here."[143] Taijen even defended Hizbullah. This nominally Sunni Lebanese stressed: "Hizbullah does not exist in Paraguay, but at any rate, this group is a political party that struggles for the liberation of its land, as you, Argentines, struggled for the Falkland Islands."[144] Taijen likened Hizbullah's struggle with Israel to Argentina's past war with

Britain. Taijen dismissed the Argentine Interior Minister's allegation of Hizbullah support at the border, reflecting "Is it right that we
send cash to the Islamic cause? We would have no problem sending
money. But it just so happens that Hizbullah has a lot more cash
than we do." But the *Clarín* newspaper headline read "All of us Arabs
here are of Hizbullah." Taijen criticized Argentina's scapegoating
of Arabs at the border, but his position was glossed as monolithic
support for Hizbullah.

Though critical of the Argentine state and media, Taijen's stance
"was not well received" by some Shia Lebanese.[145] Whether misread-
ing the headline or misconstruing his words, some Shia Lebanese
thought that their Sunni counterpart had characterized Ciudad del
Este as a "cueva de terroristas" (cave of terrorists) or labeled Shia or
Hizbullah as terrorists. Viewed as Sunni, Hussein Taijen had a better image beforehand, but he lost some respect among Shia after
his remark from the Argentine press circulated on the Brazilian and
Paraguayan sides of the border. Although Taijen criticized Argentine attempts to blame Muslims and Arabs for unresolved violence
in Buenos Aires, Shia Lebanese and others hardly thought of Taijen
as defending them. As scapegoats of the Argentine state's failure to
thwart or resolve the 1992 bombing of the Israeli embassy and the
1994 bombing of AMIA in Buenos Aires, Muslim Arabs at the border likewise failed to shore up the politics of religious difference
among themselves.

Such circumstances exacerbated violence against Muslim Arabs
at the border, as three leaders were gunned down in the span of a
year.[146] In one case, Sheikh Ziad Fahs was shot twice in the head and
survived.[147] Fahs ran the Shia-majority Centro Educacional Libanés
in Ciudad del Este, brought up earlier. Suspicions were raised that
the shooting was an attempt to silence his criticisms of the impunity surrounding the prior shooting of Taijen himself, addressed
in the next chapter. In one of Fahs's sermons, the religious leader
"demanded more seriousness on the part of Paraguayan authorities to investigate the assassination."[148] In fact, the Centro Educacional Libanés pleaded for his case to be investigated as an act of
terrorism.[149] But the anti-terrorist division of Paraguay's National
Police alleged that the violence stemmed from Muslims' internal

"sectarian" divisions.[150] Accordingly, the Paraguayan state side-stepped Fahs's own request "to investigate my case, which is very grave, because we still don't know what happened."[151] Assailants were arrested and charged, but Sunni and Shia were increasingly uncertain of due legal process at the border more than a decade after the formal end of authoritarian rule.


Muslim Arabs were subject to, and not executors of, authoritarian legacies. Lebanese, Palestinians, and Syrians brought Islam into Foz do Iguaçu and Ciudad del Este, and that border into a wider Ummah. Tending to steer clear of authoritarian and post-authoritarian regimes, their Islamic community-organizing accommodated state exceptions. But as the anti-terrorist or counterterrorist mantras of past authoritarian regimes crept into subsequent post-authoritarian administrations, Muslim Arabs saw themselves as taking the blame for anti-Israeli and anti-Jewish attacks that the Argentine government neither prevented nor prosecuted in a checkered history of state-sponsored violence. Arabs on the Brazilian and Paraguayan sides of the border distanced the Islam they practiced from the exceptional demands made by Argentine and US authorities, but the concomitant rise of liberal economic blocs made matters more uncertain.

# PART II

# COUNTERTERRORIST LIAISONS

(1990S–2010S)

# CHAPTER 4

# Free Trade Security

**Arabs at the border** could hardly foretell the Southern Common Market, better known as Mercosur, mentioned at the start of this book. Unexpectedly, their cross-border businesses came to face restrictive terms of trade and security in what historian Aylê-Salassié Filgueiras Quintão called a "common destiny" in a "vector of Americanity."[1] Ratified by Brazilian, Paraguayan, Argentine, and Uruguayan states, the Mercosur bloc took little account of Arab-led commerce at the border, but kept tabs on the US-led North American Free Trade Agreement (NAFTA) as well as the unsuccessful Free Trade Area of the Americas (FTAA).

Lebanese, Palestinians, and Syrians carried on doing business through Mercosur's standardized tariffs and monitoring mechanisms in the 1990s. On the Brazilian side of the border, Arabs curtailed exportation and imported into Brazil from outside the bloc using Mercosur's Common External Tariffs (CETs). On the Paraguayan side of the border, Arabs continued selling to Brazilian clientele by obtaining exemptions from Mercosur's CETs, importing goods from the Colón free trade zone, discussed earlier, and increasingly from South Floridian free trade zones. However, after US and Argentine authorities alleged that Arab trade threatened the bloc and hemisphere, Brazilian officials set up checkpoints on the Friendship Bridge at the border with Paraguay, detaining and releasing Arabs who resided on the Brazilian side and ran stores on the Paraguayan side. Categorized as "non-Mercosur" subjects, Arabs shored up their insecure status with heavy stakes in real estate. Amid illiberal exceptions in a liberal economic bloc, Arabs promoted and persevered in this free trade America.

This chapter builds on scholarship that eschews the dichotomies of domination and resistance in "free trade," a misnomer for otherwise "inherently asymmetric" tariff reduction agreements.[2] But I turn from government officials, corporate elites, activists, and consumers to cross-border traders in a continental bloc of economic belonging. Lebanese, Palestinians, and Syrians adjusted or defended their trade as integral to Mercosur at the same time the US pressured the bloc's member states to join the unsuccessful FTAA, which historian Moniz Bandeira saw as an attempt to "revive the Monroe Doctrine."[3] On the Brazilian and Paraguayan sides of the border, Arabs adopted and appealed for exemptions to Mercosur tariffs in efforts to shore up the cross-border commerce that they had led over the previous decades. Nonetheless, Arabs were targeted, apprehended, and discharged by mostly Brazilian state officials seeking to redress the demands of Argentine and US counterparts. Neither dominating nor resisting Mercosur, Arabs finessed and folded into this free trade America.

Arabs at the border reveal that Mercosur was not only a "customs union" but also an "incipient security community" that made illiberal exceptions to liberal democratic expectations in the bloc's accords.[4] In dialogue with scholarship on liberal democratic states that adopted market and security reforms in the 1990s, this chapter charts Mercosur member states' neoliberal and counterterrorist policies that intersected and reinforced each other at the border.[5] I show that after having adapted to the liberal economic strictures of Mercosur, hundreds of Arabs were detained and discharged as "non-Mercosur" subjects in operations that suspended due process and expanded security sharing between Brazil and other Mercosur member states. By stopping, searching, and sending on their way mostly Arabs, government authorities put into place monitoring mechanisms that controlled the cross-border flows of persons, goods, and monies that preceded, and competed with, the bloc. Through exceptional measures targeting Arabs at the border, liberal democratic member states of Mercosur sanctioned free trade security.

## Changing Customs in Foz do Iguaçu

Arabs were not necessarily welcome in this common market with continental pretensions. On the Brazilian side of the border, they and other exporters were "extremely pessimistic" when Mercosur eliminated "tariffs on 95 percent of intraregional trade."[6] Mahmud Dawas, owner of the Calce Bem shoe store, lamented, "Ninety-five percent of my sales were to Paraguayans, and now with the implementation of Mercosur, business at the border has ended," since Brazilian "manufacturers are selling directly to Paraguayans" at a price "40 to 50 percent cheaper."[7] His counterpart, Ali Ahmad Ismail, owner of Malhas Tex, agreed that Paraguayan clients found cheaper textiles, shoes, and other goods elsewhere.[8] Mohamed Saleh observed that his and others' Paraguayan customers simply stopped coming.[9] Mohamed Ali Osman concluded "The city looks like it's dying . . . with Mercosur, practically everything we had got sunk."[10] Arabs' export-driven commerce at the border was undersold by the Mercosur agreement that opened the exportation of Brazilian manufactures across the continent.

Neither exporting in nor escaping from the US dollar, Arabs' aforementioned struggle to export Brazilian merchandise in Brazilian and not US currency backfired with the real (reais, pl.), the new Brazilian money introduced in 1994. Mohamad Rahal of Exportadora Real complained that Brazilian goods became more costly because "the real appears with a value of US$1.10."[11] Aref Bakri of Exportadora Marina explained, "an increase of ten cents on the US dollar is considered abusive by Paraguayan standards." According to Zein Barakat of Exportadora Vemo, the "overvalued" real made "Brazilian merchandise 10 percent more expensive, and for this reason, Paraguayans have disappeared."[12] Hassan Waken of the Casa da Sogra later summarized that "Paraguayans generated 70 to 80 percent of sales," but "they stopped buying" with "high-priced Brazilian merchandise."[13] Ali Osman opined that the overpriced Brazilian real forced him and other exporters to mark up prices. "We export to Paraguay" in Brazilian currency, Osman noted, so "we now compete in disadvantaged terms" with a cheaper US dollar.[14] Mustafa Osman surmised, "The situation is very critical. Due to our prices rising a lot in Brazil, we end up losing a competitive advantage in the Paraguayan market. The crisis has been coming."[15] Mohamad Barakat concluded that "the trajectory of export commerce is ending because there is no way to compete."[16] Though accustomed to exchange rate fluctuations, discussed in the first chapter, Arabs had never before experienced a Brazilian currency worth more than the US dollar, which led to plummeting sales.

Even more consequentially, "free trade" meant more, not less, governmental regulation. Mercosur inverted authoritarian-era state exceptions that had facilitated cross-border trade, as explored in the first chapter. According to an Arab storeowner in Ciudad del Este, the "customs integration" between Brazil and Paraguay shared more data about cross-border sales and shipments through integrated computerized systems.[17] The "most adversely affected," recounted a news article, were the "exporters of Vila Portes [in Foz do Iguaçu] and the small merchants of Ciudad del Este."[18] The integrated customs systems detected major irregularities in 1995. While Brazil's Secretariat of International Commerce (Secex) counted nearly four hundred million dollars of Brazilian goods sent to Paraguay, the Paraguayan Dirección General de Aduanas (General Directorate of Customs) tallied less than two hundred million. This discrepancy meant that half of "Brazilian products irregularly enter Paraguay" or that "fictitious (Brazilian) exports" to Paraguay were sold in Brazil, discussed earlier.[19] "Many Brazilian traders," surmised Rubén Fadlala, the head of Paraguayan customs, declared "false exports to Paraguay" in order to evade "high taxes."[20] Mercosur's regulatory mechanisms brought greater, not lesser, scrutiny to the cross-border trade that Arabs dealt in.

Subsequently, significant numbers of Arabs in Foz do Iguaçu shut down commercial export firms, especially in the neighborhoods of Jardim Jupira and Vila Portes next to the Friendship Bridge. In 1996, Abdul Rahal observed that most of the five hundred or so export businesses closed. The news reporter qualified that only a third did, but nonetheless ascertained that "one of the showpieces

of success of the Arab community," the Jardim Jupira neighborhood specializing in export-commerce, is "today bankrupt." Amid
a wave of business closures, the rental value of Rahal's property
plummeted: "We weren't able to rent for one thousand reais a piece
of property with a thousand square meters."[21] In 1994, Jardim Jupira
became a "ghost-neighborhood," exacerbated by the construction
of the off-ramp for the BR-277 highway that complicated access for
Paraguayan customers and cut in half the neighborhood, jeopardizing Mohamad Rahal's Exportadora Tupi and Aref Bakri's Exportadora Marina.[22] On the Brazilian side of the border, Arabs expressed
greater uncertainty in the free market.

Yet some Arab businesses in Foz do Iguaçu found a niche in Mercosur.[23] Mostly in the neighborhood of Vila Portes, some five dozen
firms continued exporting to Paraguay.[24] By 1999, their stores specialized in *exportação formiga* (ant-like exportation), catering to Paraguayan buyers who crisscrossed the Friendship Bridge in order to
purchase consumables and carry them back over to the Paraguayan
side.[25] Magrão, mentioned in the introduction, served such customers in his Loja Descontão (Big Discount Store) that carried clothing for men, women, and children.[26] In 2000, Magrão's and other
stores numbered among a hundred or so, selling "manufactured
products, made in other [Brazilian] cities" to Paraguayan retail clients. Consequently, Foz do Iguaçu became the Paraná "state champion of exportation," and lost its former title as "one of the largest
centers of exportation in the entire country," as shown in the first
chapter. Although the *Anuário Estatístico* (Statistical Yearbook) of
Foz do Iguaçu the same year surmised that commercial exportation
came to an "end" with "the formation of Mercosur," some Arab businesses on the Brazilian side of the border continued to "export" to
small-scale Paraguayan clients within Mercosur.[27]

Many other Arabs on the Brazilian side of the border began
importing into Brazil's own domestic market through Mercosur's
Common External Tariffs. Introduced in the first chapter, Fouad
Fakih opened the Fouad Center—New Time in 1997, bringing in
sporting goods, clothing, and household goods that lined the
store's aisles from "all parts of the world," according to former Acifi
president, César Cabral.[28] Cabral characterized Fakih as possessing

a "totally international mentality" and knowing "where such-and-such a product exists and where it is most needed." [29] Cabral concluded that Fakih "is leading one of the boldest and most dynamic commercial undertakings that exists in the world," which "honors the blood that he carries, the blood of a businessman that comes from his origins, the origins of world commerce, started by the Phoenicians."[30] Fakih's new store had over one hundred employees, seventy thousand clients on the books, and over four thousand square meters of retail space. Fakih opened his store not beside the Friendship Bridge where commercial exporters struggled, but rather on Avenida Juscelino Kubitschek in the "heart" of Foz do Iguaçu and targeted "clients on the periphery." Fakih explained that his new business "catered to clients with less buying power," fifteen thousand of whom were registered on opening day.[31] Asked about the "crisis so often heard about nowadays," Fakih responded, "I believe in my state, in my country, and principally in Foz do Iguaçu and its people."[32] In reversing the direction of transnational trade, Arabs used Mercosur tariffs to import and invest in Brazil's side of the border.

Arabs also expanded real estate investments beyond the neighborhoods of Vila Portes and Jardim Jupira where their commercial export firms closed down. Having founded his Kamalito store a decade previously, Kamal Osman invested in two real estate agencies, Fly Móveis (Fly Real Estate) and Mobilye Móveis e Decorações (Mobilye Real Estate and Decorations), and founded a third, Amo Foz (I love Foz), that specialized in middle-class residential developments.[33] Working with one of Brazil's largest civil construction firms, Encol (until it closed in 1999), Osman chose the name Amo Foz because he "loves this city a lot and it's here that his first seeds were planted, and it's here that his work in local commerce has developed." Osman's choice to invest was based in "love" and not "real estate speculation," though many considered him to be a *latifundiário urbano* (large urban land owner).[34] Likewise, Mohamad Barakat had accumulated so "many properties" in Jardim Jupira and elsewhere in Foz do Iguaçu that he ended up donating a piece of land for a public school named in honor of his mother, Escola Municipal Najla Barakat (Najla Barakat Municipal School). In 1995, the school expanded services with a children's daycare that was named after his wife, Creche Municipal Amina Barakat (Municipal Daycare Amina Barakat).[35] On the Brazilian side of the border, Arabs solidified their status as a propertied, and not just mercantile, class.

Far from using profits to threaten the security of the bloc or hemisphere, Arabs invested in myriad property ventures and drew the "invidious comparison" of other elites.[36] Rodrigo, a propertied Brazilian of Italian origins, recounted with delight that he was mistaken for a *turco* by the brother of the then governor of the state of Paraná, Roberto Requião (1991–1994, first mandate), mentioned in the second chapter. Rodrigo had just purchased a spacious apartment in an upper-middle class building in Foz do Iguaçu, and Requião's brother, part of a well-known Jewish Brazilian family and a real estate investor, bought another apartment on the same floor. Requião's brother expressed interest in buying Rodrigo's apartment, even asking a realtor, "Quem é esse turco que tem o apartamento na frente?" (Who is this Turk who has the apartment in front?). Later, this realtor relayed to Rodrigo that the governor's brother wanted to buy his apartment, and thought he was Arab, calling him by the common label of *turco*. Rodrigo soon after ran into Requião's brother, joking that he was the *turco* with the coveted apartment.[37] In contrast to Argentine and US suspicions of Arabs harboring ulterior financial motives, to be discussed later, Arabs were taken for granted as real estate owners at the border.

Hardly in unison, and often at odds with one another, Arabs with businesses on the Brazilian side made their own invidious comparisons with counterparts on the Paraguayan side of the border. According to the son of an early migrant in the Rahal family in Foz do Iguaçu, "Ciudad del Este is full of Lebanese who buy merchandise in a store and sell it a hundred meters ahead. They make their lives that way, slowly, saving money, until the day when they have their own business."[38] Such transactions, for Mohamad Barakat, benefited "the traders from Ciudad del Este, many of them are *meus patrícios*" (my countrymen), at the cost of Foz do Iguaçu.[39] Barakat claimed that "the Friendship Bridge only serves the Paraguayans," criticizing *sacoleiros* and Brazilian consumers that used Foz do Iguaçu as a stopover to and from Ciudad del Este.[40] He and others on the Brazilian side of the border lamented that "the buildings once home to long-time traditional commercial exporters" came to serve as restaurants, storage, or parking for Brazilian consumers who arrived from all over Brazil to buy consumer items in Ciudad del Este.[41] Not long after, Barakat proposed a "shopping festival of the três fronteiras," which would "attract Brazilian buyers" to shop on the Brazilian, and not Paraguayan, side of the border.[42]

## Exempting Imports in Ciudad del Este

Arab traders in Ciudad del Este continued to attract Brazilian clientele due to the exemptions that the Paraguayan state obtained in Mercosur. After signing the treaty in 1991, the Paraguayan general-cum-president threatened to pull out if thousands of imports into Paraguay were not exempted from the customs treaty.[43] In 1994, he reiterated this stance when member states negotiated the list of products exempted from Mercosur's standardized tariffs in relation to non-Mercosur countries. While Brazil listed some thirty items and Argentina roughly three hundred, Paraguay asked to exempt over four thousand products.[44] Noted in the first chapter, the authoritarian Paraguayan state taxed some 7 to 10 percent on imports in Ciudad del Este, but the Mercosur treaty would have replaced that customs norm with a more expensive rate equivalent to that of other Mercosur member states vis à vis non-Mercosur or external countries. Amid fears that business in Ciudad del Este would languish, Domingo Daher, then vice president of the Cámara y Bolsa de Comercio (Chamber and Stock Exchange) in Asunción, himself of Syrian origin, doubted that Paraguayan leaders would "assume the socioeconomic costs" of failing to obtain exemptions from Mercosur's Common External Tariffs.[45] Subsequently, Paraguayan authorities convinced Mercosur member states to exempt thousands of imported items in Ciudad del Este from the bloc's external tariffs.[46]

In contrast to Argentine and US images of jeopardizing security, Arabs and others netted profits in Ciudad del Este made possible by the exemptions obtained by the Paraguayan state within Mercosur. This governmental backdrop was overshadowed by almost immediate record-breaking sales registered by Arabs and others in the six thousand or so stores of Ciudad del Este's downtown.[47] *Forbes* allegedly estimated that they moved more than sixteen billion US dollars in 1994, though the *New York Times* claimed a "$10-billion-a-year trade" in 1995.[48] Hussein Taijen retorted, "We don't accept any number above the estimate of US$4 billion."[49] Whatever the case, Arabs in Ciudad del Este remember that profits hit a climax in the mid-1990s. A Palestinian Brazilian, Fátima, recalled the flood of hard currency inundating her husband's electronics store. "We would close the store at 6 p.m., and we would count money until 10 p.m.," she stated.[50] She alleged that the store pulled in anywhere from US$20,000 to US$30,000 a day. As will be discussed in Chapter 6, traders in Ciudad del Este often received payments in Brazilian currency that they could deposit and exchange for dollars in Foz do Iguaçu. At least momentarily, Arabs in Ciudad del Este secured trade in Mercosur.

Importing goods from outside Mercosur that were exempted from the Common External Tariffs, Arabs on the Paraguayan side of the border drew the interest of major brand name companies in computers and electronics.[51] In 1995, Samsung invited over five hundred merchants from Ciudad del Este to a dinner and show at a five-star hotel in Foz do Iguaçu. Daewoo sent special emissaries. Brand-name manufacturers supplied shops in Ciudad del Este with monitors, recorders, and other merchandise carrying Brazilian and Argentine types of analog transmission signals.[52] Indeed, most of the imports in the Paraguayan border town ended up in Brazilian or Argentine homes, according to the Central Bank itself in Paraguay.[53] Even the newsweekly *Veja* claimed that Paraguay was the source of nearly half of the electronics being sold in Brazil and the lion's share of computer keyboards.[54] Many goods passed through the hands of so-called *compristas* or *sacoleiros*, who charted buses from all over Brazil to shop in Ciudad del Este, as they had done for decades, noted in the first chapter. Arabs on the Paraguayan side of the border continued to serve a still overwhelmingly Brazilian clientele through corporate provisions and tariff exemptions in Mercosur.

Arabs on the Paraguayan side of the border served as hemispheric protagonists, not antagonists, in this free trade America. In the 1990s, they increasingly imported from free trade zones around Miami, rather than those in Colón, as noted previously. Said Tai-jen recalled that he, his brother, and others shifted from Colón to Miami at this time, depending on product availability and price.[55] Mihail Bazas believed that most turned toward Miami and South Florida as part of a US strategy to replace Colón since the Panama Canal was being returned to the Panamanian government in 1999. Bazas added that free trade zones in Miami afforded merchants the added benefits of beaches, restaurants, and other tourist attractions lacking in Panama's Colón.[56] Fátima traveled regularly to Miami, taking advantage of the tourist infrastructure and making purchases that were shipped to her husband's business and then sold to mostly Brazilian consumers.[57] Another merchant in Ciudad del Este quipped that free trade zones in and around Miami "called almost daily" when Brazilians curtailed their shopping, "because if we don't sell, we can't buy imports" from Miami.[58] Exempted from standardized external tariffs in Mercosur, Arabs helped make Ciudad del Este into a "Paraguayan Miami" for mostly Brazilian clientele in this hemispheric America.

Arabs on the Paraguayan side of the border likewise continued to accommodate Brazilian influence. In 1995, the Brazilian state lowered the monetary limit of goods that Brazilians purchased abroad and brought into the country. *A Gazeta do Iguaçu* specified that the "import quota of merchandise at the border" was reduced "from $250 to $150 per person."[59] The Brazilian state justified the quota reduction as a way to stem the increase of imports into Brazil that dwarfed exports and negatively affected the trade balance. But news of the quota reduction provoked a temporary surge in the numbers of *sacoleiros* in the weeks before the actual measure took effect. Mohamed Sleiman on the Paraguayan side of the border joked that his store turned into an "anthill" with Brazilian shoppers, wondering whether "the Brazilian government could prolong the debate surrounding the quota, that way we'd sell more."[60] This short-term boom, however, tailed off, allegedly decreasing Paraguay's GNP growth from 4.5 percent in 1995 to 2 percent in 1996.[61] Arabs on the Paraguayan side of the border worked within the limits posed by Brazilian influence, even after the dawn of Mercosur.

Rather than directly challenge the Brazilian state's quota reduction, Arabs on the Paraguayan side of the border voiced appeals
in the language of Mercosur. Faisal Saleh, a director in the "Paraguayan American Chamber of Commerce," called upon the leaders of Mercosur's capitals in "Montevidéu, Buenos Aires, Asunción,
and Brasília" to learn "about integration" from store owners near
the Friendship Bridge as the true "representatives of our region."[62]
Saleh concluded that Ciudad del Este was "treated as a problem
city," though it "could leverage the economic redemption of the
region."[63] Hussein Taijen, in the Chamber of Commerce of Ciudad
del Este, blamed greater restrictions at the border not on the bloc
but rather on the aforementioned media allegations that tens of
billions of US dollars changed hands on the Paraguayan side of the
border. But "with the drop in the quota from $250 to $150," Taijen
concluded, "this value fell a lot."[64] Saleh, Taijen, and other Arabs
in the Paraguayan border town avoided defying Brazil in order to
secure economic livelihoods in Mercosur.

Sharif Hammoud likewise steered clear of criticizing Brazilian
or Paraguayan states in his attempt to draw "attention to the problems faced by commercial importers" in Ciudad del Este.[65] As a
founder of the Centro de Importadores y Comerciantes del Alto
Paraná (Center of Importers and Traders of Alto Paraná, known by
its acronym in Spanish, CICAP), Hammoud had just participated in
the commemoration of the thirty-ninth anniversary of the founding
of Ciudad del Este.[66] Avoiding any direct discussion of the Brazilian
quota reduction, Hammoud called for stores to "paralyze" business
and shut down for a day while storeowners partook in a rally. Hammoud proffered a speech while CICAP released an official statement,
condemning "illicit activities carried out in Ciudad del Este" that
contributed to the city's image as "the haven of terrorist organizations and the paradise for counterfeit goods."[67] In faulting traders
for tax evasion and commercial forgery as well as censuring the
media's demonization of the city, Hammoud made no mention of
the states that made exceptions for Ciudad del Este.

Hussein Taijen also used Mercosur keywords but opposed Hammoud's call to paralyze business. Taijen spoke of the importance
of the "integration" between the "peoples of all the region of the

**Figure 4.1.** Map of the Paraná Country Club on the Paraguayan side of grounds that belong to the bi-national Itaipu hydroelectric damn between Paraguay and Brazil. © OpenStreetMap contributors

Triple Border."[68] He surmised that "the biggest problem faced by commerce at the border is the pressure exerted by the Brazilian government . . . and it is not up to traders in Ciudad del Este to debate it."[69] In opposing Hammoud's call to paralyze business, Tai-jen stated, "We do not accept this position of the importers who shut down commerce since it's not up to them to resolve the problems" in

**Figure 4.2.** Detail map of the Paraná Country Club gated community. © Open-

Brazil.[70] Taijen admonished fellow importers in Ciudad del Este with Brazilian customers that "the protest has to come from the Brazilians, who are capable of inverting the situation and loosening the fence erected by" Brazil's "national industry and government." He concluded that "if nothing is done, Ciudad del Este will pass through the same situation as Puerto Iguazú in Argentina" and follow the "commercial crisis" in Foz do Iguaçu. Having been incorporated into

Brazil's expansive consumer market since authoritarian times, Arabs on the Paraguayan side hardly expected higher tariffs in Mercosur.

Indeed, Arabs in the Paraguayan border city still served mostly Brazilian consumers, selling an array of consumer imports, including electronics, toys, spirits, and cigarettes, as well as seasonal items, with generally lower prices thanks to exemptions from Mercosur's standardized external tariffs. "We have the latest releases in the world of technology, fashion, cosmetics, and perfume," opined Hammoud. "And to top it off," he concluded "the prices in Ciudad del Este are as competitive or even cheaper than those in Miami or Hong Kong."[71] Hammoud emphasized that his store served "Brazilian consumers" from São Paulo, Rio de Janeiro, and Belo Horizonte, who were the "most important," though he implied that most purchases in the Paraguayan border city were actually for resale in Brazil. Among a select number of businesses, Hammoud catered not only to middle classes but also high rollers, carrying luxury brands such as Armani, Cartier, and Gucci, more fully explored in Chapter 6. In fact, in 1997, Hammoud celebrated the 150-year anniversary of Cartier at the border, making the high-society pages of Brazilian and Paraguayan newspapers.[72]

Far from undermining security, Arabs in Ciudad del Este invested in exclusive sanctuary. Putting "a lot of capital" into Paraguay's side of the border, the Hammoud family helped bankroll the Paraná Country Club located between the Rio Paraná and the Rio Acaray, sharing the same entrance with the Itaipu dam complex. Sharif Hammoud and another Lebanese migrant, Emile Sayegh, as well as other (non-Arab) Paraguayans, came together in 1989 to build the gated community of more than a thousand acres on what had originally been a golf course in the 1970s. In the condominium's foundational act and statutes passed in 1992, Arabs numbered three of the original thirty signatories, but they took up two of the six board posts, including Sharif Hammoud whose own residence was said to be worth millions of US dollars.[73] The Paraná Country Club's residential zone has family mansions spread across 1,500 lots, in addition to two hotels, a golf course, and a "club house" with sports and banquet facilities. The commercial zone has a campus branch of the Catholic University, the Anglo American Paraguayan School, banks, restaurants, and high-end stores. Less than ten minutes from their businesses in Ciudad del Este's downtown next to the Friendship Bridge, Arabs bought into a gated community.

## Burden on the Bloc

But Arabs on the Brazilian and Paraguayan sides of the border found themselves targeted by the "close alliance" between US and Argentine authorities, studied by political scientist J. Patrice McSherry.[74] In his visit with Argentine president Carlos Menem in late 1997, US president Bill Clinton (1992–2000) not only pushed for the FTAA but also expressed "concern" about "Hizbullah in Ciudad del Este."[75] Two months later, a US counterterrorism task force visited Brazilian, Paraguayan, and Argentine capitals.[76] In the last stop in Buenos Aires, an Argentine official confided that "the Argentine government has been converted into the spearhead for a US plan to impose new standards of police and political control onto Paraguay."[77] Indeed, the Clinton administration had restructured the Southern Command of the US armed forces in prioritizing "counterterrorism" among "Latin American militaries."[78] Consequently, from late 1997 onward, US and Argentine authorities similarly associated Arabs at the border with "Islamic fundamentalist terrorism."[79]

Weeks after meeting the US counterterrorism task force, Argentine officials vilified the border at a Mercosur summit.[80] "Top-level Argentine authorities identified the border zone with Brazil and Paraguay as 'a difficult point' in the fight against ... 'fundamentalist Islamic terrorism'" related *ABC Color*.[81] Argentina's interior minister Carlos Corach derided the Paraguayan border city as "a unique refuge" for terrorists.[82] Two months afterward, in Washington, DC, Corach visited the CIA, FBI, and State Department, warning of the border's alleged risk to US and Argentine "shared security concerns" for "the entire continent."[83] The FBI director subsequently claimed "a terrorist threat" lurked at the border during his follow-up meeting with President Menem, minister Corach, and army and police officials in Buenos Aires.[84] Though never finding any terrorists at the border, the Menem administration's "alignment" with US *anti-terror* (counterterror) and flirtation with the FTAA ensured greater leverage in relation to other Mercosur member states.[85]

Arabs on the Brazilian and Paraguayan sides of the border adjusted and appealed to Mercosur, but US and Argentine media circulated images of them as an actual or possible fifth column throughout the 1990s. *US News and World Report* glossed "Lebanese and Palestinians" in Foz do Iguaçu and Ciudad del Este as Hizbullah accomplices in the unresolved bombings in Buenos Aires.[86] The *New York Times* highlighted "Lebanese merchants" with "profitable border businesses" at the "remote junction of Argentina, Brazil, and Paraguay" that the CNN En Español network described as a "triangle of terror."[87] In Argentina, *El Cronista Comercial* opined that "15,000 Arabs, with their prosperous businesses . . . have been identified as supposed financial supporters of Hizbullah."[88] *La Nación* cast "Lebanese" and "Arabs" as merchants of mayhem, pushing knock-off cigarettes and "unbelievable counterfeit goods."[89] *Clarín* reported that Lebanese and Arabs in the Paraguayan border town profited from tens of thousands of Brazilian shoppers but also provided "support and shelter to presumed terrorists."[90] For Brazilian diplomats, these baseless images of treacherous Arabs in lawless Brazilian and Paraguayan border towns shielded the Argentine state from being "pressured to resolve the case of the terrorist attacks against the Jewish community" in Buenos Aires.[91]

Advocating for Arabs in a free trade America, Faisel Saleh hoped to change the narrative by arranging for Mannah, Hammoud, and others to appear in Brazilian corporate media, namely *Veja*. Mentioned earlier, Saleh is a Brazilian citizen of Lebanese origin from the neighboring state of Mato Grosso do Sul who settled at the border and worked for Hammoud's Monalisa before opening the store Prisma in Ciudad del Este. Despite Saleh's intentions, *Veja* ended up reinforcing suspicions about Arabs.[92] *Veja* related that "some Lebanese merchants" in Ciudad del Este and Foz do Iguaçu dodged taxes and dabbled in forgery, with putative ties to the unresolved bombings in the Argentine capital. Introduced in the first chapter, Mohamed Said Mannah (nicknamed Alexandre) was cited as saying: "Here [in Ciudad del Este] the sun rises for everyone. Whoever didn't get rich didn't want to." With nothing said of Paraguayan state exemptions in Mercosur that benefited his and other businesses in the Paraguayan border city, Mannah appeared as suspiciously owning shopping centers that annually generated tens of millions of dollars. Faisal Hammoud, one of the brothers who own Monalisa, likewise seemed too wealthy, purportedly raking in a half billion a year and owning a multi-million-dollar mansion. After *Veja* reproduced the dominant image of "reel bad Arabs" conniving at the border, Saleh admitted that his colleagues "chastised me for bringing people only interested in denigrating and shaming our business activities."[93] Saleh asked *A Gazeta do Iguaçu* to publish his rebuke of *Veja*'s representation of the border in terms of tax evasion, counterfeit merchandise, and "organized crime."

Far from being a burden on the bloc, Arabs represented themselves as a kind of free trade vanguard. Ahmed (Armando) Kassem spoke in such terms about the Arab-Paraguayan Chamber of Commerce in Ciudad del Este that he helped to found, perhaps to wrest some influence from the Cámara de Comercio de Ciudad del Este.[94] Paying a visit to the offices of *A Gazeta do Iguaçu* on the Brazilian side of the border, Kassem criticized the "avalanche of accusations" against Arabs. Kassem began by rhetorically asking, "We are in difficult times with this commercial crisis in Foz do Iguaçu and Ciudad del Este. . . . How are we going to send [money] to terrorists?"[95] Having inaugurated his chamber alongside Carlos Barreto Sarubbi, then governor of Alto Parana and a political strongman since the days of Stroessner, Kassem spoke of Arabs as a "link for integration" between Latin America and Asia.[96] At the border, Arabs embodied a "direct contact between Paraguay and China," which for Kassem, could disrupt US plans for "China to sell to Miami and Miami to sell to Latin America."[97] Kassem rebuked the scapegoating that infringed on civil rights and instead located Arabs at the forefront of a free trade America.

Arabs pointed to the exceptional suspension of democratic norms under counterterrorism. During a Mercosur meeting in Foz do Iguaçu, Mohamad Barakat, Fouad Fakih, and Abdul Rahal delivered an open letter to Brazil's Justice Minister, Iris Rezende, who was the official Brazilian representative in the bloc.[98] Their letter emphasized the "integration" of the "Arab community of Foz do

Iguaçu," just a day after Kassem's statements. At the time, Barakat was the Foz do Iguaçu government's Secretary of Social Action and Fakih and Rahal had posts in Acifi. "Arabs," the letter stated, have been "always considered hard-working, orderly, pacific." Implying the adjustments and appeals that Arabs made in Mercosur, the letter emphasized that they were "dumbfounded by defamatory news regarding alleged 'terrorist cells in this region.'" The letter concluded that Arabs were more than willing to help "competent authorities" but rebuked accusations against the "colônia árabe iguaçuense" (Arab Iguaçu Community, named after the Iguaçu falls) at "this important pole" of Mercosur.

Nonetheless, Mercosur member states enacted extraordinary monitoring mechanisms and expenditures that went far beyond Arabs themselves. In 1998, Mercosur authorities met in Buenos Aires and approved the US-supported "General Plan for Security at the Tri-Border."[99] For Argentine minister Corach "who served as host," the accord "established mechanisms of cooperation" in the "fight against terrorism" and signified a "huge step" for "regional integration" that would be "followed by cooperation and solidarity in the rest of the American continent."[100] The plan proposed the Sistema de Intercambio de Información de Seguridad del Mercosur (Security Information Interchange System, in English), known by its acronym, SISME, an "automated database for storing and exchanging intelligence information" that connects "the operational activities of those organisms responsible for the security of each member state."[101] The system enables police and military forces in Brazil, Paraguay, Argentina, and other member states to share information on persons, goods, and monies across borders. Another Mercosur accord passed shortly thereafter paved the way for the Center for the Coordination of Police Training (CCCP), bringing together "security and police forces of the countries of the region" to combat "drug trafficking, terrorism, and arms smuggling."[102] Mercosur used speculations about Arabs in order to increase security mechanisms that went far beyond Arabs themselves in the bloc.

Meanwhile, Arabs dealt with the added burden of US authorities questioning their visas, which they had used to enter Miami's free trade zones to requisition the merchandise sold at the border. In

1998, the *New York Times* reported that Arabs and Asians were "pro-filed" as "fraud suspects" by US foreign service officers in South America and elsewhere.[103] Said Taijen specified that it was the US that "treated us Arabs badly."[104] Taijen recounted his experience attempting to renew his expired visa at the US embassy in Asunción around this time. A line led to the "counselor" behind a glass window with a microphone. The counselor stated that Taijen's visa renewal application "was denied." Taijen asked why, and was again told, "you are denied." He recounted, "it was humiliating," because everyone in the line behind him heard the counselor. The next Paraguayan applicant in the line tapped him on the shoulder, and remarked, "*Baisano* . . . it's not worth arguing with them.'" Taijen emphasized that his interlocutor replaced the *p* in *paisano* (coun-tryman) with a *b*, mimicking an Arabic accent in Spanish. Without knowing of the *New York Times* report on US consular profiling, Tai-jen felt minoritized by the US embassy in ways that contradicted his and other Arabs' propertied and elite status at the border. Taijen and other Arabs traded between Ciudad del Este and Miami in ways that did not fit into dominant US visions of a free trade America.

Even with proper US visas, Arab Paraguayans traveling to Miami free trade zones were targeted by US customs and border control. Taijen recounted that Alexandre Mannah, the owner of La Petis-queira, "had to wait twelve hours in the airport."[105] Having been portrayed as a suspect nouveau riche in *Veja*, Mannah carried the proper documentation but was stopped by officials from the Immi-gration and Naturalization Services (INS) that obliged him to wait in a separate room. They asked him questions about what he intended to do in the US. He explained his business and reiterated his will-ingness to answer questions. INS officials brought a metal detector and scanned him and his shoes. Without clarification, hour after hour, Mannah waited and bore the "humiliation," which Taijen saw as directed at both Arabs and Paraguayans. Mikhail Bazas like-wise qualified that the US government made it difficult for Arabs and others in Ciudad del Este to do business in Miami's free trade zones.[106] More fully explored in the sixth chapter, such experiences in the US arguably led Arabs and others at the border to turn toward East Asia in their own endeavors to secure trade in the coming years.

But other Arabs on the Paraguayan side of the border still sought to accommodate the US in Mercosur. In 1995, one of the brothers who own Monalisa, Faisal Hammoud, became the first president of the Ciudad del Este branch of the Paraguayan-American Chamber of Commerce (CCPA). In the inauguration ceremony, the US ambassador to Paraguay stated that the branch opening in Ciudad del Este symbolized the closer relationship that the US hoped to cultivate with "Mercosur member countries."[107] As "a private, independent, nonprofit association founded in 1981 by a group of Paraguayan and [US] American firms" in Asunción, CCPA garners close ties to the US embassy and, according to Taijen, worked to attract traders in Ciudad del Este to Miami's free trade zones since its founding.[108] Members included Arab-owned businesses, such as the Mannah brothers' La Petisquera, Moussa Ali and Heider Hijazi's Megatek Importadora/Exportadora, Nasser Chamseddine's Nasser Cubiertas S.A.C.I., and Ali Mohamed Osman's Macedonia S.R.L.. Though often seen to threaten trade and security, Arabs continued to do business on the terms set by the US and Mercosur member states.

## Exceptional Measures in Mercosur

In a liberal economic bloc, due process could be suspended in order to redress the "concerns" of member states, specifically about undocumented migrants, or in official parlance, "irregular foreigners."[109] Shortly after the respective visits of Clinton and the US counterterrorism task force, in early 1998, the Brazilian Federal Police set up a checkpoint on the Brazilian side of the Friendship Bridge that stopped cars and pedestrians heading toward the Paraguayan side during the morning rush. This Brazilian operation "searched for foreigners who reside in Foz do Iguaçu and work in Ciudad del Este," according to Cleber Alves, the Federal Police chief in the Maritime, Air, and Border Division.[110] Over ninety persons were detained, "the majority Arabs and Asians"; four were deported to Paraguay and eighty-eight were fined or notified to vacate the country. Alves noted that those apprehended had home residences in Foz do Iguaçu with Paraguayan IDs or visa stamps on passports, but lacked Brazilian IDs or visas. In a subsequent Mercosur meeting that addressed the question of undocumented migrants and "security at the tri-border," Argentine ministers fretted about the possibility of "another action by Islamics [*sic*], who already authored two attacks in the country," while Brazilian and Paraguayan counterparts instead called for the need to counter "arms-smuggling and money-laundering."[111]

Arab traders again were targeted the day after the Mercosur security meeting in another operation led by Brazil's Federal Police. Mostly Arabs, one reporter observed, "are easily stopped near the Friendship Bridge, principally in the early morning when they go to work in the neighboring country and also in the late afternoon, when they return" to the Brazilian side.[112] An estimated forty police officers checked the documentation of some 200 "clandestine foreigners," around 150 of whom were brought to the precinct for further questioning as relatives and friends waited in front of the police station. According to Alves, over one hundred were from Lebanon, three from Syria, two from Kuwait, one from Jordan, and one from Morocco. Living in Foz do Iguaçu and working in Ciudad del Este, they were fined less than the equivalent to one thousand dollars. Alves added, "We sent them all back to Paraguay because they carried legal documents from there." In a harsh criticism of the geopolitics of the operation, *A Gazeta do Iguaçu* suggested that "Argentina is pressuring Brazil so that Brazil pressures Paraguay into cleaning up its side of the border."[113]

After rounding up mostly Arabs, Brazil's Federal Police delivered a report to Mercosur member states, asking to "intensify the control" over "non-Mercosur [*extra-Mercosur*] citizens, especially at the tri-border." *A Gazeta do Iguaçu* went on to define "non-Mercosur citizens" as "all those who were born in countries outside" of Mercosur, "made up by Brazil, Argentina, Paraguay, and Uruguay." The police report explained, "The majority of those with irregular documentation were found in the Arab community. But Foz do Iguaçu is home for . . . the majority of these citizens" who "carry legally Paraguayan documents." Mercosur accords enabled Paraguayan citizens with state-issued IDs to legally enter Brazil, but a migrant from a non-Mercosur member state with a Paraguayan visa in his or her passport would still be required to obtain a visa to enter

Brazil. Mercosur ministers claimed not to be profiling Lebanese and other migrants with Paraguayan visas living in Brazil, but rather fugitives and traffickers as well as anyone "financing political-terrorist actions in the territory of Mercosur," though none were ever found.[114]

Accordingly, "non-Mercosur" subjects were stripped of liberal democratic norms that Mercosur member states otherwise safeguarded. Irregular or missing documentation among migrants was not a crime in Brazil, but federal police officers nonetheless brought "Arab citizens to be interrogated at the police headquarters" after being detained on the bridge to Paraguay. Fouad Fakih remembered that some lacked documentation, but those apprehended were handcuffed without an explanation. Others objected to the inter-rogations taking place during Ramadan, with little consideration of some detainees' fasting. The Foz do Iguaçu city councilor Dil-ton Vitorassi condemned the "discriminatory persecution against Arabs" and lamented that "Brazil is acting like a Third World colony." Vitorassi "blamed Argentina to be behind the pressure and accused the neighboring country of trying to repay debts to the United States through such favors." Vitorassi, however, qualified that "one can't overstep one's place in the hierarchy," so he aired grievances about such exceptional measures with the local police chief, not Brazil's Minister of Justice who coordinated the operation "in the context of Mercosur." Without checks on extraordinary measures in a bloc of states, Brazil's Federal Police led another exceptional operation at the Friendship Bridge.[115] In the morning rush, the police detained between "twenty-four and thirty-seven people." The police deported one and issued summons and fines to others in a kind of profiling that masqueraded as due process.

Arabs living or working on the Paraguayan side of the border responded by asking for more, not less, security. Armando Kassem of the Arab-Paraguayan Chamber of Commerce requested a meet-ing with Paraguayan President Juan Carlos Wasmosy (1993–1998), the handpicked successor of Andrés Rodríguez who had ensured the continued rule of the political party of the dictatorship even after the dictator had been overthrown. Kassem asked Wasmosy for "more security for the border" by taking "a census of all the Arabs of the region as a first step to regulating the migrant situation at the tri-border."[116] Diplomats and police officers on each side of the border commented that Kassem's idea was "very well viewed and considered positive." According to *A Gazeta do Iguaçu*, "the census in Paraguay would support the activities of the Federal Police in Brazil and migration control in Argentina." Though nothing came of the problematic plan, and no one else spoke up, Kassem repeated, the "Arab-Paraguayan Chamber of Commerce works for the border. Foz do Iguaçu, Ciudad del Este, and even Puerto Iguazú are like one city."

Having been once privileged by tariff exemptions in Mercosur, Arab-owned stores on the Paraguayan side of the border were subsequently targeted in order to be brought under "control," in the Argentine Interior Minister Carlos Corach's phrasing.[117] SISME, the aforementioned security data network in Mercosur, "marked" and monitored Arabs as "as non-Mercosur foreigners."[118] The data in SISME seems to have expanded during the Brazilian police roundup of hundreds of mostly Arab migrants at the bridge to Paraguay, which Corach applauded as "progress" and an "advance" in the "security of the tri-border."[119] Corach saw Arabs at the border as a matter of security, not trade, in Mercosur, and he saw Mercosur in purely transactional terms. "I am neoliberal," Corach once remarked to Paraguayan strongman Carlos Barreto Sarubbi. "And for this reason," he quipped, "I believe that the rich have to get richer in order to help the poor."[120] With US and Argentine insistence, Mercosur emerged as a security network by tracking Arab border-crossing between Foz do Iguaçu and Ciudad del Este, and in so doing, undermined farther flung commercial networks that preceded and vied with the bloc itself.

By effectively suspending due process for Arabs and other migrants, the Brazilian state also put to rest empty accusations of terrorism and shored up the "security" of Mercosur. One of the last and most injurious operations "planned by the ministers of Mercosur countries" targeted Arabs "more intensely in Foz do Iguaçu," with "inspections [*vistorias*] of apartment buildings, restaurants, and bars."[121] Vicente Chelotti, head of Brazil's Federal Police, took charge. Dubbed Rede Brasil (Brazil Net), the operation involved nearly seven thousand inspections over six days and arraigned nearly five hundred foreigners.[122] Dilton Vitorassi, Mohamad Barakat, and authorities from the Ordem dos Advogados do Brasil (OAB), akin to the American Bar Association, visited the individuals and families victimized by the operation. They reported on "abuses of power" that drew the interest of the local Procuradoria da República, akin to the office of the district attorney in the US, which affirmed that "the constitutional rights of foreigners" were violated in the "inspection."[123] Brazil's then Minister of Justice, Renan Calheiros, also asked for Brazil's Federal Police to be investigated for violating the rights of foreigners in Foz do Iguaçu.[124] Indeed, agents failed to show the required judicial warrant when entering homes in Foz do Iguaçu "and put residents, the majority Arabs and descendants, in a difficult position."[125] Through this suspension of liberal democratic rights, Brazilian police chief Chelotti declared at a subsequent Mercosur meeting that "no evidence was found of terrorist groups or groups who support them in the tri-border region."[126]

Arabs grew accustomed to contradictory state exceptions that not only constrained but also enabled their presence at the border. Some months after the anti-migrant operations, the Brazilian state declared a nationwide amnesty for foreigners to apply for permanent residence.[127] Lebanese "led the statistics" of foreign groups applying for amnesty and Foz do Iguaçu had the second largest number of grantees.[128] The state needed to take such steps, one federal police officer reiterated, instead of searching for "terrorist folklore."[129] He added, "our (Brazilian) children live with the children of foreigners" including "Arabs, Chinese, and Koreans," and so everyday citizens are best positioned to "advise them about the Statute of the Foreigner" (Estatuto do Estrangeiro). But not long after, ABIN, the Brazilian Agency of Intelligence mentioned in the previous chapter, opened a "public call" (concurso publico) for a new agent in Foz do Iguaçu.[130] In secret documents subsequently leaked to the press, ABIN was monitoring "Islamic Ethnic Groups," including the "Identification and Localization of Islamic Ethnic groups in the Country," especially at the border.[131]

Arabs likewise faced the extraordinary measures taken by Paraguayan authorities. Lebanese, Palestinians, Syrians, and others were extorted by "lawyers, judges, [and] police officers" in Ciudad del Este, according to Hector Guerín, a journalist for *ABC Color* and long-time resident.[132] Based on a news report or any speculation regarding terrorism, a Paraguayan judge would issue an arrest warrant for a given Arab or migrant storeowner.[133] After serving the warrant, police officers or others would informally offer acquittal in exchange for payment to be divided up among governmental authorities. This issuing of arrest warrants that rarely produced a conviction, for Guerín, exposed an "industry of extortion."[134] Brazilian diplomats similarly reported that Hussein Taijen complained that traders shouldered this "permanent pressure" for "extorted money" in Ciudad del Este, though not pointing fingers at the Paraguayan state itself.[135] As in the undue arrest warrants issued for some *shuyukh*, explored in the previous chapter, Paraguayan authorities capitalized on counterterrorist liaisons, especially after 9/11, as will be seen in the following chapter.

Paraguayan state officials ruled by exception, manipulating false accusations of terrorism to extort Arab businessmen as well as unscrupulously emitting Paraguayan passports and visas to "hundreds of Lebanese who entered irregularly into Paraguay."[136] In 1996 and 1997, the scheme drew "official support" from the Migration Department at the international airport near Ciudad del Este and the Paraguayan consulate in Foz do Iguaçu. The alleged brain of the operation was Lebanese-Paraguayan Ali Ahmed Zaioun, to be discussed more in detail next chapter.[137] After paying off the Paraguayan consul on the Brazilian side of the border, a thirty-day tourist visa to Paraguay was emitted and sent to Lebanon. With a Paraguayan tourist visa from Foz do Iguaçu, Lebanese could depart Beirut and reach the Minga Guazú airport in Paraguay, where Zaioun allegedly paid off other officials to stamp a Paraguayan residential visa onto Lebanese passports. With support from Paraguayan authorities, Lebanese and other migrants possessed irregular documentation that made them easy targets in a vicious circle of state exceptions.

Amid such increasingly ordinary exceptions to the rule of law, Arabs in Ciudad del Este were detained and released by the Paraguayan state in shows of force inspired by Brazilian anti-migrant operations in Foz do Iguaçu.[138] Reda Soueid wondered whether Argentine, Brazilian, and Paraguayan powers had "exchanged

**Figure 4.3.** The monument dedicated to Hussein Taijen in Ciudad del Este. Picture taken by author.

information," perhaps through SISME or the Tripartite Command.[139] As brought up last chapter, after the US and others demanded progress on the still unresolved bombings in Buenos Aires, Argentine authorities had "presented to Mercosur ministers" a report that doubted Brazilian and "Paraguayan governmental abilities to exercise effective control" over the "increasing settlement of Arab immigrants."[140] By targeting Arabs, Brazilian and Paraguayan states offset Argentine as well as US pressures in the context of the bloc

**Figure 4.4.** A close up of the plaque on the monument dedicated to Hussein Taijen in Ciudad del Este. The plaque reads, "Hussein Taijen, defender, fighter, and martyr for a better city." Picture taken by author.

and hemisphere. With the suspension of due process, Mohamad Barakat in Foz do Iguaçu declared that the targeting of "Arabs and their descendants," especially on the Paraguayan side of the border, "served as a pretext to destroy the region's economy" and remake it as a putative "zone of peace" in a liberal economic bloc that served other interests further afield.[141]

This growing precariousness culminated in the killing of Hussein Taijen, gunned down as he opened his store, Casa Colombia, in Ciudad del Este on November 8, 1998.[142] The wake occurred in the house of his son-in-law Hassan Osman, near the Sunni-majority Omar Ibn Al-Khattab mosque in Foz do Iguaçu. The fifty-eight year old was buried in the Islamic section of the Jardim São Paulo cemetery on the Brazilian side of the border.[143] A thousand border residents, Arab, Argentine, Paraguayan, Brazilian, and others, participated in a tribute to the slain leader held at the Shia-majority Mezquita del Profeta Mohamed in Ciudad del Este a week later.[144] His assassination sent shockwaves of outright fear across the "Arab collectivity" at the border.[145] Arabs felt "unsafe, if not outright persecuted," declared the Lebanese ambassador to Paraguay, Nizar Ahmed Chamas.[146] Paraguay's National Police arrested and convicted two gunmen, a (non-Arab) Brazilian resident and (non-Arab) Paraguayan citizen in Ciudad del Este, while Brazilian diplomatic staff wondered whether the real author of the assassination was a Chinese citizen in São Paulo who had been "expelled from Paraguay."[147] Although *ABC Color* alleged at one point that Hizbullah was the mastermind,[148] Ali Assi, Taijen's Shia colleague in the Chamber of Commerce of Ciudad del Este, dismissed the rumor.[149] Speaking "as a friend of Taijen," Assi stressed that Taijen not only "cultivated friendship with Brazilian and Paraguayan politicians" but also "always defended the Brazilian shoppers as well as the storeowners of Ciudad del Este."[150] On the occasion of the one-year anniversary of his murder, Arabs, Brazilians, Paraguayans, and Argentines inaugurated a statue of his bust and renamed the street where his store was once located Calle Hussein Taijen in Ciudad del Este.

The murder of Taijen transpired and remained without resolution under free trade security. Paraguayan president Raúl Cubas Grau (1998–1999) condemned the murder and reiterated his "obligation to provide security to all citizens" just as he signed another round of Mercosur accords that ensured essential exemptions for imports to the Paraguayan border city.[151] The Brazilian ambassador to Paraguay similarly regretted Taijen's death as well as the "negative climate" it "creates" for Brazilian commercial investments across the border that would "not stop," he reassured Paraguayan counterparts.[152] Paraguayan elites in Asunción denounced the killing and lauded "redoubled security measures" against purported "permissiveness" in safeguarding the country's image "among partners in Mercosur."[153] The Paraguayan-American Chamber of Commerce president, and Monalisa co-owner Charif Hammoud eulogized Taijen as a "pioneer" and called on the Paraguayan state to promote a "positive and respectable image" of the border. Only mayor Juan Carlos Barreto tried to imply Taijen was involved in *cosas raras* (odd things) that putatively prevented police from "saving" him.[154] Regardless, those close with Hussein Taijen's family suspected the "Paraguayan police" of conspiring in the assassination. It was an open secret that officers in the counterterrorist division of

Paraguay's National Police were "molestando en demasía" (harassing too much, in Spanish) "Arabs and Chinese" through extortion and blackmail, to be taken up again next chapter.[155]

At the border, Arabs leveraged and leaned on Mercosur throughout the 1990s. On the Brazilian side, they used standardized external tariffs, importing from outside the bloc into Brazil's consumer market. On the Paraguayan side, they also continued to serve Brazilian consumption through exemptions to the bloc that ensured lower tariffs on imports from the free trade zones in Colón as well as Miami. Meanwhile, US authorities pushed FTAA and counterterrorist agendas that enabled Argentine counterparts to play off other member states in Mercosur. Subsequently, US and Argentine allies pointed fingers at Arabs on the Brazilian and Paraguayan sides of the border as jeopardizing the bloc and hemisphere. But Arabs continued making their own adjustments and appeals to a free trade America. In order to shore up Argentine demands in Mercosur and preempt the US, the Brazilian state clamped down on Arab border-crossings. With Arabs detained and denied due process in a relatively unaccountable bloc, Mercosur member states triumphantly cracked down on antecedent and rival cross-border commercial circuits. With their rights suspended and Mercosur secured by member states, Arabs could hardly predict that their destiny would be to summarily "begin" a "war without end."

# CHAPTER 5

# Beginning the "War without End"

**Arabs and everyone else** at the border sought shelter and safety after the attacks on September 11, 2001. As part of the soon-to-be-declared war on terror, the FBI asked akin "Brazilian and Paraguayan federal police" agencies "to identify all of the Arabs" in Foz do Iguaçu and Ciudad del Este.[1] A month later, a US diplomat fretted, "What are all these Muslims doing at the border?"[2] Lebanese, Palestinians, and Syrians responded through Brazilian and Paraguayan states with distinct agendas vis à vis the US. In the ensuing series of incriminations and recriminations, Arabs at the border became entangled in what American Studies critics Amy Kaplan and Melani McAlister respectively called a "war without end."[3]

Arabs took on the roles of activists as well as informants in a war on terror. Some mobilized for peace in a mass-mediated spectacle, Paz sem Fronteiras / Paz sin Fronteras / Peace without Borders, mentioned at the very start of this book. Bringing together tens of thousands of spectators from each side of the border for a one-day event in Foz do Iguaçu, their calls for peace garnered support from Brazilian civilian and military leaders leery of US suspicions of terrorism at the border. Meanwhile, a few Arabs in Ciudad del Este served as Paraguayan police informants, pointing fingers at business competitors of Arab or Muslim origin as terrorist suspects.

Their unfounded allegations served Paraguayan state interests still dominated by the same political party of the old military regime, which unsuccessfully tried to corroborate US suspicions. In a war-torn America, some Arabs rebuked US counterterrorist claims in Foz do Iguaçu while others attempted to substantiate those same claims in Ciudad del Este. In accommodating Brazilian state demur as well as Paraguayan state deference to the war on terror, Arabs neither openly confronted nor entirely conformed to the US.[4]

Centering Arab transnational mobilization in a post-9/11 hemispheric America, this chapter reformulates a key question in the vast literature on the US war on terror. How did this "war without end" begin? I return to Edward Said's point that "beginnings" are "intentional acts of power," entailing a "reversal" as well as "an authorization for what comes after."[5] Declared and covered as a war allegedly without historical precedence, state and media authorities ignored prior US-supported South American dictatorships that analogously alleged to combat terror.[6] Instead of recalling this beginning of a war on terror, US, Brazilian, Paraguayan, Argentine, and Mercosur officials ahistorically fixated on Arabs at the border and the suspicions still looming over them from the aforementioned 1992 and 1994 attacks in Buenos Aires, despite the sheer lack of evidence in ongoing investigations. In response, Arabs downplayed their own histories under US-backed South American military regimes, folding the near-erasure of authoritarian antecedents into this truncated origin story of a war-torn America.

Whether censuring or condoning war, state authorities similarly used Arabs at the border as pretexts in what anthropologist Catherine Lutz called "militarization" that "legitimate[d] the use of force" across the hemisphere.[7] Under George W. Bush (2001–2009), the Department of Defense's Southern Command justified larger budgets and sway through "mission creep" over Arabs in the "tri-border area" or "TBA," as it became called in English.[8] In Brazil, Fernando Henrique Cardoso (1995–2003) and Luiz Inácio Lula da Silva (2003–2011) refuted US claims of lawlessness at the border amid their "revitalization" of the "defense industry."[9] In Paraguay, Luis Ángel González Macchi (1999–2003) and Nicanor Duarte Frutos (2003–2008) witnessed dozens of US military missions on the

Paraguayan side of the border.[10] US and South American states justified military influence under ostensible civilian rule by creating, debating, and exchanging information about Arabs at the border. In this exceptional militarization, Arabs censured, capitalized, and came to terms with counterterrorism.

## America at War

Arabs at the border found themselves in the crosshairs of civilian and military authorities after the 9/11 attacks in the US. Interpol (the acronym for the International Criminal Police Organization) inundated police bureaus in Foz do Iguaçu and Ciudad del Este with the "names and sketches" of terrorist suspects and requests for more information that produced no leads.[11] FBI agents from the US "were in Brazil" and crossed the border into Paraguay but they failed to find any evidence.[12] Staff in the Pentagon, the headquarters of the US Department of Defense, circulated and discarded an "unsigned, top secret memo" that proposed an armed "attack on terrorists" at "the border of Paraguay, Argentina, and Brazil."[13] The US State Department expressed panic about non-existent "terrorist groups" operating "in the tri-border area of Argentina, Brazil, and Paraguay."[14] Francis Taylor, a former military commander who became the counterterrorism coordinator in the State Department, went so far as to declare, without evidence, "The terrorists operating at the tri-border worry us. We want to work with governments to disrupt these operations."[15] The US ambassador in Brazil echoed, though later retracted, that Arabs at the border harbored a "terrorist support network."[16]

Even refuting such claims of terrorism at the border underscored militarization in an ostensibly civilian-led hemisphere. Brazil's General Alberto Cardoso, head of the Gabinete de Segurança Institucional (GSI, or Office of Institutional Security, similar to the Joint Chiefs of Staff in the US government), urged the aforementioned Francis Taylor in the US State Department "to not 'satanize' the region of the tri-border," or accuse it of being an area of terrorism "without proof."[17] General Cardoso publicly stated in Brazilian media, "we didn't detect anything at the tri-border" from investigations that began "ten years ago" after the "attacks that occurred in Argentina."[18] Top Brazilian officials also met with the US Southcom commander, qualifying that "illicit activities" at the border include "money-laundering, tax evasion, and smuggling," but not "international terrorism."[19] In consonance with this military standpoint, Brazilian president Fernando Henrique Cardoso (known by the acronym FHC) downplayed US president Bush's unease "about the tri-border" a month after 9/11.[20] Mentioned later in this chapter, the Brazilian ambassador in Washington, DC, Rubens Barbosa, likewise "expressed concern" about US accusations "without proof of terrorist activities in the tri-border," when he met with Steven Monblatt, the State Department's deputy coordinator of counterterrorism.[21] Whether making or refuting claims of terrorism at the border, the military exercised influence in civilian-led governments with continental reach.

Arabs at the border found some refuge from US accusations in the Brazilian state, which overlooked its own militarization after the formal end of military rule. The Foz do Iguaçu mayor, Sâmis da Silva, of the center-right Party of the Brazilian Democratic Movement (PMDB) opined that "the US government has a bone to pick with trade in the region, coupled by the fact that there are many immigrants of Arab origin."[22] The city council passed a motion that "condemned" the backlash against the "Arab community of this *tríplice fronteira* after the attack on the US" as well as expressed "solidarity with the Arab community in Foz do Iguaçu."[23] The author of the motion, Chico Brasileiro of the Communist Party of Brazil (PC do B), admonished the "brutal persecution that the Arab community was suffering at the border."[24] Then city council president, Dilton Vitorassi, of the center-left Worker's Party (PT), "condemned the persecution of Arab people," while Vilmar Andreola, of the centrist Party of Brazilian Social Democracy (PSDB), rebuked policemen in Ciudad del Este who were "blackmailing Arabs under the pretext of looking for terrorists."[25] Even the one-time opposition leader to the Brazilian military regime who became FHC's Minister of Justice, José Gregori, resigned because, as he explained, "I suffered . . . pressure from various sectors, internal and external, who wanted me to find a terrorist."[26]

Arabs in Foz do Iguaçu embraced Brazilian rebuffs of US counterterrorist suspicions, which they saw as beginning not during authoritarian rule but rather after the unresolved bombings in Argentina. In the Argentine *Clarín*, Ali Said Rahal lamented "for the past eight years," since the AMIA bombing, "the FBI plays the same music, and everyone dances."[27] In a local Brazilian newspaper, Rahal continued that US politicians and pundits "are trying to say that our region is at risk for terrorism because we live here."[28] Kamal Osman condemned "misleading new stories" about the border that had begun some eight years previously with the AMIA bombing. He protested, "We led a life to build our names. Now, any news will destroy the image of the city" that Arabs helped build.[29] Mentioned in the introduction and fourth chapter, Magrão also recalled "For nearly a decade, after attacks . . . in Argentina, there's been a hunt for terrorists in this border zone, but no one was ever jailed and no one ever found any terrorists."[30] Leila Ahmed, a Lebanese-born professor of English with a Brazilian permanent residence visa, warned "the eyes of the world turned to Arabs" after 9/11.[31]

An "anti-terrorist witch hunt" targeting "foreigners of Arab origin" in Ciudad del Este was set into motion by the Paraguayan state in consonance with US suspicions.[32] Paraguay's National Police raided the Galería Pagé and other shopping centers, detaining dozens of Arabs and scurrying them off.[33] Some lacked appropriate documentation in Paraguay. Others did not have business receipts or proper tax documentation. José Antonio Moreno Ruffinelli, the Paraguayan foreign minister, stated that "Paraguay is not against citizens from Arab countries" but stressed that the "national government will combat terrorism" as "the best ally" of the US.[34] Indeed, "counterterrorism" had become "a more important component, if not requirement" in Paraguay-US relations.[35] But Paraguay's own vice-minister of foreign relations let it slip that most Arabs in custody had "problems with documentation" and were not "linked to extremist groups."[36] A police commissioner on the Paraguayan side of the border, Carlos Alsina, also affirmed that "we believe" Arabs "are good people."[37] Indeed, Arabs in Ciudad del Este were released from custody since "there was no proof of their involvement with terrorism."[38]

Arabs understandably avoided dwelling on Paraguay's authoritarian legacies, appealing instead to precarious democratic civics now engulfed by a war on terror. One of the Hammoud brothers, Alex, wrote an open letter to *ABC Color*, "express[ing] his concern with the treatment . . . that Arabs in Paraguay have been receiving since the terrorist attacks of September 11 in the United States."[39] Noting that he arrived in Paraguay in 1975, Hammoud witnessed the "birth of Ciudad del Este," not mentioning the previous name of the city's eponymous founder, Stroessner, and the uninterrupted rule of the latter's erstwhile Colorado Party. Hammoud called upon the Paraguayan state to defend the "public interest and attract investment . . . so that Paraguay protects itself from the wave of violence and injustice that the world is immersed in." He dismissed the "distorted information" and "baseless rumors" about "some members of the Arab community" who were "accused of deeds not proven by any judicial, legislative, or executive power." Hammoud concluded, "Arabs dedicated themselves to the construction and development of this region through the decades," making Paraguay "our second country and the first country for our children."

Feeling under attack, Arabs in Ciudad del Este sought accommodation with the status quo. Samir Jebai, owner of the shopping center mentioned earlier, stated "we are ready to collaborate in any way we can" because "we are confident" in "the investigations."[40] He reflected that "we came here escaping war in Lebanon," and that "the community here is very small, we all know one another, so if there was some activity linked to terrorism, we would know about it."[41] Said Taijen, whose brother had been murdered without accountability, as addressed last chapter, declared that "we would be the first to condemn" terrorism but "there is no evidence."[42] Mikhal Meskin Bazas "dismissed claims that terrorist groups exist in the border zone" because authorities spent years investigating and never found anything.[43] Arab traders in Ciudad del Este emphasized past and present records of cooperating with state officials and investigations that failed to find any terrorist link in the Paraguayan border city.

Arabs in Ciudad del Este feared the further erosion of civil rights in a Paraguayan state that the US praised as "an active and prominent partner in the war on terror," not unlike the decades-long alliance between Washington, DC, and Stroessner's dictator-ship.[44] The new president of the Arab-Paraguayan Chamber of Commerce in Ciudad del Este, Ahmed (Armando) Khalil Chams, declared that Paraguayan militarized forces were "selling out the security of the United States" as well as undermining "citizenship rights" in the Paraguayan border city. He "accused policemen in Paraguay's anti-terrorism secretariat of being part of a group carrying out extortion against Arab traders in Foz do Iguaçu and Ciudad del Este."[45] Chams stated that "anti-terrorist policemen" were "blackmailing us" for reasons such as irregular visa status or seemingly tax-evasive transactions. Chams was allegedly accused of fraud in Panama's free trade zone of Colón, but it was the anti-terrorist division of the Paraguayan police who paid a visit to his store without arresting him.[46] Chams explained that "the Arab who pays [extortion] is the good Arab, if he doesn't pay, he's a bad one."[47] Meanwhile, Reda Soueid accused the Paraguayan state of "terrorizing" and "spreading panic" in a "climate of insecurity" exacerbated by the US-led war on terror. Soueid put it simply, "We [Arabs] are afraid."[48] In Foz do Iguaçu, Mohamad Barakat repeated that the "Paraguayan government" failed "to defend . . . Ciudad del Este" in the US-led war.[49] Lebanon's diplomat Hicham Hamdan likewise expressed concern over whether "his compatriots detained in Paraguay" would be considered "innocent until proven guilty."[50]

Arabs on the Brazilian and Paraguayan sides of the border also felt scrutinized by post-9/11 Argentina. "After September 11," remembered Fawas, the son of the founder of Galeria Rahal, "a lot of journalists from Argentina came here" to the Paraguayan side of the border. These journalists, he surmised, "queriam pegar os grandes," (they wanted to get the big ones, in Portuguese), ostensibly trying to associate wealthy families such as the Hammouds, Jebais, and Mannahs with terrorism.[51] In 2001, *Clarín* conjectured that none other than Bin Laden and the Taliban passed through Foz do Iguaçu and Ciudad del Este.[52] This and other Argentine media warned of "security gaps" on the Brazilian and Paraguayan sides of the border.[53] The Argentine gendarmerie chief in Puerto Iguazú, Hugo Miranda, likewise juxtaposed "what we are doing" on the Argentine side of the border in relation to the allegedly "minimal . . . border controls between Brazil and Paraguay."[54] The former president Carlos Menem called on Argentines to join the US fight against terror and for a "joint action with Brazil and Paraguay" to improve "security at the tri-border."[55] In response, the US State Department highlighted Argentina's "continuing strong support for the global war on terrorism throughout 2002."[56] In the "close ties" between Buenos Aires and Washington, DC, the US lauded Argentine counterterrorist visions of Arabs at the border.[57]

Suspicion was the sine qua non of not only past authoritarianism but also present-day counterterrorism. A month after 9/11, the "Tripartite Command" reported "nothing concrete" at the border, after looking into alleged "terrorist activities."[58] Neither incriminated nor fully exonerated, Arabs remained in a double bind, exacerbated by the transnational security network of military and civilian authorities initiated years before 9/11. As mentioned in the third chapter, the Tripartite Command was then headed by Brazil's Federal Police chief in Foz do Iguaçu, Joaquim Mesquita, who had repeatedly investigated suspicions that produced no evidence. Argentina's representative, José Domingo Battaglia, the gendarmerie commander in Misiones, admitted that "for now, the subject" of "cells that shelter or support terrorists" is "totally discarded, but monitoring continues." Augusto Lima, the Paraguayan National Police spokesman who started his career during Stroessner's thirty-five year reign, echoed, "we haven't found anything that ties the region to the presence of terrorists." But Lima qualified that "the Paraguayan judicial system continues its investigations of foreigners, principally those of Arab origin" as well as "their legal identification on Paraguayan territory," in a state apparatus still run by the defunct dictatorship's political party.[59]

Any transnational activity undertaken by Arabs at the border became "truncated, questioned, (and) re-politicized" amid counterterrorist suspicions and authoritarian silences, to again paraphrase anthropologists Sally Howell and Andrew Shryock.[60] Take for example Lebanese-led call centers scrutinized by Interpol and raided by Brazil's Federal Police soon after the US declaration of war on terror.[61] The US State Department claimed that "possible links" existed between these "clandestine telephone centers" and "terrorist activities."[62] But a month of investigations discovered that the accused would run a telephone switchboard from a rented house and abandon it after two or three months "leaving behind a series of bills that sometimes surpassed R$100,000" (nearly $90,000 US dollars at the time).[63] A suspect, Lebanese Brazilian Mohamed Omar Matar, said that the call center had nothing to do with terrorism but was rather "motivated by the high cost of making international phone calls," monopolized by the Brazilian telecommunications company, Embratel. Originally founded in 1965 and owned by the authoritarian state, Embratel expanded control over long-distance communication after re-democratization and privatization in 1998.[64] Brazil's Federal Police chief Joaquim Mesquita concluded that the Lebanese-Brazilian-run "call center was used to fool telephone companies" and offer cheaper calls "mainly to the Middle East."[65] Neither saints nor subversives, Arabs were being called out on a hemispheric field of exceptional rule.

## Peace without Borders in Foz do Iguaçu

Some Arabs responded by organizing an *ato* (act of observance), "Paz sem Fronteiras / Paz sin Fronteras / Peace without Borders." They explicitly avoided characterizing the event as a protest, demonstration, or rally, language which could exacerbate media coverage of an allegedly unruly border. Their "act of observance" was slotted for November 11, 2001, the two-month anniversary of 9/11, in order to condemn "acts of terrorism practiced on American soil" as well as reaffirm the "integration" and "peace" of the border stigmatized by the US war on terror. A founding member, Marcelle, one of the few Christian Lebanese at the border, recalled that the movement originated before 9/11 when she and two other women, a Muslim Lebanese Brazilian and an Israeli-born Jewish Argentine, planned an event "for peace in the Middle East." They intended to plant trees at a tourist spot, Três Marcas (three border markings) between Brazil, Paraguay, and Argentina. They invited the press to cover what was then idealized as an event for peace among adherents of the three Abrahamic faiths. After September 11, 2001, they decided to put on a larger event for peace as well. The movement grew to more than two hundred rank-and-file members with nine directory board members: the Maronite Christian Marcelle; four Sunni Muslim Arab Brazilians; and others from Brazil, Paraguay, Argentina, and Israel. Though affirming peace without borders, the movement's directory planned for the event to take place on the Brazilian side of the border, on the grounds of the Itaipu complex, folding into the Brazilian government's own demur toward war.

Fouad Fakih was a key figure in this multi-ethnic, multi-religious movement for "peace without borders" at a time of war. Mentioned in the first and fourth chapters, Fakih helped run the Acifi business association since the 1970s, undertook trade ventures across the Friendship Bridge in the 1980s, and opened a successful department store in the 1990s. He and others from each side of the border oversaw the production and distribution of more than twenty-thousand shirts imprinted with the symbol of a dove and the slogan "Peace without Borders," which financed some of the movement's costs.[66] Fakih, Marcelle, and other idealists reasoned that US counterterrorist allegations were against not just Arabs, but also Brazilians, Paraguayans, Argentines, and others at the border.[67] "This border region," Fakih explained, "brings together communities of around sixty different ethnicities, who have lived together for more than one hundred years," that is, until "the 9/11 attacks" when Arabs were "irresponsibly included in the list of suspects."[68] Despite such framing, some local detractors characterized the movement as "eminently Arab," so another director in the movement, Jacob Schneider, went on record that, "I am of Jewish origin and at my side are members with dozens of other backgrounds."[69] Planning for the "participation of ethnic groups" and "the participation of religious authorities," movement leaders acknowledged Arabness but also avoided being framed as only Arab in efforts to gain wider appeal on the three sides of the border and beyond.

Accordingly, Arab board members renewed their protagonism in a hemispheric America, reaching out to government authorities from Foz do Iguaçu, Ciudad del Este, Puerto Iguazú, and beyond. Marcelle convinced border authorities that US-government claims of terrorism implied they were "incompetent" and "unaware" of what was happening "under their noses." Fouad Fakih traveled to Brasília and met with the Brazilian president's secretary, delivering a personal letter that asked him to attend and to "defend the society of Foz do Iguaçu," while *A Gazeta do Iguaçu* reported on the invitations that had been extended to not only Brazilian but also Paraguayan and Argentine presidents.[70] Fakih and other movement leaders also relayed an official invitation to George W. Bush through the US embassy in Brasília.[71] The respective city government leaders at the border as well as several state-level officials participated in the event, whereas South and North American presidents sent representatives. Drawing upon their history of civic engagement since authoritarian times, discussed in the second and third chapters, Arabs sought to include the US on the terms set in South America atop a hemispheric stage.

Indeed, Peace without Borders endeavored to change the dominant narrative of the war on terror, not by accusing the accusers but rather by conscientiously opting "to not pay with the same currency in order to uphold 'peace,'" as *A Gazeta do Iguaçu* put it.[72] With a business-friendly "currency" at a time of war, the movement's communications team, made up of mostly Brazilian media authorities in the Foz do Iguaçu government, Acifi, Itaipu, and a local journalists' union, worked on local as well as "regional and world levels," reaching out to the Atlanta-based CNN network (which had just publicized negative images of the border, addressed in the next chapter). Paraguay's *Diario Vanguardia* likewise wrote that this "'movement of peace and against war' . . . forms part of another kind of war that unites the inhabitants of Foz do Iguaçu, Ciudad del Este, and Puerto Iguazú: war against the economic crisis and against the 'evil image' that has ruined this season's tourist business."[73] Charif Hammoud echoed that "we are organizing the great event Paz sin Fronteras" in order to reinvigorate border commerce that had been "drastically reduced" by the negative image of Foz do Iguaçu and Ciudad del Este disseminated by corporate media.[74]

Paz sem Fronteiras staged the border's national, ethnic, and religious accommodation as a counterpoint to dominant images of intolerance and lawlessness. After the national anthems of Brazil, Paraguay, and Argentina at the event, representatives of seventy-two ethnic groups at the border marched through the audience and took their place in front of the stage. Subsequently, "national representatives" from Brazil, Argentina, Paraguay, and the US, alongside the "religious representatives" of Islam, Christianity, Judaism, Spiritism, and Buddhism, read respective messages of peace and fraternity. The event culminated in the signing of a "trinational agreement" between Brazilian, Paraguayan, and Argentine authorities, without the US.[75] Indeed, the "mission of unity and integration between Brazil, Paraguay, and Argentina" was not to criticize the US-led war on terror but rather to change its narrative that vilified the border.[76] As the Paraná state governor Jaime Lerner (PFL) declared, the *ato* was "proof of tolerance, respect, and solidarity of the border community."[77]

Arabs at the border tried to shift the dominant narrative of a war they neither began nor could finish. They emphasized accommodation by echoing Brazilian, Paraguayan, and Argentine leaders' emphasis on solidarity and peace without explicit criticisms of US counterterrorist claims. Fakih declared, "the power of mobilization at the tri-border is greater than the criticisms and accusations made about the region."[78] Foz do Iguaçu mayor Sâmis da Silva repeated that the border is "an example of peaceful coexistence [*convivência*],"[79] while Governor Lerner repeated: "The unity of the border is stronger than any attempt at stigmatizing it."[80] The governor of Alto Paraná in Paraguay, Jorvino Urunaga, stated that the border's "message of peace to the world" should not be overshadowed by terror.[81] And the intendente of Puerto Iguazú in Argentina, Timoteo Liera, called upon residents of the three sides of the border to "fight" unproven "accusations" in order to defend their shared tourist economy. Having sought security in a free trade bloc that suspended due process, as explored in the previous chapter, Arabs now mobilized with local border authorities for peace at a time of war.

Effectively eliding a hemispheric history of state exceptions, the headliners in the *ato* declared solidarity with Arabs and Muslims, as a market-friendly assertion of the plurality of an otherwise maligned borderland. Calls for Third Worldist or Global South solidarity, as explored in the second chapter, were replaced by pronouncements of "peace" and "faith," resonating with the movement's aims to build an alternative narrative to war and sanitize the border through the strategic display of "diversity." In avoiding the vitriol of US authorities, business and government leaders in the event also made no mention of past authoritarian regimes or present-day counterterrorist controls in ostensibly civilian-led governments that ruled by exception. The *ato*'s liberal democratic ethos remained silent about the aforementioned suspension of basic liberal democratic norms for many Arabs at the border, which was occurring at that very moment.

The *ato's* message of peace that avoided confrontation fell short of neutralizing the dominant narrative of war and barely caught the attention of big media in Brasília, Asunción, Buenos Aires, and Washington, DC. Covering the ostensible start of a war with no end, US mainstream media nearly ignored the act for peace at a border that did not fit into what Ulf Hannertz critiqued as a counterterrorist "story line."[82] Only brief notes were issued by news media such as *Folha de S. Paulo*, *O Estado de S. Paulo*, and *O Globo* in Brazil, or *Ultima Hora*, *Diario ABC Color*, and *La Nación* in Paraguay.[83] Major media in these cities downplayed the message of peace at the border and gave equal weight to counterterrorist accusations. Meanwhile, newspapers in Foz do Iguaçu and Ciudad del Este ran front-page stories that read: "Brazil, Paraguay, and Argentina said no to terror in the Peace without Borders event";[84] "Peace without Borders, a message of communion in Foz do Iguaçu";[85] and "War on the evil image,"[86] not dwelling on the limited reach of the movement's message.

Indeed, US authorities again voiced suspicion of the border. Some months after "Peace without Borders," US vice-president Dick Cheney expressed concern with "terrorist activities in Latin America, specifically in the tri-border region."[87] During the New Realities in the Hemisphere conference in Washington, DC, Cheney stated that "terrorists continue to take root in the region." This vitriol continued in Paraguay during the visit of the US Southern Commander, General James Hill, who claimed that the tri-border not only financed terrorist organizations but was home to "sleeper cells" as well.[88] A week later, his vice-commander General Peter Page added that the border "remains relatively free from the activity of security controls." The Foz do Iguaçu mayor asked for Brazil's foreign ministry to issue a formal rebuke while Fouad Fakih decried the resultant "economic and social terror" at the border.[89]

Historically denied full enfranchisement at the border, as seen in the second chapter, Arabs and others were well aware of the *ato*'s limited impact. As one rank and file participant put it, after Peace without Borders ended, "everything went back to the way it was."[90] A *Gazeta do Iguaçu* editor-in-chief Rogério Bonato surmised that "the Peace without Borders movement was a failure. . . . We supported the movement in the newspaper and what happened? . . . We can't make headlines in big media?"[91] Even Fouad Fakih's rising "popularity" provoked fears of his political aspirations among some local government power brokers who "expelled" him from Acifi and "instigated" students to protest against him at the university that he co-founded.[92] Peace without Borders was no match for war without end.

Arabs likewise left intact a border among themselves, as addressed in Chapter 3. Shia stated that they were the *peões* (peons), *mão-de-obra* (manual labor), and *serviçais* (servants) in the movement, whether driving visitors around town or delivering materials. Sunni Muslims, Christians, and Jews made up the movement's upper circles, with no Shia Muslims on the directory board.[93] Allegedly, the movement's leaders failed to extend an invitation to the Shia-majority Sociedade Islâmica Beneficente, though the *ato* was attended by Bilal Mohsen Wehbi, the Lebanese Shia shaykh from São Paulo who had inaugurated the mosque in Ciudad del Este a decade previously. In 1997, Wehbe naturalized as a Brazilian citizen but remained on the radar of the US.[94] A second-generation Brazilian of Arab origins whose father is Shia ended up serving as the guide for Bilal, and for this reason, "many of my Sunni friends," he remarked, "stopped talking to me." Sunni Muslims "don't want to give space" for Shia to have a real say, he noted. Arabs redrew boundaries between themselves in this war on terror.[95]

## Counterterrorist Informants in Ciudad del Este

Some Arabs criticized their own role in post-9/11 extraordinary measures taken by state powers, especially on the Paraguayan side of the border. The aforementioned Armando Chams called out Arabs who were "fake informants" of "Paraguayan authorities," conspiring with the "police to take action" against other Arabs "without the slightest investigation" after 9/11.[96] "Informants" were "traders of Arab origin who accuse their co-nationals of having ties with terrorist groups in order to commercially extort or 'eliminate them.'"[97] Chams approached the Paraguayan Ministry of Justice, Interpol, and the US embassy in Asunción "to expose the blackmailing" that Arabs "were subject to." He explained that Arab "traders with ties to police authorities utilized their contacts to prejudice competitors with false allegations." On the day before the Peace without Borders *ato* in Foz do Iguaçu, complicit officers in Paraguay's National Police raided stores in Ciudad del Este, detained Arab owners, and apprehended computers, documents, and safes. An onlooker shouted, "This is nonsense! Everyone here is at work! We are tired of all these lies. It's all a show!"[98] Not long after, the police officers themselves became the target of scrutiny in Ciudad del Este's city council.[99] When city councilors considered legal action, one of the Arab informants "was quicker and accused the city council president, Alício Peralta Martinez, of being the accountant of the terrorists."[100] Complicit police officers followed up, threatening city councilors with allegations of collusion with terrorists.[101] Said Taijen expressed dismay at this vicious cycle: "There aren't any Arab terrorists at the tri-border . . . the accusations are lies. . . . Local and national authorities and the Ministry of Foreign Relations assure us that the accusations are slanderous but they keep coming." His colleague added, "more than thirty persons" accused of terrorism "were freed" because there is "no connection."[102]

A handful of Arabs accommodated Paraguayan state deference to the US-led war on terror. Ali Ahmed Zaioun was allegedly an informant for a Paraguayan state apparatus still overseen by the political party of the defunct dictatorship. Introduced last chapter, Zaioun gained notoriety in the fraudulent Paraguayan state-supported emission of visas for Lebanese migrants during the 1990s.[103] After 9/11, Amnesty International accused Zaioun of "extortion, death threats, and the appropriation of businesses . . . in the Lebanese community of Ciudad del Este."[104] Hector Guerín, the journalist then working at the *Diario Vanguardia*, explained that Zaioun was "an informant for the Anti-terrorist Police" accusing "his commercial rivals of being terrorists."[105] Guerín suspected that another Lebanese Paraguayan, Kassan Hijazi, was also an informant because Paraguayan public prosecutors suspended probes into his purportedly million-dollar, tax-evasive remittances to "the Middle East, Asia, and the US."[106] Based on these cases, Guerín argued that the "accusations about the presence of terrorists" investigated by state powers actually "stem from the [border] zone itself."[107]

Arab informants capitalized on the Paraguayan state's alignment with the US agenda "to find terrorists," since "counterterrorism" had become a "major component" in Paraguayan-US relations, as political scientists Frank Mora and Jerry Cooney observed.[108] In particular, Zaioun allegedly colluded with Esteban Aquino Bernal, the "counterterrorist counsel of the Supreme Court of Justice" and influential in the Secretaría de Prevención e Investigación del Terrorismo (SEPIT, or Secretary of the Prevention and Investigation of Terrorism).[109] One of the so-called "questionable figures" of the Colorado Party that stayed in power after the end of the dictatorship,[110] Aquino publicly took credit for the US State Department's "praise" that "Paraguay continues being an active partner in the war on terror in 2002."[111] Through Aquino's influence, the anti-terrorist division of the Paraguayan National Police allegedly gave "protection" to the merchandise that Zaioun shipped to his store.[112] Zaioun and Aquino together were said to "make a living by extorting other merchants" through accusations of terrorism, and Aquino himself was later investigated for owning "luxurious residencies" on a modest government salary.[113]

Bringing notoriety to Ciudad del Este in this war-torn America, Zaioun pointed to a rival businessman, Assad Ahmed Barakat, as a "terrorist." In turn, Barakat himself accused Zaioun of turning "a commercial dispute with me . . . into a terrorist war."[114] Shortly before 9/11 in 2001, Zaioun and Barakat met before a Paraguayan judge to settle a "commercial dispute" over distribution rights to a popular video game for which both claimed to be the sole distributor.[115] The owner of the video game, A.B. United of Hong Kong, sent documentation to Paraguay's public prosecutors and

Ministry of Industry and Commerce, "complaining" that the licensing agreement had been made with Barakat, not Zaioun.[116] According to Guerín, Zaioun had falsely registered the game in his name in order "to demand large sums of money from Arab merchants" who would "commercialize the product."[117] Just as the court leaned toward Barakat, Zaioun allegedly raised the question, "Madame judge, are you going to pronounce the verdict in favor of a terrorist?"[118] Zaioun's claim against a rival merchant as an alleged terrorist drew upon a Paraguayan state-supported extortion racket, discussed last chapter, exacerbated by the US war on terror. Under scrutiny of investigative reporting, Zaioun declared himself to be a victim of Guerín and an unidentified "group of persons with international arrest warrants."[119]

The Barakat case served as a proxy war between Brazil and the US over Paraguay. Born in Lebanon and naturalized as a Paraguayan citizen, Barakat ran a profitable electronics business in Ciudad del Este and resided with his Brazilian wife and their Brazilian-born sons in Foz do Iguaçu. The day before the Peace without Borders event, Zaioun's accusation against Barakat led Paraguayan police to raid Barakat's store, Casa Apolo, in Ciudad del Este. As Barakat remained free on the Brazilian side of the border, a Paraguayan prosecutor related that "no proof" but rather only "signs" of terrorist affiliation were found, specifically, Arabic recordings of and a mass-produced red parchment card from Hassan Nasrallah, Hizbullah's secretary-general, as well as money transfer receipts, discussed later.[120] Subsequently, the Paraguayan foreign minister requested that Brazilian authorities detain and hand over Barakat, but Brazilian legislation at the time prohibited the extradition of anyone with a Brazilian-born child, and considered Barakat's own appeals. As the Brazilian judicial system deliberated over the case, the US State Department publicly praised "Paraguayan authorities" who "pursued the extradition from Brazil of local Lebanese Hizballah leader Assad Ahmad Barakat."[121] Only later did the highest court in Brazil agree to extradite Barakat to Paraguay on the condition that he would not be tried for allegedly supporting Hizbullah in what Brazilian government ministers considered to be a "politically motivated" case.[122]

Barakat himself accused Paraguayan government officials of defrauding the state in the aforementioned extortion schemes, marked by both authoritarian legacies and counterterrorist liaisons. He alleged that Carlos Cálcena, the Paraguayan *fiscal* (public prosecutor, in Spanish) and future vice-minister of the Interior who led the raid on his store, tried to blackmail him in exchange for looking the other way, and Cálcena had been, in fact, denounced to the Organization of American States and later put on trial for pocketing drug money after another arrest.[123] Barakat explained that the raid on his store found only a red parchment card from Hassan Nasrallah, secretary general of Hizbullah, which "does not mean that I support terrorism or terrorists," but was rather a mass-produced "thank you" acknowledgement for donations Barakat made to orphanages, not prohibited by Brazilian or Paraguayan law.[124] Asked about money transfer receipts, Barakat explained, "I do business with Miami, New York, Chile, so there's remittances to Lebanon for these purchases, through the credit card, for products that pass through Hong Kong."[125] Barakat's wife characterized her husband as a "scapegoat" and affirmed, "he wouldn't support a terrorist group that goes around killing children like our own."[126] While awaiting a judicial decision in Brazil and leery of US involvement, Barakat categorically stated, "I don't trust the police in Paraguay."

Arabs at the border tended to view Barakat's commercial affairs as "business as usual" in a Paraguayan state that sought to conceal its own illiberal ways under intense US scrutiny. Nasser, an importer in Ciudad del Este and resident of Foz do Iguaçu, opined that Barakat's problem probably started with "one of those money exchanges" in Ciudad del Este where he wired the payment for goods ordered from China. Once the shipment of merchandise arrived in Paraguay, Barakat likely arranged for a "manager" to pay import taxes. Nasser explained that "managers" often offer to "despachar por mais barato" (deal for cheaper, literally, in *portanhol*), evading the payment of the total amount of government taxes by up to two-thirds. Generally, a "manager" pays off government officials and pockets the remaining amount in state-sponsored fraud, similar to dynamics explored in Chapters 1 and 4. Barakat was perhaps issued a tax receipt for imports at a third or so of their actual value that could have been recorded in his own accounting records. With post-9/11 US scrutiny, the real amount of money that Barakat transferred could be traced back to him and authorities perhaps found that the value was far greater than that registered in his own records. With the discrepancy between the amount of money transferred and the lower sum in his accounting books, Barakat could be tried for tax evasion in Paraguayan courts. Not only would the Paraguayan state then avoid investigating its own illiberal liaisons, but US authorities could also spin the case as a victory in the war on terror, though there was no actual evidence regarding terrorism.

Alleged informants exerted a perverse power that bent the self-declared Bush doctrine to serve the purpose of personal profiteering. They were said to "create boogeymen among their countrymen" (*crean zozobras entre sus paisanos*, in Spanish), with unaccountable economic and imaginative influence that expanded in the US-led war on terror.[127] Zaioun was even asked to testify that Barakat owned the business in question, Casa Apolo, since their stores faced each other, shoring up Paraguayan fiscal auditing that demonstrated Casa Apolo transferred money without paying taxes of almost a billion guaraníes (at the time, nearly US$500,000) between 1999 and 2001.[128] The amount was hardly significant in comparison to the tens of billions of US dollars irregularly wired from the Brazilian side of the border to Ciudad del Este and then elsewhere, to be discussed in the following chapter. After Barakat was found guilty of tax evasion and jailed in Paraguay, Zaioun stepped up "pressuring merchants of Arab origin," to buy products imported by Zaioun, including a new electronic console game, at elevated prices.[129] Zaioun shot back that "there are many who sell this product" in Ciudad del Este.[130]

These counterterrorist informants signaled Paraguay's move toward the US and away from Mercosur. The US State Department praised the conviction of who it called "Hizballah fundraiser Assad Ahmad Barakat on charges of tax evasion" as a "major accomplishment," without saying anything of informants like Zaioun who seemed to operate above the law.[131] In the next two years, the US put "$37 million of investment" into "various areas" in Paraguay, including "continued cooperation on counterterrorism and anti-money-laundering activities in the Tri-Border area."[132] Indeed, Paraguayan president Duarte had "made a strategic decision to align Paraguay with the United States" and exercised some distance from Brazil and Argentina.[133] Duarte's shift toward the US grew out of a "disenchantment" with the "regional solidarity" that he once professed alongside fellow Mercosur member states, which refused to renew long-standing economic concessions in the bloc, discussed earlier.[134] Accordingly, Barakat's conviction for tax evasion became framed as a Paraguayan victory in a US-led war on terror, and not another illiberal outcome in a Paraguayan state still overseen by the defunct dictatorship's political party in league with US counterterrorism.[135]

Arabs in Ciudad del Este accommodated but tended to keep a low profile under these exceptions to the rule of law. Indeed, accusations of being a terrorist continued to be "used for extortion and blackmail . . . in the cut-throat marketplace in Ciudad del Este, where most storeowners likely have some accounts to settle, whether due to tax evasion or forgery," in the view of Brazilian investigative reporter Lourival Sant'anna.[136] One Arab storeowner reflected, "we won't be surprised" if other Arabs were arrested "as terrorists. They've been doing that for some time now. For them, this tri-border zone is a shelter for terrorists." His colleague confided, "Today we cannot speak in public, because if we say something, tomorrow they'll come for us and here, who will defend us?"[137]

## Exceptional Equivocations and Enlistments

But the US government equivocated. In 2002, the State Department's new deputy coordinator of counterterrorism, Cofer Black, admitted "no concrete signs of a terrorist presence" during the meeting of the 3+1 group, a security network made up of Brazil, Paraguay, and Argentina "plus" the US.[138] At the same time, Black raised suspicions of "piracy and money-laundering" at the border in "financing terrorism," qualifying that the US would support the 3+1 group to combat "possible remittances . . . to Arab extremists." The State Department reiterated Black's position, writing that "available information did not substantiate reports of operational activities by terrorists," but rather pointed to "international terrorist financing and money laundering in the area."[139] For Brazilian diplomats, the US government's "more moderate" posture indicated a "rebuke of the fallacies" regarding putative "terrorist activities" at the border.[140] Since the matter of terrorist finance is addressed in the following chapter, suffice it to say that some other US authorities echoed this shift, including Stephen Monblatt, then serving on the Organization of American States' Committee against Terrorism,[141] the new ambassador to Brazil, Donna Hrinak,[142] and Southern Command General James Hill.[143]

Seemingly upending this foreign policy stance, then FBI director Robert Mueller declared "al-Qaeda . . . has a presence in the Tri-Border Region in South America."[144] Rather than follow the State Department, the FBI exacerbated matters by lending greater credence to a *Washington Post* story that broke months previously, alleging that none other than Osama Bin Laden visited the Omar Ibn Al-Khattab mosque on the Brazilian side of the border.[145] The Hollywoodesque plot originated with the Brazilian newsweekly *Veja*. The "world's most wanted terrorist," wrote *Veja*, "passed three pleasant days in Foz do Iguaçu" and met with "Arab community members in the Sunni mosque of the city."[146] A "twenty-eight-minute video" of Bin Laden's visit to the mosque, further embellished the magazine, "still exists today," though no sources were ever found.[147] As seen in the second chapter, the cornerstone-laying ceremony of the actual mosque took place at the end of authoritarian rule and the inauguration was held after the return of civil society. Ignoring that history of accommodation, *Veja* alleged that Bin Laden visited the mosque in the 1990s, when the congregation was led by Egyptian-born shaykh Mahmoud Badran. The latter's replacement, Taleb Jommaa, underscored that Badran "deserves respect," having fulfilled the responsibility that the Egyptian government gave him in the mosque at the time.[148] Far from being a closet al-Qaeda sympathizer, Badran had actually made headlines celebrating commonalities between Judaism, Christianity, and Islam.[149] The news story about Bin Laden also "baffled" the Centro Cultural Beneficente Islâmico that constructed the mosque. A founding member,

Ali Said Rahal, felt obligated to state on record: "Bin Laden was never in Foz" do Iguaçu.[150]

Arabs at the border enlisted the help of a homeland statesman in what cultural critics Ella Shohat and Robert Stam call the "burden of representation," the pressure that historically misrepresented subjects shoulder in representing themselves.[151] At the border, they hosted none other than Lebanon's prime minister Rafic Hariri. Upon arriving in Foz do Iguaçu, the Lebanese prime minister was greeted by flower-bearing students from the Escola Libanesa Brasileira. Praised for building a bridge between the border and Lebanon, Hariri had been invited to a business conference in São Paulo and was entertained in Brasília by the then newly elected president, Luiz Inácio Lula da Silva.[152] Amid a busy schedule, Hariri allegedly asked Lula to intervene on behalf of Barakat.[153] In his address to the welcoming party at the border, Hariri declared that "we are with you" and empathized with "the problems you are suffering from in this sensitive area of Brazil and Paraguay."[154] Although "there is talk of many plots being weaved against those living in this area" where "the eyes of the world are all turned," Hariri "heard from the Brazilian authorities" of the "moral and noble" stances of Lebanese at the border. His entourage, which included his future successor, Fouad Siniora, privately met with "public figures" and "expatriates" at the border. Hariri openly acknowledged the "pressures being felt by the Lebanese, whether in Brazil or Paraguay," and questioned the "large group of countries and intelligence agencies" that made unfounded allegations against them. For Fouad Fakih, "the Lebanese Prime Minister reaffirmed" the absence of "terrorist cells" and "disproved the unfounded and calumnious news stories of the international press."[155]

Fakih, Magrão, and other members soon organized the Conselho Anfitrião da Comunidade Árabe Libanesa (Welcome-Party Council of the Arab Lebanese Community) in order to host the visit of another entourage of homeland statesmen.[156] Three months after the visit of the Lebanese prime minister, they welcomed the Lebanese vice minister of foreign relations, Mohammad Issa, the director of emigrant affairs, Haitham Joumaa, and the Lebanese ambassador in Brazil, Joseph Sayagh.[157] Hariri's emissaries explored the establishment of a Lebanese consulate in Foz do Iguaçu, which never materialized. Not necessarily strengthening ties with the homeland, Lebanese authorities joined the Foz do Iguaçu mayor to commemorate Brazil's independence day in the official parade on September 7, the Dia da Pátria; they were photographed together under a banner that read "181 Years of the Independence of Brazil."[158] Providing a spotlight otherwise dimmed by suspicion, Lebanese and Arabs at the border again felt vindicated by Lebanese state officials who praised "civic spirit" at the border.[159]

Perhaps at the urging of migrants themselves, Lebanese prime minister Hariri announced the "re-opening of the Embassy of Lebanon in Paraguay" during his 2003 visit. However, the task of representing Lebanese and Arabs in Paraguay was a greater challenge due to Paraguayan-US rapprochement.[160] Around the same time of the announcement, the Paraguayan vice president Luiz Castiglioni had spent a week in Washington, DC, where he expressed pride in the State Department's "satisfaction" with the Barakat conviction and bilateral counterterrorist agreements.[161] Not long after, the Lebanese diplomat Hicham Hamdan met with this Paraguayan vice president, publicly downplaying the case of Barakat and other Lebanese detainees as "problems" whenever "there is a large collective."[162] Mentioned earlier, Hamdan had asked Paraguayan authorities to maintain due process for Lebanese citizens a month after the 9/11 attacks. After being officially appointed ambassador and taking up the post in 2004, Hamdan again asked why Lebanese citizens from Ciudad del Este were held without charges at the Tacumbú penitentiary in Asunción where the political prisoners of the dictatorship used to be locked up.[163] Authoritarian legacies haunted counterterrorist liaisons today.

With no exorcism in sight, military influence and expenditures increased in tandem. Brazilian President Lula's administration increased military personnel in intelligence and public security while remaining vigilant that no terrorist ties had been found at the border. Lula appointed his "close friend," General Jorge Armando Félix, to head the Gabinete de Segurança Institucional, mentioned previously.[164] In 2003, General Félix testified before the Committee on Foreign Relations of Brazil's Chamber of Deputies. General Félix explained that the Federal Police and army had carried out investigations at the border since 1990 and never found any sign of terrorism.[165] He admonished the federal government to avoid "disrespecting" and "discriminating" against migrants. At the same time, General Félix and others allegedly exerted pressure on President Lula to dismiss then head of ABIN, Mauro Marcelo Lima e Silva, since he "was the first civil police officer to command this intelligence department."[166] In agreement, President Lula appointed Márcio Paulo Buzanelli, "a veteran of the extinct SNI" as head of ABIN.[167] In 2004, Buzanelli observed that no signs of terrorism were found at the border, but wrote that it was "imperative" to improve the "state apparatus" to carry out further investigations and counter "potential threats."[168] Indeed, Buzanelli's call for militarization presaged the doubling of arms purchases between 2005 and 2009 as well as the 25 percent surge in public safety expenditures.[169]

This increasingly militarized Brazil not only demurred to US counterterrorism but also quietly monitored Arabs at the border. At the UN in 2003, President Lula denounced the human and civil costs of the US war on terror. At the same time, he dodged discussing Arabs at the border by skipping part of his speech's original text previously distributed to the press and posted on the Brazilian Foreign Relations Ministry website.[170] In the excerpt that was not read, Lula would have stated, "there is no proof of any activity linked to terrorism at the tri-border between Argentina, Paraguay, and Brazil." In 2005, General Félix likewise distanced the US war on terror and carefully acknowledged Brazil's continued surveillance of the border during his meeting with the US ambassador.[171] In response to the US ambassador's question about the border, General Félix remarked that ABIN "targeted individuals of interest" through a private border security firm, RMAS (Regional Movement Alert System). General Félix reassured the US ambassador that ABIN and Brazil's Federal Police were addressing the "serious problems in the region," including the "illegal movement of arms, money, and drugs." The US ambassador noted General Félix's fastidious avoidance of the terms "terrorists" and "terrorism." The Brazilian general stressed that security measures must be "packaged properly so as not to negatively reflect upon the proud and successful Arab community in Brazil."

Instead of acknowledging the authoritarian legacies of counterterrorist interventions today, the Brazilian state took aim at persistent US stereotypes of a South American border supposedly run amok by Middle Eastern boogeymen. In 2004, the aforementioned Brazilian ambassador in Washington, DC, Rubens Barbosa, rebuked a US writer in *Foreign Affairs* who called the border a "new Libya" where terrorists "meet to swap tradecraft."[172] For Ambassador Barbosa, the US writer "perpetuate[d] a damaging stereotype that in no way does justice to Brazil's struggle against terrorism" through state surveillance of the border for over the previous decade.[173] Ambassador Barbosa pointed out that "no evidence has been produced to prove the presence of terrorist organizations (or even the existence of fund-raising activities) in the area." He cited a list of corroborating US authorities, including Monblatt, Hrinak, and General Hill, mentioned earlier. Serving in Washington, DC, during the mandates of FHC and Lula, Barbosa questioned US visions by underscoring Brazil's own militarized presence at the border.

Not as leverage against but rather in alignment with the US, the Paraguayan state also used Arabs at the border as a pretext for militarization. In 2002, Paraguay's ambassador in Washington, DC, Leila Rachid, herself of Syrian-Lebanese origins, stated, "We have been working very closely with the State Department's office of counterterrorism" against what she thought was a Hizbullah outpost at the border.[174] At the time, Rachid claimed that the Paraguayan government "lent more support to Washington's anti-terrorism efforts than any other country in Latin America," allegedly detaining and extraditing subjects of interest from the border. After becoming foreign minister in the Duarte government, in 2004, Rachid stressed that the 3+1 working group "was able to demonstrate to the world that the tri-border has no terrorist cells." In step with the equivocation in the US State Department, the now Paraguayan foreign minister alleged that "followers of Hizbullah" allegedly send money "to support this political party" in Lebanon.[175] The same year, she neither confirmed nor denied Duarte's concession that permitted US military operations on Paraguayan territory.[176] Whether demurring or deferring to war on terror, civilian governments across the hemisphere justified militarization through Arabs at the border.

Beyond the border, Arab transnational ties even became entangled in the 2006 Israeli war on Lebanon. According to long-time Islamic Benevolent Society member Mohamed Hijazi, many families from Foz do Iguaçu and Ciudad del Este had been vacationing in southern Lebanese villages when the US-backed Israeli airstrikes and shelling began.[177] The Fakih family recounted that members were vacationing in the Beqaa Valley, and with the start of the Israeli offensive, they crammed into a single vehicle and fled into Syria. They needed at least two or three cars, but reasoned that several vehicles might have drawn Israeli artillery, and if one of them had been hit, the other would have been faced with an unimaginable choice to either continue on or stay with those killed or wounded.[178] Downplaying these tolls on everyday civilians, President George W. Bush claimed Israeli military incursions were, in fact, part of the US war on terror.[179] At the same time, President Lula sent the Brazilian military to evacuate Brazilians of Lebanese origin.[180] President Duarte's "Paraguayan government," though, failed to take action to assist "Paraguayan citizens [of Lebanese origin] trapped in Lebanon."[181] Meanwhile, back in Foz do Iguaçu, some two thousand Brazilians and Paraguayans of Arab origin, among others, organized a peaceful protest against Israeli military aggression, which the US embassy in Asunción claimed could "turn violent, anti-Semitic, or anti-American in nature."[182] Disturbingly, US diplomats in Paraguay saw Arabs at the border as capable of acting militaristically, instead of how they were actually being acted upon by ever more powerful militarized forces across and beyond the hemisphere.

After the September 11, 2001, attacks, US officials in the Pentagon, State Department, and elsewhere alleged that "Arabs at the tri-border" were organizing or supporting terrorism in a putatively lawless South America. This chapter instead showed that Arabs folded into Brazilian and Paraguayan state agendas that respectively demurred and deferred to this "war without end." Being accused of terrorist complicity, some Arabs responded by organizing the event Paz sem Fronteiras / Paz sin Fronteras / Peace without Borders, with support from Brazilian authorities who dismissed US accusations.

Meanwhile, a few Arabs in Ciudad del Este became informants and pointed out their business rivals as terrorists, who were then jailed for tax evasion by Paraguayan government officials from the same political party that had backed the thirty-five-year-long dictatorship. With no terrorists to be found at the border, US authorities equivocated and instead emphasized terrorist finance, explored in the next chapter. Whether Arabs at the border rebuffed or tried to substantiate such stances, they and their interlocutors overlooked the past of state-led terror in the present-day. In this beginning of a "war without end," terrorism was never found among Arabs at the border, but its endless search advanced exceptional military influence in civilian governments across the hemisphere.

## CHAPTER 6

# Speculative Accounts

**Arabs remained subject to** speculation amid systemic financial irregularities at the border. They remitted money from the border "to relatives in Lebanon," unduly drawing suspicions of "terrorist" finance among some authorities and pundits, according to Mohamad Barakat.[1] In fact, far larger fortunes had dubiously moved from Brazilian banks to the Paraguayan side of the border and then elsewhere in what became known as the *caso Banestado* (Paraná State Bank case).[2] After signs of state complicity in the bank scandal, Fouad Fakih asked officials to absolve the "remittances that Arabs sent," but suspicions nonetheless loomed.[3]

This chapter asks how Arabs performed and were cast in such accounts from the 1990s through the 2010s. Lebanese, Palestinians, Syrians, and others traded in Brazilian and Paraguayan currencies relative to the US dollar, remitting a portion of their livelihoods to Middle Eastern homelands. After 9/11, however, US authorities more vocally conjectured that such remittances could finance terrorism and tried to convince Brazilian and Paraguayan counterparts likewise. In an attempt to neutralize such speculation, Arabs joined the Foz do Iguaçu city government's lawsuit against the Atlanta-based CNN network that depicted them as terrorist financiers. The US Treasury Department subsequently blocked the assets of some Arabs at the border, a few with reputations as *trambique-iros* (tricksters) but not terrorists. Under such circumstances, Arab charity-giving diminished in Foz do Iguaçu but coalesced around a new mosque in Ciudad del Este, buoyed by sales in upscale imports from East Asia. Arabs tried to offset illiberal security with liberal exchange that neither absolved nor incriminated them. Arabs drew upon and were drawn into a speculative America.

Building on Anna Tsing's work, I grasp speculative accounts at the border as "economic" and "dramatic," or as Bill Maurer likewise theorized, "numeric and narrative."[4] My point of departure is a special account, called the CC5, used at Paraná State Bank agencies to remit tens of billions of dollars from Foz do Iguaçu to Ciudad del Este, and then elsewhere, during the 1990s and 2000s. Much earlier, Brazil's authoritarian regime created CC5 accounts as exceptional conduits for money sent abroad. However, Brazilian, Paraguayan, Argentine, Mercosur, and US officials debated not this authoritarian-era financial exception but instead whether Arabs at the border could fund terrorism. Likewise lacking a broader understanding of financial exceptions and irregularities, CNN represented border trade as terrorist finance after 9/11, leading the Foz do Iguaçu public prosecutor, a vocal critic of authoritarian rule in his youth, to initiate a lawsuit with Arab witnesses. Taking on economic and dramatic roles, Arabs folded into speculative accounts of a hemispheric America.

The suspicions of economic duplicity that had loomed over Arabs since authoritarian times, as noted previously, morphed into more recent counterterrorist financial conjectures that Marieke de Goede called "speculative security."[5] This state exception to liberal democratic and market norms purports to identify and interrupt monies that presumably fund terrorist acts not yet conceived or carried out. The resultant "finance-security assemblage," for de Goede, is a "transnational landscape of laws, institutions, treaties, and private initiatives that play a role in fighting terrorism financing."[6] In step with de Goede's emphasis that "speculative security" criminalizes migrant monies and overlooks big capital, I focus on the tactics employed by the accused. At the border, Arabs kept doing business and publicly mobilizing amid Brazilian, Paraguayan, Argentine, Mercosur, and US speculations. Neither freed from suspicions of financial wrong-doing nor formally charged with funneling money

for terrorist ends, Arabs at the border accommodated state exceptions in economic and dramatic ways.

## Not Banking on Scandal and Suspicion

Arabs at the border sent money to the places they migrated from,
such as Baaloul, Kabrikha, Lela, and elsewhere in the Beqaa Valley as well as in South Lebanon, and to a lesser extent, the West
Bank, Jordan, and Syria. Their wealth underwrote what geographer
Husein Amery called the "remittance economy" of Lela specifically.[7]
In 1989, Amery found that "ninety-seven out of 125 sampled house-
holds in Lela received remittances" from the Americas. This money
financed house construction as well as public works, such as the
building of a new mosque, repairs to an electrical grid, and a water
well. Remitters thought of new houses not as permanent dwellings
but rather as "summer retreats," which they hoped would "attract
and attach migrants' foreign-born children to their parents' homeland."[8] Indeed, *veranear* ("to pass the summer," in Spanish and
Portuguese) in Lebanon is a common transnational practice that
required significant investment. As the largest migrant group at the
border, Lebanese remitted most funds, but other Arabs sent monies
too. Having been displaced from Palestine to Jordan before settling
"in Brazil twenty years ago," Mustafá Jaber likewise related, "I would
send $150, $200, even $300 dollars every month to my family, always
with the expectation of returning to my land after the independence
of Palestine."[9] Remittances from the border funded intermittent
family vacations or eventual returns to respective homelands.

Multiple state powers monitored such financial flows. In 1992,
Brazil's Federal Revenue Secretariat (RF) expressed concern over
"cases of repatriating money without taxation," in the words of the
RF director of Foz do Iguaçu, Adonis da Cunha Ramos.[10] At the same
time, US Treasury Department authorities met with Paraguayan
counterparts to institute "binational mechanisms for the control
and prevention of money-laundering" at this and other borders.[11] Six
years later, in 1998, central banks from Argentina, Brazil, and Paraguay signed accords to track bank accounts suspected of tax evasion
and "money deposited in international accounts in bank agencies at

the border."[12] In a Mercosur meeting at the border in the same year, the then General Director of Brazil's Federal Police, Vicente Chelotti, stated that he and his counterparts investigated "money remittances sent outside the region," finding that they "didn't have anything to do with money remittances for terrorist groups."[13]

Meanwhile, liberal democratic governments made exceptions for big capital to traverse this border though an authoritarian-era type of financial account. The account was known by the acronym CC5, after the Carta Circular n° 5 of 1969, issued by the then authoritarian regime.[14] In 1996, the now liberal democratic Brazilian state passed an extraordinary measure for this account to operate specifically in Foz do Iguaçu, so that business owners in Ciudad del Este could continue to "exchange [Brazilian] reais spent in Paraguay for US dollars in Brazil," as they had done up until that time, mentioned in the first chapter.[15] State officials sought to encourage high-grossing businesses in Ciudad del Este to deposit Brazilian currency from Brazilian customers in CC5 accounts in Foz do Iguaçu, which could then be exchanged for US dollars and remitted back to businesses in Paraguay. For a Brazilian foreign ministerial official, who I call Victor, it was thought that enabling businesses on the Paraguayan side of the border to purchase US dollars on the Brazilian side would stabilize exchange rates as well as "facilitate and make more dynamic commercial relations at the border."[16] Brazil's Central Bank selected branches of the Paraná State Bank (Banestado) in Foz do Iguaçu and chose managers in those branches to oversee the accounts.[17] Consequently, traders in Ciudad del Este allegedly remitted "truckloads full of reais," and later, electronic money transfers, to be exchanged for US dollars in Foz do Iguaçu and then sent back to Ciudad del Este.[18]

Instead of attracting only Brazilian currency disbursed in Ciudad del Este, this state exception enabled domestic Brazilian fortunes to be irregularly sent abroad. "Word spread" about CC5 accounts, according to Victor, and "a lot of people" set them up in order to send money from Brazil to Paraguay, and then elsewhere.[19] Using the names of Paraguayan *laranjas* (fig., stooges, in Portuguese) to open the accounts in Foz do Iguaçu, Paraná State Bank managers received kickbacks by approving CC5 accounts for clients to send money first to Paraguay, and then elsewhere. Money trans-fers through this kind of account in the 1990s and early 2000s were "colossal," to use the Victor's expression. One report estimated that some $124 billion US dollars were sent abroad between 1992 and 1998, a staggering amount that persisted in subsequent years.[20] "Money was coming from every corner and funneled through Foz," related a report from Brazil's Federal Police.[21] Victor reflected that "the rising cost of the US dollar between 1997 and 2004 had to do with this hole that opened up in Foz do Iguaçu."[22] As remitters bought US dollars in Brazil and then transferred those US dollars to Para-guay, the US dollar became more expensive and the Brazilian real became cheaper. Though one of the many players was the *doleiro* ([black-market] money-exchanger) Alberto Youssef, of Lebanese ori-gin, originally from Londrina, a city some seven hours away by car from the border, Arabs in Foz do Iguaçu and Ciudad del Este were not suspects in these financial irregularities.[23]

Arabs at the border did not bank on state scandal and scrutiny, but they had grown accustomed to subsequent fluctuations in hemispheric currencies. On the Paraguayan side, in 1999, Cherif Hammoud from Monalisa reflected that "the devaluation of the real" curtailed Brazilian buying power that hurt business in Ciu-dad del Este "because Brazilians make up 80 percent of our sales."[24] Hassan Diab echoed that the weak Brazilian currency would "bank-rupt" traders in Ciudad del Este, citing the case of his brother who lost 25 percent of the value of the "thirty thousand reais" he had "in his safe" when he exchanged them "for dollars."[25] An electronics store manager, Hassan el Farras put it simply, "the dollar rose and everything got worse."[26] Meanwhile, on the Brazilian side of the bor-der, Ali Osman noted that Paraguayan clientele hoped for "a greater reduction in the price of Brazilian products" with the ongoing over-valuation of the US dollar.[27] His cousin in textiles noted that despite the "uncertainty in exchange rates," the expensive dollar lowered the prices of Brazilian goods for Paraguayan customers. Akin busi-nesses in the neighborhood of Vila Portes adjacent to the Friend-ship Bridge, featured in the first and fourth chapters, saw sales slightly improve due to a cheaper Brazilian currency that attracted clientele from the other sides of the border.

Arabs folded transnational projects into these hemispheric exchange rates. Mohamad, a twenty-something Brazilian of Palestinian origins, narrated his family's relocation in terms of Brazilian currency fluctuations relative to the US dollar. Mohamad was born in Foz do Iguaçu, but when he was five or so, his father moved the family to Jordan, in order for him and his siblings "to learn the language and religion." With a business at the border, the father converted earnings from the Brazilian real to the US dollar, and then into Jordanian dinars. In the 1990s, the family lived on these money transfers, and "every once in a while" they would visit "friends and relatives" in Foz do Iguaçu as his father oversaw the business at the border. But Mohamad specified that the real's devaluation and the dollar's overvaluation in the 1990s and early 2000s "didn't make it worthwhile," so the family returned to live in Foz do Iguaçu, where he studied at a nearby university. For Mohamad and others, the value of the Brazilian currency diminished after being remitted to the homeland. With a more expensive US dollar, Arabs themselves narrated the diminishing numeric value of their remittances to Arab homelands.

Consequently, "the Arab community" *pagou o pato* (fig., took the fall) for the multi-billion-dollar financial irregularities in the Paraná State Bank scandal, according to the Brazilian foreign ministerial official Victor.[28] In his view, US authorities speculated, "Why is there so much money sent" from the border? Mentioned last chapter, the US ambassador to Brazil Cristobál Orozco ostensibly answered the question by presuming "an economic support network of terrorism" around Foz do Iguaçu, though he admitted lacking proof.[29] The US State Department's counterterrorism coordinator Francis Taylor "worried" about "the darker side of commercial trade" at the border that could shelter "clandestine networks of persons and money" which "support terrorist organizations in the Middle East."[30] The US Subsecretary of State, Otto Reich, likewise speculated that "financial networks" at the border might garner "terrorist ties" without "necessarily" being "terrorist groups."[31] Monblatt, Hrinak, and other US diplomats referenced last chapter, having failed to substantiate allegations of actual terrorists, repeated these conjectures concerning terrorist finance at the border.

US suspicions of terrorist finance at the border enabled the Brazil-ian state to avoid its own entanglement in irregular financial flows. Without any mention of the bank scandal, President FHC acknowl-edged that he did not know if "international terrorism could be laundering money in South America."[32] The highest-ranking gen-eral, Alberto Cardoso, surmised that the border "remains more conducive for laundered money to finance illegal activity, includ-ing terrorism."[33] FHC's foreign minister Celso Lafer went on the record that "money laundering" concerned "the Brazilian govern-ment," and "the possibility" of financing terrorism "exists," but any allegation needed to be investigated by the pertinent authorities.[34] Brazil's ambassador to Paraguay, Luiz Augusto de Castro, hypothe-sized that some of the money laundered in Ciudad del Este "could finance Arab terrorism."[35] But Brazil's Justice Minister, José Gre-gori, dismissed "suspicions" of terrorist finance for the lack of evi-dence, verified by the Federal Police in an "anti-terror" working group under his command.[36] In the group, one officer expressed the hope to find "some financier of terror" while another qualified that the remittances "came from elsewhere" in Brazil.[37] Indeed, looking for terrorist financiers clouded rather than clarified domestic irreg-ularities in state-approved financial conduits.

The drama of terrorist finance ended up rhetorically subsum-ing state investigations of financial irregularities committed by others with greater sums of wealth. The head of Paraguay's Secre-taría de Prevención de Lavado de Dinero (Money-Laundering Pre-vention Secretariat), César Arce, looked for but did not find "finan-cial flows" to "terrorists" at the border, having just participated in a seminar on how to track terrorist monies in Washington, DC, after 9/11.[38] Paraguay's Central Bank president, Raúl Vera Bogado, likewise opined that "there is grounds to suspect possible money-laundering . . . could be connected . . . to terrorist activities."[39] He added that Paraguay and the US "closely collaborated" in order "to detect suspicious financial operations." But a Paraguayan econo-mist opined that tycoons, not "terrorists," remitted fortunes from Brazil to Paraguay and then elsewhere because the Paraguayan state had lacked the technical means to follow monies sent abroad.[40] A Paraguayan journalist echoed that Brazilian moguls undertook the lion's share of remittances to evade taxes, but the "blame" was placed on Paraguay.[41]

Under US pressures to pursue terrorist monies and Brazilian concerns with complicity in irregular money-transfers, the Paraguayan state "prevented" Arabs in Ciudad del Este "from sending money remittances abroad" a month after 9/11.[42] Paraguay's Central Bank (BC) "blocked the bank accounts of holders of Arab origin due to suspicions that local traders could be helping to finance terrorist organizations that operate in the Middle East." The BC allegedly possessed a list of some forty names, mostly of Arab origin, who allegedly "sent more than US$50 million to the Middle East in the last five years."[43] Fouad Fakih condemned the "recent steps to block bank accounts and imprison traders of Arab origin in Ciudad del Este."[44] Having led the Peace without Borders movement in Foz do Iguaçu, Fakih stated that money transfers from the border "pass through the Clearing House of New York and all that is needed is to identify the sender and receiver."[45] Government authorities subsequently failed to find any evidence between the frozen bank accounts and terrorist finance, but established a drama that drew attention away from state complicity in much larger financial irregularities.

## From Terrorist-Finance Suspects to Victimized Appellants

Some state authorities tried to cast Arabs at the border as terrorist-finance suspects soon after 9/11. Celso Três, the Brazilian federal prosecutor who investigated CC5 accounts, entertained the possibility of "terrorist participation" in the banking scandal. Três conjectured that perhaps "there were many CC5 [accounts] utilized by persons of Arab origin," offering no evidence but mentioning Foz do Iguaçu's "dense population linked to the Arab world" and the "intercepted phone calls" from the border that he claimed were connected to the "terrorist act that occurred in Argentina."[46] Três's showboating drew little support in Brazil but likely aided the state-supported extortion rackets shaking down Arabs on the Paraguayan side of the border, addressed in Chapters 4 and 5. Mentioned last chapter, Paraguay's federal prosecutor Carlos Cálcena cited Três to claim that Ciudad del Este was one of the "strongholds of the financial support of terror," before Cálcena was denounced to the Organization of American States and tried for embezzling hundreds of thousands of dollars.[47]

At the same time, other state authorities cast Arabs at the border as victimized appellants. Ten days after the baseless allegations, Antônio Vanderli Moreira, then public prosecutor of the Foz do Iguaçu government, filed a lawsuit for "compensatory damages" against Três.[48] Without stipulating a monetary amount, Moreira reasoned that the claims made by Três would worsen the "prejudice" against Arabs at the border and carry "negative repercussions" for the "imminently touristic" city of Foz do Iguaçu. Moreira implied that Três made the accusations as a self-serving publicity stunt because he took "no measures" to investigate.[49] Moreira called on long-time traders to testify, including Fouad Fakih. In his deposition, Fakih stated that Três "was offensive" to not only Foz do Iguaçu but also "Arabs who reside here," voicing fears of a plummeting economy amid talk of terror. At the time, Fakih criticized similar US speculations that "hurt all commerce in the region," evident in "flight cancellations" and drops in hotel reservations that would enable the "US to finish off with the Treaty of Mercosur."[50] In this account, Arabs at the border were not suspects but rather litigants in a defamation case.

Arabs at the border were both constrained and enabled by extraordinary measures, not only as suspects of terrorist finance but also as subjects of solidarity. Moreira, the public prosecutor taking up the defense of Arabs and the border, was born into a family of Italian and Portuguese origins in Rio Grande do Sul and moved to Foz do Iguaçu as a young lawyer, penned criticisms of authoritarian rule in the 1970s, and mounted the defense of Juvêncio Mazzarollo and *Nosso Tempo* in the 1980s, mentioned in the second chapter.[51] Moreira explained, "since I arrived here [at the border], I've lived with Arabs and I knew that everything that was being published about them was a lie."[52] His defense earned accolades from Rogério Bonato, editor of *A Gazeta do Iguaçu*, which took up a similar public stance.[53] Bonato remembered an anonymous call made to his newspaper after 9/11, claiming that "Muslims were fundraising for a terrorist organization" at an event hosted by the Omar Ibn al-Khattab mosque. A Gazeta do Iguaçu refuted the accusation because a journalist from the newspaper had covered the event, an 'eid (holy day) marking the end of the fast during Ramadan, annually making headlines since the 1990s, as shown in the third chapter. The journalist stated, "I went to that event and nothing was collected for terrorists!"

Notwithstanding such civic solidarity, Arabs made prime-time news as seemingly rich racketeers on the Atlanta-based CNN. In the broadcast "Terrorists Find Haven in South America," CNN portrayed the border as one of the world's "busiest black markets" that sheltered and supplied "terrorists."[54] The author, Harris Whitbeck, then a CNN correspondent based in Mexico City, twisted Arabs' economic and political patrimony at the border as suspicious terrorist finance.[55] Whitbeck saw Arab businesses not as a half-century-long investment in real estate and civil society, but rather as a "revolving door for Islamic extremists" and "hundreds of millions of dollars of transactions" that allegedly "support terrorism." Citing nameless authorities from Paraguay, Argentina, and the US, the CNN reporter ignored the objections of Brazilian officials, who were then investigating CC5 accounts. Attentive not to authoritarian legacies, but rather to counterterrorist liaisons, CNN twisted Arab trade and finance, occulted Brazilian demur, and emphasized Paraguayan and Argentine deference to the US after 9/11.

But Arabs at the border found recourse in the next day's local news headline that read, "CNN Practices Terrorism against the Border," which criticized the network for driving away tourists and wreaking "immeasurable" damage to "our economy."[56] The Foz do Iguaçu mayor Sâmis da Silva characterized the CNN report as "verbal terrorism" and led an official delegation to meet with Brazil's Justice Minister, José Gregori.[57] With Fouad Fakih by his side, Silva related that tourists cancelled hotel reservations due to the speculative news coverage. Gregori responded that "the entire city" of Foz do Iguaçu "is victim of a defamatory campaign" akin to a "true witch-hunt" and he vowed to take measures to "redress the economic damage already done."[58] Two weeks later, none other than Brazilian president FHC went on CNN and "guaranteed" that no evidence of terrorism at the border was found in ongoing investigations.[59] Brazilian government and media authorities safeguarded Arabs and the border against what they perceived to be the deleterious repercussions of US speculations.

In efforts to change the dominant narrative, Arabs tried to accommodate foreign correspondents who reported on the border from metropoles like São Paulo, Buenos Aires, or even Mexico City, as in the case of CNN's Harris Whitbeck.[60] In one of several such instances, Magrão recounted his interaction with a US foreign correspondent for the Associated Press (AP) who reported on the border from his base in São Paulo.[61] The AP reporter requested a phone interview, but Magrão insisted that he would only speak in person at his store near the Friendship Bridge. As discussed in the first and fourth chapters, the neighborhood of Vila Portes where Magrão opened his store reached prominence in the 1980s and endured Mercosur in the 1990s. Upon meeting Magrão, the AP correspondent admitted that he expected to land on a secret airstrip and travel through the jungle until reaching "Taliban-type soldiers" at the border. Instead, the reporter passed through an international airport, four-lane highways, urban neighborhoods, and more than a dozen and a half military or government posts around the Friendship Bridge. According to Magrão, the correspondent ditched his initial story based on speculation and ended up writing an account actually about this border.

But US media continued to cast Arabs at the border as suspects in a counterterrorist drama. CNN's Christiane Amanpour found a photograph of what she purported to be the Iguaçu/Iguazú waterfalls while she was embedded with US armed forces in Kabul, Afghanistan in 2001. On camera, Amanpour reported, "while we were scouring this now-abandoned house, we came across this picture on the wall. These are the falls of Iguazu [*sic*] in Brazil, and this is where US intelligence officials say they've identified terrorist cells that they say are linked to Osama bin Laden and the Al Qaeda network."[62] The photograph was not of Iguaçu/Iguazú, but CNN avoided issuing any rectification. A year later, in 2002, another CNN reporter, Mike Boettcher, speculated that a "terrorist meeting" in Ciudad del Este brought together "groups linked to Osama Bin

Laden," a recurrent charge made some six months before the *Veja* and *Washington Post* reporting, discussed last chapter.[63] Boettcher ignored Brazilian authorities with contrary views and referenced Argentine and Paraguayan counterparts who alleged "an increase of terrorist activity in the region." Ignoring the multi-billion dollar state bank scandal, Boettcher thickened the plot of a counterterrorist drama, observing that "thousands of dollars move through Lebanese[-owned] currency exchanges, millions of dollars are spent on telephone bills, and there is an intense transfer of bank funds between the [South American] region and the Middle East."[64]

Both Brazilian and Paraguayan state authorities rebuked CNN's vilification of Arabs at the border.[65] As in the previous year, the Foz do Iguaçu mayor characterized media coverage as the "terrorism of CNN."[66] The mayor called for a "greater monitoring of the media to identify defamatory material" against the border. Likewise, Foz do Iguaçu city councilors unanimously approved a "motion of repudiation against the news story released by the CNN network."[67] Javier Zacarías Irún, the mayor of Ciudad del Este, echoed that the border was "prejudiced by the irresponsible publication."[68] Even the city council of Ciudad del Este voted to take legal action "against whomever accuses Ciudad del Este and the tri-border zone of being a nest of terrorists," but opted for silence after alleged threats ostensibly made by the informant mentioned last chapter.[69] Having witnessed the steady decrease of historically high profits since the mid-1990s, Arabs at the border asked state authorities to "demand explanations" from CNN.[70]

Arabs drew upon an established track record of seeking legal recourse on Brazil's side of the border. In 2002, then secretary of tourism in Foz do Iguaçu, Neuso Rafagnin, compared "Arabs and Chinese" to "clouds of locusts" because they "devastate everything wherever they pass and afterwards go away."[71] Arabs threatened to sue the official for "xenophobia, racism, and prejudice and they demanded explanations for such declarations." This litigious strategy worked. The following year, the same official dismissed US counterterrorist suspicions of Arabs, speculating that the US "began looking for terrorists" only after Arabs at the border bypassed Miami and the US by importing directly from East Asia.[72] Rafagnin characterized Arab residents as "good people" and the border as "being a victim of the international press."[73] The point is that Arabs knew and exercised their rights at the border.

Arabs served as *testemunhas* (legal witnesses) in the lawsuit filed by the Foz do Iguaçu public prosecutor mentioned earlier, Antônio Vanderli Moreira. The lawsuit asked "for the reparation of moral damages" against Turner Internacional do Brasil Ltda., the owner of the now defunct website cnn.com.br, which translated and published Boettcher's story.[74] Moreira declared that "the US government and its media stations" alleged "terrorism" at the border "due to the concentration of Arab immigrants" and "cannot continue stigmatizing an orderly people who helped shape this border."[75] Moreira reasoned, "it was the duty of the public prosecutor to defend the people and the region."[76] He showed that the number of tourists to the border decreased after calumnious reports of sheltering terrorists, and called upon Fouad Fakih, Mohamed Barakat, Mohamad Ismail, and others to provide depositions, narrating their decades long history at the border as well as attesting to the "moral damage" caused by the unfounded reportage.[77]

Through this legal performance, Arab traders were recast by themselves and others as appellants and witnesses, rather than terrorist financiers, in a speculative America. In 2004, the Second District Court of Foz do Iguaçu convened the first judicial conciliation between the Foz do Iguaçu city government and the CNN network. It ended without an agreement because the defendant, Turner Internacional do Brasil Ltda., alleged that it was not "the one responsible for the journalistic content produced by the network's headquarters' in the US and reproduced in Brazil."[78] It argued that the lawsuit would have to be filed against the headquarters, Turner Broadcasting System, Inc., in Atlanta. At the time, Moreira considered this sort of response as "part of big international capital; they don't want to know anything, they are above it all." Moreira added that he did not expect to win the case but rather to "show that we didn't agree with the defamatory campaign that was made" against Arabs and the border.[79]

## US Drama of Pursuing Terrorist Finance

Nonetheless, US authorities maintained that Arabs were shady money handlers at the border. In 2004, New York district attorney Robert Morgenthau testified to the US senate that his probe into Manhattan banks uncovered "millions of dollars" being "transmitted on behalf of parties from the tri-border region of Brazil, Argentina, and Paraguay," with no mention of the authoritarian-era bank accounts being investigated in Brazil.[80] A couple years afterwards, Morgenthau mused that he "broke up" a Middle Eastern terrorist-finance network at the border, though admitting "we know very little about the ultimate recipients and who the transmitters were."[81] In fact, some named in his report had been already indicted by a Brazilian task-force on the CC5 account scandal.[82] Officials in Foz do Iguaçu and Ciudad del Este considered that more senior US officials invalidated Morgenthau's claims, having declared that the border showed no signs of terrorism in a previous 3+1 meeting, mentioned last chapter.[83]

But the US government had revised, not relinquished, this drama, which became about pursuing "terrorist finance," and not just "terrorism." In this new plot, in 2006, the US Treasury and State departments classified nine residents and two organizations at the border as "Specially Designated Nationals," an exceptional euphemism for suspected terrorists and narcos.[84] Overseen by the Treasury Department's Office of Foreign Assets Control (OFAC), this black-listing was made possible by US president George W. Bush's Executive Order 13224, "Blocking Property and Prohibiting Transactions with Persons Who Commit, Threaten to Commit or Support Terrorism," signed into law soon after 9/11.[85] It aimed to freeze assets of "individuals and entities that commit, or pose a significant risk of committing, acts of terrorism," including those who knowingly or unknowingly donate to groups denominated as terrorist by the US.[86] The executive order contributed to jurisdictional tensions between the US Treasury Department and the US State Department. In the pursuit of terrorist finance, Treasury and State department officials would have equal discretion over how to designate and block the assets of Specially Designated Nationals. As a brief instance, the aforementioned case of Assad Ahmed Barakat was particularly complex. As a Specially Designated National, Barakat possessed assets in Paraguay and Brazil, and at the time, Paraguayan officials had requested his extradition from Brazil.[87] US government authorities were conflicted over how to freeze business and residential assets across domains under other sovereign states.

In this drama of pursuing terrorist finance, US embassies in Brasília and Buenos Aires recommended the Treasury "postpone" the plan to announce the "special designation" of some Arabs at the border.[88] A foreign service officer in Brasília requested more time to apprise Brazilian officials, who would otherwise "react poorly" and "decline to move forward with any asset freezes" if they were not previously given "evidence" of terror-finance that they "repeatedly questioned."[89] Referring to the "tri-border area" by the acronym TBA, this officer called for "a strategy on TBA terror finance" that took seriously Brazilian requests for the US to "share . . . evidence of terror finance in the TBA."[90] To do otherwise would "alienate the decision-makers whose actions are required to freeze any Brazilian assets belonging to these individuals" and "would leave the door wide open to asset flight," as designees could move their finances elsewhere.[91] An officer in Buenos Aires wrote that he "fully supports AmEmbassy Brasilia arguments" for the need to consider "local sensitivities" and coordinate "with local and regional security and intelligence agencies."[92] Two years previously, he remembered, the US agreed that no "operational acts of terrorism" existed at the border in the 3 + 1 meeting.[93] So the "public designation" of some residents as terrorist financiers would be understood as a US equivocation.[94] The designation was slightly postponed in a thickening plot.

Intrigue developed between US attorney-general Alberto González and Brazil's Minister of Justice Márcio Thomaz Bastos, himself of Lebanese origins. In 2007, González stated that "more can be done" about terrorist financing at the border, but Bastos shot back that Brazilian intelligence used the latest technology to "constantly monitor the situation" at the border.[95] Brazilian officials from the ministries of Justice, Defense, and Foreign Relations, moreover, related to US counterparts that "Arab immigrants at the border with Argentina and Paraguay send money to the Middle East that goes to their families. They're personal remittances."[96] Though "difficult" to differentiate between donations "all immigrants make," and "supposed actions to finance terrorism,"[97] the ABIN director, Márcio Paulo Buzanelli, mentioned last chapter, affirmed that the "money going there [Lebanon] doesn't feed terrorism," but rather charity and social services. He added, "since we [in Brazil] don't work with terrorist lists," as the US does, it would be "very difficult to pinpoint if some of this money goes to terrorism," adding that even the US government permits fundraising among Shia Lebanese in Dearborn, Michigan.[98] Still keeping Arabs under watch, Brazilian authorities rebuked the US.

In an unexpected plot twist, the US Treasury Department's OFAC issued a press release, publicizing the actual names of nine "special designated nationals" at the border, Muhammad Yusif Abdallah, Hamzi Ahmad Barakat, Hatim Ahmad Barakat, Mohammad Fayez Barakat, Saleh Mahmoud Fayad, Sobhi Mahmoud Fayad, Ali Muhammad Kazan, Farouk Omairi, and Mohamad Tarabain Chamas. It characterized them as members of "Assad Ahmad Barakat's network in the Tri-Border Area" and a "major financial artery to Hizbullah in Lebanon." OFAC's director declared that freezing their assets would "disrupt this channel" and "further unravel Barakat's financial network."[99] Over the course of the next year, Brazilian, Argentine, Paraguayan, and US news stories cited this press release from the Treasury Department's OFAC.[100] In 2007, *Revista Época* published an article about these "Muslims settling in Brazil and Paraguay," noting they "appear in a report of the US Department of Treasury."[101] "According to the document," wrote *Revista Época*, they allegedly raised money through "contraband, drugs and arm-trafficking, counterfeiting dollars and passports," which allegedly "would help bankroll the activities of terrorist groups from the Middle East." Though noting that "Brazilian authorities complain" of unsubstantiated US claims, *Revista Época* and big media tended to de facto legitimize US counterterrorist speculations.

In another dramatic twist, some Arabs suspected that counterparts at the border deceptively accused other Arabs as terrorists, similar to the dynamics explored last chapter which fuel and fool counterterrorist measures. The *shaykh* of the Islamic Benevolent

Society, Mohamad Khalil, pointed out that the nine men on the list of terrorist-financiers *não são da mesma massa* (fig., are not cut from the same cloth), some are honest while others are unscrupulous. Khalil was born and raised in Lebanon, educated in Qom, and lived in Iran for some thirteen years. In 1998, he arrived in Curitiba to administer the mosque and came to serve the Islamic Benevolent Society in Foz do Iguaçu, whose members often run businesses in Ciudad del Este. After asking about the "specially designated nationals" on each side of the Friendship Bridge, Khalil and others discerned that all were owed money by the same Arab trader in Ciudad del Este, himself suspected of being an informant of Paraguayan law enforcement. The sheikh reasoned that the individual perhaps tried to free himself of debts by listing his Arab creditors as terrorist financiers at the border. Animating this America, Arabs speculated about their own business rivalries at the border in a US-led drama of pursuing terrorist monies.

Hardly upstaged, US government authorities expressed increasing suspicion over Arab donations and remittances. In 2003, Steven Monblatt, then the US head of the Inter-American Committee against Terrorism, called upon Arabs at the border to make more "transparent" their donations to charities in Lebanon and Palestine, in order to prevent such money from being suspected as terrorist finance.[102] Two years later, the State Department warned against the "bulk cash smuggling and the abuse of charities" in "potential terrorist fundraising activities" at the border.[103] In agreement, the US Treasury Department speculated that alleged terrorist financiers at the border may use "corrupt charities" and take advantage of "those who wittingly and unwittingly donate to them."[104] In a 2006 interview with Brazil's *Folha de S. Paulo*, the FBI director of international operations likewise qualified that "the money that was or is being transmitted to the Middle East" from the border is "a grey area," because Arabs "donate money with good intentions."[105] But Brazil's ambassador to Paraguay observed that "Arab community members in the region of Ciudad del Este" make "remittances . . . with the sole objective of financially supporting their families."[106] Recurrently questioned by Brazilian counterparts, US authorities failed to provide the sort of evidence to consolidate their performance.

Nonetheless, Arab fundraising became emblematic not of civic engagement but rather of its suspension in an exceptional order. In 2010, the US Treasury Department's press release alleged that Ali Kazan and Sheikh Sayyed Bilal Mohsen Wehbe "raised more than $500,000 for Hizballah from Lebanese businessmen in the TBA [Tri-Border Area]" after Israel bombed Lebanon four years previously.[107] Indeed, the US Treasury had already listed Kazan as one of the Specially Designated Nationals, and later added Wehbe. But at the border, most associated each of them with organizing civic associations and running educational institutions. According to Reda Soueid, Wehbe assisted the Islamic Benevolent Society in Foz do Iguaçu, raising support for the Escola Libanesa Brasileira that opened in Foz do Iguaçu in 2000.[108] As mentioned previously, Wehbe appointed Kazan as director of that school, but the US list of terrorist finances distorted community fundraising that has a long history at the border. In the 1990s, Ziad Fahs, featured in Chapter 3, claimed that on the occasion of 'Ashura, traders donated some US$800,000 for the Centro Educacional Libanés in Ciudad del Este.[109]

Arabs speculated that government authorities twisted this and other acts of charity in order to validate the drama of terrorist finance. In the 1990s and 2000s, some Lebanese-owned stores at the border made room near cash registers for small donation boxes whose proceeds were destined for war victims in Lebanon and Palestine. In these taken-for-granted containers, customers would place small bills of reais or guaranis, whose worth relative to the US dollar was low, for reasons mentioned earlier. Immediately after 9/11, however, Paraguayan authorities raided the stores in Ciudad del Este and confiscated the boxes, and some storeowners that had the donation boxes on countertops were listed as potential financiers of terrorism. "That's how they [government authorities] fabricated the connection" between Arab trade and terrorism, explained Khalil, "collecting money in these small boxes for families in Lebanon turned into 'financing the terrorists of Hizbullah and Hamas.'"[110]

Accordingly, public-spirited collections diminished amid fears of what Sociedade Beneficente Muçulmana (SBM) president Jamil Ibrahim Iskandar called Islamophobia, which for him meant

"Muslims becoming synonymous with terrorists."[111] According to Iskandar, the CNN report in 2001 that associated Islam with terrorism at the border worsened some six years later when *Revista Época* publicized the US Treasury Department allegations. As a result, he reflected, "the community is reluctant in expressing its culture and religion," especially through charity. This aversion arose when SBM's religious leader Sheikh Khalil floated the idea of sponsoring a dinner to raise money for victims of the Israeli war on Lebanon in 2006, mentioned at the end of last chapter. He got the idea from a similar event in Curitiba that raised a humble sum of money for war relief in Lebanon. But most at the border feared that any act to raise funds for the homeland would be twisted as "financing Hizbullah."[112] Khalil explained that many lack any sympathy for Hizbullah, despite assumptions to the contrary. Though the SBM president and religious leader concurred that migrants continued remitting "money to family members in the Middle East," some shied away from fundraising under such surveillance.

The Arab Unity Club in Foz do Iguaçu, the first civic association at the border explored in the first and second chapters, temporarily closed its doors under such circumstances in the 2000s. Previously, the club had made local news for board elections and commemorative galas.[113] Twenty or so traders had served as major patrimonial donors, each contributing R$50,000 to provide the club's financial basis of some R$1,000,000 "or 500,000 dollars" (then currency exchange estimates).[114] But the club's regular members stopped giving amid US-derived suspicions of charity donations, exacerbated by *Revista Época* and the widely disseminated US Treasury Department list with names of specially designated Brazilians and Paraguayans of Arab origin. Indeed, Arab Unity Club members failed to raise even a modest sum requested by the board of directors to keep the club's doors open. Given the fact that Arabs at the border would not even contribute to maintain a non-profit entity with civic ends that was established decades previously, Nasser rhetorically asked, why would they be sending millions of dollars to "terrorists in the Middle East"?[115]

"The community feels very watched," emphasized Sheikh Khalil from the Islamic Benevolent Society.[116] Khalil recalled a visit from a young man with Lebanese parents, born in Brazil, who "speaks

Arabic well." The young man gave his card, and asked to be contacted if any questionable activity arose. "If I discover something," reasoned Khalil, "I'm going directly to the police. Why would I call this man?"[117] With mosques and religious gatherings open to the public, Khalil explained, "I'm not afraid of informants. I'm afraid of the informant who lies, who adds or invents things." Khalil, and everyday Arabs, drew attention to the role of state authorities and unaccountable informants with vested interests in speculative security.

## The Exceptional Rise of the *Este*

Arabs in Ciudad del Este expanded supply chains through, and not in spite of, state exceptions to democracy and the market. In the mid-1990s, Samir and Ibrahim Jaber, naturalized Paraguayan citizens of Lebanese origin, opened the Centro Pioneer, specializing in car audio and home theatre electronics.[118] Importing from China, Japan, the US, Panama, and elsewhere, their business earned annual profits of over US$100 million by the 2000s. At the same time, the Centro Pioneer and other businesses in Ciudad del Este made headlines for alleged "tax evasion" whereby Paraguayan tax officials initiated and later suspended audits for what *ABC Color* called "huge" kick-backs.[119] Without referencing state tax irregularities, the Pioneer Corporation in Japan honored Samir Jaber "for the quantities of sales reached" in 2012. A Paraguayan colleague stated that Jaber deserved this "international distinction" for "working in legal, formal, and transparent" ways "that have their costs."[120] He noted Jaber's "entrepreneurial spirit" and his leadership in the Chamber of Commerce of Electronics and Appliances of Paraguay (CIEEP) as "summarily positive for Ciudad del Este."

In Ciudad del Este, Arabs' own accounts of their trade underscore not Paraguayan or US exceptional pursuits of financial assets but rather the rise of China. Arabs increasingly imported from China in the 2000s, though trade relations between Paraguay and East Asia date back decades.[121] Within the first decade of the twenty-first century, a manager in La Petisquera, Khaled, witnessed Chinese businesses grow seven-fold in trade fairs across Europe, Asia, and elsewhere. Khaled migrated from Lela to Ciudad del Este, like the Mannah brothers who own the business. As the acquisitions manager in perfumery, Khaled explained that the pump, glass, and packaging of the perfume are produced in China, which now supplies much of the higher-end line in La Petisquera. Matter-of-factly taking note of what anthropologist Arjun Appadurai called "production fetishism," Khaled explained that "the end-product" is "Made in France" because "the perfume itself," which "is more difficult to produce," is "still made in France."[122] Khaled implied that many in Ciudad del Este share the same understanding in importing luxury brands, such as Armani, Gucci, Louis Vuitton, and others, which are mostly manufactured in China.[123] Having brought in goods from Panama since the 1960s and Miami since the 1990s, as explored previously, La Petisquera and other businesses in Ciudad del Este helped China make up 34 percent of all imports into Paraguay as of 2011.[124] Arab transnational trade at the border, like elsewhere in South America, turned to the *Este*.

Arabs gave distinct reasons for the border's turn toward Asian-centered supply chains. Said Taijen reflected that he and others initially shifted away from US free trade zones due to the politics of obtaining a US visa. Arabs experienced difficulty traveling to Miami in the 1990s, as related in Chapter 4, but Taijen explained that, after 9/11, a rumor spread that Arab Paraguayans were asked to become informants when they requested or applied to renew a visa at the US embassy in Asunción. "We want to help you . . . to give you a visa," US consular officers supposedly told Taijen's interlocutors, "but you need to help us too."[125] As this perhaps apocryphal tale spread, Taijen concluded, Arabs started to look for other places to do business, namely in "Popular China, Taiwan, Korea, and India," as well as in "Singapore, Malaysia, and even Pakistan." For Fouad Fakih, though, Arab businesses, "as in any other part of the world went to China for the price."[126] He explained that the turn toward Asian market suppliers has not diminished the power that the US still possesses over patents and intellectual property that underwrite such manufacturing.[127] Taijen and Fakih made distinct speculations about the US in the border's economic shift toward Asia.

Arabs also led Paraguayan-US joint commercial ventures in order to serve a still predominantly Brazilian clientele. In 2005, Ghassan

Nassar and his brother Hicham brought together Paraguayan and US investors in the group Initial SA.[128] As naturalized Paraguayan citizens of Lebanese origins, the Nassar brothers ran the firm Pioneer Internacional that competed with the Jaber's, mentioned earlier. Their transnational group acquired property to build a new shopping center one hundred meters from the Friendship Bridge that Brazilians still crisscross to shop in Ciudad del Este. Paraguayan government officials sold this property, once owned by the "deceased dictator Alfredo Stroessner," at allegedly below-market values, raising suspicions of pay-offs.[129] The construction of the shopping center's marble-like floors and clear glass windows proceeded and retail space was rented out by 2008. Named Shopping del Este, this "sophisticated side" of Ciudad del Este featured high-end boutiques of clothing and accessories as well as shops for home decoration and design. Imported from mostly Asia, name brands like Calvin Klein, Casa Bella, Nike, and Ralph Lauren "attract consumers with greater buying power," overwhelmingly from Brazil.[130] Financed by US investors and patronized by Brazilian consumers, the Nassar brothers' ventures were apparently investigated but never formally charged by Paraguayan fiscal authorities.[131]

Arabs invested profits back into the Paraguayan border city still governed by the same political party of the defunct dictatorship. In 1996, the children of Ali Said Rahal from the Casa de la Amistad, introduced in the first chapter, inaugurated the Grupo Rahal, after their father's store had expanded into the Galeria Rahal with more than seventy-five retail spaces. Under this group, they opened the Fenix Trading Company, an authorized dealer for Panasonic with distribution rights for Nokia in Paraguay and Bolivia, as well as Anovo, which serviced respective warranties and provided other assistance for East Asian–led electronics companies.[132] Their suppliers and buyers can stay at the Hotel California they also own in Ciudad del Este, which annually receives tens of thousands of visitors. Most importantly, the Grupo Rahal runs the multi-million-dollar Fenix Emprendimientos Inmobiliarios SA (Fenix Real Estate Developments). In 2011, it constructed the Don Alí building, named after the father, in an upper–middle-class part of Ciudad del Este.[133] For the group's CEO, Maaty Rahal, the technologically integrated

building introduced a new legal model for apartment building ownership and land trusts in Paraguay.[134] The mayor, Sandra
MacLeod, whose Colorado Party ruled the Paraguayan border town
for more than six decades, stated that the building represents "all
the pride of Ciudad del Este."[135]

Arabs have grown used to doing business at the border under
exceptional rule. Next to the Galeria Rahal but across from the Shopping del Este is S.A.X. in the King Fong shopping center, inaugurated by Armando (Ahmad) Nasser in 2008. Featured in the Brazilian
*Isto É*, Armando explained that the store's insignia stands for "Style,
Arts, and Xtras," in reference to the Saks on Fifth Avenue.[136] Dior,
Giorgio Armani, Prada, and Versace brands occupy a retail space
as large as a NFL football field that includes a bistro and café too.
Nasser reflected, "I wanted to offer Brazilians and Paraguayans the
chance to buy quality products, in a sophisticated atmosphere, and
without the exorbitant prices like those of São Paulo." The store's
website shows illustrious clients such as Brazilian Minister of Justice José Eduardo Cardozo and Brazilian senator Álvaro Dias, as
well as the Paraguayan minister and vice-minister of Industry and
Commerce.[137] Today, Nasser noted that 60 percent of his customers are Brazilian and their purchases individually average around
two thousand US dollars. Only fourteen years old when he arrived
in Paraguay in 1979, his first store specialized in imported spirits
and cigarettes, and with the profits, a decade later Nasser founded
the Grupo Fenícia.[138] In 2014, the group's real estate arm, 5 Star
Empreendimentos Imobiliários Ltda, sealed a "management services agreement" with Hyatt Hotel Corporation for a Park Hyatt
hotel in Foz do Iguaçu.[139] At the same time, his business drew the
scrutiny of Paraguayan state authorities who pressed charges of tax
evasion and considered dismissing the charges a year later.[140]

Arabs contributed to what a Paraguayan economist called Ciudad del Este's "more independent position," less beholden to Asunción, Brasília, and even Miami. In 2007, Arabs co-founded Fedecamaras, the Federation of Chambers of Commerce of Ciudad del
Este.[141] Fedecamaras brought together several trade associations,
including Samir Jaber's Cámara de Importadores de Electrónica y
Electrodomésticos del Paraguay, mentioned earlier in this chapter;

the Hammoud brothers' Cámara de Importadores y Comerciantes del Alto Paraná, discussed in the fourth chapter; the Cámara de Comércio de Ciudad del Este that Said Taijen helped found and run, introduced in the first chapter; and others headed by Chinese, Koreans, and Paraguayans. In 2008, they hosted a delegation of Miami free trade zone representatives, US and Paraguayan state authorities, and Paraguayan-American Chamber of Commerce members. The CEO and officers of the Miami free zone promised "a faster, more efficient, and cheaper supply chain" for Ciudad del Este through the free trade zones in southern Florida.[142] In the Q&A, Taijen asked the delegation to explain why US consular offices in Asunción revoked or failed to renew visas for Arab Paraguayans and why US customs singled them out in Miami. US representatives replied that they were not aware of such matters.[143] For Taijen, the delegation made an unconvincing pitch to regain its once volumi- nous trade with Ciudad del Este.

Arabs' snub of a US commercial mission occurred just as Para- guayan president Fernando Lugo (2008–2012) interfered in the six-decades-long rule of the Colorado Party, the political party of Stroessner's regime that had remained in power after the inter- nal military coup. Soon after his surprise electoral victory, Lugo declared his intention to debunk the myth of "sleeper cells" at the border because "Ciudad del Este, just like Paraguay, has the right to look at the world with its head high."[144] Around this time, Assad Ahmad Barakat earned parole from prison in Paraguay and returned to Foz do Iguaçu.[145] Sobhi Mahmoud Fayad, previously jailed for tax evasion by Paraguayan law enforcement,[146] and "spe- cially designated" by the US Treasury Department, was released in 2008 as well. Shortly afterward, in Foz do Iguaçu, Fayad made an appearance at a three-hundred-person dinner that the Sociedade Beneficente Islâmica held in honor of visiting Lebanese deputy Ali Khalil of the AMAL party, who represented the Lebanese state at Lugo's inauguration in Asunción. At the resort hotel where the reception for the visiting Lebanese dignitary was held, an Arab Brazilian colleague characterized the release of Barakat and Fayad as "signs" of Lugo's "attempt to curb" US influence in Paraguay.[147] In 2008, the US State Department's annual report on terrorism commented not on the release of Barakat and Fayad, but only continued concerns "that Hizballah and HAMAS sympathizers were raising funds in the Tri-Border Area by participating in illicit activities and soliciting donations," and repeated those concerns in subsequent years.[148] Before President Lugo was forced to leave office through what neighboring states judged to be an unconstitutional impeachment process in 2012, Arabs speculated that Paraguay had tried to limit US influence at the border.

Arab investments in Ciudad del Este interrupted the drama of terrorist finance. Under Lugo's administration, in 2011 Arabs began mobilizing for a new mosque.[149] One of the organizers, Khaled from La Petisquera, called the new mosque a "contribution to . . . Ciudad del Este as well as a *destino* (destination) that people like to visit."[150] At the ground-breaking ceremony in 2012, Lugo's vice-minister of culture, Hugo Brítez, characterized the mosque in similar terms. "This city will have a new icon," he began. "It will be a meeting place, not only for the exercise of faith, but also . . . for those who visit us from afar."[151] Community organizers and state authorities alike spoke of the new mosque in terms of tourist development, citing the example of the mosque in Foz do Iguaçu that attracts thousands of tourists each month, brought up in the third chapter.[152] Accordingly, Sunni Lebanese organizers avoided publicly discussing the previously mentioned Mezquita del Profeta Mohammed where Shia Lebanese prayed in Ciudad del Este during the past two decades. Khaled emphasized that in the new mosque, "anyone can enter, Shia, Sunni, and so on, like a Muslim can enter in any church."[153] In 2015, Paraguayan president Horácio Cartes (2013–2018) of the Colorado Party inaugurated the new mosque.[154] The Sunni Lebanese organizers chose the official name of Alkhaulafa Al-Rashdeen (Rightly-Guided Caliphs or Rulers, in Arabic, a phrase not used by Shia), but the mosque is usually referred to as the Mezquita del Este (Mosque of the East, in Spanish), some blocks south of the microcenter. The Ciudad del Este mayor, Sandra McLeod of the Colorado Party, and the Foz do Iguaçu mayor, Rení Pereira, among others, participated in the inauguration of the mosque that Said Taijen called a "symbol of cosmopolitan multiculturalism" in Paraguay.[155]

But Hollywood refused to let go of the drama. A "big budget action film" about "organized crime" at this "notorious" border, called *Triple Frontier*, was announced by Kathryn Bigelow and Paramount Pictures in 2009.[156] Bigelow reunited with screen writer Mark Boal, from the Academy Award-winning *The Hurt Locker*, but they put aside the project after Brazilian, Paraguayan, and Argentine authorities declared their unanimous opposition.[157] The Foz do Iguaçu city government issued an official statement that asked to approve the script before "the release of any touristic image" because "the supposed theme of the film" may ignore "the lack of proof that traders, associations, or persons of Arab origin at the border are connected to the financing of Islamic terrorist groups."[158] The Paraguayan Minister of Tourism in Lugo's government, Liz Cramer, likewise warned of the "prejudice" that the film "will bring to us all" at the border.[159] A year later, however, José Padilha of the famed *Tropa de Elite* (*Elite Squad*) announced his intention to make a similar movie called *Tri-Border*. In his words, the movie would be set at "the frontier of three countries, in which one finds many different players operating . . . including Lebanese smugglers suspected of helping Hamas and Hizbullah, as well as corrupted police and politicians from Brazil, Paraguay and Argentina."[160] Padilha went on to co-produce and co-direct *O Mecanismo* (*The Mechanism*) on Netflix.[161] It dramatizes a political crisis surrounding corruption investigations and features scenes from the Friendship Bridge and Ciudad del Este that perpetuate long-standing Argentine, Brazilian, and US denigrations of Paraguay.[162] In 2019, Bigelow's script writer, Mark Boal, teamed up with director J. C. Chandor for another Netflix production starring Ben Affleck, Oscar Isaac, and other A-list actors. With the original title, *Triple Frontier*, the film was shot on the outskirts of Bogotá in Colombia, southern California, and the O'ahu island of Hawaii, but the fictional storyline of money and mayhem still took place at a vague South American borderland.[163] Big media globalized US-derived visions of a fictional, lawless land "down south of the Rio Grande."

Meanwhile, Arabs remained under suspicions of terrorist finance while (non-Arab) suspects in the multi-billion-dollar financial irregularities of the Banestado case went unpunished. A then little-known federal judge in Curitiba, Sérgio Moro, presided over the case between 2003 and 2007. Moro subsequently served as judge in the *lava-jato* or Car Wash case, investigating systemic financial irregularities overshadowing the impeachment of President Dilma Rousseff (2012–2016) and leading to the imprisonment of former President Lula, each of the center-left PT. In both cases, Moro gained nationwide recognition through proceedings against hundreds of suspects and was even mythologized by the aforementioned José Padilha in the first season of *O Mecanismo*. But according to former governor and senator Roberto Requião, most of the proceedings in the Banestado case overseen by Moro resulted in "acquittal due to lack of evidence" or were de facto suspended by the "inertia of the Federal Police and of the Attorney General's Office" (Ministério Público Federal).[164] Used to irregularly remit tens of billions of dollars in the 1990s and 2000s, the CC5 accounts in the Banestado case allegedly implicated the center-right PSDB-led coalition that commanded the federal government at the time. But the elite Brazilian suspects implicated in the Banestado scandal remained exempt from investigations. This exceptional rule of justice threw the book at some, turned a blind eye to others, and failed to exonerate speculations about Arabs at the border.

Arabs in Foz do Iguaçu and Ciudad del Este were subject to speculation in multiple accounts, economically and imaginatively, from the 1990s to the 2010s. Importing and exporting goods since they settled at the border, Arabs were suspected of evading taxes or unduly taking advantage of liberal trade policies at the border under authoritarian military rule. But their cross-border trade and finances came under closer scrutiny after the transition to civilian-led democratic and market regimes, which produced exceptions that selectively expedited and exploited as well as distorted and defended them. Investing in transnational lifestyles by sending monies to Lebanon, Palestine, and other Middle Eastern homelands, Arabs became embroiled in probes of irregular bank transfers as well as pursuits of terrorist monies. Though Arabs in Foz do Iguaçu and Ciudad del Este were not involved in the state bank accounts that irregularly remitted massive sums of money from Brazil to Paraguay and then elsewhere, their trade and finances remained as matters of speculation among Argentine, Brazilian, Paraguayan, Mercosur, and US powers.

# Make America Exceptional Again?

**Arabs animate and abide** in an American hemisphere where US power was once considered a "manifest destiny." In 2019, a Brazilian colleague of Lebanese origin, who I call Guilherme here, provided a telling instance that took place in the US Immigration and Customs Area of the Miami International Airport, infamous for the profiling of Arabs from South America discussed in the fourth chapter.[1] Guilherme handed over his Brazilian passport with the appropriate visa. The visibly nervous US immigration and customs official inquired about his ostensibly Arabic-sounding last name. Though not surprised by this particular line of questioning, Guilherme grew perplexed when asked if he lived in Foz do Iguaçu or near the "waterfalls." In response, Guilherme explained that he was from Brasília, the capital of Brazil. The border official promptly stamped his passport and bid him entry to the US. At American border-crossings in Foz do Iguaçu, Ciudad del Este, or even Miami, Arabs grew accustomed to not democratic due process but rather the state exception denying or granting it. Their decades-long accommodation reveals a hemispheric history of making America exceptional again.

In what I have called a "manifold destiny," Arabs came to terms with exceptional rule, connecting and connected by a hemispheric America. From the 1960s to the 1990s, Arabs helped the authoritarian and post-authoritarian rise of Brazil over historically US- and Argentina-dominated Paraguay. Their trade and activism lent greater autonomy in a semiperipheral America, bore the limits to liberation in a Third World America, and tested faith in an Ummah America. Subsequently, from the 1990s to the 2010s, Arabs negotiated the counterterrorist reach of Mercosur and the US. Their trade and activism paid a high price for a free trade America, negotiated peace but also profited in a war-torn America, as well as dramatized a speculative America. Lebanese, Palestinians, and Syrians were constrained, enabled, and came to terms with authoritarian and counterterrorist powers. Though spurious security studies allege their border presence contravenes the hemisphere, my work contends that Arabs drew and were drawn into this American crossroads of exceptional rule.

Attentive to this folding, the account here extended the transnational turn of Middle East studies into American studies, Brazilian studies, and Latin American and Latino studies. I inserted a mobile Middle East into what Juan Poblete called the "unmarked center" of area and ethnic studies once inhabited by the US.[2] By redrawing fields with hemispheric proportions through a Middle Eastern border presence, the aim was to achieve a more "fully globalized study of the Americas," to again paraphrase José David Saldívar.[3] At the border, Arabs' transnational projects draw upon and are drawn into a hemispheric America. Instead of beginning or ending in Euro-American metropoles, Arabs at the border bring the "trans-" of a transnational Middle East into the "trans-" of a transamerican hemisphere. Though not questioning the categories of coloniality that created this hemisphere,[4] they are hardly bearers of a false consciousness, acknowledging their own relative accommodation of extraordinary measures in Brazil, Paraguay, Argentina, Mercosur, and the US.

Arabs at the border are circumstantial protagonists in nothing less than a novel understanding of the contemporary American hemisphere. They bore witness to the past decades of authoritarian rule that did not simply culminate in liberal democracy, but rather presaged present-day counterterrorist controls, involving militarized forces that never entirely returned to the barracks but instead took up positions in domestic security and intelligence operations. Heretofore presumed as separate subjects, authoritarian and counterterrorist politics constitute the crossroads where Arabs have lived and worked in Brazilian and Paraguayan states, under the watch of Argentina, Mercosur, and the US. Accordingly, the first part of this book, set between the 1960s and the 1990s, explored Arab trade and activism under authoritarian and post-authoritarian governments that made liberal exceptions to an illiberal status quo, and illiberal exceptions in a liberalizing transition. The second part of this book looked at Arab trade and activism in Mercosur and the US war on terror, which made mostly illiberal exceptions to liberal market and democratic norms. During the second half of the twentieth century and the first decades of the twenty-first century, Arabs experienced not democratic fulfillment but rather exceptional measures in this hemispheric America.

In contrast to books titled "before and after 9/11" that emphasize September 11, 2001,[5] my work centers around the 1990s as the key decade of change and continuity. While the book's first half culminates in the aftermath of the still unresolved bombing of AMIA in Buenos Aires in 1994, the second half takes off with the Mercosur accords that had been signed previously but went into effect in 1995. Military rulers had been replaced by, or reinvented themselves as, civilian successors, but states continued making exceptions in trade and diplomacy. Arabs at the border accommodated extraordinary measures, but shifted from semiperipheral to free trade, from Third World to war-torn advocacy, as well as from Ummah to more speculative ventures. Attentive to such changes at the border, this study has put greater emphasis on the degree of continuity that Arabs have experienced under varying forms of exceptional rule. Under circumstances not entirely of their own choosing, Arabs at the border have come to terms with authoritarian legacies as well as counterterrorist liaisons.

Arabs' accommodation, and not rejection, of state powers took shape under seemingly "strange" authoritarian norms and continue today under more "familiar" counterterrorist intrusions. Indeed, anthropology's old tenet, "to make the strange familiar, and the familiar strange" guided my approach to hemispheric formation.

Rather than relativize the boundaries between "us" and "them" originally indexed by the expression, I blurred those categories by projecting the "strange" and "familiar" onto a hemispheric field of exceptional rule. I sought to make familiar the authoritarian and post-authoritarian governments whose strange exceptions enabled semiperipheral commerce, Third World activism, and Ummah organization. I likewise endeavored to make strange democratic regimes that oversee counterterrorist controls whose familiar exceptions authorized free trade security, war with neither a beginning nor an end, as well as dramatic and economic speculation. This anthropological approach to the hemisphere relativizes authoritarian and counterterrorist rule in "our America." It critically redirects attention from what Arabs at the border did, and didn't do, to what sorts of state exceptions they and others came to terms with, in a process not yet over.

At a crossroads of exceptional rule, Arabs renewed what Ella Shohat and Robert Stam called the "struggle over representation," mentioned earlier.[6] In 2016, on the Brazilian side of the border, some of the traders and activists from the Barakat, Ghazzaoui, Hassan, Hijazi, Osman, and Rahal families participated in the documentary *Árabes no Paraná*.[7] Sponsored by Itaipu, with support from the Foz do Iguaçu city government, Arabs told their own stories within the matrix of modernity/coloniality that decolonial critics Aníbal Quijano and Walter Mignolo theorized.[8] The documentary opened with black and white images of Guaraní Indians and a quote from the Spanish explorer Álvar Núñez Cabeza de Vaca, the first European chronicler of the Iguaçu/Iguazú falls, introducing Arabs as one of the more recent groups that settled at this crossroads. On the Paraguayan side, Said Taijen, Khaled Ghotme, and others in the city's newly constructed Mezquita del Este and the older Centro Educacional Libanés collaborated in "Migración Árabe en Paraguay," an episode of the *Invisibles* program of RPC (Red Paraguaya de Comunicación, Paraguayan Network of Communication).[9] Also within the modernity/coloniality matrix, this program referenced both the Guaraní and Spanish languages in the "cosmopolitan spirit" of Ciudad del Este where Arabs "don't feel like strangers." Taijen expressed his "sincere thanks to successive government administrations, not only the present-day one" (in 2016), carefully acknowledging both the Paraguayan military regime's political party that monopolized power for some six decades as well as the only elected president not from that party, Fernando Lugo, under whose mandate the Mezquita del Este began to be built, noted last chapter. Without the "epistemic difference" of "border thinking," Arabs sought accommodation, not "radical exteriority," to the status quo in an exceptional order not yet over.

Folding into the hemisphere, their transnational ties varied in respective national settings. On the one hand, Arabs in Foz do Iguaçu and Ciudad del Este had a long-standing interplay with national metropoles in Brazil and Paraguay. As noted, Arabs on the Brazilian side of the border engaged in commercial and civic exchanges with suppliers and community associations in São Paulo while Arabs on the Paraguayan side did so with Asunción. Today, some of their children and grandchildren, born and raised at the border, now pursue undergraduate and graduate study or work opportunities in São Paulo, Asunción, or elsewhere. On the other hand, however, Arabs at the border occupy distinct positions in respective national public spheres. In Foz do Iguaçu, Arabs speak or are spoken about as "a segunda maior comunidade árabe do Brasil" (the second largest Arab community in Brazil), after São Paulo. Once a colleague remarked that Foz do Iguaçu would become the largest because "a colônia em São Paulo está morrendo," (the community in São Paulo is dying), allegedly.[10] But I never heard Arabs in Ciudad del Este represented in such ways. As discussed, many who operate stores on the Paraguayan side actually reside on the Brazilian side of the border, but even those who both live and work in Ciudad del Este prefer to keep a lower profile. Indeed, José Daniel Nasta's moving documentary *Árabes en el Paraguay: Migrantes y descendientes* mentioned Ciudad del Este only once in passing, attending to early and mid-twentieth-century Lebanese and Syrian migrants and their descendants in Asunción, Encarnación, and Villa Rica, before the Paraguayan border town was even built.[11] However, these national comparisons and contrasts, of which there are many, must not distract from the hemispheric scale of analysis that I emphasized in this book.

Whatever the national context, Arabs at the border, like everyone else, witnessed the rise and fall of the hemispheric "pink tide" of progressive rule. In Brazil, Arabs and others leveraged the market- and Global South–friendly policies of Luis Inácio Lula da Silva (2003–2011), though less so under Dilma Rousseff before her aforementioned impeachment (2012–2016). In Paraguay, some viewed Fernando Lugo (2008–2012) as standing up to Brazil and the US before Lugo's own forced removal from office. In Argentina, Arabs at the border continued to be suspected of some sort of collusion in the still unresolved 1992 and 1994 bombings in Buenos Aires during the mandates of Néstor Kirchner (2003–2007) and Cristina Fernández de Kirchner (2007–2015). But Arabs at the border expressed more frustration with the US, even under Barack Obama (2009–2017). On the eve of the latter's election, one elderly Lebanese gentleman at the border remarked that "US Americans say that there is terrorism here . . . because Arabs did well in business here . . . and the US Americans don't like it."[12] With their criticism directed at "the [US] government" and "not the people," Arabs at the border saw themselves being vilified as an "enemy" in order to influence "public opinion in the United States."[13] But it was not uncommon for some to personalize the "US government," having grown accustomed to visits from US officials and reporters. One member of the Rahal family, for instance, recalled his own encounter with an unnamed US politician visiting the border as part of an official delegation.[14] At the border, Arabs tended to accommodate the US government, from Bush through Obama, faring neither better nor worse in this hemisphere's seemingly progressive wave.

Arabs now tried to keep a measured distance from revanchist efforts that "make America exceptional again." They neither condemned nor condoned the Cúpula Conservadora das Américas (Conservative Summit of the Americas, in Portuguese), originally slated for July 2018 and later held on the Brazilian side of the border.[15] In the middle of his underestimated presidential bid, then candidate Bolsonaro organized the summit as his "most ambitious initiative in foreign policy," which would declare the hemisphere's conservative era after decades of progressive rule.[16] Erroneously, *Veja* reported that Bolsonaro would "participate in an event of the Arab community . . . in Foz do Iguaçu."[17] In response, Arab and Muslim institutions at the border issued a *carta aberta* (open letter) on social media.[18] Muslim Arabs wrote that they held nothing against then candidate Bolsonaro, but felt a public statement was necessary after *Veja*'s mistaken news reporting, given their past experience of "xenophobia and Islamophobia" spread by "big commercial media" and "echoed" by unnamed "politicians." Neither declaring support for nor opposition against Bolsonaro, the letter was signed by the Islamic Benevolent Society, the Islamic Benevolent Cultural Center, the Arab-Palestinian Brazilian Society, as well as the Arab Palestinian Federation. Whether or not due to this letter, the conservative summit with hemispheric pretensions was postponed. It took place after Bolsonaro was sworn in as president. The summit's headliner ended up being Jair Bolsonaro's son Eduardo, then a Federal Deputy who had just returned from Washington, DC, where he met with White House officials, attended Steve Bannon's birthday party, and sported a "Trump 2020" baseball cap.[19] Though Bolsonaro's stated aim to "fazer o Brasil grande" (make Brazil great, in Portuguese) borrowed from the Trump campaign and administration's slogan "Make America Great Again," this Conservative Summit of the Americas failed to shore up otherwise disparate right-wing exceptional movements that call for an allegedly "new course in the world."[20] Their goal to make America exceptional, again, has a much longer history.

Arabs at the border avoided wholesale alignments in American politics, but they continued to express solidarity with Palestinian self-determination, as they had done for decades. On the Brazilian side of the border, they disapproved of the Bolsonaro administration's stated goal to move the Brazilian embassy in Israel from Tel Aviv to Jerusalem, which would defy not only the UN but also decades of Brazil's own foreign policy.[21] On the Paraguayan side, Arabs at the border backed "Marito," Mario Abdo Benítez, who promised to "stop the blackmailing in Ciudad del Este," though he was the son of dictator's fixer and defended the Paraguayan dictatorship throughout his career.[22] In a reversal of his predecessor's decision, Marito moved the Paraguayan embassy in Israel from Jerusalem back to Tel Aviv.[23] Meanwhile, on the Argentine side of the border, Mauricio Macri (2015–2019) renewed the militarization of Puerto Iguazú with Israeli technology, and his successor, Alberto Fernández (2019–present) embarked on his first foreign trip to Israel.[24] In response to Donald Trump's declaration of Jerusalem as "the capital of Israel," Palestinians, Lebanese, and others organized an event in the Foz do Iguaçu city council chambers that called for the "peaceful coexistence" among all peoples and a more inclusive recognition of Jerusalem.[25] As Argentine, Brazilian, Paraguayan, and US administrations now leaned toward Israel, Arabs took collective stands at the border for causes and homelands farther afield.

Exceptional rule continues in the increasing ordinariness of extraordinary legal enactments or suspensions. As the hemisphere's so-called "pink tide" neared a crescendo in 2007, Argentina's president added an article to the penal code that punished terrorist finance, and four years later, his successor and spouse revised the code to include any "illicit association with terrorist ends."[26] In 2011, the aforementioned Fernando Lugo signed Paraguayan Law 4024 that made "terrorism," "terrorist association," and "terrorist finance" into punishable offenses.[27] In 2016, Dilma Rousseff approved Brazil's Law 13,260 that defined terrorism in terms of "xenophobia, discrimination, or prejudice . . . with the goal of causing widespread or social terror."[28] Across hemispheric American metropoli, progressive activists and organizations made the most vocal critiques of such legislation, fearing that such a broad legal definition of *terrorismo* could criminalize any civic dissent as had been the case under authoritarian regimes. With consequences for and far beyond Arabs at the border, state powers now exercised authoritarian discretion through counterterrorist oversight.

An increasing array of authorities became what philosopher Judith Butler calls "petty sovereigns . . . delegated with the power to render unilateral decisions, accountable to no law and without any legitimate authority."[29] As such, US Treasury Department officials and proxies renewed accusations that Arabs at the border financed

Hizbullah, using Obama-era regulations after Trump became president.[30] In the US House of Representatives in 2018, experts recycled inflammatory claims about Arabs at the border and concurrently tried to justify Treasury Department budget increases.[31] As the Subcommittee on Counterterrorism and Intelligence conducted a hearing on Iran's Global Terrorism Network, a "witness" from the Foundation for Defense of Democracies (FDD), gave testimony on "Iran's proxy terror networks in Latin America," headed by Hizbullah operatives allegedly in "Foz do Iguassu [*sic*]" as well as "Ciudad Del Este [*sic*]," naming Assad Ahmad Barakat among others referenced in this book.[32] Citing a narrow selection of media articles and government press releases, the witness noted that despite "corrupt" local officials susceptible to terrorist financiers, "the governments of Argentina, Brazil, and Paraguay are more receptive than at any time in the past 10 years to US leadership in the fight against terror."[33] His written testimony concluded by asking the US congress to "provide additional resources to treasury," requesting an increase of more than 10 percent for the upcoming year, noting the more than 10 percent increase authorized the previous year.[34] Echoed in conservative and right-wing media,[35] and exerting pressure on South American states, this non-governmental authority justified ever-increasing counterterrorist government spending by representing Arabs at the border as a threat to the hemisphere. His narrative ignores the nearly three decades that Arabs at the border have been recurrently investigated and the many extraordinary measures that states took to do so.

His alarmist tone was echoed by Argentina's Financial Intelligence Unit (UIF) in a press release about "suspected financiers of Hizbullah" supposedly in the "tri-border area."[36] With newfound clout under the aforementioned legislation in Argentina, the UIF head also garnered praise from the director of the US Treasury Department's Financial Crimes Enforcement Network (known by the acronym FinCEN). The FinCEN director had been just appointed by the Trump administration. The FinCEN head expressed pride in "the role that FinCEN played" in "recent anti-terrorism financing actions by Argentina's Financial Intelligence Unit."[37] Not long afterward, these Argentine and US bureaucrats co-wrote newspaper articles that were simultaneously published in Argentina and the US, congratulating their "fact-finding mission" that assessed "the money laundering and terrorist finance threats in the Tri-Border Area between Argentina, Paraguay and Brazil."[38]

These Argentine and U.S. officials exercised what Butler called "spectral sovereignty."[39] They came to "'deem' as dangerous" none other than Assad Ahmad Barakat for having carried out suspicious million-dollar transactions in a casino in Puerto Iguazú on the Argentine side of the border.[40] As already examined in this book, around the time of the 9/11 attacks, Barakat was accused of laundering money with alleged terrorist ends by a Lebanese business rival, leading to Barakat's conviction for tax evasion in Paraguay. After serving his sentence, Barakat returned to live with his Brazilian wife and children on the Brazilian side of the border. But with the new round of accusations, it was Paraguay, not Brazil, that was pressured by neither Argentine nor US officials but rather the FDD witness who had previously testified to the US House of Representatives.[41] The FDD witness stated that Paraguay is a "fiscal paradise for terrorism" due to "the very low level of public integrity among those who govern in Paraguay."[42] This "FDD member," as characterized in Paraguayan media, lacked the legal authority that he effectively exercised by claiming such lawlessness at the border.

His "exaggerated" and "catastrophic" allegations of terrorism elicited critical responses from the Paraguayan foreign minister, finance minister, interior minister, and vice-president.[43] But Paraguayan judges filed arrest warrants for Barakat, alleging not financial crimes with purportedly terrorist ends but rather the irregular acquisition of a Paraguayan passport despite having been stripped of Paraguayan nationality.[44] The right-wing Paraguayan president called for an investigation into the irregular emission of passports while his ministers held meetings with US diplomats who praised the Paraguayan state for cooperating on matters of money laundering. As "law is either used tactically or suspended," writes Judith Butler, "populations are monitored, detained, regulated, inspected, interrogated, rendered uniform in their actions, fully ritualized and exposed to control and regulation in their daily lives."[45] This "indefinite" status of Arabs at the border, to again cite Butler, "does not signify an exceptional circumstance, but, rather, the means by which the exceptional become established as a naturalized norm."[46]

Arabs on the Paraguayan side of the border attested to this ordinariness of extraordinary rule. Ali Farhat, cited in the third chapter, surmised that "every year or two we are confronted by a wave of allegations about Hizbullah and the terrorist threat in the region."[47] Jihad Aoun, with his business in the Galeria Zuni in Ciudad del Este, echoed, "it is an account that no one ever buys" at the border, explaining that "tax-evasive smuggling, money laundering, arms and drugs trafficking" exist but not "terrorist cells" or "traders . . . giving away their money to extremist groups."[48] "Alwie Moustaff Hijazi [*sic*]" affirmed that Lebanese "came to this area because they are tired of terrorist attacks that only cause pain and war, they want peace, and to say that they are encouraging violence and hatred is something that does not enter anyone's head. . . . We do not understand this."[49] Farhat, Aoun, Hijazi, and others grew accustomed to being denied the rule of law through what Butler called "the differential allocation of grievability that decides what kind of subject is and must be grieved, and which kind of subject must not."[50]

Under such circumstances, Barakat applied for asylum from Paraguay and turned himself into Brazil's Federal Police in Foz do Iguaçu.[51] His appeal for accommodation drew support from *Gazeta Diário* (formerly *A Gazeta do Iguaçu*), whose editorial column declared that whatever financial irregularity Barakat may have engaged in, "it doesn't have anything to do with terrorism." The (non-Arab) Brazilian editorial writer called for mobilization among Lebanese "countrymen" and "we Brazilians" as well as vigilance against using "an isolated case . . . to denigrate the Lebanese community of the border."[52] Meanwhile, Barakat's family led a protest of "at least 100 people," in front of Brazil's Federal Police headquarters in Foz do Iguaçu. Barakat's son declared, "We are not terrorists. We are here asking for support from the Lebanese Embassy in Brasília and even [former Brazilian] President Michel Temer who is a Lebanese descendant and whose father also came from Lebanon as a refugee."[53] Supreme Court judge Raquel Dodge declared that Barakat would remain in "preventive detention" in Brazil until the "National Committee for Refugees of the Ministry of Foreign

Relations" evaluated his request for asylum, after Argentine and US allegations provoked Paraguayan officials to issue a warrant for his arrest, neither for financial infringements nor alleged ties to Hizbullah.[54] Since "to seek asylum is precisely to seek legal status," wrote Butler, states can scrutinize cases by fiat in an actual suspension of international law.[55] After nearly two years, the Brazilian state extradited Barakat to Paraguay where he now again stands trial, this time for the irregular possession of a Paraguayan passport, and not for financial transactions in Puerto Iguazú alleged by Argentine and US authorities.[56] In this "manifold destiny," Arabs still await a final verdict in the more than sixty-year history of exceptional rule at an American crossroads.

# Notes

## INTRODUCTION

1. Mohamad Barakat, 24 July 2007.
2. Said Taijen, 28 November 2008. The Portuguese acronym is Mercosul, which also refers to the Southern Common Market. The Spanish acronym, Mercosur, is more commonly used in the US.
3. Mohamad Ismail, 12 July 2007; Mohamad Ismail appears in Jon Jeter's "Laughing in the Face of Terrorist Reports," *Washington Post*, 11 April 2004.
4. Brazil alone has nine tri-national borders, but the term is commonly used to refer to this crossroads.
5. "Marco inicial para a integração continental," *Folha de S. Paulo*, 28 March 1965, 10; "Presidentes inauguram Ponte Brasil-Paraguai," *Folha de S. Paulo*, 28 March 1965, 1; "Testemunho de fé nos destinos da América," *Folha de S. Paulo*, 28 March 1965, 10; "Castelo a Stroessner: 'Não nos deteremos na justa contemplação da tarefa que foi realizada," *Diário do Paraná*, 29 March 1965, 5.
6. Ceres Moraes, *Paraguai: A consolidação da ditadura de Stroessner, 1954–1963* (Porto Alegre: EdiPUCRS, 2000), 97. In Portuguese, the bridge is called Ponte da Amizade and, in Spanish, Puente de la Amistad. In 1961, the base of the Friendship Bridge was commemorated by Brazil's democratically elected Juscelino Kubitschek and Paraguay's military head of state Alfredo Stroessner. After completion in 1965, the fully operational bridge was inaugurated by Brazil's Marechal Castelo Branco and Paraguay's Stroessner. In 2019, another bridge between the Brazilian and Paraguayan sides of this border began to be constructed.
7. The Argentine state had long kept watch over this border. After the Friendship Bridge was built between Brazil and Paraguay in 1965, a series of reports from the Buenos Aires–based *Clarín* expressed malaise about the "stagnant" Argentine side of the border. See "Por la Ruta de Alvar Nuñez Cabez de Vaca," *Clarín*, 17, 18, 19, 21 June 1968. See also Isaac Francisco Rojas, *Intereses*

*argentinos en la Cuenca del Plata* (Buenos Aires: Ediciones Líbera, 1969). Rojas saw Brazil eroding Argentine interests in these borderlands of the Rio de la Plata Basin. The bridge that connected the Argentine side to the Brazilian side of the border was inaugurated only in 1985, mentioned later.

8. Philip Abbot, "Terrorist Threat in the Tri-Border Area," *Military Review*, Fall 2004, 51–55; Mariano Bartolomé, "A tríplice fronteira: Principal foco de insegurança no cone sul americano," *Military Review*, Summer 2003, 22–35; Cristiana Brafman Kittner, "The Role of Safe Havens in Islamist Terrorism," *Terrorism and Political Violence* 19 (2007): 307–29; Thomaz Guedes Costa and Gastón Schulmeister, "The Puzzle of the Iguazu Tri-Border Area," *Global Crime* 8.1 (2007): 26–39; Carlos Escudé and Beatriz Gurevich, "Limits to Governability, Corruption, and Transnational Terrorism," *Estudios interdisciplinarios de America Latina y el Caribe* 14.2 (2003): 127–48; Rex Hudson, *Terrorist and Organized Crime Groups in the Tri-Border Area (TBA) of South America* (Washington, DC, Federal Research Division—LOC and Central Intelligence Crime Center, 2003); Rensselaer Lee, "The Triborder-Terrorism Nexus," *Global Crime* 9.4 (2008): 332–47; Howard Meehan, "Terrorism, Diasporas, and Permissive Threat Environments" (MA thesis, Naval Postgraduate School, 2004); William Mendel, "Paraguay's Ciudad del Este and the New Centers of Gravity," *Military Review*, March 2002, 51–57; Mark Steinz, *Middle East Terrorist Activity in Latin America: Policy Papers on the Americas* (Washington, DC: Center for Strategic and International Studies, 2003); Mark Sullivan, *Latin America: Terrorism Issues* (Washington, DC: CRS Report for Congress, 2005); Ana Sverdlick, "Terrorists and Organized Crime Entrepreneurs in the 'Triple Frontier' among Argentina, Brazil, and Paraguay," *Trends in Organized Crime* 9.2 (2005): 84–93.

9. Edward Said and Christopher Hitchens, eds., *Blaming the Victims: Spurious Scholarship and the Palestinian Question* (New York: Verso, 2001).

10. Linda Basch, Nina Glick Schiller, and Cristina Szanton Blanc, *Nations Unbound: Transnational Projects, Postcolonial Predicaments, and Deterritorialized Nation-States* (New York: Routledge, 2005); Alejandro Portes, "Towards a New World: The Origins and Effects of Transnational Activities," *Ethnic and Racial Studies* 22.2 (1999): 463–77.

11. Felipe Fernández-Armesto, *The Americas: A Hemispheric History* (New York: Random House, 2005), 11, 19.

12. Giorgio Agamben, *State of Exception* (Chicago: University of Chicago Press, 2005); Carl Schmitt, *The Concept of the Political* (Chicago: University of Chicago Press, 2007).

13. For an exhaustive treatment of authoritarianism, see Jerry Dávila, *Dictatorship in South America* (Malden, MA: Wiley-Blackwell, 2013); and for counterterrorism, see Joseph Masco, *The Theater of Operations: National Security Affect from the Cold War to the War on Terror* (Durham, NC: Duke University Press, 2014).

14. Walter Mignolo, "Decolonial Reflections on Hemispheric Partitions: From the 'Western Hemisphere' to the 'Eastern Hemisphere,'" in *The Routledge Companion to Inter-American Studies*, ed. Wilfried Raussert (New York: Routledge, 2017), 59–67; José David Saldívar, *Trans-Americanity: Subaltern*

*Modernities, Global Coloniality, and the Cultures of Greater Mexico* (Durham, NC: Duke Univeristy Press, 2011).

15. Paul Gilroy, *The Black Atlantic: Modernity and Double Consciousness* (London: Verso, 1993); Jacqueline Brown, "Black Liverpool, Black America, and the Gendering of Diasporic Space," *Cultural Anthropology* 13.3 (1998): 291–335.

16. Camilla Fojas and Rudy P. Guevarra Jr., eds., *Transnational Crossroads: Remapping the Americas and the Pacific* (Lincoln: University of Nebraska Press, 2012). For previous work, see Rob Wilson and Arif Dirlik, eds., *Asia/Pacific as a Space of Cultural Production* (Durham, NC: Duke University Press, 1995); Arif Dirlik, ed., *What Is in a Rim? Critical Perspectives on the Pacific Region Idea* (Boston: Rowman and Littlefield Publishers, 1998).

17. Pedro Cabán, "The New Synthesis of Latin American/Latino Studies," in *Borderless Borders: US Latinos, Latin Americans, and the Paradox of Interdependence*, eds. Frank Bonilla et al. (Philadelphia: Temple University Press, 1998); Juan Flores and George Yúdice, "Living Borders/Buscando America: Languages of Latina/o Self-Formation," *Social Text* 24 (1990): 57–84; Matthew Gutmann and Jeffrey Lesser, eds., *Global Latin America: Into the Twenty-First Century* (Berkeley: University of California Press, 2016); Juan Poblete, ed., *Critical Latin American and Latino Studies* (Minneapolis: University of Minnesota Press, 2003); Juan Flores and Renato Rosaldo, eds., *A Companion to Latina/o Studies* (Malden, MA: Blackwell, 2007); José David Saldívar, *The Dialectics of Our America: Genealogy, Cultural Critique, and Literary History* (Durham, NC: Duke University Press, 1991); Lourdes Torres, "Editorial: Imagining the Future of Latino Studies," *Latino Studies* 11.3 (2013): 269–70.

18. Yousef Awad, *The Arab Atlantic: Resistance, Diaspora, and Trans-Cultural Dialogue in the Works of Arab British and Arab American Women Writers* (Berlin: Lambert Academic Publishing, 2012); Christina Civantos, "Orientalism and the Narration of Violence in the Mediterranean Atlantic: Gabriel García Márquez and Elias Khoury," in *The Global South Atlantic: Region, Vision, Method*, eds. Kerry Bystrom and Joseph Slaughter (New York: Fordham University Press, 2017), 165–85; Stacy Fahrenthold, "An Archaeology of Rare Books in Arab Atlantic History," *Journal of American Ethnic History* 37.3 (2018): 77–83; Ella Shohat, "The Sephardi-Moorish Atlantic: Between Orientalism and Occidentalism," in *Between the Middle East and the Americas: The Cultural Politics of Diaspora*, eds. Evelyn Alsultany and Ella Shohat (Ann Arbor: University of Michigan Press, 2013), 42–62.

19. Andrew Arsan, Akram Khater, and John Tofik Karam, "Editorial Forward," *Mashriq & Mahjar: Journal of Middle East and North African Migration Studies* 1.1 (2013): 1, 3; Evelyn Alsultany and Ella Shohat, eds., *Between the Middle East and the Americas: The Cultural Politics of Diaspora* (Ann Arbor: University of Michigan Press, 2013); Andrew Arsan, *Interlopers of Empire: The Lebanese Diaspora in Colonial French West Africa* (Oxford: Oxford University Press, 2014); Lily Pearl Balloffet, *Argentina in the Global Middle East* (Stanford: Stanford University Press, 2020); Stacy D. Fahrenthold, *Between the Ottomans and the Entente: The First World War in the Syrian and Lebanese Diaspora, 1908–1925* (Oxford: Oxford University Press, 2019); Sarah M. A. Gualtieri, *Arab Routes: Pathways to Syrian California* (Stanford: Stanford University Press, 2020); Sarah M. A.

Gualtieri, *Between Arab and White: Race and Ethnicity in the Early Syrian American Diaspora* (Berkeley: University of California Press, 2009); Steven Hyland, *More Argentine Than You: Arabic-Speaking Immigrants in Argentina* (Albuquerque: University of New Mexico Press, 2017); Akram Fouad Khater, *Inventing Home: Emigration, Gender, and the Middle Class in Lebanon, 1870–1920* (Berkeley: University of California Press, 2001); Camila Pastor, *The Mexican Mahjar: Transnational Maronites, Jews, and Arabs under the French Mandate* (Austin: University of Texas Press, 2017).

20. John Carlos Rowe, "Areas of Concern: Area Studies and the New American Studies," *Alif: Journal of Comparative Poetics* 31 (2011): 11–34.

21. Amy Kaplan and Donald Pease, eds., *Cultures of United States Imperialism* (Durham, NC: Duke University Press, 1993); Inderpal Grewal, *Transnational America: Feminisms, Diasporas, Neoliberalisms* (Durham, NC: Duke University Press 2005); Caroline F. Levander and Robert S. Levine, eds., *Hemispheric American Studies* (Rutgers, NJ: Rutgers University Press, 2008).

22. Ann Laura Stoler, "Imperial Formations and the Opacities of Rule," in *Lessons of Empire: Imperial Histories and American Power*, eds. Craig Calhoun, Frederick Cooper, and Kevin Moore (New York: New York University Press, 2006), 48–60; Winfried Fluck, Donald Pease, and John Carlos Rowe, eds., *Re-framing the Transnational Turn in American Studies* (Lebanon, NH: Dartmouth College Press, 2011); Brian Edwards and Dilip Parameshwar Gaonkar, eds., *Globalizing American Studies* (Chicago: University of Chicago Press, 2010); William V. Spanos, *Redeemer Nation in the Interregnum: An Untimely Meditation on the American Vocation* (Oxford: Oxford University Press, 2016).

23. Donald Pease, "Exceptionalism," in *Keywords for American Cultural Studies*, eds. Bruce Burgett and Glenn Hendler (New York: New York University Press, 2007), 108–11.

24. Kristin Hoganson and Jay Sexton, eds., *Crossing Empires: Taking US History into Transimperial Terrain* (Durham, NC: Duke University Press, 2020).

25. Shohat, "The Sephardi-Moorish Atlantic," 59–60.

26. Paulo Roberto de Almeida, "Brazilian Studies in the United States: Trends, Perspectives, and Prospects," in *Envisioning Brazil: A Guide to Brazilian Studies in the United States, 1945–2003*, eds. Marshall Eakin and Paulo Roberto de Almeida (Madison: University of Wisconsin Press, 2005), 3–29; Leslie Bethell, "Brazil and 'Latin America,'" *Journal of Latin American Studies* 42.3 (2010): 457–85; Vinicius Mariano de Carvalho, "Brazilian Studies and Brazilianists: Conceptual Remarks," *Brasiliana: Journal for Brazilian Studies* 5.1 (2016): 344–66; K. David Jackson, "History of the Future: Luso-Brazilian Studies in the New Millennium," *Luso-Brazilian Review* 40.2 (2003): 13–30; Anthony Pereira, "Brazilian Studies Then and Now," *Brasiliana: Journal for Brazilian Studies* 1.1 (2012): 3–21; Charles A. Perrone, "Fred P. Ellison and Interamerican Imperatives," *Hispania* 99.4 (2016): 526–29.

27. José Briceño-Ruiz and Andrés Rivarola Puntigliano, *Brazil and Latin America: Between the Separation and Integration Paths* (Lanham, MD: Lexington Books, 2017); Lúcia Helena Costigan and Leopoldo M. Bernucci, "O Brasil, a América Hispânica e o Caribe: Abordagens comparativas," *Revista Iberoamericana* 68.200 (2002): 871–74; Maria Ligia Coelho Prado, "O Brasil e a distante

América do Sul," *Revista de História* 145 (2001): 127–49; Marshall Eakin, "Does Latin America Have a Common History?" *Vanderbilt e-Journal of Luso-Hispanic Studies* 1.1 (2004): 29–49; Robert Patrick Newcomb, *Nossa and Nuestra América: Inter-American Dialogues* (West Lafayette, IN: Purdue University Press, 2012); Ori Preuss, *Bridging the Island: Brazilians' Views of Spanish America and Themselves, 1865–1912* (Madrid: Iberoamericana-Vervuert, 2011); Jorge Schwartz, "Abaixo tordesilhas," *Estudos Avançados* 7.17 (1993): 185–200.

28. Luiz Alberto Moniz Bandeira, *Relações Brasil-EUA no contexto da globalização: I—Presença dos EUA no Brasil* (São Paulo: Editora SENAC, 1998); Luiz Alberto Moniz Bandeira, *Relações Brasil-EUA no contexto da globalização: II—Rivalidade emergente* (São Paulo: Editora SENAC, 1999); Ana Luiza Beraba, *América aracnídea: Teias culturais interamericanas* (Rio de Janeiro: Civilização Brasileira, 2008); Maria de Fátima Fontes Piazza, "A arte estadunidense no suplemento *Pensamento da América*, do jornal *A Manhã*," *Revista FSA* 11.2 (2014): 247–62; Luis Cláudio Villafañe Gomes Santos, *O Brasil entre a América e a Europa: O império e o interamericanismo* (São Paulo: Editora Unesp, 2003); Antonio Pedro Tota, *O imperialismo sedutor: A americanização do Brasil na época da segunda guerra* (São Paulo: Companhia das Letras, 2000); Luiz Werneck Vianna, *A revolução passiva: Iberismo e americanismo no Brasil* (Rio de Janeiro: Editora Revan, 1997).

29. Luiz Alberto Moniz Bandeira, *Brasil, Argentina e Estados Unidos: Conflito e integração na América do Sul: Da tríplice aliança ao Mercosul, 1870–2003* (Rio de Janeiro: Editora Revan, 2003); Jerry Dávila, *Hotel Trópico: Brazil and the Challenge of African Decolonization, 1950–1980* (Durham, NC: Duke University Press, 2013); Marshall Eakin, *Becoming Brazilians: Race and National Identity in Twentieth-Century Brazil* (Cambridge, UK: Cambridge University Press, 2017); Jeffrey Lesser, *Immigration, Ethnicity and National Identity in Brazil* (Cambridge, UK: Cambridge University Press, 2013); Paulo Schilling, *O expansionismo brasileiro: A geopolítica do General Golbery e a diplomacia do Itamarati* (São Paulo: Global, 1981); Ruy Mauro Marini, "Brazilian 'Interdependence' and Imperialist Integration," *Monthly Review* 17.7 (1965): 10–29; Ruy Mauro Marini, "Brazilian Subimperialism," *Monthly Review* 23.9 (1972): 14–24; Paulo Gilberto Fagundes Vizentini, *O regime militar e a projeção internacional do Brasil: Autonomia nacional, desenvolvimento econômico e potência média, 1964–1985* (São Paulo: Almedina Brasil, 2020).

30. Paul Amar, ed., *The Middle East and Brazil: Perspectives on the New Global South* (Bloomington: Indiana University Press, 2014).

31. Ella Shohat and Robert Stam, *Unthinking Eurocentrism: Multiculturalism and the Media* (New York: Routledge, 1994), 48.

32. Emanuelle Santos and Patricia Schor, "'Brazil Is Not Traveling Enough': On Postcolonial Theory and Analogous Counter-Currents. An Interview with Ella Shohat and Robert Stam," *Portuguese Cultural Studies* 4 (2012): 13–40.

33. Gloria Anzaldúa, *Borderlands/La Frontera* (San Francisco: Aunt Lute Books, 1987); Sonia Álvarez, Arturo Árias, and Charles Hale, "Re-visioning Latin American Studies," *Cultural Anthropology* 26.2 (2011): 225–46; Allison Margaret Bigelow and Thomas Miller Klubock, "Introduction to Latin American Studies and the Humanities: Past, Present, Future," *Latin American Research*

*Review* 53.3 (2018): 573–80; Flores and Yúdice, "Living Borders/Buscando America"; Saldívar, *The Dialectics of Our America*; Ana del Sarto, Alicia Ríos, and Abril Trigo, eds., *The Latin American Cultural Studies Reader* (Durham, NC: Duke University Press, 2004).

34.  Cabán, "The New Synthesis of Latin American/Latino Studies."
35.  Juan Poblete, introduction to *Critical Latin American and Latino Studies*, ed. Juan Poblete (Minneapolis, MN: University of Minnesota Press, 2003), xxvi, xxxv; Juan Poblete, introduction to *New Approaches to Latin American Studies: Culture and Power* (New York: Routledge, 2017), 1–13.
36.  Juan Poblete, review of *Between the Middle East and the Americas*, eds. Evelyn Alsultany and Ella Shohat, *Mashriq & Mahjar: Journal of Middle East and North African Migration Studies* 2.1 (2015): 174–78.
37.  Saldívar, *Trans-Americanity*.
38.  Aníbal Quijano and Immanuel Wallerstein, "Americanity as a Concept, or the Americas in the Modern World-System," *International Journal of Social Sciences* 134 (1992): 583–91.
39.  Partha Chatterjee, *The Nation and Its Fragments: Colonial and Postcolonial Histories* (Princeton, NJ: Princeton University Press, 1998).
40.  Vasco Graça Moura, *O Tratado de Tordesilhas / The Treaty of Tordesillas* (Lisbon: CTT Correios, 1994); Mary Wilhelmine Williams, "The Treaty of Tordesillas and the Argentine-Brazilian Boundary Settlement," *Hispanic American Historical Review* 5.1 (1922): 3–23; Thomas Wilson and Hastings Donnan, "Border and Border Studies," in *A Companion to Border Studies*, eds. Thomas M. Wilson and Hastings Donnan (Malden, MA: Blackwell, 2012), 7.
41.  Bartolomé Bennassar, "Tordesillas: El primer reparto del mundo," *Política Exterior* 6.25 (1992): 151–59; Ademir Gebara, Herib Caballero Campos, anhd Leandro Baller, eds., *Leituras de fronteiras: Trajetórias, histórias e territórios* (Jundiaí: Paco Editorial, 2019).
42.  Alejandro Grimson, "Fronteras, estados e identificaciones en el Cono Sur," in *Estudios latinoamericanos sobre cultura y transformaciones sociales en tiempos de globalización* 2 (Buenos Aires: CLACSO, 2001); Alejandro Grimson, "Nations, Nationalism and 'Borderization' in the Southern Cone," in *A Companion to Border Studies*, eds. Thomas M. Wilson and Hastings Donnan (Malden, MA: Blackwell, 2012), 194–213; Adriana Dorfman and Arthur Borba Colen França, "Estudos fronteiriços no Brasil: Uma geografia da produção científica," in *Geografia política, geopolítica e gestão do território,* ed. Augusto César Pinheiro da Silva (Rio de Janeiro: Gramma, 2016), 65–84.
43.  Haroldo Dilla Alfonso, "Los complejos urbanos transfronterizos en América Latina," *Estudios fronterizos* 16.31 (2015): 15–38; Jacob Blanc and Frederico Freitas, eds. *Big Water: The Making of the Borderlands between Brazil, Argentina, and Paraguay* (Tucson: University of Arizona Press, 2018); Camilo Pereira Carneiro, *Fronteiras Irmãs: Transfronteirizações na Bacia do Prata* (Porto Alegre: Ideograf—Gráfica e Editora, 2016); Ramón Fogel, "La region de la triple frontera: Territorios de integración y desintegración," *Sociologias* 10.20 (2008): 270–90; Ieva Jusionyte, *Savage Frontier: Making News and Security on the Argentine Border* (Berkeley: University of California Press, 2015); Silvia Montenegro and Veronica Giménez Béliveau, *La Triple Frontera:*

*Globalización y construcción social del espacio* (Madrid: Miño y Dávila, 2006); Silvia Montenegro and Veronica Giménez Béliveau, eds., *La Triple Frontera: Dinámicas culturales y procesos transnacionales* (Buenos Aires: Editorial Espacio, 2011); Rosana Pinheiro-Machado, *Counterfeit Itineraries in the Global South: The Human Consequences of Piracy in China and Brazil* (New York: Routledge, 2018); Fernando Rabossi, "Nas Ruas de Ciudad del Este: Vidas e vendas num mercado de fronteira." PhD diss., Universidade Federal do Rio de Janeiro, 2004.

44. Poliana Fabíula Cardozo, "O Líbano ausente e o Líbano presente: Espaço de identidades de imigrantes libaneses em Foz do Iguaçu." PhD diss., Universidade Federal do Paraná, 2012; Rosana Pinheiro-Machado, "A ética confucionista e o espírito do capitalismo: Narrativas sobre moral, harmonia e poupança na condenação do consumo conspícuo entre chineses ultramar," *Horizontes Antropológicos* 13.28 (2007): 145–74; Fernando Rabossi, "Árabes e muçulmanos em Foz do Iguaçu e Ciudad del Este: Notas para uma reinterpretação," in *Mundos em movimento: Ensaios sobre migrações*, eds. Giralda Seyferth, Helion Póvoa Neto, Maria Catarina Chitolina Zanini, and Miriam de Oliveira Santos (Santa Maria: Editora UFSM, 2007), 287–312; Marcia Anita Sprandel, "Brasileiros na fronteira com o Paraguai," *Estudos Avançados* 20.57 (2006): 137–56; Blanc and Freitas, *Big Water.*

45. Prefeitura Municipal de Foz do Iguaçu, *Anuário estatístico* (Foz do Iguaçu: Secretaria Municipal—Departamento de Informações Institucionais, 2001); Instituto Brasileiro de Geografia e Estatística (IBGE), *Censo 2010* (Brasília: Ministério do Planejamento, Orçamento e Gestão, 2010).

46. Jorge Rodríguez Vignoli, *Distribución espacial de la población de América Latina y el Caribe: Tendencias, interpretaciones y desafíos para las políticas públicas*, publication 32 (Santiago de Chile: CEPAL, 2002), 1831-P; United Nations Economic Commission for Latin America and the Caribbean (CEPAL), *América Latina: Urbanización y evolución de la población urbana, 1950–2000* (Santiago de Chile: CELADE, 2005), 40, 116; Mabel Causarano, *Dinámicas metropolitanas en Asunción, Ciudad del Este y Encarnación* (Asunción: UNFPA/ADEPO, 2006); Dirección General de Estadísticas, Encuestas y Censos (DGEEC), *Anuario 2012* (Asunción: UNFPA/ADEPO, 2013).

47. Centro de Estudios Regionales del Nordeste Argentino (CERNEA), *El Macro Sistema Territorial de la Frontera Nordeste Argentina* (Corrientes: CERNEA, 1978); United Nations Economic Commission for Latin America and the Caribbean (CEPAL), *América Latina*; Instituto Nacional de Estadística y Censos (INDEC), *Censo 2010* (Buenos Aires: Ministerio de Economía, 2010).

48. The bridge was named in honor of the Brazilian civilian leader who died before assuming the presidency. For the inauguration of this bridge, see: "Sarney e Alfonsín pregam soluções latino-americanas," *Jornal do Brasil,* 30 November 1985, 12; Fernando de Mello Barreto, "Olavo Setúbal," in *A política externa após a redemocratização* (Brasília: Fundação Alexandre Gusmão, 2012), 27; Luiz Alberto Moniz Bandeira, "Las relaciones en el Cono Sur: Iniciativas de integración," in *El Cono Sur: Una historia común*, eds. Mario Rapoport and Amado Luiz Cervo (Buenos Aires: Fondo de Cultura Económica, 2001), 310; Olivier Dabène, *The Politics of Regional Integration in Latin America:*

*Theoretical and Comparative Explorations* (New York: Palgrave Macmillan, 2009), 73.

49. It should be noted that there is no bridge between Argentina and Paraguay where each meet Brazil at this border. Five hours southwest from Foz do Iguaçu on the Paraná River, there is a bridge between Argentina and Paraguay, specifically between Posadas, the capital of the Argentine province of Misiones, and Encarnación, the third largest city of Paraguay. The Paraná River is the hemisphere's second largest river, second only to the Amazon. The Iguaçu/Iguazú River is a tributary of the Paraná River. Of course, physical land composes most of the border between Argentina and Paraguay, as that of Brazil and Paraguay, as well as Brazil and Argentina.

50. Bruce Knauft, "Provincializing America: Imperialism, Capitalism, and Counterhegemony in the Twenty-First Century," *Current Anthropology* 48.6 (2007): 781–99.

51. Dipesh Chakrabarty, *Provincializing Europe: Postcolonial Thought and Historical Difference* (Princeton, NJ: Princeton University Press, 2000).

52. Bruce Knauft, "Reply," *Current Anthropology* 48.6 (2007): 799.

53. Aihwa Ong, *Neoliberalism as Exception: Mutations in Citizenship and Sovereignty* (Durham, NC: Duke University Press, 2006), 5.

54. Ibid., 3.

55. Peter Lambert, "The Myth of the Good Neighbour: Paraguay's Uneasy Relationship with Brazil," *Bulletin of Latin American Research* 35.1 (2016): 34–48; Werner Baer and Melissa Birch, "The International Economic Relations of a Small Country: The Case of Paraguay," *Economic Development and Cultural Change* 35.3 (1987): 601–27; Andrew Nickson, "Brazil and Paraguay: A Protectorate in the Making?" *Mural Internacional* 10 (2019): 1–14.

56. Lily Pearl Balloffet, "Argentine and Egyptian History Entangled: From Perón to Nasser," *Journal of Latin American Studies* 50.3 (2018): 549–77; Seme Taleb Fares, "O pragmatismo do petróleo: As relações entre o Brasil e o Iraque," *Revista Brasileira de Política Internacional* 50.2 (2007): 129–45; Jessica Stites Mor, "The Question of Palestine in the Argentine Political Imaginary: Anti-Imperialist Thought from Cold War to Neoliberal Order," *Journal of Iberian and Latin American Research* 20.2 (2014): 183–97; Frank O. Mora, "Paraguay: From the *Stronato* to the Democratic Transition," in *Small States in World Politics: Explaining Foreign Policy Behavior*, ed. Jean A. K. Hey (Boulder, CO: Lynne Rienner Publishers, 2003), 13–31; Frank O. Mora, "Paraguay: The Legacy of Authoritarianism," in *Latin American and Caribbean Foreign Policy*, eds. Frank O. Mora and Jeanne A. K. Hey (Lanham, MD: Rowman and Littlefield, 2003), 309–27; Marta Tawil Kuri, ed., *Latin American Foreign Policies toward the Middle East: Actors, Contexts, and Trends* (New York: Palgrave Macmillan, 2016); Paulo Gilberto Fagundes Vizentini, *A política externa do regime militar brasileiro: Multilateralização, desenvolvimento e a construção de uma potência média (1964–1985)*, 2nd ed. (Porto Alegre: UFRGS Editora, 2004).

57. Nathaniel Greenberg, "Amia and the Triple Frontier in Argentine and American Discourse on Terrorism," *A Contracorriente* 8.1 (2010): 61–93.

58. J. Patrice McSherry, "Strategic Alliance: Menem and the Military-Security Forces in Argentina," *Latin American Perspectives* 24.6 (1997): 68; Nickson, "Brazil and Paraguay"; Andrea Oelsner, "Mercosur's Incipient Security

Governance," in *The Security Governance of Regional Organizations*, eds. Emil Kirchner and Roberto Domínguez (New York: Routledge, 2011): 190–217; Jorge Zaverucha, "Poder militar: Entre o autoritarismo e a democracia," *São Paulo em Perspectiva* 15.4 (2001): 76–83.

59. Melissa Birch, "Paraguay and Mercosur: The Lesser of Two Evils?," *Latin American Business Review* 15.3–4 (2014): 269.

60. Arthur Bernardes do Amaral, *A Tríplice Fronteira e a Guerra ao Terror* (São Paulo: Apicuri Editora, 2009).

61. Ciro Leal M. da Cunha, *Terrorismo internacional e política externa brasileira após 11 de setembro* (Brasília: Fundação Alexandre de Gusmão, 2010); Peter Lambert, "Dancing between Superpowers: Ideology, Pragmatism, and Drift in Paraguayan Foreign Policy," in *Latin American Foreign Policies: Between Ideology and Pragmatism*, eds. Gian Luca Gardini and Peter Lambert (New York: Palgrave Macmillan, 2014), 67–86.

62. Marieke de Goede, *Speculative Security: The Politics of Pursuing Terrorist Monies* (Minneapolis: University of Minnesota Press, 2012).

63. Money-laundering at this particular border has a longer history. See, for example: "Contrabando de dinheiro, sangria nacional," *Nosso Tempo*, 4 February 1981, 6.

64. Fouad Fakih, "O Brasil é a segunda pátria dos árabes," *H2Foz*, 19 September 2003, www.h2foz.com.br/noticia/o-brasil-e-a-segunda-patria-dos-arabes-13885.

65. Fouad Fakih, 25 November 2008.

66. José Martí, "Nuestra América," in *Nuestra América*, ed. Juan Marinello (Caracas: Ayacucho, 1977), 30–1.

67. Jeffrey Belnap and Raúl Fernandez, eds. *José Martí's 'Our America:' From National to Hemispheric Cultural Studies* (Durham, NC: Duke University Press, 1998).

68. Belnap and Fernandez, *José Martí's 'Our America'*; Laura Lomas, *Translating Empire: José Martí, Migrant Latino Subjects, and American Modernities* (Durham, NC: Duke University Press, 2008); Saldívar, *The Dialectics of Our America*.

69. Alsultany and Shohat, *Between the Middle East and the Americas*; Amar, *The Middle East and Brazil*; Gualtieri, *Arab Routes*; Waïl Hassan, "Brazil," in *The Oxford Handbook of Arab Novelistic Traditions*, ed. Waïl Hassan (Oxford: Oxford University Press, 2017), 543–57; Aisha Khan, ed., *Islam in the Americas* (Gainesville: University Press of Florida, 2015); María del Mar Logroño Narbona, Paulo G. Pinto, and John Tofik Karam, *Crescent over Another Horizon: Islam in Latin America, the Caribbean, and Latino USA* (Austin: University of Texas Press, 2015).

70. Mohamad Barakat, 24 July 2007.

71. Ahmad Mattar, *Guia social de la colonia de habla arabe en Bolivia, Colombia, Ecuador, Peru, Venezuela y las islas holandesas de Curacao y Aruba* (Barranquilla: Empresa Litográfica S.A., 1945); Philipp Bruckmayr, "Syro-Lebanese Migration to Colombia, Venezuela and Curação: From Mainly Christian to Predominantly Muslim Phenomenon," *European Journal of Economic and Political Studies* 3 (2010): 151–97.

72. Mattar, *Guia social de la colonia de habla arabe*.

73.  Brian Aboud, "Re-reading Arab World–New World Immigration History: Beyond the Prewar/Postwar Divide," *Journal of Ethnic and Migration Studies* 26.4 (2000): 653–73.

74.  Márcio Rickil Costa, "Árabes formam a maior colônia estrangeira em Foz," *A Gazeta do Iguaçu,* 10 August 1995, 10. See also Antônio França, "Fronteira esperneia contra desmprego," *A Gazeta do Iguaçu,* 15 February 1996, 6; Montenegro and Giménez Béliveau, *La triple frontera,* 26, 148–50, 173.

75.  "Deputado canadense vem a Foz para avaliar meio ambiente: Mohamad Omairi tem parentes e muitos amigos na cidade," *A Gazeta do Iguaçu,* 13 August 1999.

76.  Jackson Lima, "Notas de turismo: Visto Já Era (Mohamed Omairi, em Foz: Deputado defende fim do visto)," *A Gazeta do Iguaçu,* 15 August 1999.

77.  Fernando Rabossi, "Terrorist Frontier Cell or Cosmopolitan Commercial Hub? The Arab and Muslim Presence at the Border of Paraguay, Brazil, and Argentina," in *The Middle East and Brazil: Perspectives on the New Global South,* ed. Paul Amar (Bloomington: Indiana University Press, 2014), 99.

78.  George Galsze, *Die fragmentierte Stadt: Ursachen und Folgen bewachter Wohnkomplexe im Libanon* (Opladen: Leske + Budrich, 2003), 149–52.

79.  Aihwa Ong, *Flexible Citizenship: The Cultural Logics of Transnationality* (Durham, NC: Duke University Press, 2001), 6.

80.  Paulo Gabriel Hilu da Rocha Pinto, "Ritual, etnicidade e identidade religiosa nas comunidades muçulmanas no Brasil," *Revista USP* 67 (2005): 228–49.

81.  Fahrenthold, *Between the Ottomans and the Entente.*

82.  Zé Beto Maciel, "De olho na telinha: Yo não entendo nadie, Histórias do multilinguísmo na fronteira," *A Gazeta do Iguaçu,* 15 May 1993.

83.  Khan, *Islam in the Americas.*

84.  Costa, "Árabes formam a maior colônia estrangeira em Foz"; Jackson Lima, "Os árabes da fronteira," *Classe 10* 1.3 (1996) 11–13; Antônio França, "Árabes na fronteira: Xeque lamenta notícias de que seria terrorista," *A Gazeta do Iguaçu,* 16 February 1996, 1, 7.

85.  John Tofik Karam, "Historias musulmanas en América Latina y el Caribe," *Istor: Revista de Historia Internacional* 12.45 (2011): 22–43.

86.  John Tofik Karam, María del Mar Logroño Narbona, and Paulo G. Pinto "Latino America in the *Umma* / the *Umma* in Latino America," in *Crescent over Another Horizon: Islam in Latin America, the Caribbean, and Latino USA.,* eds. María del Mar Logroño Narbona, Paulo G. Pinto, and John Tofik Karam (Austin: University of Texas Press, 2015), 1–21.

87.  Eric Wolf, *Europe and the People without History* (Berkeley: University of California Press, 1982).

88.  Engseng Ho, "Empire through Diasporic Eyes: A View from the Other Boat," *Comparative Studies of Society and History* 46.2 (2004): 210.

89.  Akhil Gupta and James Ferguson, "Discipline and Practice: 'The Field' as Site, Method, and Location in Anthropology," in *Anthropological Locations: Boundaries and Grounds of a Field Science,* eds. Akhil Gupta and James Ferguson (Berkeley: University of California Press, 1997), 1–46.

90.  See John Tofik Karam, "Belly Dancing and the (En)Gendering of Ethnic Sexuality in the 'Mixed' Brazilian Nation," *Journal of Middle East Women's Studies* 6.2 (2010): 86–114; John Tofik Karam, "Romancing Middle Eastern Men

in North and South America: Two Mid-Century Texts," in *Constructions of Masculinity in the Middle East and North Africa: Literature, Film, and National Discourse*, eds. Mohja Kahf and Nadine Sinno (Cairo: American University in Cairo Press, 2020); and the third chapter in John Tofik Karam, *Another Arabesque: Syrian-Lebanese Ethnicity in Neoliberal Brazil* (Philadelphia: Temple University Press, 2007).

91. George Marcus, "Ethnography in/of the World System: The Emergence of Multi-Sited Ethnography," *Annual Review of Anthropology* 24 (1995): 95–117.

92. In 2017, the *Gazeta Diário de Foz do Iguaçu* was founded by the son of the former owner of *A Gazeta do Iguaçu*.

93. Michael Kearney, *Changing Fields of Anthropology: From Local to Global* (Lanham, MD: Rowman & Littlefield, 2004).

94. George Marcus and James Faubion, eds., *Fieldwork Is Not What It Used to Be: Learning Anthropology's Method at a Time of Transition* (Ithaca, NY: Cornell University Press, 2009).

95. John Tofik Karam, "Fios árabes, tecido brasileiro," *Revista de História da Biblioteca Nacional* 4.46 (2009): 22–4.

96. Carmen Alicia Ferradás, "Security and Ethnography on the Triple Frontier of the Southern Cone," in *Borderlands: Ethnographic Approaches to Security, Power, and Identity*, eds. Hastings Donnan and Thomas Wilson (New York: University Press of America, 2010), 35–53; Carmen Alicia Ferradás, *Power in the Southern Cone Borderlands: An Anthropology of Development Practice* (Westport, CT: Bergin and Garvey, 1998).

97. Ella Shohat and Robert Stam, *Flagging Patriotism: Crises of Narcissism and Anti-Americanism* (New York: Routledge, 2007), 63–64.

## CHAPTER 1

1. Cassiano Ricardo, *Marcha para Oeste* (Rio de Janeiro: Livraria José Olympio, 1942); Cassiano Ricardo, *Marcha para Oeste*, vol. 2 (São Paulo: Editora da Universidade de São Paulo, 1970); William Raymond Steiger, "What Once Was Desert Shall Be a World: Getúlio Vargas and Westward Expansion in Brazil, 1930–1945." PhD diss., UCLA, 1995; Robert Wegner, *A conquista do Oeste: A fronteira na obra de Sérgio Buarque de Holanda* (Belo Horizonte: Editora UFMG, 2000).

2. Ramón César Bejarano, *El Paraguay en busca del mar* (Asunción: Casa Editorial Toledo, 1965); Marcial Riquelme, "Notas para el estudio de las causas y efectos de las migraciones brasileñas en el Paraguay," in *Enclave sojero, merma de soberanía y pobreza*, eds. Ramón Fogel and Marcial Riquelme (Asunción: Centro de Estudios Rurales Interdisciplinarios, 2005), 113–39; Christine Folch, "Surveillance and State Violence in Stroessner's Paraguay: Itaipú Hydroelectric Dam, Archive of Terror," *American Anthropologist* 115.1 (2013): 44–57; Edgar Ynsfrán, *Un giro geopolítico: El milagro de una ciudad* (Asunción: Instituto Paraguayo de Estudios Geopolíticos e Internacionales, 1990).

3. Paul Amar, *The Security Archipelago: Human-Security States, Sexuality Politics, and the End of Neoliberalism* (Durham, NC: Duke University Press, 2013).

4. Amar, *The Security Archipelago*, 245.

5. Michael Conniff, *Panama and the United States: The End of the Alliance* (Athens, GA: University of Georgia Press, 2001), 103; Andrew Zimbalist and John Weeks, *Panama at the Crossroads: Economic Development and Political Change in the Twentieth Century* (Berkeley: University of California Press, 1991), 65–66; Thomas Leonard, "Colón Free Trade Zone (CFTZ)," in *Historical Dictionary of Panama* (Lanham, MD: Rowman and Littlefield, 2015), 85.

6. Frank O. Mora and Jerry W. Cooney, *Paraguay and the United States: Distant Allies* (Athens: University of Georgia Press, 2007), 179; Baer and Birch, "The International Economic Relations," 606, 613.

7. Knauft, "Reply," 799.

8. Werner Baer, *The Brazilian Economy: Growth and Development* (Boulder, CO: Lynne Rienner, 2013); David Collier, ed., *The New Authoritarianism in Latin America* (Princeton, NJ: Princeton University Press, 1979); Juan Gabriel Valdés, *Pinochet's Economists: The Chicago School of Economics in Chile* (Cambridge, UK: Cambridge University Press, 1995); Guillermo O'Donnell, *Modernization and Bureaucratic Authoritairanism: Studies in South American Politics* (Berkeley: University of California Press, 1973); Thomas Skidmore, *The Politics of Military Rule in Brazil, 1964–1985* (Oxford: Oxford University Press, 1989).

9. Andrew Nickson, "The Itaipu Hydro-Electric Project: The Paraguayan Perspective," *Bulletin of Latin American Research* 2.1 (1982): 1–20; Christine Folch, *Hydropolitics: The Itaipu Dam, Sovereignty, and the Engineering of Modern South America* (Princeton, NJ: Princeton University Press, 2019); Jacob Blanc, *Before the Flood: The Itaipu Dam and the Visibility of Rural Brazil* (Durham, NC: Duke University Press, 2019).

10. Jackson Lima, "Colônia Árabe: 60 anos de Foz do Iguaçu," *Revista 100 Fronteira*, May 2009, 60–62.

11. José Maria de Brito, *Descoberta de Foz do Iguaçu e fundação da colônia militar* (Curitiba: Travessa dos Editores, 2005 [1907]).

12. "Rahal: De Mascate a Empresário," *Nosso Tempo,* 17 February 1989, 8; Lima, "Os árabes da fronteira," 11–13.

13. Nadir Aparecida Cancian, *Cafeicultura paranaense (1900–1970)* (Curitiba: Grafipar, 1981); Maxine Margolis, "The Coffee Cycle on the Paraná Frontier," *Luso-Brazilian Review* 9.1 (1972): 3–12; Verena Stolke, *Cafeicultura: Homens, mulheres e capital (1850–1980)* (São Paulo: Brasiliense, 1986); Ruy Wachowicz, *Norte Velho, Norte Pioneiro* (Curitiba: Vicentina, 1987).

14. Lincoln Gordon, *A New Deal for Latin America: The Alliance for Progress* (Cambridge, MA: Harvard University Press, 1963); Jeffrey Taffet, *Foreign Aid as Foreign Policy: The Alliance for Progress in Latin America* (New York: Routledge, 2007).

15. "A comunidade Árabe de Foz do Iguaçu," *Nosso Tempo,* 5 May 1981, 6.

16. Lima, "Os árabes da fronteira," 12.

17. Baer and Birch, "The International Economic Relations of a Small Country."

18. Mora and Cooney, *Paraguay and the United States*, 184.

19. Harris Gaylord Warren, *Rebirth of the Paraguayan Republic* (Pittsburgh, PA: University of Pittsburgh Press, 1985), 134–35.

20. Isaac Francisco Rojas, *Intereses argentinos*. A decade later, he authored *La ofensiva geopolítica brasileña en la Cuenca del Plata* (Buenos Aires: Ediciones Nemont, 1979).

21. "Por la Ruta de Alvar Nuñez Cabez de Vaca," *Clarín*, 17, 18, 19, 21 June 1968.

22. In Posadas, which itself borders on the Paraguayan city of Encarnación, a distinct wave of mostly Christian Lebanese and Syrians lived and traded since the first decades of the twentieth century. See Lily Pearl Balloffet, "A Digital History of the Arab Argentine *mahjar*," paper presented at the symposium, "The Middle East in Latin America," Duke University, 2016; Lily Pearl Balloffet, *Argentina in the Global Middle East* (Stanford: Stanford University Press, 2020); *Guia Assalam del comercio sirio-libanes en la República Argentina* (Buenos Aires: Empresa Assalam, 1928), 200, 313.

23. The entire bridge is roughly five hundred meters long. Its iron frame was constructed by Brazil's Companhia Siderúrgica Nacional de Volta Redonda, forming the giant arc that defines the bridge; the bridge is made from fourteen thousand tons of cement, three thousand tons of iron, and sixty tons of nails and screws. "Ponte da Amizade: 25 anos unindo Brasil e Paraguai," *A Gazeta do Iguaçu*, 28 March 1990, 4.

24. "Convênios entre o Brasil e o Paraguai: Convênio para o estabelecimento, em Paranaguá, de um entrepôsto de depósito franco para as mercadorias exportadas ou importadas pelo Paraguai," *Correio da Manhã*, 18 May 1956, 4; Alberto da Costa e Silva, "Da Guerra ao Mercosul: Evolução das relações diplomáticas Brasil-Paraguai," in *A Guerra do Paraguai: 130 anos depois*, ed. Maria Eduarda Castro Magalhães Marques (Rio de Janeiro: Relume Dumará, 1995), 170.

25. Baer and Birch, "The International Economic Relations of a Small Country"; Werner Baer and Luis Breur, "From Inward- to Outward-Oriented Growth: Paraguay in the 1980s," *Journal of Interamerican Studies and World Affairs* 28.3 (1986): 125–40; Ceres Moraes, "Interesses e colaboração do Brasil e dos Estados Unidos com a ditadura de Stroessner," *Diálogos* 11 (2007): 55–80.

26. Phil Kelly and Thomas Whigham, "La geopolítica del Paraguay: Vulnerabilidades regionales y respuestas nacionales," *Perspectivas Internacionales Paraguayas* 3 (1990): 41–78; Alfredo da Mota Menezes, *La Herencia de Stroessner: Brasil-Paraguay 1955–1980* (Asunción: Carlos Schauman Editor, 1990); José Luis Simón, ed., 1990. *Política exterior y relaciones internacionales del Paraguay contemporáneo* (Asunción: Centro Paraguayo de Estudios Sociológicos, 1990).

27. Ciudad Puerto Presidente Stroessner was initially named Puerto Flor de Lis. Roberto Paredes, *Stroessner y el stronismo* (Asunción: Servilibro, 2004), 65, 147.

28. Dibb's "Gran Hotel Casino Acaray" in Ciudad Presidente Stroessner advertised in Foz do Iguaçu tourist brochures as early as 1969. See "Gran Hotel Casino Acaray" *Cataratas: A Rainha do Turismo* 1.5 (1969). Later on, Dibb was called "one of the richest businessmen of Paraguay" by the Brazilian newsweekly *Veja*: "Roupa suja: Escândalo mistura genro de Stroessner com Somoza," *Veja*, 18 June 1980, 42; "Já se pode jogar até mesmo no mundo socialista," *Veja*, 17 June 1981, 117; see also Fidel Miranda Silva, *Historia de Alto Paraná* (Ciudad del Este: AGR, 2007).

29. "Nuevas instalaciones serán inauguradas por Iciersa . . . ABC entrevistó al señor Humberto Domínguez Dibb," *ABC Color*, 31 October 1970, 9; John Tofik Karam, "The Levant in Latin America," in *Global Middle East: Into the*

*Twenty-First Century*, eds. Asef Bayat and Linda Herrera (Berkeley: University of California Press, 2021), 253–66.

30. "Don Elias Saba," *ABC Color*, 10 April 1973, 3; "Padre espiritual de este diario: Don Elías Saba," *ABC Color*, 2 April 1973, 8; Andrew Nickson, "Gustavo Saba (1950– )," *Historical Dictionary of Paraguay* (Lanham, MD: Rowman and Littlefield, 2015), 517; See also the website for the Saba family-owned real estate agency, Abas Inmobiliaria, www.abas.com.py/home/nosotros (date of access: 3 April 2015).

31. Armando Rivarola, 23 February 2009.

32. Mihail Meskin Bazas, 17 September 2008.

33. In Portuguese, "vendia uiskie, bebida importada que não tinha aqui e jeans Lee." Ali Said Rahal and son Fawas, 16 September 2008.

34. Said Taijen, 28 November 2008.

35. Mohamad Barakat, 23 May 2009; Said Taijen, 28 November 2008.

36. Mohamad Barakat, 23 May 2009; Said Taijen, 28 November 2008.

37. John Tofik Karam, "On the Trail and Trial of a Palestinian Diaspora: Mapping South America in the Arab-Israeli Conflict," *Journal of Latin American Studies* 45.4 (2013): 751–77; "Atentado hecho criminal perpetrado esta mañana contra funcionarias de la embajada israelí," *La Tarde*, 4 May 1970, 1–2; "Atentaron contra la embajada de Israel en nuestra capital," *ABC Color*, 5 May 1970, 1; "Editorial: Agresión a Nuestra Paz," *Patria*, 5 May 1970, 3.

38. "'Fatah' ataca em Assunção," *O Estado de S. Paulo*, 5 May 1970, 10; "Oriente Médio-Assunção: Árabe mata mulher de um diplomata israelense," *Última Hora*, 5 May 1970, 6; "Armas brasileiras no terror árabe: A polícia de Assunção acha que os árabes que atacaram a embaixada de Israel compraram as armas no Brasil," *O Estado de S. Paulo*, 6 May 1970, 3; "Êstes homens iam matar o Embaixador: Ordem da Al Fatah em Assunção era matar embaixador," *O Globo*, 6 May 1970, 1, 7.

39. "Atividades das Organizações Terroristas Árabes no Brasil," Sheets 17, 18, 19, Folder 499A, Delegacia de Polícia de Foz de Iguaçu. Arquivo Público do Paraná.

40. Said Taijen, 16 June 2009; María Helena, 5 June 2009.

41. Decreto No. 707. "Por el cual se aprueba el cambio de denominación de la entidad denominada 'Cámara de Comercio de Ciudad Presidente Stroessner.'"

42. "Fotos e Destaques da Cidade: A Nova Diretoria da Acifi," *Revista Painel*, November 1974, 4; "A madeira como fator de desenvolvimento de Foz," *Memoria de Foz do Iguaçu*, December 1982, 14–16; Associação Comercial e Industrial de Foz do Iguaçu (ACIFI), *Relatório de Gestão, 2000/2002* (Foz do Iguaçu: ACIFI, 2003), 2.

43. J. Adelino de Souza and Chico de Alencar, "Fouad Fakih: 'Foz tem um grande futuro com os novos projetos: O presidente que construiu a sede própria da Acifi tem muita confiança na cidade," *A Gazeta do Iguaçu*, 23 July 2001, 6–7

44. Fouad Mohamad Fakih, "Mensagem da Associação Comercial e Industrial de Foz do Iguaçu (ACIFI)," *Revista Painel*, June 1978, 3; "A comunidade Árabe de Foz do Iguaçu," *Nosso Tempo*, 5 May 1981, 6.

45. Souza and Alencar, "Fouad Fakih."

46. Ibid.

47. Juvêncio Mazzarollo, *A taipa da injustiça: Esbanjamento econômico, drama social e holocausto ecológico em Itaipu* (Curitiba: Comissão Pastoral da Terra do Paraná, 1980).

48. Lima, "Os árabes da fronteira," 11–13.

49. Paulino Viapiana, "Atração energética: A hidrelétrica de Itaipu vira um foco turístico e estimula a economia das cidades ao redor do lago," *Veja,* 22 July 1987, 65–66.

50. "Lela, a cidade irmã no Mediterrâneo," *A Gazeta do Iguaçu,* 26 August 1990, 8.

51. Baer, *The Brazilian Economy,* 187; Skidmore, *The Politics of Military Rule in Brazil,* 143; Antonio Nilson Quezado Cavalcante and Etienne F. Cracco, "Os incentivos às exportações de manufaturados: Analise e sugestão," *Revista de Administração de Empresas* 12.1 (1972): 63–69.

52. "Decreto-Lei No 491, de 5 de Março de 1969: Estímulos fiscais à exportação de manufaturados," Presidência da República, Casa Civil, Subchefia para Assuntos Jurídicos, 12 March 1969, www.planalto.gov.br/ccivil_03/decreto-lei/Del0491.htm.

53. "A ordenada marcha da Capital do Turismo: Foz 65 anos," *Revista Painel,* June 1979, 10–11.

54. "Políticos condenam prefeitos biônicos: Mesa redonda promovida por Nosso Tempo debate livremente as implicações da intervenção no Município e julga a administração Cunha Vianna," *Nosso Tempo,* 17 to 24 December 1980, 7–9.

55. Menezes, *La Herencia de Stroessner,* 19, 37.

56. Mohamad Barakat, 28 May 2009.

57. "ACIFI quer protelar o funcionamento do Siscomex: A entidade teme inviabilizar o setor de exportação." *A Gazeta do Iguaçu,* 5 January 1993, 6–7; J. Adelino de Souza and Chico de Alencar, "Wádis Benvenutti: 'A Acifi está no caminho certo—O presidente que falou até com Delfim Neto para manter as exportações em cruzeiros," *A Gazeta do Iguaçu,* 23 July 2001, 4–5.

58. In Portuguese, "eu ia buscar o dinheiro nestas exportadoras em sacos de linhagem. Girava muito dinheiro e as exportadoras foram crescendo muito." J. Adelino de Souza and Chico de Alencar, "Tibiriça Botto Guimarães: 'A consolidação da Acifi se deu a partir do Fouad: A participação de quem veio para uma temporada e se apaixonou pela cidade," *A Gazeta do Iguaçu,* 23 July 2001, 18.

59. "Anteprojeto de Lei No. 28/1974," Câmara Municipal de Foz do Iguaçu.

60. "Indicação No. 02/1976," Câmara Municipal de Foz do Iguaçu; "Decreto No. 2.064, Prefeito Municipal, Clóvis Cunha Vianna," Câmara Municipal de Foz do Iguaçu.

61. Lima, "Os árabes da fronteira"; "Exportadora Tupy," *Revista Painel,* June 1975, 14–22.

62. Nino Palazzo and Adolfo Giménez, "Todo un pais vestido de contrabando," *HOY,* 29 July, 1983, 9.

63. "Lela, a cidade irmã no Mediterrâneo," *A Gazeta do Iguaçu,* 26 August 1990, 8.

64. "Projeto de Lei No. 83/2007, Altera a denominação da Rua das Missões, para Rua Mustapha Ali Osman," Câmara Municipal de Foz do Iguaçu; "Projeto de Lei No.76/2010, Altera a denominação da Praça da Amizade, para Praça *Mustapha Ali Osman*," Câmara Municipal de Foz do Iguaçu.

65. Viapiana, "Atração energética."
66. "Crise e desemprego assolam o Paraguai," *Nosso Tempo,* July 1983, 7.
67. Viapiana, "Atração energética."
68. "Jardim Jupira recebe pavimentação através do plano comunitário," *Revista Painel*, July 1980; "O difícil tráfego na Ponte da Amizade," *Revista Painel*, April 1980; Wadis Benvenutti, "A força do comércio e do turismo iguaçuense," *Revista Painel*, July 1981; "Crise e desemprego assolam o Paraguai," *Nosso Tempo*, 6 July 1983, 7.
69. "Crise e desemprego assolam o Paraguai," *Nosso Tempo*, 6 July 1983, 7.
70. Lima, "Os árabes da fronteira."
71. "Exportadores realizam mais negócios em 1991," *A Gazeta do Iguaçu*, 12 January 1992, 3; "Dia de Calmaria na Fronteira," *A Gazeta do Iguaçu*, 4 March 1992, 3; "Ponte da Amizade registrou ontem movimento recorde," *A Gazeta do Iguaçu,* 3 March 1992, 7.
72. "'Estou com todo e qualquer movimento de libertação,' entrevista com Mohamed Barakat," *Nosso Tempo*, 1 September 1988, 10.
73. "*Kamalito* magazine: A loja de todos nos," *Nosso Tempo*, 12 October 1981, 15.
74. "Kamal Osman: 'Foz do Iguaçu precisa ser transformada em Zona de Livre Comércio': Qual fenício dos tempos atuais, o libanês . . ." *A Gazeta do Iguaçu*, 20 November 1993, 20–1.
75. "Notas: Loja de departamentos," *Nosso Tempo*, 6 October 1981, 8; "*Kamalito* magazine: A loja de todos nos," *Nosso Tempo*, 12 October 1981, 15; Antônio França, "Árabes decidem voltar para o Oriente," *Folha de Londrina*, 7 September 1997, 3–4; "Kamal Osman: 'Foz do Iguaçu precisa ser transformada em Zona de Livre Comércio,'" *A Gazeta do Iguaçu,* 20 November 1993, 20–1.
76. Souza and Alencar, "Fouad Fakih."
77. Karam, *Another Arabesque.*
78. Maureen O'Dougherty, *Consumption Intensified: The Politics of Middle-Class Daily Life in Brazil* (Durham, NC: Duke University Press, 2002), 63.
79. "Colônia Árabe homenageará Sérgio Spada," *Nosso Tempo*, 12 May 1988, 1.
80. In Portuguese, "um intercâmbio mais livre entre os três países (Brasil, Paraguai e Argentina) já que ninguém tinha dólares."
81. "O difícil tráfego na Ponte da Amizade," *Revista Painel,* April 1980, 5.
82. "Crise paraguaia afeta duramente Foz," *Nosso Tempo*, 6 September 1985; Marcial Antonio Riquelme, "Dificultades para la transición en Paraguay," *Investigación Económica* 186 (1988): 172.
83. Ricardo Grinbaum, "A fronteira da muamba," *Veja*, 26 July 1995, 75.
84. Said Taijen, 16 June 2009.
85. Fernando Rabossi, "Terrorist Frontier Cell," 99.
86. "Destaque: Mohamed Said Mannah," *Nosso Tempo*, 29 April 1988; Said Taijen, 16 June 2009.
87. "Stroessner: Audaz y millonario robo," *HOY*, 30 July 1983, 17.
88. "Ciudad Puerto Stroessner: O paraíso das falsificações e da corrupção," *Nosso Tempo,* 20 December 1984, 13; "Pdte. Stroessner: Uma cidade que já foi jardim," *Nosso Tempo*, 29 January 1988, 10–11; "Paraguay: Onde Comprar," *A Gazeta do Iguaçu*, 4 December 1988, B1–B2.

89. "Señalan que tarjeta de facilitación turística causa graves trastornos: Hoteleros, comerciantes y sectores vinculados están preocupados," *ABC Color*, 19 November 1973, 28; "Foz de Yguazu: La aplicación de la tarjeta de facilitación turística y sus problemas: La tarjeta habilita a visitar sólo Pto. Pte. Stroessner durante ocho horas," *ABC Color*, 23 November 1973, 11; "Esta tarjeta es válida por 5 días en períodos de 8 horas cada salida," *ABC Color*, 23 November 1973, 11; "Visto Policial de Saída para o Exterior," *Revista Cataratas* 1.5 (1969); Adão Luiz Almeida, Secretaria Municipal de Cooperação para Assuntos de Segurança Pública, 22 August 2008.

90. Such shopping complexes are often run as condominium associations, whereby an individual or group financed the construction, and then sold off individual store spaces.

91. "Ciudad Puerto Stroessner: O paraíso das falsificações e da corrupção," *Nosso Tempo*, 20 December 1984, 13; "Em liquidação: Uísque no mercado negro tem desconto de 30%," *Veja*, 15 July 1981, 27; "Contrabando: Começa a degringolar entrega a domicílio," *Nosso Tempo*, 5 March 1987, 14; "Paraguai: Onde Comprar," *A Gazeta do Iguaçu*, 4 December 1988, B1–B2.

92. "Ciudad Puerto Stroessner: O paraíso das falsificações e da corrupção, *Nosso Tempo*, 20 December 1984.

93. Menezes, *La Herencia de Stroessner*, 20, 28–29; Carlos Nuñez, a Paraguayan tourism operator active at the border in the 1970s, recounted that the "large movement" of "Brazilian shoppers" mostly purchased "whiskey and cigarettes," but when the "mini-television was released," they came in search of electronics as well. Carlos Nuñez, 26 April 2009.

94. "Compristas de todo o Brasil invadem Foz do Iguaçu," *Nosso Tempo*, 26 June 1986, 11.

95. Baer and Birch, "The International Economic Relations of a Small Country," 604

96. "Comércio en Stroessner estaria dominado por los extranjeros," *ABC Color*, 3 September 1973, 30.

97. Only a trickle moved to Puerto Iguazú in the aforementioned province of Misiones on the Argentine side of the border. See Karina Andrea Bidaseca, *Los sin tierra de Misiones: Disputas políticas y culturales en torno al racismo, la 'intrusión' y la extranjerización del excluido en un espacio social transfronterizo* (Buenos Aires: CLACSO, 2012).

98. Marcial Riquelme, "Notas para el estudio," 113–139; Ricardo Menegotto, *Migrações e fronteiras: Os imigrantes brasileiros no Paraguai e a redefinição da fronteira* (Santa Cruz do Sul: EDUNISC, 2004).

99. Andrew Nickson, "Brazilian Colonization of the Eastern Border Region of Paraguay," *Journal of Latin American Studies* 13.1 (1981), 129; Carlos Wagner, *Brasiguaios: Homens sem pátria* (Rio de Janeiro: Vozes, 1990), 11; José Lindomar C. Albuquerque, *A dinâmica das fronteiras: Os brasiguaios na fronteira entre o Brasil e o Paraguai* (São Paulo: Annablume, 2010).

100. The Paraguayan economist Reinaldo Penner affirmed that the tax exceptions for Ciudad Presidente Stroessner arose out of convergent Paraguayan and Brazilian state interests. Reinaldo Penner, "Segundo informe sobre el

comercio de productos informáticos en Ciudad del Este" (Ciudad del Este: Paraguay Vende y USAID, 2006), 9.

101. Penner, "Segundo informe sobre el comercio."

102. Reinaldo Penner, 15 April 2009; "Serán ampliados depósitos de Puerto P. Stroessner," *ABC Color*, 14 October 1974, 32; "Finalizó en P. Stroessner un Curso de Valoración Aduanera," *ABC Color*, 19 October 1974, 32; "Construirán una nueva vía en la Aduana de Stroessner," *ABC Color*, 25 February 1980, 42.

103. "Rodriguez revoga lei de importação," *A Gazeta do Iguaçu*, 30 January 1990, 1.

104. Victor Torres, 15 February 2009.

105. Miranda Silva, *Historia de Alto Paraná*; "Tumulto na Ponte: 'Paseros' e policiais trocam palavrões," *Nosso Tempo*, 6 July 1983, 7; "Ciudad Puerto Stroessner: O paraíso das falsificações e da corrupção," *Nosso Tempo*, 20 December 1984, 13; "Governo paraguaio fecha pistas clandestinas em Alto Paraná," *A Gazeta do Iguaçu*, 9 April 1991, 16.

106. Galsze, *Die fragmentierte Stadt*, 149–52; Rabossi, "Nas ruas de Ciudad del Este," 60, 214.

107. Said Taijen, 28 November 2008; "M. H. Jebai," *ABC Color*, 3 February 1982, 14.

108. Menezes, *La Herencia de Stroessner*, 20.

109. "Ameaça de bomba no Jebai Center: Tensão e medo na fronteira, ponte fechada por 3 horas," *A Gazeta do Iguaçu*, 24 July 1994, 1.

110. Mihail Meskin Bazas, 17 September 2008; Zimbalist and Weeks, *Panama at the Crossroads*, 26.

111. Ahmad Mattar, *Guia social de la colonia de habla arabe.*

112. Said Taijen, 28 November 2008.

113. "Serán ampliados depósitos de Puerto P. Stroessner," *ABC Color*, 14 October 1974, 32; "Construirán una nueva vía en la Aduana de Stroessner," *ABC Color*, 25 February 1980, 42.

114. "Um 'mundo fantástico' para el turismo," *ABC Color*, 3 February 1982, Suplemento especial, 28.

115. Sérgio Spada, "O equilíbrio das Três Fronteiras," *Nosso Tempo*, 28 August 1986, 14.

116. "A espera de um final de Semana Santa," *A Gazeta do Iguaçu*, 11 April 1990; "Cruzeiro forte na fronteira," *A Gazeta do Iguaçu*, 11 September 1990, 7; "Aumenta número de compristas no Paraguai," *A Gazeta do Iguaçu*, 25 September 1990, 11.

117. "Dólar dispara na fronteira: Ciudad del Este chegou a cotar a moeda em Cr$1.300," *A Gazeta do Iguaçu*, 30 October 1991, 1, 3; "Feridão e queda do dólar aumentam movimento no Paraguai," *A Gazeta do Iguaçu*, 16 November 1991, 3.

118. Knauft, "Reply," 799.

119. Anna Tsing, *Friction: An Ethnography of Global Connections* (Princeton, NJ: Princeton University Press, 2005), 57.

120. Reinerio Parquet, *Las empresas transnacionales en la economia del Paraguay* (Santiago de Chile: Comisión Economica para America Latina y el Caribe de las Naciones Unidas, 1987), 30–1.

121. "O difícil tráfego na Ponte da Amizade," *Revista Painel,* April 1980, 5; "Camiones de carga ocasionan dificultades en el tránsito," *ABC Color*, 18 February 1981, 22; "Mucha demora en el control de vehículos," *ABC Color*, 21 February 1981, 24.

122. "Colônia árabe comemora a "festa muçulmana," *Diário do Paraná*, 16 October 1981, 8.

123. "A comunidade Árabe de Foz do Iguaçu," *Nosso Tempo,* 5 May 1981, 6; "'Estou com todo e qualquer movimento de libertação,' entrevista com Mohamed Barakat," *Nosso Tempo*, 1 September 1988, 10; "A imigração de árabes," *A Gazeta do Iguaçu,* 20 June 1992, 21.

124. Nino Palazzo and Adolfo Giménez, "Todo un pais vestido de contrabando," *HOY*, 29 July, 1983, 9; Adolfo Giménez, "El ingreso ilegal desde el Brasil," *HOY,* 18 November 1983, 8–9.

125. Giménez, "El ingreso ilegal desde el Brasil," 8–9.

126. Giménez, "El ingreso ilegal desde el Brasil," 8–9.

127. "Usarian facturas falsas para traer contrabando," *ABC Color*, 7 January 1973, 11; "Entregaron a Barrientos nuevas informaciones sobre contrabando: Se refiere a Guías o Avisos de retorno procedentes del Brasil," *ABC Color*, 27 October 1973, 10; "Camara y bolsa de comercio desea reanudar las conversaciones sobre contabando: La entidad privada elevó para ello una nota a dicha secretaría de Estado," *ABC Color*, 31 December 1973, 9.

128. "Camara y bolsa de comercio," 9.

129. "O ano foi muito ruim para o comércio," *A Gazeta do Iguaçu,* 5 January 1992, 4; "Exportadores realizam mais negócios em 1991," *A Gazeta do Iguaçu,* 12 January 1992, 3.

130. Wagner, 19 September 2008.

131. "Foz do Iguaçu Hoje," *Revista Painel,* June 1975, 14–22; "A ordenada marcha da Capital do Turismo: Foz 65 anos," *Revista Painel,* June 1979, 10–11.

132. "Passagem alternativa," *Diário do Paraná,* 21 October 1980, 7.

133. "Passagem alternativa de Foz entra em operação," *Diário do Paraná,* 25 October 1980, 7.

134. "Fiscais da Receita fazem representação contra Polícia Federal," *Nosso Tempo,* 29 December 1983, 4–5.

135. "Fiscais da Receita fazem," 4–5.

136. "Tres Fronteras—II—Foz de Yguazu es un polo de desarrollo, Pto. Stroessner espera la planificación: En toda la zona, sin embargo, el crecimiento avanza igual," *ABC Color*, 3 November 1974, 23; "'Extraordinario progreso de la zona," *ABC Color*, 25 January 1979, 11; "Alto Paraná: Hay nuevos planes para su desarrollo," *ABC Color*, 31 January 1979, 27.

137. "Um 'mundo fantástico' para el turismo," *ABC Color*, 3 February 1982, Suplemento especial, 28.

138. "Aduana: Se busca una mayor fluidez," *ABC Color*, 3 February 1982, Suplemento especial, 14.

139. "Ciudad Puerto Stroessner: O paraíso das falsificações e da corrupção," *Nosso Tempo,* 20 December 1984, 13; "Mesmo no 'Paraíso,' Atenção e Cuidado," *Veja*, 22 July 1987, 52; "Destaque: Mohamed Said Mannah," *Nosso Tempo*, 29 April

1988. Brazilian media erroneously characterized Ciudad Presidente Stroessner as a "zona franca" for much of its history.

140. "Editorial: Zona Franca Comercial en Puerto Pte. Stroessner II," *ABC Color*, 19 December 1970, 10.

141. "Centro de importadores elevó una nota a la camara de diputados acerca del ingreso ilegal de whisky al país: Solicita disminución de gravámenes como medio para combatir el auge del contrabando de esta bebida," *ABC Color*, 13 August 1971, 10.

142. "Centro de importadores elevó una nota," 10; Humberto Domínguez Dibb, *La evasión de divisas: Historia del mayor fraude al país* (Asunción: Ediciones HOY, 1986).

143. Dibb, *La evasión de divisas*; "Corrupção levou o Paraguai à completa ruina financeira: Evasão fraudulenta de divisas, contrabando e caos cambial," *Nosso Tempo*, 12 September 1985, 13.

144. Hector Guerín, 16 April 2009

145. Miranda Silva, *Historia de Alto Paraná*; "Tumulto na Ponte: 'Paseros' e policiais trocam palavrões," *Nosso Tempo*, 6 July 1983, 7; "Ciudad Puerto Stroessner: O paraíso das falsificações e da corrupção," *Nosso Tempo*, 20 December 1984, 13; "Governo paraguaio fecha pistas clandestinas em Alto Paraná," *A Gazeta do Iguaçu*, 9 April 1991, 16.

146. "Tráfico en el Puente de la Amistad," *ABC Color*, 26 February 1982, 22; "Tumulto na Ponte: 'Paseros' e policiais trocam palavrões," *Nosso Tempo*, 6 July 1983, 7; "Crise e desemprego assolam o Paraguai," *Nosso Tempo*, 6 July 1983, 7; "Crise econômica amplia a tensão no Paraguai," *Nosso Tempo*, 1 June 1984, 9; "Terror e mordomia na Ponte da Amizade," *Nosso Tempo*, 23 May 1985, 19; "Corrupção na Ponte de Amizade," *Nosso Tempo*, 29 August 1985, 17.

147. "Collor de Mello também é a solução para a crise paraguaia," *A Gazeta do Iguaçu*, 3 March 1990, 16.

148. "Pacote de medidas do novo governo gera expectativas na frontiera," *A Gazeta do Iguaçu*, 14 March 1990, 16.

149. Sérgio Spada, "O Equilíbrio das Três Fronteiras," *Nosso Tempo*, 28 August 1986, 14.

150. "Exportadores de Foz do Iguaçu rompem o cerco da Cacex," *Nosso Tempo*, 30 June 1989, 2; "ACIFI pede liberação de cota de exportação," *A Gazeta do Iguaçu*, 29 June 1990, 3.

151. Rabossi, "Nas ruas de Ciudad del Este," 28.

152. "Kamal Osman: 'Foz do Iguaçu precisa ser transformada em Zona de Livre Comércio'," *A Gazeta do Iguaçu*, 20 November 1993, 20–21.

153. "Caos na Vila Portes: Comerciantes querem uma solução," *A Gazeta do Iguaçu*, 27 December 1990, 1, 3.

CHAPTER 2

1. Vijay Prashad, *The Darker Nations: A Biography of the Short-Lived Third World* (New Delhi: Leftword Books, 2007); Vijay Prashad, *The Poorer Nations: A Possible History of the Global South* (London: Verso Books, 2014).

2. "Atentado a la Embajada de Israel: Hay 6 muertos," *Clarín*, 18 March 1992; United States Department of State, *Patterns of Global Terrorism 1992* (Washington, DC: Office of the Secretary of State, 1993).

3.  Mark Berger, "After the Third World? History, Destiny, and the Fate of Third Worldism," *Third World Quarterly* 25.1 (2004): 9–39.
4.  Pamila Gupta, Christopher Lee, Marissa Moorman, and Sandhya Shukla, Introduction to special issue "The Global South: Histories, Politics, Maps," *Radical History Review* 131 (2018): 1–12; Clovis Maksoud, "Redefining Non-Alignment: The Global South in the New Global Equation," in *Altered States: A Reader in the New World Order*, eds. Phyllis Bennis and Michel Moushabeck (New York: Olive Branch Press, 1993), 28–37; Jean Comaroff and John Comaroff, *Theory from the South: Or How Europe Is Evolving toward Africa* (Boulder, CO: Paradigm Publishers, 2011).
5.  Gupta, Lee, Moorman, and Shukla, Introduction, 2.
6.  Associação dos Diplomados da Escola Superior de Guerra (ADESG), *A região de Foz do Iguaçu*; Mora and Cooney, *Paraguay and the United States*, 44; Menezes, *La Herencia de Stroessner*, 64, 69; Ananda Simões Fernandes, "A política externa da ditadura brasileira durante os 'anos de chumbo' (1968–1974): As intervenções do 'Brasil Potência' na América Latina," *História Social* 18 (2010): 157–76; Pio Penna Filho, "O Itamaraty nos anos de chumbo: O Centro de Informações do Exterior (CIEX) e a pressão no Cone Sul (1966–1979)," *Revista Brasileira de Política Internacional* 52.2 (2009): 49.
7.  Fares, "O pragmatismo do petróleo," 129–145; Shiguenoli Miyamoto, "O Brasil e as negociações multilaterais," *Revista Brasileira de Política Internacional* 43.1 (2000): 119–37; Frank O. Mora, "Paraguay: From the *Stronato*," 13–31; Frank O. Mora, "Paraguay: The Legacy of Authoritarianism," 309–27; Vizentini, *A política externa do regime militar brasileiro*.
8.  Cecilia Menjívar and Néstor Rodríguez, eds., *When States Kill: Latin America, the US, and Technologies of Terror* (Austin: University of Texas Press, 2001); J. Patrice McSherry, *Predatory States: Operation Condor and Covert War in Latin America* (Lanham, MD: Rowman & Littlefield, 2005).
9.  "Clube União Árabe de Foz do Iguaçu," 21 September 1978, Câmara Municipal de Foz do Iguaçu.
10. Serviço de Informações da Superintendência Regional da Polícia Federal no Estado do Paraná, "Colônia Árabe no Estado do Paraná," 26 July 1983, Arquivo Nacional; Serviço Nacional de Informações, "Atividades Árabes no Brasil," 27 October 1983, Arquivo Nacional; Assessoria Especial de Segurança e Informações de Itaipu Binacional, "Atividades Árabe-Palestinas em Foz do Iguaçu/PR," 23 October 1986, Arquivo Nacional; Assessoria Especial de Segurança e Informações de Itaipu Binacional, "Atividades Árabe-Palestinas em Foz do Iguaçu/PR," 15 July 1988, Arquivo Nacional.
11. Ibid.
12. "'Estou com todo e qualquer movimento de libertação," *Nosso Tempo*, 1 September 1988, 10.
13. Monique Sochaczewski, "Palestine-Israel Controversies in the 1970s and the Birth of Brazilian Transregionalism," in *The Middle East and Brazil: Perspectives on the New Global South*, ed. Paul Amar (Bloomington: Indiana University Press, 2015), 76. See also Thomas Skidmore, *Politics in Brazil, 1930–64: An Experiment in Democracy* (New York: Oxford University Press, 1968), 199; Comissão de Relações Exteriores, "Aprova o acordo cultural entre os Estados Unidos do Brasil e a República

Árabe Unida," PDC 111/1961, www.camara.leg.br/proposicoesWeb/fichadetramitacao?idProposicao=167557.

14. "El gobierno nacional dispuso ayer tres días de duelo oficial en tributo póstumo al Presidente Gamal Nasser," *ABC Color*, 1 October 1970, 9; Karam, "On the Trail and Trial of a Palestinian Diaspora," 751–77.

15. Matthew Hull, *Government of Paper: The Materiality of Bureaucracy in Urban Pakistan* (Berkeley: University of California Press, 2012), 1.

16. José Luiz Silva Preiss, "Brasil e Argentina no Oriente Médio: Do Pós-Guerra Mundial ao Final da Guerra Fria," PhD diss., Pontifícia Universidade Católica do Rio Grande do Sul, 2013; Tawil Kuri, *Latin American Foreign Policies toward the Middle East*; Fehmy Saddy, ed., *Arab-Latin American Relations: Energy, Trade, and Investment* (New Brunswick: Transaction Books, 1983); Fehmy Saddy, ed., *The Arab World and Latin America: Economic and Political Relations in the Twenty-First Century* (London: I. B. Tauris, 2016).

17. "Brasil não apoiará as sancões contra o Irã," *Correio Braziliense*, 29 December 1979, 9; "Brasil não vende uma arma sequer ao Irã," *Ultima Hora*, 29 November 1983, 6; Monica Yanakiew, "O termômetro das mudanças," *Jornal do Brasil*, 30 December 1985, B6; Vizentini, *A política externa do regime militar brasileiro*, 253; William Beeman, *The Great Satan vs. the Mad Mullahs: How the United States and Iran Demonize Each Other* (Chicago: University of Chicago Press, 2005).

18. "Entrevista com o Embaixador do Irã: A República Islâmica do Irã é um exemplo para o mundo," *Nosso Tempo*, 26 July 1984, 10–12; Serviço Nacional de Informações, "Presenças de Mohamed Taghi Tabatabaie e do Embaixador do Irã em Foz do Iguaçu/PR," 10 August 1984, Arquivo Nacional.

19. Ibid.

20. "Um jogo definido," *Veja*, 8 August 1984, 106–7; Serviço Nacional de Informações, "Mohamed Taghi Tabatabaie," 11 October 1984, Arquivo Nacional; Centro de Informações da Polícia Federal, "Atividades de membro da seita xiita no Brasil—Mohammad Taghi Tabatabaie Einaki—Foz do Iguaçu—Curitiba/PR," 4 April 1986, Arquivo Nacional.

21. Agência Central, "Comércio Brasil—Irã," 9 April 1985, Arquivo Nacional; Ministério das Relações Exteriores, "Atividades de membro da seita xiita no Brasil, Mohammad Taghi Tabatabaie," 31 January 1985, Arquivo Nacional; Douglas Farah, "Iran in Latin America: An Overview," in *Iran in Latin America: Threat or 'Axis of Annoyance'?*, eds. Cynthia Arnson, Haleh Esfandiari, and Adam Stubits (Washington, DC: Woodrow Wilson International Center for Scholars, 2009) 13–25; José Luiz Silva Preiss, "As Relações Brasil—Irã: Dos antecedentes aos desdobramentos no século XXI," *ANMO: África del Norte y Medio Oriente* 1.1 (2011): 45–60; Fernando de Mello Barreto, "Roberto de Abreu Sodré," in *A Política Externa após a redemocratização* (Brasília: Fundação Alexandre Gusmão, 2012), 93–94.

22. Ministério do Exército, "Centro Cultural Árabe Brasileiro de Foz do Iguaçu," 11 July 1983, Arquivo Nacional.

23. Carlos Ribeiro Santana, "O aprofundamento das relações do Brasil com os países do Oriente Médio durante os dois choques do petróleo da década de 1970: Um exemplo de ação pragmática," *Revista Brasileira de Política*

*Internacional* 49.2 (2006): 157–77; Vizentini, *A política externa do regime militar brasileiro*, 244, 250.

24. "Aprenda a Língua Árabe," "Convite," *Nosso Tempo*, 15 April 1982, 10; "Protesto dos árabes ao terrorista Beguim," *Nosso Tempo*, 15 June 1982, 15; "Mais de mil pessoas foram buscar comida," *Nosso Tempo*, 20 July 1983, 7; "Professor da Líbia em Foz," *Nosso Tempo*, 15 December 1983, 17; "Cônsul geral da Síria em Foz," *Nosso Tempo*, 19 January 1984, 9; "Comunidade árabe lembra Gamal Abdul Nasser," *Nosso Tempo*, 2 August 1984, 18; "Comunidade árabe comemora o nascimento de Maomé," *Nosso Tempo*, 20 December 1984, 1; "Corpo diplomático líbio em Foz do Iguaçu," *Nosso Tempo*, 12 January 1985.

25. "A Líbia de Kadafi: Vista por Mohamad Barakat . . .," *Nosso Tempo*, 5 May 1983; "Centro Árabe repudia tentativa de invasão," *Nosso Tempo*, 13 July 1983, 19; "As causas do povo do terceiro mundo . . .," *Nosso Tempo*, 13 December 1984; "Um duro golpe contra o imperalismo e as forças de dominação," *Nosso Tempo*, 26 September 1985.

26. "'Livro Verde' de Kadhafi será distribuído em todo o Paraná," *Nosso Tempo*, 15 December 1983, 17; "Líbia de Kadhafi derrotou o imperialismo: Data é lembrada pelo Centro Árabe-Brasileiro Cultural," *Nosso Tempo*, 20 June 1985, 11; "Em 16 anos, Revolução de Kadhafi mudou a face da Líbia," *Nosso Tempo*, 26 September 1985, 8; "Declaração do Centro Cultural Árabe Brasileiro do Paraná," *Nosso Tempo*, 12 December 1985, 14; "A Vitória da Líbia sobre o imperialismo," *Nosso Tempo*, 16 May 1986, 22; "Comunidade árabe lembra ataque americano à Líbia," *Nosso Tempo*, 10 April 1987, 5; "Ato de solidariedade à Líbia e repúdio ao imperialismo," *Nosso Tempo*, 24 April 1987, 2; "100 Aniversário da Revolução Líbia," *Nosso Tempo*, 4 September 1987, 3; "Comunidade árabe lembra ataques terroristas contra a Líbia," *Nosso Tempo*, 28 April 1988, 3.

27. "Pregação revolucionária em Foz do Iguaçu," *Nosso Tempo*, 1 July 1981, 8.

28. "A comunidade Árabe de Foz do Iguaçu," *Nosso Tempo*, 5 May 1981, 6.

29. "Embaixador da Líbia apoia Argentina na questão das Ilhas Malvinas," *Diário do Paraná*, 25 April 1982, 3; Serviço Nacional de Informações, "Manifestações Árabes em Foz do Iguaçu/PR," 12 July 1983, Arquivo Nacional.

30. Secretaria da Receita Federal do Ministério da Fazenda, Cadastro Geral de Contribuintes, Ficha de Inscrição do Estabelecimento-Sede do Centro Cultural Beneficente Islâmico de Foz do Iguaçu, 3 January 1982; Centro Cultural Beneficente Islâmico de Foz do Iguaçu, "Ata de Assembleia Extraordinária," 3 January 1982, Câmara Municipal de Foz do Iguaçu.

31. "A cultura islâmica—publicação do Centro Cultural Beneficente Islâmico de Foz do Iguaçu," *Nosso Tempo*, 15 April 1982, 2; "A cultura islâmica—publicação do Centro Cultural Beneficente Islâmico de Foz do Iguaçu," *Nosso Tempo*, 20 April 1982, 2; "Para compreender o Islamismo—A cultura islâmica—publicação do Centro Cultural Beneficente Islâmico de Foz do Iguaçu," *Nosso Tempo*, 15 Junho 1982, 2; "Condenado pela espúria Lei de Segurança Nacional," *Nosso Tempo*, 30 July 1982, 6, 8.

32. Letter from Ali Said Rahal, President of Centro Cultural Beneficente Islâmico de Foz do Iguaçu to Foz do Iguaçu mayor, 2 March 1982, Câmara Municipal de Foz do Iguaçu.

33. Câmara Municipal de Foz do Iguaçu, "Autoriza a doação de uma área de terras ao Centro Cultural Beneficente Islâmico de Foz do Iguaçu," Projeto de Lei No. 12/1982, 8 June 1982, Câmara Municipal de Foz do Iguaçu, "Autoriza o Chefe do Executivo Municipal a doar ao Centro Cultural Beneficente Islâmico de Foz do Iguaçu, uma área de terras," Lei Municipal No. 1.148, 13 June 1983.

34. "Mesquita em Foz." *Nosso Tempo,* 19 March 1983; "Com embaixadores e sheikhs é iniciada construção da mesquita," *Nosso Tempo,* 6 April 1983; "Muçulmanos constroem a primeira mesquita no Oeste," *Nosso Tempo,* 23 August 1984, 1.

35. For the first meeting, see Ahmad H. Sakr, "The First Islamic Conference of South America," *Muslim Standard* 25 (November 1977): 23. On the Muslim World League, see Jacob Landau, *The Politics of Pan-Islam: Ideology and Organization* (Oxford: Oxford University Press, 1990).

36. "Manifestações Árabe-Palestinas em Foz do Iguaçu / PR," Assessoria Especial de Segurança e Informações, 14 February 1984, Arquivo Nacional; Fares, "O pragmatismo do petróleo"; Paulo Gilberto Fagundes Vizentini, *Relações Internacionais do Brasil: de Vargas a Lula* (São Paulo: Editora Fundação Perseu Abramo, 2003), 51.

37. "Atividades da Associação Cultural Sanaúd, Relembrando o Massacre de Sabra e Chatila—Foz do Iguaçu," Serviço de Informações da Superintendência Regional da Polícia Federal no Estado do Paraná, 23 October 1984, Arquivo Nacional.

38. "Palestinos de Foz relembram o massacre de Sabra e Chatila," *Nosso Tempo,* 27 September 1984, 14; "Árabes vão as ruas em Foz do Iguaçu," *Nosso Tempo,* 24 November 1988, 5; Zé Beto Maciel, "Falta contigüidade ao território da Palestina," *A Gazeta do Iguaçu,* 26 November 2000, 10.

39. Itaipu Binacional, "Atividades Árabe-Palestinas em Foz do Iguaçu," Assessoria Especial de Segurança e Informações, 23 October 1986; "Dia internacional de solidariedade ao povo palestino," *Nosso Tempo,* 4 December 1986, 3, 10, 14.

40. "Dia internacional de solidariedade ao povo palestino," *Nosso Tempo,* 4 December 1986, 3, 10, 14.

41. "Árabes vão as ruas em Foz do Iguaçu," *Nosso Tempo,* 24 November 1988, 5.

42. "Protesto dos árabes ao terrorista Beguim," *Nosso Tempo,* 15 Junho 1982, 15; "Protesto da Colônia Árabe," *Diário do Paraná,* 27 June 1982.

43. "Solidariedade ao Povo Palestino," *Revista Painel,* July 1982.

44. Howard Winant, *Racial Conditions: Politics, Theory, Comparisons* (Minneapolis, MN: University of Minnesota Press, 1994), 141; Mohamad Barakat, 5 June 2009.

45. "Atividades de organizações árabes no Paraná," Serviço Nacional de Informações, Informação no. 0934, 23 March 1984, Arquivo Público do Paraná. In the original Portuguese, the passages read, "a Sociedade Islâmica de Foz do Iguaçu, cujos membros são Xiitas e apoiam o Irã" and "the Centro Cultural Beneficente Islâmico de Foz do Iguaçu, formado por Sunitas que se ligam ao Iraque."

46. "Entrevista com o Embaixador do Irã: A República Islâmcia do Irã é um exemplo para o mundo," *Nosso Tempo,* 26 July 1984, 10–12; "Sociedade Beneficente Islâmica de Foz do Iguaçu, Culto Religioso, em nome de Deus, Clemente, o

Misericordioso," *Nosso Tempo,* 9 June 1989, 30; "Eng. Mir Hussein Mussaw da República do Irã," *A Gazeta do Iguaçu,* 2 June 1990, 7; "Simpósio," *A Gazeta do Iguaçu,* 2 June 1990, 7; "Alimentos à população carente: A Sociedade Beneficente Islâmica distribuirá hoje," *A Gazeta do Iguaçu,* 3 June 1990, 9; "Sociedade Islâmica distribui alimentos," *A Gazeta do Iguaçu,* 6 June 1990, 8; "Delegação Iraniana em Foz," *Nosso Tempo,* 14 June 1990, 3.

47. "Entrevista com o Embaixador do Irã: A República Islâmcia do Irã é um exemplo para o mundo," *Nosso Tempo,* 26 Julho 1984, 1, 12.

48. Mohamad Barakat, 5 June 2009.

49. Jerry Dávila, *Dictatorship in South America* (Malden, MA: Wiley-Blackwell, 2013).

50. Sameul Alves Soares, *Controles e autonomia: As Forças Armadas e o sistema político brasileiro (1974–1999)* (São Paulo: Editora Unesp, 2006), 65–6.

51. Antônio Vanderli Moreira, 27 October 2008.

52. "Eleições diretas: Foz inicia campanha," *Nosso Tempo,* 26 July 1983, 18; "Lição de moral no PDS: PMDB faz comícios e o povo pede a cabeça de Vianna," *Nosso Tempo,* 4 August 1983, 8–9; "O povo é o patrão do governo," *Nosso Tempo,* 18 August 1983, 3; "PDS adere ao PMDB na luta por eleições diretas em Foz," *Nosso Tempo,* 18 August 1983, 10–12; "Vereadores de Foz estão em 'greve' contra o prefeito," *Nosso Tempo,* 25 August 1983, 2.

53. "O comício dos 50 mil: Povão adere à tese das diretas," *Nosso Tempo,* 27 January 1984, 10–1; Débora Ferreira, "12 de janeiro, uma data histórica," *Nosso Tempo,* 27 January 1984, 12.

54. "Atividades de Mohamad Ibrahim Barakat, junto a comunidade árabe em Foz do Iguaçu/PR e Presidente Stroessner/Paraguai," Serviço Nacional de Informações, Pedido de Busca no. 0127, 30 September 1983.

55. Mohamad Barakat, 23 May 2009.

56. Serviço Nacional de Informações, Agência Central, "Atividades Árabes no Brasil," 27 October 1983; Agência Central (ACE), "Visita do corpo diplomatico líbio a Foz do Iguaçu e Curitiba/PR," 8 February 1985; Agência Central (ACE), "Apoio do partido comunista brasileiro à candidatura de Mohamed Ibrahim Barakat—Foz do Iguaçu/PR," 30 September 1988; Itaipu Binacional, Assessoria Especial de Segurança e Informações, "Atividades Árabe-Palestinas em Foz do Iguaçu/PR," 15 July 1988; Agência Central (ACE), "Atividades da comunidade árabe em Foz do Iguaçu," 8 January 1990, Arquivo Nacional.

57. "Condenado pela espúria Lei de Segurança Nacional," *Nosso Tempo,* 30 July 1982, 6, 8; "Juvêncio Condenado," *Nosso Tempo,* 7 October 1982, 2; "Juvêncio: A solidariedade da nação ao preso político do regime," *Nosso Tempo,* 13 October 1983, 2.

58. Juvêncio Mazzarollo, 6 December 2008.

59. "LSN: Deboche nacional," *Nosso Tempo,* 6 July 1983, 4; Jacob Blanc, "The Last Political Prisoner: Juvêncio Mazzarollo and the Twilight of Brazil's Dictatorship," *Luso-Brazilian Review* 53.1 (2016): 153–78.

60. Juvêncio Mazzarollo, 6 December 2008.

61. Ibid.

62. Ibid.

63. "Entrevista com o Embaixador do Irã: A República Islâmica do Irã é um exemplo para o mundo," *Nosso Tempo,* 26 July 1984, 10–12.

64. Aluízio Palmar, *Onde foi que vocês enterraram nossos mortos?* (Curitiba: Foto-Laser Gráfica e Editora Ltda., 2007). See also his website, Documentos Revelados, documentosrevelados.com.br.

65. Aluízio Palmar, "Sete dias na terra dos aiatolás," *Nosso Tempo*, 25 October 1984, 8–9.

66. "Congresso Internacional em solidariedade com a revolução Líbia," *Nosso Tempo*, 16 August 1984, 12; "Juvêncio vai à Líbia," *Nosso Tempo*, 23 August 1984, 2; "Brasileiros vão à Líbia festejar aniversário da Revolução de Kadhafi," *Nosso Tempo*, 30 August 1984, 8; Juvêncio Mazzarollo, "Em grande estilo, a Líbia de Kadhafi celebrou 150 aniversário da revolução: 'O único país do Oriente Médio que está dando certo,'" *Nosso Tempo*, 4 October 1984, 8; Juvêncio Mazzarollo, "A maior riqueza da Líbia não é o petróleo, mas o socialismo," *Nosso Tempo*, 11 October 1984, 4; "Uma viagem pelo Oriente em tapete mágico: Arialba Freire . . .," *Nosso Tempo*, 25 October 1984, 12.

67. "Brasileiros vão à Líbia festejar aniversário da Revolução de Kadhafi," *Nosso Tempo*, 30 August 1984, 8.

68. Juvêncio Mazzarollo, 16 December 2008.

69. Câmara Municipal de Foz do Iguaçu, "Concede licença a Vereadora Arialba do Rocio Cordeiro Freire, para ausentar-se do País, pelo prazo de 30 (trinta) dias, para desempenhar missão de interesse do Município," Resolução legislativa No. 5, 10 September 1984. In Portuguese, "para desempenhar missão de interesse do Município . . . no Congresso Internacional em Solidariedade ao Povo Árabe Líbio."

70. Arialba Freyre, 9 September 2008.

71. "Congresso Internacional em solidariedade com a revolução Líbia," *Nosso Tempo*, 16 August 1984, 12; "Juvêncio vai à Líbia," *Nosso Tempo*, 23 August 1984, 2; "Brasileiros vão à Líbia festejar aniversário da Revolução de Kadhafi," *Nosso Tempo*, 30 August 1984, 8; "Destaques: Mohamed Barakat," *Nosso Tempo*, 27 February 1986, 12.

72. "Os ventos da liberdade vão sacudir o Paraguai: Uma plêiade de intelectuais e líderes populares latinoamericanos estará em Foz dias 11 e 12," *Nosso Tempo*, 9 August 1984, 11; "Saudação de Abertura da "Jornada," *Nosso Tempo*, 23 August 1984, 4; "Sete Países Latinoamericanos estiveram representados na Jornada de Solidariedade Ao Povo Paraguaio," *Nosso Tempo*, 23 August 1984, 8–9; Juvêncio Mazzarollo, "Jornada de Solidariedade ao povo paraguaio," *Nosso Tempo*, 18 July 1985, 12.

73. "Informe [sobre opositores paraguayos en Foz]," 8 May 1984; "Jornada de Solidariedade ao Povo Paraguaio," 12 August 1984; "IIa Jornada de Solidariedade ao Povo Paraguaio," 10–11 August 1985, CDyA.

74. Paul Sondrol, "The Emerging New Politics of Liberalizing Paraguay: Sustained Civil-Military Control without Democracy," *Journal of Interamerican Studies and World Affairs* 34.2 (1992): 141. See also Menezes, *La Herencia de Stroessner*, 128; Vizentini, *A política externa do regime militar brasileiro*, 155; Mora and Cooney, *Paraguay and the United States*, 195–6.

75. "200 empresários num jantar de apoio aos candidatos do PMDB," *Nosso Tempo*, 13 September 1985, 5.

76. Ibid.

77. "Sarney e Stroessner dizem que Continente deve caminhar unido," *Jornal do Brasil*, 10 October 1985, 25; "Nota de repúdio ao terrorismo sionista," *Nosso Tempo*, 4 October 1985, 14.

78. "Sarney e Stroessner dizem que Continente deve caminhar unido," *Jornal do Brasil*, 10 October 1985, 25.

79. "Mesquita poderá ser inaugurada em abril," *Nosso Tempo*, 3 January1987, 2; "Mesquita muçulmana: Novo monumento de Foz do Iguaçu," *Revista Painel*, June 1987; "Em nome de Alá e Maomé: Mesquita Omar Ben ElKhatab," *Nosso Tempo*, 20 October 1988, 1; "Personalidades em destaque," *Nosso Tempo*, 20 October 1988, 4.

80. Arialba Freyre, 9 September 2008.

81. Ibid.

82. Skidmore, *The Politics of Military Rule in Brazil*, 267–68; Wendy Hunter, *Eroding Military Influence in Brazil: Politicians against Soldiers* (Chapel Hill, NC: University of North Carolina Press, 1997), 57.

83. "Aniversário da 'Intifada,'" *Nosso Tempo*, 9 December 1988; "Paraguai: Marchas do Silêncio terminam sob pancadaria e prisões," *Nosso Tempo*, 9 December 1988; "A vitória do PMDB foi imoral," *Nosso Tempo*, 9 December 1988.

84. "Terror fiscal em Foz," *A Gazeta do Iguaçu*, 11 December 1988, 3.

85. "Fiscais do ICM na Cidade," *A Gazeta do Iguaçu*, 21 December 1988, 7.

86. Mora and Cooney, *Paraguay and the United States*, 129–30; Paul Lewis, *Paraguay under Stroessner* (Chapel Hill, NC: University of North Carolina Press, 1980); Andrew Nickson, "Tyranny and Longevity: Stroessner's Paraguay," *Third World Quarterly* 10.1 (1988): 237–59.

87. Marcial Antonio Riquelme, "Toward a Weberian Characterization of the Stroessner Regime in Paraguay (1954–1989)," *European Review of Latin American and Caribbean Studies* 57 (1994): 41–42; Mora and Cooney, *Paraguay and the United States*, 126.

88. Paul Sondrol, "Totalitarian and Authoritarian Dictators: A Comparison of Fidel Castro and Alfredo Stroessner," *Journal of Latin American Studies* 23.3 (1991): 617.

89. Riquelme, "Toward a Weberian Characterization," 41–42; Mora and Cooney, *Paraguay and the United States*, 126.

90. Sondrol, "The Emerging New Politics of Liberalizing Paraguay," 141

91. Humberto Domínguez Dibb, *Presencia y vigencia Arabes en el Paraguay* (Asunción: Editorial Cromos, 1977); John Tofik Karam, "I, Too, Am the Americas: Arabs in the Redrawing of Area and Ethnic Studies," *Journal of American Ethnic History* 37.3 (2018): 93–101.

92. Bader Rachid Lichi and Alejandro Hamed Franco, "Estudos políticos e estratégicos sobre a Palestina," *Nosso Tempo*, 15 April 1982, 10; Alejandro Hamed Franco, *Los árabes y sus descendientes en el Paraguay: Un largo recorrido histórico* (Asunción: Arandurã Editorial, 2002), 180; Lewis, *Paraguay under Stroessner*, 140–1; Nickson, "The Overthrow of the Stroessner Regime," 185–209.

93. Armando Rivarola, 23 February 2009.

94. Hector Guerín, 6 April 2009.

95. Miranda Silva, *Historia de Alto Paraná*, 438.

96. Andrew Nickson, "Reestablishing the Status Quo," in *The Paraguay Reader: History, Culture, Politics*, eds. Peter Lambert and Andrew Nickson (Durham, NC: Duke University Press, 2013), 329.

97. Ley No. 06/89. "Que denomina "Ciudad del Este" a la ciudad capital del departamento de Alto Paraná, que hasta hoy lleva el nombre de 'Ciudad Presidente Stroessner'"; "Corrupção na fronteira: Ciudad del Este está sob intervenção federal," *A Gazeta do Iguaçu*, 24 March 1991, 20.

98. Miranda Silva, *Historia de Alto Paraná*, 438.

99. Hector Guerín, 16 April 2009.

100. Renato Dalto and João Domingos, "Comércio bilateral é maior preocupação," *Jornal do Brasil*, 22 January 1990; "Presidentes do Brasil e do Paraguai inauguram Itaipu," *O Fluminense*, 7 May 1991.

101. "Árabes estão indignados com Collor de Mello," *Nosso Tempo*, 11 August 1989, 1, 3; "A questão da Palestina e a sucessão," *Nosso Tempo*, 20 October 1989, 12; "Árabes fazem ato contra Collor em Foz," *Jornal do Brasil*, 12 August 1989, 3.

102. In Portuguese, the "estrepitosa manifestação de repúdio," from the article, "A questão da Palestina e a sucessão," *Nosso Tempo*, 20 October 1989, 12.

103. "Dia internacional de solidariedade ao povo palestino," *Nosso Tempo*, 4 December 1986, 3, 10, 14; "Liberdade para Lamia e repúdio ao sionismo," *Nosso Tempo*, 15 May 1987, 1; "O dia da terra," *Nosso Tempo*, 9 April 1987, 6; "Árabes protestam contra massacre," *A Gazeta do Iguaçu*, 23 May 1990, 9; "Árabes protestam contra massacre de palestinos," *Nosso Tempo*, 25 May 1990, 3; "Dia de solidariedade ao povo palestino," *A Gazeta do Iguaçu*, 29 November 1990, 11; "Proclamação do Estado Palestino," *A Gazeta do Iguaçu*, 15 November 1991, 5; "Palestinos: Um dia de solidariedade internacional, *A Gazeta do Iguaçu*, 30 November 1991, 1; "8 de Dezembro: O significado histórico da intifada," *A Gazeta do Iguaçu*, 8 December 1991.

104. "A libertação da Palestina é uma questão de tempo," *Nosso Tempo*, 6 March 1989, 9.

105. "Árabes festejaram Proclamação do Estado Palestino," *Nosso Tempo*, 15 December 1989, 3.

106. "Rodriguez revoga lei de importação," *A Gazeta do Iguaçu*, 30 January 1990, 1.

107. Said Taijen, 28 November 2008.

108. "Protesto dos árabes ao terrorista Beguim," *Nosso Tempo*, 15 June 1982, 15; "Em 16 anos, Revolução de Kadafhi mudou a face da Líbia," *Nosso Tempo*, 26 September 1985, 8; "Colônia árabe recebeu missão diplomática da Líbia," *Nosso Tempo*, 23 December 1987, 41.

109. Ricardo Jiménez, Mário, and Ayala, PRF, 22 April 2009.

110. Ibid. In Spanish, "ideologicamente . . . no coinciden . . . son anti-imperialistas."

111. Berger, "After the Third World?"

112. Mário Ricardo Jiménez and Ayala, PRF, 22 April 2009.

113. "Corrupção na fronteira: Ciudad del Este está sob intervenção federal," *A Gazeta do Iguaçu*, 24 March 1991, 20; "Governo paraguaio fecha pistas clandestinas em Alto Paraná," *A Gazeta do Iguaçu*, 9 April 1991, 16.

114. "Eleições para prefeito em Ciudad del Este," *A Gazeta do Iguaçu*, 27 January 1991, 8; "A briga entre colorados e liberais," *A Gazeta do Iguaçu*, 27 January 1991, 9; "Partido Colorado vence a eleição em Ciudad del Este," *A Gazeta do Iguaçu*, 28 May 1991, 4.

115. "Corrupção derruba funcionários da Aduana em Ciudad del Este," *A Gazeta do Iguaçu,* 22 June 1994, 5.
116. "Atentado a la Embajada de Israel: Hay 6 muertos," *Clarín*, 18 March 1992, 3; "Atentado destruyó Embajada de Israel," *El Territorio*, 18 March 1992, 1–2.
117. Ibid.
118. In Argentina, see "Afirman que un argentino musulmán detonó el coche bomba en la embajada: La Jihad Islamica se adjudicó en Beirut el ataque," *Clarín*, 19 March 1992, 2–3; "Atribuyen autoría del atentado a Hizllabolha" [*sic*], *El Territorio*, 22 March 1992, 3. In Paraguay, see "Unánime repudio en Argentina por atentado terrorista," *ABC Color*, 19 March 1992, 26–27; "El Yihad Islámico prometió seguir ataque contra Israel," *ABC Color,* 24 March, 1992, 23. In Brazil, see "A conexão brasileira," *Veja*, 1 April 1992, 30–31. In the US, see "Shiite Group Reasserts Link to Argentine Embassy Attack," *New York Times,* 24 March 1992, 10; S. Dillon, "Argentina's Shiites Thrust into Spotlight," *Miami Herald,* 25 March 1992, 12.
119. Nathaniel Nash, "At Least 6 Die as Blast Destroys Israel's Embassy in Buenos Aires," *New York Times,* 18 March 1992.
120. United States Department of State, *Patterns of Global Terrorism, 1992* (Washington, DC: Office of the Secretary of State, 1993).
121. United States Department of State, "Daily Briefing," Washington, DC, March 18, 1992, dosfan.lib.uic.edu/ERC/briefing/daily_briefings/1992/9203/040.html.
122. "Buscan aquí a simpatizantes de terroristas que volaron la Embajada isralí: Son árabes y viven en Ciudad del Este," *ABC Color*, 26 March 1992, 1, 11.
123. Ibid.
124. Howard J. Wiarda and Hilary Collins, "Constitutional Coups? Military Interventions in Latin America," *Security and Defense Studies Review* 12.1&2 (2011): 189–98.
125. In Spanish, "los extranjeros con radicación definitiva tendrán los mismos derechos en las elecciones municipales."
126. Constitución de Paraguay de 1992, Asunción: Red ediciones SL, 2013: p. 38, "Ley N. 834/96," Código Electoral Paraguayo, tsje.gov.py/static/ups/legislaciones/1996-ley-834.pdf.
127. Said Taijen, 28 November 2008.
128. "Palestinos fecham comércio na fronteira em sinal de protesto," *A Gazeta do Iguaçu,* 20 February 1992, 6.
129. Ibid.
130. In Spanish, "nosotros estamos en contacto permanente con el ministro del Interior de Argentina—José Luis Manzano—y hacemos intercambio de datos." See "Buscan aquí a simpatizantes de terroristas que volaron la Embajada israelí: Son árabes y viven en Ciudad del Este," *ABC Color*, 26 March 1992, 1, 11.
131. Ibid.
132. In Portuguese, "aquelas ações que ocorreram em Buenos (Aires) tinham tido origem muito diferente do que era propalado . . . não havia . . . no nosso território planejamento ou o apoio logístico ou de pessoal para aqueles atentados." Alberto Cardozo, statement made in meeting of the Comissão de Segurança Públia e Combate ao Crime Organizado, Câmara dos Deputados, 21 August 2007; Márcio Paulo Buzanelli, "Abin precisa ser

conhecida para ser respeitada, afirma diretor-geral da agência," ABIN, 20 December 2006, www.abin.gov.br/modules/mastop_publish/?tac=Entrevista_ do_Diretor-Geral_ao_Inforel; Paulo de Tarso Resende Paniago, "O papel dos serviços de inteligência na prevenção e no combate ao terrorismo internacional," *Revista Brasileira de Inteligência* (ABIN) 3.4 (2007).

133. Departamento de Inteligência, Escritório do Rio de Janeiro, da Secretaria de Assuntos Estratégicos, "Atentado à Embaixada de Israel em Buenos Aires," 25 March 1992; GAB/CI/DPF/CFR/PSC, "Alerta à Embaixada de Israel em Brasília," Radiograma no 644/92, 26 May 1992; SI/SR/DPF/RJ, "Riscos de atentados à representações judaicas ou hotel em São Paulo, onde se hospedariam judeus," Informe na 142/92, 26 May 1992, Arquivo Nacional.

134. "Documento condena atentado terrorista," *A Gazeta do Iguaçu*, 28 March 1992, 1, 24.

135. Ibid.

136. "Toques e Retoques: Nota Incômoda," *A Gazeta do Iguaçu*, 1 April 1992, 2.

137. Chico de Alencar, "De olho na telinha: Colônia árabe, uma força de Foz," *A Gazeta do Iguaçu*, 21 May 1993.

138. "Jardim Jupira será restaurado: Comerciantes fazem parceria com municipio para asfaltar as ruas e reassentar famílias," *A Gazeta do Iguaçu*, 13 May 1994, 20.

139. "Dia de solidariedade ao povo palestino," *A Gazeta do Iguaçu*, 29 November 1990, 11; "Proclamação do Estado Palestino," *A Gazeta do Iguaçu*, 15 November 1991, 5; "Palestinos: Um dia de solidariedade internacional," *A Gazeta do Iguaçu*, 30 November 1991, 1; "8 de dezembro: O significado histórico da intifada," *A Gazeta do Iguaçu*, 8 December 1991; Ronildo Pimentel, "Causa Palestina: Ato em Foz pede paz ao povo palestino," *Três Poderes*, December 2000, 3.

140. Agência Central (ACE), "Atividades da comunidade árabe em Foz do Iguaçu," 8 January 1990, Arquivo Nacional.

## CHAPTER 3

1. "Esta madrugada seguían removiendo escombros en busca de más víctimas," *Clarín*, 19 July 1994, 4–5.

2. Olivier Roy, *Globalized Islam: The Search for a New Ummah* (New York: Columbia University Press, 2004), 287.

3. Sally Howell and Andrew Shryock, "Cracking Down on Diaspora: Arab Detroit and America's War on Terror," *Anthropological Quarterly* 76.3 (2004): 443–62.

4. Edna Aizenberg, "Argentine Space, Jewish Memory: Memorials to the Blown Apart and Disappeared in Buenos Aires," *Mortality* 12.2 (2007): 109–23; Carlos Escudé and Beatriz Gurevich, "Limits to Governability, Corruption, and Transnational Terrorism," *Estudios interdisciplinarios de America Latina y el Caribe* 14.2 (2003): 127–48; Federico Pablo Feldstein and Carolina Acosta-Alzura, "Argentinean Jews as Scapegoat: A Textual Analysis of the Bombing of AMIA," *Journal of Communication Inquiry* 27.2 (2003): 152–70; Luis Fleischman, "The Case of the Bombing of the Jewish Headquarters in Buenos Aires (AMIA): A Structural Approach," *MACLAS Latin American Essays* 12 (1999) 119–34; Beatriz Gurevich, "After the AMIA Bombing: A Critical Analysis of Two Parallel

Discourses," in *The Jewish Diaspora in Latin America and the Caribbean: Fragments of Memory*, ed. Kristin Ruggiero (Sussex: Sussex Academic Press, 2005), 86–112.

5. Charles T. Call, "War Transitions and the New Civilian Security in Latin America," *Comparative Politics* 35.1 (2002): 1–20; Juan Linz and Alfred Stepan, *Problems of Democratic Transition and Consolidation: Southern Europe, South America, and Post-Communist Europe* (Baltimore, MD: Johns Hopkins University Press, 1996); Brian Loveman, *For La Pátria: Politics and the Armed Forces in Latin America* (Wilmington, DE: Scholarly Resources, 1999); J. Patrice McSherry, *Incomplete Transition: Military Power and Democracy in Argentina* (New York: Macmillan, 1997); Anthony Pereira and Diane Davis, "Introduction: New Patterns of Militarized Violence and Coercion in the Americas," *Latin American Perspectives* 27.2 (2000): 3–17.

6. "El Hizbullah en colores," *Clarín*, 31 July 1994, 3; "La frontera caliente," *Clarín*, 13 November 1995, 12; Denise Chrispim Marin, "Brasil faz acordo para combater terror," *Folha de S. Paulo*, 17 October 1995.

7. Pablo Vila, *Crossing Borders, Reinforcing Borders: Social Categories, Metaphors, and Narrative Identities on the US-Mexico Frontier* (Austin: University of Texas Press, 2000).

8. "Centro Islâmico oferece curso de língua árabe," *Nosso Tempo*, 17 February 1989, 8; "Um centro para preservar a cultura árabe," *Nosso Tempo*, 6 March 1989, 9.

9. "'Em nome de Alá e Maomé: Mesquita Omar Ben ElKhatab," *Nosso Tempo*, 20 October 1988.

10. "Constroem mesquitas os que amam a Deus," *Nosso Tempo*, 20 October 1988, 2.

11. Secretaria de Informações do Exterior, Divisão de Segurança e Informações, Ministério das Relações Exteriores, "Guerra no Golfo Pérsico," 29 January 1991, Arquivo Nacional; David Sheinin, *Argentina and the United States: An Alliance Contained* (Athens, GA: University of Georgia Press, 2006), 200; Mora and Cooney, *Paraguay and the United States*, 239.

12. Mohamad Khalil, 18 July 2007.

13. "Conflito no Golfo: 'Guerra entre irmãos,'" *A Gazeta do Iguaçu*, 22 August 1990, 8; "Iraque x Kuwait: Histórias que poucos sabem," *A Gazeta do Iguaçu*, 5 January 1991, 4; "Árabes de Foz estão ao lado do Iraque," *A Gazeta do Iguaçu*, 10 January 1991, 16; "Crise no Golfo repercute na colônia árabe em Foz," *A Gazeta do Iguaçu*, 11 January 1991, 16; "Árabes de Foz realizam manifestação pela paz," *A Gazeta do Iguaçu*, 16 January 1991, 7; "Colônia árabe não acredita na imprensa americana," *A Gazeta do Iguaçu*, 18 January 1991; "Incidente na passeata dos árabes em Foz," *A Gazeta do Iguaçu*, 25 January 1991, 1, 16; Jackson Lima, "Árabes da fronteira opinam sobre o conflito no Iraque," *A Gazeta do Iguaçu*, 22 January 1993, 4.

14. Beeman, *The Great Satan*.

15. Juvêncio Mazzarollo, "Fanatismo religioso," *Nosso Tempo*, 2 March 1989, 7.

16. Beeman, *The Great Satan*.

17. "Psiu: Espantoso," *Nosso Tempo*, 16 June 1989, 9. For the seminal critique of orientalism, see Edward Said, *Orientalism* (New York: Vintage, 1979). For the

critique of orientalism in Brazil, see Waïl Hassan, "Carioca Orientalism: Morocco in the Imaginary of a Brazilian *Telenovela*," in *The Global South Atlantic: Region, Vision, Method*, eds. Kerry Bystrom and Joseph Slaughter (New York: Fordham University Press, 2017).

18. "Centro Islâmico oferece curso de língua árabe," *Nosso Tempo*, 17 February 1989, 8; "Um centro para preservar a cultura árabe," *Nosso Tempo*, 6 March 1989, 9.

19. Ibid.

20. Sociedade Beneficente Islâmica de Foz do Iguaçu, "Culto Religioso, em nome de Deus, Clemente, o Misericordioso," *Nosso Tempo*, 9 June 1989, 30.

21. Ibid.

22. Ibid. In Portuguese,"culto religioso em louvor de sua alma que será celebrado no dia 11 de junho de 1989."

23. Agência Central, "Fatos e consequências em torno do falecimento do líder espiritual e da República Islâmica do Irã, Ayatollah Khomeini," 21 July 1989, Arquivo Nacional.

24. "Eng. Mir Hussein Mussaw da República do Irã," *A Gazeta do Iguaçu*, 2 June, 1990, 7; "Simpósio," *A Gazeta do Iguaçu*, 2 June 1990, 7; "Alimentos à população carente: A Sociedade Beneficente Islâmica distribuirá hoje," *A Gazeta do Iguaçu*, 3 June 1990, 9; "Sociedade Islâmica distribui alimentos," *A Gazeta do Iguaçu*, 6 June 1990, 8; "Delegação Iraniana em Foz," *Nosso Tempo*, 14 June 1990, 3.

25. "Sociedade Islâmica distribui alimentos," *A Gazeta do Iguaçu*, 6 June 1990, 8.

26. Agência Central, "Visita do Presidente da República à Hidrelétrica de Itaipu— Foz do Iguaçu," 24 November 1989.

27. "A imigração de árabes," *A Gazeta do Iguaçu*, 20 June 1992, 21.

28. Paulo Gabriel Hilu da Rocha Pinto and Silvia Montenegro, "As comunidades muçulmanas na tríplice fronteira: Identidades religiosas, contextos locais e fluxos," paper presented at the 26a Reunião Brasileira de Antropologia (Porto Seguro, 2008), 7.

29. Nickson, "The Overthrow of the Stroessner Regime," 185–209.

30. Loveman, *For La Pátria*, 219; Sondrol, "The Emerging New Politics of Liberalizing Paraguay," 127–63.

31. Mohamad Barakat, 5 June 2009; Fawas, 4 December 2008; MYA conceded an interview to reporter Jeffrey Goldberg, "In the Party of God," *New Yorker*, 22 October 2002.

32. Pinto and Montenegro, "As comunidades muçulmanas na tríplice fronteira," 7.

33. Muhammad Ayyub Shahimi, *Dirasat ightirabiyah: Al-intishar al-lubnani fi al-baraghway* (Beirut: al-Tab'ah 2000), 178–80.

34. Franco, *Los árabes*, 214; Silvia Montenegro, "La inmigración árabe en Paraguay," in *Los árabes en América Latina*, ed. Akmir Abdeluahed Akmir (Madrid: Siglo XXI, 2009), 299–300.

35. "Líder guerrilheiro da AMAL visita Foz do Iguaçu," *Nosso Tempo*, 13 February 1986, 2.

36. In the 1990s, Brazilian and Paraguayan civilian rulers avoided legislation that classified "terrorist organizations," specifically Hizbullah, which would

soon be adopted in the US. In 2019, the administration of Paraguayan president Mário Abdo Benítez classified Hizbullah as a terrorist organization as a step toward implementing financial oversight, the backdrop to which is discussed in Chapter 6. See "Abdo reconoce a Hezbollah como terrorista y anuncia más controles financieros," *ABC Color*, 19 August 2019.

37. Franco, *Los árabes*, 216. In Spanish, "nuestra religión no hace distingo de nacionalidades, ni culturas, ni etnias. Todo musulmán es hermano de religión, iguales en derecho, en todos los aspectos."

38. Republica Argentina, Gendarmería Nacional, "Comunicado de Prensa," *A Gazeta do Iguaçu*, 19 July, 1994, 3; "Aisladas las tres fronteras," *ABC Color*, 19 July 1994, 4; "Bloqueo de fronteras, rutas y estricto control en aeropuerto," *El Territorio*, 19 July 1994, 10.

39. "Igual que la Embajada," *Clarín,* 19 July 1994, 19.

40. Decreto Nacional 2,023/94, "Actividades Subversivas," Buenos Aires, 16 November 1994, published in the Boletin Oficial, 21 November 1994.

41. Beatriz Sarlo, "Argentina under Menem: The Aesthetics of Domination," *NACLA Report on the Americas* 27.2 (September/October 1994): 33–37.

42. "El Hizbullah en colores," *Clarín,* 31 July 1994, 3. But Hizbullah released a statement in Beirut: "We deny any relationship with the attack of Buenos Aires," "Hezbollah negó haber tomado parte del atentado en la AMIA," *Clarín,* 21 July 1994, 22.

43. Eduardo Estévez, "Intelligence Community Reforms: The Case of Argentina," in *Intelligence Elsewhere: Spies and Espionage Outside the Anglosphere*, eds. Philip Davies and Kristian Gustafson (Washington, DC: Georgetown University Press, 2013), 222–23; Priscila Carlos Brandão Antunes, "Establishing Democratic Control of Intelligence in Argentina," in *Reforming Intelligence: Obstacles to Democratic Control and Effectiveness*, eds. Thomas Bruneau and Steven Boraz (Austin: University of Texas Press, 2007), 195–218.

44. "Sospechan que la base de los terroristas está funcionando en el sur de Brasil," *Clarín,* 19 July 1994, 2–3; See Paraguayan and Brazilian reportage that cited this Clarín news article: "¿Terroristas operan en Ciudad del Este?" *ABC Color,* 20 July 1994, 24; "Inteligência argentina aponta central de terrorismo na fronteira," *A Gazeta do Iguaçu,* 20 July 1994, 24.

45. "Paraguay no niega que haya 'bases,'" *Clarín,* 22 July 1994, 20.

46. "Terroristas estuvieron aquí en abril pasado," *ABC Color,* 19 July 1994, 5. In Spanish, it reads, "tendria la protección de la numerosa colonia extranjera (presumiblemente árabe libanesa) radicada en la fronteriza Ciudad del Este."

47. "El terrorista sirio se 'esfumó' de Ciudad del Este, según la Policía," *ABC Color*, 2 September 1994, 100.

48. "El tríangulo de los fantasmas," *La Nación*, 19 October 1997.

49. Josias de Souza, "Governo investiga conexão árabe no Brasil," *Folha de S. Paulo*, 31 July 1994.

50. Ibid.

51. Consbras Buenos Aires, "Brasil-Argentina-Paraguai," 28 November 1997, Itamaraty.

52. Ibid.; "Abin precisa ser conhecida para ser respeitada, afirma diretor-geral da agência," ABIN, 20 December 2006, www.abin.gov.br/modules/mastop_publish/?tac=Entrevista_do_Diretor-Geral_ao_Inforel; Priscila Carlos

Brandão Antunes, *SNI e Abin: Uma leitura da atuação dos serviços secretos brasileiros ao longo do século XX* (Rio de Janeiro: Fundação Getúlio Vargas Editora, 2002); José Maria Pereira da Nóbrega Júnior, "A militarização da segurança pública," *Revista de Sociologia Política* (Curitiba) 18.35 (2010): 125.

53.  Denise Chrispim Marin, "Brasil faz acordo para combater terror," *Folha de S. Paulo*, 17 October 1995.

54.  "El Islam, en portugués," *Clarín*, 24 July 1994, 11; "Una frontera con el control relajado," *Clarín*, 24 July 1994, 11.

55.  Ibid.

56.  "Así viven los musulmanes de Ciudad del Este," *La Prensa*, 25 November 1994, 16–17. In Spanish, "la prensa nos quisó echar la culpa de todo."

57.  Ibid. In Spanish, "siempre echan la culpa a los árabes."

58.  "Una frontera con el control relajado," *Clarín*, 24 July 1994, 11. In Spanish, "aquí no hay árabes indocumentados, son todos naturalizados y participan en las elecciones, están muy bien integrados en nuestra sociedad."

59.  Howell and Shryock, "Cracking Down on Diaspora."

60.  Jackson Lima, "Árabes de Foz condenam acusações: Lideranças da Colônia Árabe dizem não há terroristas em Foz do Iguaçu," *A Gazeta do Iguaçu*, 22 July 1994, 24; "Muçulmanos de Foz condenam atentado em Buenos Aires," *A Gazeta do Iguaçu*, 23 July 1994, 21. All quotes in the paragraph come from these two articles.

61.  "Donde hubo fuego," *Página/12*, 14 June 1998; Jorge Zaverucha, "The Degree of Military Political Autonomy during the Spanish, Argentine and Brazilian Transitions," *Journal of Latin American Studies* 25.2 (1993): 283–99; James Brennan, *Argentina's Missing Bones: Revisiting the History of the Dirty War* (Berkeley: University of California Press, 2018).

62.  "Intensas investigaciones también en Misiones por el atentado a la sede de la AMIA," *El Territorio*, 23 July 1994, 10–1.

63.  "Operação de guerra para caçar terrorista: Polícia secreta faz pente fino," *A Gazeta do Iguaçu*, 3 September 1994, 1, 3.

64.  For Argentine coverage, see "Detienen a presuntos terroristas," *El Territorio*, 13 September 1994, 1, 9; "Caso AMIA: Declararán dos libaneses," *Clarín*, 14 September 1994, 12; "Entre la cautela y el entusiasmo," *Clarín*, 14 September 1994, 12. For Brazilian coverage see "Suspeitos de terrorismo são presos em Iguazu," *A Gazeta do Iguaçu*, 14 September 1994, 1–2; "Libaneses presos na Argentina são libertados," *A Gazeta do Iguaçu*, 20 September 1994, 24.

65.  "Libaneses a Buenos Aires," *El Territorio*, 14 September 1994, 1, 9; "Juez esperaba exhorto original para el envío de los libaneses," *El Territorio*, 15 September 1994, 9; "Los dos libaneses serán indagados hoy por Galeano," *El Territorio*, 16 September 1994, 9; "Audí podría ser un terrorista proiraní buscado por la Interpol," *El Territorio*, 17 September 1994, 9; "AMIA: Allanamientos para dar con quien vendió el explosivo," *Clarín*, 15 September 1994, 12; "Llegaron y hoy los interrogarán," *Clarín*, 15 September 1994, 12; "Los libaneses, en la mira del Mossad," *Clarín*, 16 September 1994, 13; "Galeano busca conexiones entre los libaneses y la AMIA," *Clarín*, 17 September 1994, 8.

66.  "Caso AMIA: Los libaneses no tenían nada que ver," *Clarín*, 18 September 1994, 19; "Por falta de méritos liberaron a libaneses," *El Territorio*, 19 September

1994, 35; "Libaneses presos na Argentina são libertados," *A Gazeta do Iguaçu,* 20 September 1994, 24.

67. Alfredo Jalaf, 1 July 2010.

68. Alfredo Jalaf, 1 July 2010; "Trasladarán a dos libaneses y liberarán a los otros tres," *El Territorio,* 14 September 1994; "Los dos libaneses serán indagados hoy por Galeano," *El Territorio,* 15 September 1994.

69. "Barakat condena atitude do governo da Argentina," *A Gazeta do Iguaçu,* 15 September 1994, 5.

70. "Atentado a la Embajada: Israel cargó contra la Corte Suprema," *Clarín,* 4 November 1995, 30.

71. "Presiones y resistencia," *Clarín,* 24 November 1995, 3.

72. "La AMIA insiste en que no hay resultados," *Clarín,* 13 November 1995, 12. In Spanish, "La Argentina sigue siendo un lugar donde los atentados quedan impunes."

73. "Editorial—Argentina e o anti-semitismo," *A Gazeta do Iguaçu,* 17 July 1996, 2; "Corach y Jassan, otra vez el blanco preferido de Cavallo," *Clarín,* 16 October 1996; "Corach volvió a la carga," *La Nación,* 17 October 1996.

74. Christina Civantos, "Ali Bla Bla's Double-Edged Sword: Argentine President Carlos Menem and the Negotiation of Identity," in *Between the Middle East and the Americas: The Cultural Politics of Diaspora,* eds. Evelyn Alsultany and Ella Shohat (Ann Arbor: University of Michigan Press, 2013), 108–29; David Sheinin, "El judío en la mina de carbón: El inconfundible, dictadura e identidad en Argentina," in *Más allá del Medio Oriente: Las diásporas judías y árabes en América Latina,* eds. Raanan Rein, María José Cano Pérez, and Beatriz Molina Rueda, 163–96 (Granada: Editorial de la Universidad de Granada, 2012).

75. "Terrorism in Latin America / AMIA Bombing in Argentina," Hearing before the Committee on International Relations, 104th Congress, 28 September 1995 (Washington, DC: US Government Printing Office, 1996).

76. "U.S. policy toward Argentina," Hearing before the Subcommittee on Western Hemisphere Affairs of the Committee on Foreign Affairs, House of Representatives, 98th Congress, March 16, 1983 (Washington, DC: US Government Printing Office, 1983).

77. "Terrorism in Latin America / AMIA Bombing in Argentina," Hearing before the Committee on International Relations, 104th Congress, 28 September 1995 (Washington, DC: US Government Printing Office, 1996), 40.

78. Brasemb Buenos Aires, "Terrorismo," MRE, 16 September 1994; "La frontera caliente," *Clarín,* 13 November 1995, 12; Denise Chrispim Marin, "Brasil faz acordo para combater terror," *Folha de S. Paulo,* 17 October 1995.

79. Ibid.

80. ConsBras Assunção, "Informo. A primeira reunião do grupo de trabalho Brasil-Paraguai-Argentina sobre segurança na fronteira tríplice," 18 May 1996; ConsBras Buenos Aires, "Comunico . . . I Reunião do comando tripartite das três fronteras," MRE, 7 June 1996; Carlos Corach and Mario Baizán, eds., *La respuesta Argentina Frente al Terrorismo* (Buenos Aires: Fupomi Ediciones, 2002) 87–88; "Protección compartida para la triple frontera," *Clarín,* 8 March 1996; Patricio Downes, "Crean un comando especial para la triple frontera," *Clarín,* 19 May 1996; Romero Sales, "Comando Tripartite para

combater tráfico e terror: A assinatura do Acordo entre Brasil, Argentina e Paraguai foi realizada ontem entre ministros dos três," *A Gazeta do Iguaçu*, 19 May 1996, 1, 6–7.

81. "Antiterror—Árabes serão identificados e regularizados na fronteira," *A Gazeta do Iguaçu*, 19 May 1996, 7.

82. Zé Beto Maciel, "FBI volta a atacar 'tríplice fronteira': Diretor do FBI diz que vai investigar atividades árabes na fronteira de Foz do Iguaçu," *A Gazeta do Iguaçu*, 14 May 1998; Franco Iacomini, "Fronteira sem lei," *Veja*, 8 April 1998, 44. In Portuguese, "o banditismo endógeno do Paraguai."

83. Consbras Buenos Aires, "Brasil-Argentina-Paraguai. Controle da fronteira tríplice," MRE 28 November 1997; "Amia será foco de encontro sobre terror," *A Gazeta do Iguaçu*, 24 September 1998, 5; "Argentinos suspeitam de proteção do Brasil," *A Gazeta do Iguaçu*, 24 September 1998, 5.

84. Jamillah Karim, *American Muslim Women: Negotiating Race, Class, and Gender within the Ummah* (New York: New York University Press, 2009), 12.

85. "Família típica admite influência brasileira," *Folha de Londrina*, 7 September 1997, 3–4.

86. Franco, *Los árabes*. In Spanish, "libre práctica del culto islámico en el Paraguay."

87. "Muçulmanos jejuam no mês do Ramadan," *A Gazeta do Iguaçu*, 23 January 1996, 1, 16.

88. "Árabes islâmicos de Foz e a 'Festa do Sacrifício' . . . O Eid Al Adha," *A Gazeta do Iguaçu*, 18 April 1997, 8; "Árabes lembram Meca na Festa do Sacrifício," *A Gazeta do Iguaçu*, 8 April 1998, 1; "Entidades recebem doações de carne: Festa do Sacrifício," *A Gazeta do Iguaçu*, 31 March 1999, 23; "Muçulmanos jejuam no mês do Ramadan," *A Gazeta do Iguaçu*, 23 January 1996, 1, 16; "Muçulmanos jejuam para comemorar o Ramadan," *A Gazeta do Iguaçu*, 18 January 1997, 8; Sônia Inês Vendrame, "Muçulmanos encerram Ramadã," *A Gazeta do Iguaçu*, 19 January 1999, 1, 4; Silvana Canal, "Muçulmanos começam o Ramadã: Eles jejuam, rezam e pedem graças a Deus durante o período de um mês," *A Gazeta do Iguaçu*, 12 December 1999; Mônica Resende, "Ramadã termina hoje: Muçulmanos comemoram seu Natal e tem início a festa do fim do Ramadã," *A Gazeta do Iguaçu*, 7 January 2000, 25.

89. "Meninas muçulmanas celebram fim do Ramadã," *A Gazeta do Iguaçu*, 28 January 1998, 12.

90. "Provopar recebe duas toneladas de roupas: Doação partiu da Sociedade Beneficente Islâmica," *A Gazeta do Iguaçu*, 10 July 1996, 9; "Islâmicos doam três toneladas de roupas," *A Gazeta do Iguaçu*, 21 March 1997, 6; "Sociedade Islâmica doa 21 fardos de roupas . . . usadas para o Provopar," *A Gazeta do Iguaçu*, 16 December 1998, 22; "Provopar recebe doação de 300 quilos de leite," *A Gazeta do Iguaçu*, 19 January 1999, 21.

91. "Provopar recebe duas toneladas de roupas: Doação partiu da Sociedade Beneficente Islâmica," *A Gazeta do Iguaçu*, 10 July 1996, 9. In Portuguese, "Estamos comemorando uma data muito importante, pois este é o mês do Ramadã, ou seja, o mês de Deus—no qual sentimos a obrigação religiosa e humana de ajudar ao próximo. Com isto, colaboramos para diminuir o sofrimento no mundo."

92. "Mapa," *O Cordelista: Informações culturais e turísticas,* December 1991, 4–5; "Árabes inauguram o carimbo da Mesquita," *A Gazeta do Iguaçu,* 13 December 1998, 23.

93. Silvana Canal, "Mesquita abre suas portas: A Mesquita deixa um pouco da rigidez de lado e abre as suas portas para a visitação do público," *A Gazeta do Iguaçu,* 4 December 1998, 1.

94. "Marco Histórico: Em homenagem aos 15 anos da Mesquita, os correios . . .," *A Gazeta do Iguaçu,* 13 December 1998, 1; "Árabes inauguram o carimbo da Mesquita," *A Gazeta do Iguaçu,* 13 December 1998, 23.

95. "Novo cemitério reflete a miséria," *Nosso Tempo,* 8 December 1981, 13.

96. Alexandre Palmar, "Religiosos da fronteira cultuam finados: Cristãos, islâmicos e budistas da tríplice fronteira celebram data com diferentes valores," *A Gazeta do Iguaçu,* 2 November 1999, 29; Jackson Lima, "Iguaçuenses relembram seus mortos: Religiões têm rituais e cerimônias diferentes, mas morte é vista como uma 'passagem," *A Gazeta do Iguaçu,* 2 November 2000, 29; "Islamismo tem rituais diferentes," *A Gazeta do Iguaçu,* 2 November 2000, 29.

97. "Presidente do Parlamento libanês visita a fronteira," *A Gazeta do Iguaçu,* 9 March 1996, 3; "Nabih Berri . . . O líder libanês empolgou uma multidão, tanto no Aeroporto quanto na área externa do Hotel Bourbon," *A Gazeta do Iguaçu,* 13 March 1996, 3; "Editorial—Pela paz no Oriente Médio," *A Gazeta do Iguaçu,* 14 March 1996, 2.

98. "Nabih Berri em Foz: A visita do Presidente do Parlamento Libanês," *Revista Painel,* April 1996, 3.

99. Antônio França, "Argentina nega operação para identificar terroristas," *A Gazeta do Iguaçu,* 17 April 1996, 4; "Libaneses da fronteira vão protestar contra os ataques: Com a segunda maior colônia árabe da América Latina, reunindo mais de 12 mil libaneses, os moradores da fronteira vão pedir a volta da paz ao Sul do país," *A Gazeta do Iguaçu,* 17 April 1996, 4; "Casal libanês de Foz perde oito parentes," *A Gazeta do Iguaçu,* 17 April 1996, 4.

100. "Protesto de árabes contra Israel reúne mais de 3 mil: PT disse que o Brasil estava solidário ao povo árabe e pediu que também se sensibilizassem aos familiares dos 19 Sem Terra mortos ontem," *A Gazeta do Iguaçu,* 19 April 1996, 5.

101. "Religiosos se encontram em protesto contra guerra: A celebração foi realizada anteontem na Sociedade Beneficente Islâmica," *A Gazeta do Iguaçu,* 27 June 1996, 4.

102. Mônica Resende, "Árabes constroem segunda escola em Foz: Única diferença em relação aos outros estabelecimentos é o ensino da língua árabe," *A Gazeta do Iguaçu,* 9 January 2000, 7.

103. Fawas, 4 December 2008.

104. Mônica Resende, "Árabes constroem segunda escola em Foz: Única diferença em relação aos outros estabelecimentos é o ensino da língua árabe," *A Gazeta do Iguaçu,* 9 January 2000, 7.

105. Ibid. In Portuguese, "tem como objetivo atender os filhos descendentes da Comunidade Islâmica, bem como todos os alunos de outras comunidades."

106. Regina Venâncio, "Editorial," *Nossa Escola,* Foz do Iguaçu, 1.1 (2008): 3.

107. Francione Oliveira Carvalho, "Fronteiras instáveis: Inautenticidade inter-cultural na escola de Foz do Iguaçu," PhD diss., Universidade Presbiteriana Mackenzie, 2011, 123–24.

108. Franco Iacomini, "Um enclave libanês," *Veja*, 8 April 1998, 47.

109. Ibid.

110. Brasemb Assunção, "Informa sobre a repercussão, na imprensa local, das declarações do Secretário de Segurança da Argentina sobre o incremento da falta de segurança em Ciudad del Este," 28 May 1998, Itamaraty (Ministério de Relações Exteriores, MRE).

111. Iacomini, "Um enclave libanês."

112. "Crise diplomática provoca endurecimento na fronteira," *A Gazeta do Iguaçu*, 21 May 1998, 6; "'Discriminação' provocou protestos de Foz em Brasília," *A Gazeta do Iguaçu*, 21 May 1998, 7.

113. Nadine Naber, *Arab America: Gender, Cultural Politics, and Activism* (New York: New York University Press, 2012).

114. Denise Chrispim Marin, "Brasil faz acordo para combater terror," *Folha de S. Paulo*, 17 October 1995; "Protección compartida para la triple frontera," *Clarín*, 8 March 1996; "Comando tripartito de las tres fronteras," *Clarín*, 1 June 1998. See also material collected by Seguridad Estratégica Regional en el 2000, known as Ser2000, which was founded in Argentina after the failed 1990 military insurrection led by Mohamed Alí Seineldín against the demo-cratically elected government of Carlos Menem, each Argentine respectively of Lebanese and Syrian origins. Ser2000's original website brought together security-related policy briefings and news clippings from Argentina, and has since branched out elsewhere to Latin America. It led to the founding of the Red de Seguridad y Defensa de América Latina, www.resdal.org/ing/equipo_i2.html (date of access: 28 August 2020). Some of this background is recounted in Germán Soprano, "La reforma de la defense nacional y las fuerzas armadas argentinas en democracia durante la década de 1990," *Cadernos Prolam/USP* 14.133 (2015): 133–56.

115. "Sheik iraní negó estar vinculado al terrorismo," *ABC Color*, 12 February 1996, 106; "Xeque nega envolvimento com grupos de terroristas," *A Gazeta do Iguaçu*, 16 February 1996; Antônio França, "Árabes na fronteira—Xeque lamenta notícias de que seria terrorista: Apesar de estar há dois anos na fronteira, o xeque Seyed Mohsen foi confudido com terrorista e investigado pela Polícia Federal," *A Gazeta do Iguaçu*, 16 February 1996.

116. "Peligroso terrorista árabe estaría residiendo en Foz," *ABC Color*, 10 Febru-ary 1996, 81; "Policía Federal negó que religioso árabe sea un terrorista," *ABC Color*, 11 February 1996, 65.

117. Embaixada em Teerã, "Brasil-Iran. Prorrogação de visto oficial. Seyed Mohsen Tabatabei," 15 April 1998, Itamaraty; Embaixada em Teerã, "Brasil-Iran. Prorrogação de visto oficial. Seyed Mohsen Tabatabei," 15 May 1998, Itamaraty; Embaixada em Teerã, "Vicor. Mohsen Tabatabei. Entrevista do Embaixador do Irã com o DG do DAOP" 21 May 1998, Itamaraty; Embaixada em Teerã, "Vicor. Seyed Mohsen Tabatabei Enkani e família," 22 June 1998, Itamaraty; Embaixada em Teerã, "Relações Políticas e Comerciais Brasil-Irã. Concessão de Vistos. Seyed Mohsen Tabatabei Enkani, esposa e filhos," 23 June 1998, Itamaraty.

118. Mohamad Barakat, 5 June 2009.

119. Antônio França, "Árabes na fronteira—Xeque lamenta notícias de que seria terrorista," *A Gazeta do Iguaçu,* 16 February 1996, 1, 7.

120. "Representante del Amal dijo que no incentivan violencia," *ABC Color,* 12 February 1996. In Spanish, "orientando, ayudando e incentivando las costumbres religiosas de su comunidad y no tiene ninguna relación con el terrorismo."

121. "O xeque Moshen Al Tabatabay, da mesquita de Foz, visitou o presidente da Câmara Adilimar Sartori, acompanhado do secretário de Indústria e Comércio, Mohamad Barakat," *A Gazeta do Iguaçu,* 20 February 1996; "Perseguição—Políticos condenam a campanha contra árabes: A nota a seguir foi assinada por dirigentes dos seguintes partidos: PT, PDT, PSDB, PMDB, PCdoB e PSB (Nota de Solidariedade à comunidade árabe da Tríplice Fronteira)," *A Gazeta do Iguaçu,* 24 February 1996, 11.

122. "Sociedade Islâmica faz doação para o Provopar," *A Gazeta do Iguaçu,* 2 March 1996, 9.

123. "Sociedade Islâmica doa 21 fardos de roupas," *A Gazeta do Iguaçu,* 16 December 1998, 22.

124. "Egipcio prófugo es sospechoso en atentados en Luxor y contra AMIA," *ABC Color,* 22 September 1998, 83.

125. Gerardo Youn, "Triple Frontera: Un informe oficial compromete a Paraguay," *Clarín,* 30 June 1998; "Triple frontera e inseguridad," *Clarín,* 3 July 1998. In Spanish, "por el atraso del gobierno paraguayo en la implementación de las medidas de seguridad."

126. "Paraguay rechaza acusaciones sobre la Triple Frontera," *Clarín,* 1 July 1998.

127. Irina Hauser, "La voz de los intendentes," *Página/12,* 4 August 1998. In Spanish, "es gente que acá todos conocemos."

128. Ibid. In Spanish, "Acá nunca hubo atentados ni se detectaron células terroristas."

129. "Redada antiterrorista en Paraguay," *Clarín,* 5 September 1998.

130. "Corach quiere hablar con Arias sobre terrorismo," *ABC Color,* 10 September 1998, 2.

131. "Supuesto terrorista pidió garantías para entregarse: Sacerdote islamico negó ser del Hizbulá y se declaró sunita," *ABC Color,* 12 September 1998, 21.

132. "Xeque Khaled Eldin não depõe no PY: Líder religioso islâmico, naturalizado brasileiro, vai esperar encaminhamento diplomático," *A Gazeta do Iguaçu,* 22 September 1998; "Brasília teria orientado xeque para não depor no Paraguai, *A Gazeta do Iguaçu,* 23 September 1998.

133. "Xeque Khaled vai depor espontaneamente na 2a: Juíz do Paraguai oferece garantias de segurança para líder religioso," *A Gazeta do Iguaçu,* 15 September 1998, 4; "Xeque Khaled Eldin não depõe no PY: Líder religioso islâmico, naturalizado brasileiro, vai esperar encaminhamento diplomático," *A Gazeta do Iguaçu,* 22 September 1998, 31.

134. "Xeque islâmico nega relação com terrorismo: Líder religioso diz que não foi intimidado no Paraguai e que seu endereço em Foz é conhecido," *A Gazeta do Iguaçu,* 12 September 1998, 3. In Portuguese, "exerço minhas funções religiosas em estrita obediência às leis brasileiras e amparado pela Constituição, que garante a liberdade de consciência e culto religioso."

135. Edna Mendes, "Xeque acusa autoridades de colaborar com o terror," *Folha de Londrina,* 11 September 1998.

136. "Xeque Khaled vai depor espontaneamente na 2a: Juíz do Paraguai oferece garantias de segurança para líder religioso," *A Gazeta do Iguaçu,* 15 September 1998, 4.

137. Franco Iacomini, "Fronteira Sem Lei," *Veja,* 8 April 1998, 44.

138. "Supuesto terrorista pidió garantías para entregarse: Sacerdote islamico negó ser del Hizbulá y se declaró sunita," *ABC Color,* 12 September 1998, 21.

139. "Xeque islâmico nega relação com terrorismo: Líder religioso diz que não foi intimidado no Paraguai e que seu endereço em Foz é conhecido," *A Gazeta do Iguaçu,* 12 September 1998, 3. In Portuguese, "Khaled Eldin é um sacerdote sunita, o que mostra a falta de propósito das acusações."

140. "Árabes querem desmistificar suspeitas de terrorismo em Foz," *A Gazeta do Iguaçu,* 30 April 1998, 5; "Fronteira de sangue," *Época,* 6 December 1999; Mário Osava, "Triple frontera de Brasil, Argentina y Paraguay es un barril de pólvora," in *Estados Unidos en Guerra: El miedo a la libertad vigilada,* ed. Kintto Lucas (Quito: Ediciones Abya-Yala, 2001), 167.

141. "Árabes querem desmistificar suspeitas de terrorismo em Foz," *A Gazeta do Iguaçu,* 30 April 1998, 5; "Fronteira de sangue," *Época,* 6 December 1999. In Portuguese, "Temos uma guerra oculta por aqui, e nós, árabes, estamos na defensiva."

142. "Rastrean a dos libaneses integrantes de Hizbullah," *ABC Color,* 8 September 1998, 60; "Libanés dijo no tener vinculación con el Hizbullah," *ABC Color,* 9 September 1998, 30; "Supuesto terrorista pidió garantías para entregarse: Sacerdote islamico negó ser del Hizbulá y se declaró sunita," *ABC Color,* 12 September 1998, 21; "Xeque islâmico nega relação com terrorismo: Líder religioso diz que não foi intimidado no Paraguai e que seu endereço em Foz é conhecido," *A Gazeta do Iguaçu,* 12 September 1998; "Xeque Khaled vai depor espontaneamente na 2a," *A Gazeta do Iguaçu,* 15 September 1998; "Eldin ficará detido em casa de amigo," *A Gazeta do Iguaçu,* 15 September 1998.

143. "En Ciudad del este, todos los árabes somos el Hizbullah: Atentados terroristas, entrevista al líder economico de la frontera paraguaya," *Clarín,* 10 August 1998.

144. Ibid.

145. Fawas, 21 May 2009. In Portuguese, "não era muito bem visto."

146. "Asesinan al presidente de la Cámara de Comercio de Ciudad del Este," *ABC Color*, 9 November 1998, 1, 70–1; "Asesinan a otro comerciante libanés en Ciudad del Este," *ABC Color,* 20 November 1998, 30; "Balean a sacerdote islámico en centro de Ciudad del Este," *ABC Color*, 29 November 1999, 78.

147. Silvana Canal, "Xeque árabe recupera-se de atentado: Ziad Fahs, que levou dois tiros na cabeça, passa bem e faz cirugia hoje," *A Gazeta do Iguaçu,* 30 November 1999, 29; "Polícia prende dois suspeitos," *A Gazeta do Iguaçu,* 30 November 1999, 29.

148. "Xeque quer polícia investigando caso: 'Muita gente quer me prejudicar,' afirmou o líder religioso," *A Gazeta do Iguaçu,* 6 January 2000, 24.

149. "Comunidad árabe se mantiene 'cerrada'," *ABC Color*, 4 December 1999, 62.

150. "Dos hipótesis se tejen sobre atentado contra sacerdote islámico," *ABC Color*, 1 December 1999, 73.

151. "Islámico pide que brigada investigue fallido atentado," *ABC Color*, 5 January 2000, 28.

## CHAPTER 4

1. Aylê-Salassié Filgueiras Quintão, *Americanidade: Mercosul—Passaporte para a integração* (Brasília: Senado Federal, 2010), 65.
2. Kimberly Clausing, *Open: The Progressive Case for Free Trade, Immigration, and Global Capital* (Cambridge, MA: Harvard University Press, 2019), 96; Catherine Dolan and Dinah Rajak, eds., *The Anthropology of Corporate Social Responsibility* (New York: Berghan Books, 2016); Rebecca Galemba, "'Corn Is Food, Not Contraband': The Right to 'Free Trade' at the Mexico–Guatemala Border," *American Ethnologist* 39.4 (2012): 716–34; Clara Han, *Life in Debt: Times of Care and Violence in Neoliberal Chile* (Berkeley: University of California, 2012); Sandya Hewamanne, *Stitching Identities in a Free Trade Zone: Gender and Politics in Sri Lanka* (Philadelphia: University of Pennsylvania Press, 2008); Karam, *Another Arabesque*; Karla Slocum, *Free Trade and Freedom: Neoliberalism, Place, and Nation in the Caribbean* (Ann Arbor: University of Michigan Press, 2006).
3. Luiz Alberto Moniz Bandeira, "Política Exterior do Brasil–De FHC a Lula," *Projeto História* 31 (2005): 111; Marcel Nelson, *A History of the FTAA: From Hegemony to Fragmentation in the Americas* (New York: Palgrave Macmillan, 2015).
4. Stephen Brooks, *Producing Security: Multinational Corporations, Globalization, and the Changing Calculus of Conflict* (Princeton, NJ: Princeton University Press, 2005), 156; Mónica Hirst, "MERCOSUL Politics: Between Fragmentation and Integration," in *Paths to Regional Integration: The Case of Mercosur*, eds. Joseph Tulchin and Ralph Espach with Heather Golding (Washington, DC: Woodrow Wilson Center Reports on the Americas, 2002), 141.
5. Amar, *The Security Archipelago*; Daniel Goldstein, "Toward a Critical Anthropology of Security," *Current Anthropology* 51.4 (2010): 487–517; Daniel Goldstein, "Decolonialising 'Actually Existing Neoliberalism,'" *Social Anthropology / Anthropologie Sociale* 20.3 (2012): 304–9.
6. Consbras Ciudad del Este, "Comércio fronteiriço," MRE, 28 May 1997; "A realidade é de extremo pessimissmo para exportadores," *A Gazeta do Iguaçu*, 9 December 1994, 7; "Editorial: O colapso da exportação," *A Gazeta do Iguaçu*, 5 May 1995, 4; Brooks, *Producing Security*, 150–51.
7. "A realidade é de extremo pessimissmo para exportadores," *A Gazeta do Iguaçu*, 9 December 1994, 7; "Editorial: O colapso da exportação," *A Gazeta do Iguaçu*, 5 May 1995, 4.
8. Ibid.
9. Sônia Inês Vendrame, "Falta de acesso quebrou Jardim Jupira: Em cada 3 dias uma nova loja fecha as portas," *A Gazeta do Iguaçu*, 23 October 1999.
10. "Em disputa sem precedentes, duas chapas concorrem à direção da Acifi," *A Gazeta do Iguaçu*, 15 March 1996, 10.
11. "Exportação sofre queda nas vendas: Movimento caiu 80%—exportadores querem real igual ao dólar," *A Gazeta do Iguaçu*, 9 July 1994, 1.
12. Jackson Lima, "Real prejudica exportações: Exportadores de Foz viram o movimento cair 80% e querem paridade entre dólar e real," *A Gazeta do Iguaçu*, 9 July 1994, 24.

13. Cristiane Pinheiro, "Comércio da Vila Portes vive a pior crise dos últimos anos: Os exportadores, que antes davam o tom da dinâmica do local culpam o Plano Real pela situação atual," *A Gazeta do Iguaçu,* 20 June 1996, 6.

14. "Obstáculos às exportações vão se avolumando gradativamente: Exportadores estão prevendo desemprego em massa no setor," *A Gazeta do Iguaçu,* 24 November 1994, 19.

15. "Vila Portes vive a maior crise da história: A próspera Vila que chegou a ter mil trabalhadores está desabando," *A Gazeta do Iguaçu,* 2 May 1995, 6.

16. "Pacotão piora as coisas," *A Gazeta do Iguaçu,* 17 November 1994, 24.

17. Yahya, 3 October 2008; See also "Tratado de Recife," Mercosul Decrees 1280/1994—1281/1994.

18. "Aduanas iniciam processo de integração," *A Gazeta do Iguaçu,* 26 January 2000, 6; "Integração aduaneira em Foz," *Oeste: Revista de Informação,* January 2002.

19. "US$200 milhões: É o valor do contrabando do Brasil para o Paraguai: Mas há suspeitas de fraude por parte de alguns exportadores," *A Gazeta do Iguaçu,* 16 July 1995, 16.

20. Ibid.

21. Jackson Lima, "Os árabes da fronteira," *Classe 10* 1.3 (1996): 11–13; Jackson Lima, "Crise de Foz poderia ter sido evitado: Há mais de quatro anos, o jornal alerta para a crise," *A Gazeta do Iguaçu,* 1 August 1996, 4.

22. Jackson Lima, "Paralisação do viaduto inferniza comerciantes do Jupira," *A Gazeta do Iguaçu,* 29 July 1994, 20; "Pacotão piora as coisas," *A Gazeta do Iguaçu,* 17 November 1994, 24.

23. Antônio França, "Mudança no câmbio vai reaquecer a exportação: Desvalorização do real frente ao dólar, segundo exportadores e economistas, foi acertada," *A Gazeta do Iguaçu,* 1 February 1996, 13; "Foz: Campeã Estadual em Exportação," *Revista Painel,* March 2000, 6–7.

24. Sônia Inês Vendrame, "Falta de acesso quebrou J. Jupira: Em cada 3 dias uma nova loja fecha as portas: Das 500 restam apenas 40 em funcionamento," *A Gazeta do Iguaçu,* 23 October 1999; Mônica Resende, "Foz é campeã estadual em exportações," *A Gazeta do Iguaçu,* 3 February 2000, 5.

25. "Exportação cai à espera de definições: Exportador teme que indústria mantenha preços em dólar aumentando em real," *A Gazeta do Iguaçu,* 19 January 1999, 5; "Spread tira lucro dos paraguaios," *A Gazeta do Iguaçu,* 19 January 1999, 5.

26. Mhamad Mahmoud Ismail, 12 July 2007.

27. Prefeitura Municipal de Foz do Iguaçu, *Anuário estatístico* (Foz do Iguaçu: Secretaria Municipal—Departamento de Informações Institucionais, 2001).

28. César Cabral, "Globalização da economia coloca novos desafios ao comércio internacional," *A Gazeta do Iguaçu,* 9 December 1994, 6.

29. Ibid.

30. Ibid.

31. J. Adelino de Souza and Chico de Alencar, "Fouad Fakih: 'Foz tem um grande futuro com os novos projetos,'" *A Gazeta do Iguaçu,* 23 July 2001, 7.

32. "Fouad Center New Time—Uma Prova de Crença em Foz do Iguaçu," *A Gazeta do Iguaçu,* 11 December 1998.

33. "Kamal Osman: 'Foz do Iguaçu precisa ser transformada em Zona de Livre Comércio,'" *A Gazeta do Iguaçu,* 20 November 1993, 20–1.

34. "Caderno Imobiliário: Amo Foz Empreendimentos e Planejamentos imboliários ltda," *A Gazeta do Iguaçu,* 24 September 1991, 6; "Kamal Osman: 'Foz do Iguaçu precisa ser transformada em Zona de Livre Comércio,'" *A Gazeta do Iguaçu,* 20 November 1993, 20–21.

35. "Prefeitura amplia escola Najla Barakat," *A Gazeta do Iguaçu,* 8 June 1995.

36. Thorstein Veblen, *The Theory of the Leisure Class: An Economic Study of Institutions* (New York: Macmillan Company, 1902).

37. Rodrigo, 27 October 2008.

38. Lima, "Os árabes da fronteira."

39. "Barakat alerta para a falência das exportações na Vila Portes," *A Gazeta do Iguaçu,* 17 November 1994, 24.

40. Ibid.

41. "Sacoleiros invadem o Paraguai: O movimento vem aumentando com a chegada do Natal, Vila Portes começa ter estrutura voltada para muambeiro," *A Gazeta do Iguaçu,* 1 December 1996, 7.

42. ConsBras Ciudad del Este, "I Festival de Compras e Turismo das Três Fronteiras," 9 June 1997, Itamaraty (Ministério de Relações Exteriores).

43. "Paraguai fica no Mercosul: Autoridades paraguaias desmentiram notícias de que Paraguai deixaria o Mercosul," *A Gazeta do Iguaçu,* 14 May 1992, 3; "O futuro de Ciudad del Este," *A Gazeta do Iguaçu,* 14 May 1992, 3.

44. Jackson Lima, "Exportações via Foz devem chegar a US$100 milhões: Em novembro foram exportados por Foz 78,2 milhões," *A Gazeta do Iguaçu,* 18 December 1994, 6.

45. "Aranceles," *El Territorio,* 18 September 1994.

46. Luigi Manzetti, "The Political Economy of Mercosur," *Journal of Interamerican Studies and World Affairs* 35.4 (1993-94): 101–41; Thomas Andrew O'Keefe, *Latin American and Caribbean Trade Agreements: Keys to a Prosperous Community of the Americas* (Leiden: Koninklijke Brill, 2009).

47. Humberto Paglia, "Eletrônicos importados vêm para o Brasil: Segundo o Banco Central do Paraguai 70% dos produtos importados vão para os lares brasileiros e argentinos," *A Gazeta do Iguaçu,* 4 February 1995.

48. José Maschio, "'Sacoleiros' enriquecem Paraguai," *Folha de S. Paulo,* 8 December 1994; James Brooke, "Foz do Iguaçu Journal: Smuggling, Yes, but Darker Crimes are Disowned," *New York Times,* January 11, 1995.

49. Antônio França, "Cota baixa pode trazer 180 mil desempregados: Com a redução da cota, a Câmara de Comércio Paraguaio Americano estima que a fronteira receberá uma carga de efeitos negativos," *A Gazeta do Iguaçu,* 16 November 1995, 7.

50. Fátima, 3 December 2008.

51. Brooke, "Foz do Iguaçu Journal."

52. Ricardo Grinbaum, "A fronteira da muamba," *Veja,* 26 July 1995, 77.

53. Paglia, "Eletrônicos importados vêm para o Brasil."

54. Grinbaum, "A fronteira da muamba."

55. Said Taijen, 28 November 2008.

56. Mihail Meskin Bazas, 17 September 2008.

57. Fátima, 3 December 2008.

58. "Greve repercute até nos EUA: Operação Padrão entra no 25° dia e quebra-
deira pode começar no comércio de Foz e Ciudad del Este—Até os comerciantes dos EUA estão reclamando," *A Gazeta do Iguaçu*, 5 May 1994, 1, 3–5.

59. Antônio França, "O homem que derrubou a quota," *A Gazeta do Iguaçu*, 9
November 1995, 10.

60. Antônio França, "Paraguai viveu 'dia de cão' ontem: Cerca de 90 mil brasileiros atravessaram a fronteira, aproveitando o último dia da cota de US$250,"
*A Gazeta do Iguaçu*, 16 November 1995, 6; França, "Cota baixa pode trazer 180
mil desempregados; "Comércio de Ciudad del Este recupera e venda ao com-
prista," *A Gazeta do Iguaçu*, 2 July 1998.

61. "Cota de US$150—Secretário prevê falências e aumento da criminalidade," *A
Gazeta do Iguaçu*, 22 October 1995, 11; "Cota de compras—Protesto de para-
guaios pode fechar a ponte hoje," *A Gazeta do Iguaçu*, 27 October 1995, 3;
França, "O Homem que derrubou a quota."

62. "Empresário faz críticas a FHC," *A Gazeta do Iguaçu*, 16 November 1995, 7.

63. Ibid.

64. França, "Cota baixa pode trazer 180 mil desempregados"; Antônio França,
"Paraguai faz campanha para combater pirataria," *A Gazeta do Iguaçu*, 21 January 1997, 7.

65. Antônio França, "Paraguaios ameaçam fechar as portas dia 27," *A Gazeta do
Iguaçu*, 25 June 1996, 16; Antônio França, "Protesto no Paraguai vai fechar
95% do comércio," *A Gazeta do Iguaçu*, 27 June 1996, 5; "Protesto deixa Ciudad del Este com clima de feriado," *A Gazeta do Iguaçu*, 28 June 1996, 5;
"Comerciantes del Este cerrarán sus puertas," *ABC Color*, 27 June 1996, 46; "El
90% del comercio de Ciudad del Este paró ayer," *ABC Color*, 28 June 1996, 48.

66. "Ciudad del Este faz 39 anos com crise e festa," *A Gazeta do Iguaçu*, 4 February
1996, 16.

67. "Protesto deixa Ciudad del Este com clima de feriado: Comerciantes fecham
as lojas em protesto contra a falta de segurança," *A Gazeta do Iguaçu*, 28 June
1996, 5.

68. "Câmara de Comércio é contra a paralização," *A Gazeta do Iguaçu*, 25 June
1996, 16.

69. "Câmara de Comércio diz que protesto será isolado," *A Gazeta do Iguaçu*, 27
June 1996, 5.

70. "Câmara de Comércio é contra a paralização," *A Gazeta do Iguaçu*, 25 June
1996, 16.

71. Sônia Inês Vendrame, "Ciudad del Este quer o retorno de turista verdadeiro
na região: Desvalorização do real assusta importadores e provoca queda
de 80% nas vendas," *A Gazeta do Iguaçu*, 24 January 1999, 4; Sônia Inês Vendrame, "40 mil empregos estão ameaçados: Paraguai poderá implantar cota
para compras que começam a ser feitas no Brasil (Entrevista com Charif
Hammoud)," *A Gazeta do Iguaçu*, 24 January 1999, 5.

72. "Sociedade: Oswald Damião devidamente anfitrionado por Sharif Hammoud
comemora os 150 anos de Cartier," *A Gazeta do Iguaçu*, 17 December 1997,
10; "Boutique Cartier abrió sus puertas en elegante brindis," *ABC Color*, 17
December 1997, 58–59.

73. Juan Carlos, 29 August 2008; "Acta Fundacional y Estatutos del Consorcio de Proprietarios del Paraná Country Club," 31 July 1992.

74. McSherry, "Strategic Alliance," 69.

75. "Que se dijeron Menem y Clinton," *Clarín*, 17 October 1997; Brasemb Buenos Aires, "Fronteira Tríplice," MRE, 4 March 1998.

76. "La CIA informó a Menem sobre la Triple Frontera," *La Nación*, 19 December 1997.

77. Gabriel Pasquini, "Fronteras: Presión de Clinton al Mercosur," *La Nación*, 16 December 1997; "Los EEUU amenazan con sancionar a Paraguay: La Triple Frontera," *Clarín*, 19 December 1997.

78. McSherry, "Strategic Alliance," 67.

79. "Los EEUU amenazan con sancionar a Paraguay: La Triple Frontera," *Clarín*, 19 December 1997.

80. Marcelo Soares and Sérgio Léo, "Ministros do Mercosul em Foz para discutir terrorismo," *A Gazeta do Iguaçu*, 14 December 1997, 1, 5; "Agentes de vários países buscan datos de terrorismo en C. del Este," *ABC Color*, 1 December 1997, 79; "Unidad de contraterrorismo y tráfico de armas en Paraguay," *ABC Color*, 10 December 1997, 98; "Menem y Cardoso admiten presencia de terroristas en las Tres Fronteras," *ABC Color*, 16 December 1997, 100; "Situación de Ciudad del Este inquietaría a EE.UU," *ABC Color*, 17 December 1997, 103; "Vigilan a grupo de árabes sospechosos en C. del Este," *ABC Color*, 20 December 1997, 66; "No hay grupos terroristas, pero sí una mafia oriental," *ABC Color*, 24 December 1997, 70.

81. "Tres Fronteras es un 'punto difícil' en lucha contra terrorismo," *ABC Color*, 4 December 1997, 68.

82. In Spanish, "un santuario único en el mundo." W. Curia, "Triple Frontera: Graves denuncias de Corach," *Clarín*, 21 November 1997; "Menem ordenó a Corach moderar sus denuncias," *Clarín*, 22 November 1997; "El gobierno toma nuevas medidas para aumentar el control en la triple frontera," *Clarín*, 28 November 1997; "Corach ahora niega haber calificado a Ciudad del Este como 'santuario de la corrupción,'" *ABC Color*, 18 December 1997, 78.

83. "Corach logró avances por la seguridad en la Triple Frontera," *Clarín*, 25 February 1998; "Argentinos admitem progresso na segurança das 3 fronteiras," *A Gazeta do Iguaçu*, 26 February 1998, 1, 11.

84. "El jefe del FBI entregará en un mes un informe sobre la AMIA," *Clarín*, 13 May 1998; "Respaldó Freeh al juez Galeano," *La Nación*, 13 May 1998; "Puesto a punto con el FBI," *Clarín*, 14 May 1998; Brasemb Buenos Aires, "Argentina. Terrorismo e crime organizado. Visita do director do FBI. Tríplice Fronteira . . .," MRE, 20 May 1998.

85. "Governo americano vai financiar ações antiterror," *A Gazeta do Iguaçu*, 17 March 1998, 9; Brasemb Buenos Aires, "Política Externa. Argentina-EUA. Visita do chefe da SIDE a Washington," MRE, 26 February 1999.

86. Jack Epstein, "Where Tourism Meets Terrorism," *US News & World Report*, 8 August 1994, 38.

87. Brooke, "Foz do Iguacu Journal."

88. "Ciudad del Este, bajo sospecha," *El Cronista Comercial*, 23 November 1995.

89. César Sánchez Bonifato, "Paraguay: Show del contrabando," *La Nación*, 17 January 1996.

90. Javier Calvo, "Ciudad del Este, el paraíso de los narcos, el contrabando y las armas," *Clarín*, 2 May 1996; Javier Calvo, "Niegan que haya terroristas en Ciudad del Este," *Clarín*, 3 May 1996.

91. Brasemb Assunção, "Repercussões na imprensa e nos meios diplomáticos e governamentais do Paraguai . . . sobre a existência de relatório da inteligência argentina no qual autoridades paraguaias são acusadas . . .," MRE, 1 July 1998.

92. Grinbaum, "A fronteira da muamba."

93. Jack Shaheen, *Reel Bad Arabs: How Hollywood Vilifies a People* (Northhampton: Interlink Publishing Group, 2001); "Vereadores repudiam reportagem da 'Veja,'" *A Gazeta do Iguaçu*, 3 August 1995, 3; "'Fronteira da Muamba: Empresários indignados com reportagem da 'Veja,'"*A Gazeta do Iguaçu*, 8 August 1995, 3.

94. "Fronteira ganha Câmara de Comércio Árabe-Paraguaia: Entidade está aberta a participação de empresário de Foz," *A Gazeta do Iguaçu*, 12 December 1997, 10; Ricardo Jiménez, Mário, and Ayala, PRF, 22 April 2009.

95. "Câmara Árabe-Paraguaia desconhece os terroristas," *A Gazeta do Iguaçu*, 19 December 1997, 1, 7.

96. "Árabes trabajarán por la integración," *ABC Color*, 17 December 1997, 5.

97. "Câmara Árabe-Paraguaia desconhece os terroristas," *A Gazeta do Iguaçu*, 19 December 1997, 1, 7.

98. "Barakat entrega carta ao ministro," *A Gazeta do Iguaçu*, 18 December 1997, 7.

99. Jorge Elías, "Mayor apoyo de los EE.UU. al control en la triple frontera," *La Nación*, 24 February 1998.

100. "Acordaron un plan de seguridad para la Triple Frontera," *Clarín*, 28 March 1998.

101. Corach and Baizán, *La Respuesta Argentina*, 104–15; Andrea Oelsner, "Consensus and Governance in Mercosur: The Evolution of the South American Security Agenda," *Security Dialogue* 40.2 (2009): 208; Etiene Coelho Martins, *Direito internacional e segurança pública* (São Paulo: Biblioteca 24 Horas, 2011), 49, 128.

102. Corach and Baizán, *La Respuesta Argentina*, 116–18; Andrea Oelsner, "Mercosur's Incipient Security Governance," in *The Security Governance of Regional Organizations*, eds. Emil Kirchner and Roberto Domínguez (New York: Routledge, 2011), 201, 208.

103. "Unfair Visa Profiles," *New York Times*, 29 January 1998.

104. Said Taijen, 28 November 2008; Said Taijen, 16 June 2009.

105. Said Taijen, 16 June 2009.

106. Mihail Meskin Bazas, 17 September 2008.

107. "EUA mais perto de C. del Este: Empresários abrem filial da Câmara de Comércio Paraguaio-Americano, *A Gazeta do Iguaçu*, 13 May 1995, 23; "Miembros residentes Ciudad del Este," www.pamcham.com.py/afiliados_cde.php (date of access: 16 June 2009). For the new website and website owner, see usparaguaychamber.org (date of access: 28 August 2020).

108. Said Taijen, 16 June 2009; www.pamcham.com.py (date of access: 16 June 2009). For the new website and website owner, see usparaguaychamber.org (date of access: 28 August 2020).

109. Nilton Bobato, "PF inicia operações para pegar estrangeiros ilegais," *A Gazeta do Iguaçu*, 7 January 1998, 5.

110. "Tráfico de gente—PF inicia operações para pegar estrangeiros ilegais," *A Gazeta do Iguaçu*, 21 December 1997; Nilton Bobato, "PF inicia operações para pegar estrangeiros ilegais," *A Gazeta do Iguaçu*, 7 January 1998, 5.
111. "Ministros do Mercosul discutem as Três Fronteiras em Assunção," *A Gazeta do Iguaçu*, 14 January 1998, 7; "Ministro confirma as ações contra possíveis terroristas," *A Gazeta do Iguaçu*, 14 January 1998, 7.
112. "PF prende 200 estrangeiros irregulares na área da Ponte," *A Gazeta do Iguaçu*, 15 January 1998, 14; "Mais de 100 estrangeiros ilegais serão deportados," *A Gazeta do Iguaçu*, 16 January 1998, 16, "Operações contra a ilegalidade nas três fronteiras vão continuar," *A Gazeta do Iguaçu*, 17 January 1998, 7.
113. "PF prende 200 estrangeiros irregulares na área da Ponte," *A Gazeta do Iguaçu*, 15 January 1998, 14; "Mais de 100 estrangeiros ilegais serão deportados," *A Gazeta do Iguaçu*, 16 January 1998, 16; "Operações contra a ilegalidade nas três fronteiras vão continuar," *A Gazeta do Iguaçu*, 17 January 1998, 7.
114. "Ministros decidem intensificar controle na Tríplice Fronteira," *A Gazeta do Iguaçu*, 18 January 1998, 1, 5; "Quem são os fronteiriços?" *A Gazeta do Iguaçu*, 17 January 1998, 7.
115. "PF fez nova operação e deteve mais estrangeiros irregulares," *A Gazeta do Iguaçu*, 8 February 1998, 14.
116. "Câmara árabe-paraguaia pede o cadastramento de seus cidadãos," *A Gazeta do Iguaçu*, 28 January 1998, 1, 12; "Árabes e chineses ameaçam demitir todos os brasileiros," *A Gazeta do Iguaçu*, 6 February 1998, 7.
117. "Corach logró avances por la seguridad en la Triple Frontera," *Clarín*, 25 February 1998.
118. "Corach and Baizán, *La Respuesta Argentina Frente al Terrorismo*, 155–59.
119. "Argentinos admitem progresso na segurança das 3 fronteiras," *A Gazeta do Iguaçu*, 26 February 1998, 1, 11.
120. Irina Hauser, "Corach pasó de canillita a campeón," *Página/12*, 4 August 1998. In Spanish, "Soy neoliberal y por eso creo que para ayudar a los pobres hay que enriquecer más a los ricos."
121. "PF aperta fiscalização na Ponte da Amizade," *A Gazeta do Iguaçu*, 3 April 1998, 3; "Procuradoria vai investigar PF: Procurador da República viu indícios de absuos na fiscalização de estrangeiros," *A Gazeta do Iguaçu*, 8 April 1998, 25; "'Prioridade deve ser a orientação sobre o Estatuto do Estrangeiro,'" *A Gazeta do Iguaçu*, 9 April 1998, 5; "PF não encontra evidências de terror nas três fronteiras: Diretor da PF, Vicente Chelotti, diz que não encontrou terroristas ou grupos de apoio na fronteira," *A Gazeta do Iguaçu*, 10 July 1998, 27.
122. "Prioridade deve ser a orientação sobre o Estatuto do Estrangeiro," *A Gazeta do Iguaçu*, 9 April 1998, 5; "Balanço geral da 'Rede Brasil,'" *A Gazeta do Iguaçu*, 9 April 1998, 5.
123. "Procuradoria vai investigar PF: Procurador da República viu indícios de absuos na fiscalização de estrangeiros," *A Gazeta do Iguaçu*, 8 April 1998, 25; "Procurador abre inquérito na 2a," *A Gazeta do Iguaçu*, 9 April 1998, 5.
124. "Renan Calheiros pediu abertura de inquérito para investigar PF," *A Gazeta do Iguaçu*, 30 April 1998, 1, 5.
125. "Corregedor investiga operação Rede Brasil," *A Gazeta do Iguaçu*, 6 June 1998, 5.
126. "Temor Argentino: PF não encontra evidências de terror nas três fronteiras," *A Gazeta do Iguaçu*, 10 June 1998.

127. Sergio Torres, "País vai anistiar estrangeiros clandestinos," *Folha de S. Paulo*, 19 June 1998; Sônia Inês Vendrame, "Brasil vai anistiar estrangeiros ilegais," *A Gazeta do Iguaçu*, 6 September 1998; "Foz tem quase 6 mil estrangeiros ilegais," *A Gazeta do Iguaçu*, 6 September 1998; Sônia Inês Vendrame, "Começa processo de anistia a estrangeiros," *A Gazeta do Iguaçu*, 9 September 1998, 27.

128. "Empresário diz que 'arrastões' da PF provocaram fuga em massa," *A Gazeta do Iguaçu*, 9 September 1998, 27; Sônia Cristina Silva, "Ministro vai ao Paraguai negociar situação de brasileiros irregulares," *A Gazeta do Iguaçu*, 7 November 1998, 4.

129. "Sindicato da PF critica 'Rede Brasil,'" *A Gazeta do Iguaçu*, 9 April 1998, 5; "Prioridade deve ser a orientação sobre o Estatuto do Estrangeiro," *A Gazeta do Iguaçu*, 9 April 1998, 5.

130. Wilson Tosta, "Abin abre concurso para agente secreto," *A Gazeta do Iguaçu*, 11 January 2000.

131. In Portuguese, "Grupos étnicos islâmicos no País: Identificação e localização de grupos étnicos islâmicos no País." Policarpo Junior, "O Documento Secreto da Espionagem," *Veja*, 22 November 2000, 42–47.

132. Hector Guerín, "La industria de la extorsión en el Este," *ABC Color*, 4 January 1999, 14.

133. "Rastrean a dos libaneses integrantes de Hizbullah," *ABC Color*, 8 September 1998, 60; "Xeque islâmico nega relação com terrorismo," *A Gazeta do Iguaçu*, 12 September 1998, 3.

134. Hector Guerín, "La industria de la extorsión en el Este," *ABC Color*, 4 January 1999, 14.

135. Brasemb Assunção, "Assassinato do Presidente da Câmara de Comércio de Ciudad del Este," MRE, 9 November 1998.

136. "Contrabando humano no Mercosul: Esquema para libaneses desmontado no Paraguai," *A Gazeta do Iguaçu*, 22 October 1997, 1, 8–9.

137. Ibid.

138. "Soueid compara operação do PY à 'Rede Brasil' da PF," *A Gazeta do Iguaçu*, 12 September 1998, 3.

139. Ibid.

140. Gerardo Youn, "Triple Frontera: Un informe oficial compromete a Paraguay," *Clarín*, 30 June 1998; "Triple frontera e inseguridad," *Clarín*, 3 July 1998.

141. "Xeque islâmico nega relação com terrorismo," *A Gazeta do Iguaçu*, 12 September 1998, 3; Brooks, *Producing Security*, 157.

142. "Asesinan al presidente de la Cámara de Comercio de Ciudad del Este," *ABC Color*, 9 November 1998, 1; "Polícia investiga morte do empresário libanês, Hussein Teijen," *A Gazeta do Iguaçu*, 10 November 1998, 29, "Amigo de Hussein descarta ação terrorista," *A Gazeta do Iguaçu*, 10 November 1998, 29.

143. "Llegó al Paraguay hace 32 años," *ABC Color*, 9 November 1998, 70.

144. "Para Bower, pesquisa policial no convence en reunión con árabes," *ABC Color*, 17 November 1998, 85.

145. "Libanés duda de que Taijén haya sido asesinado por deudas," *ABC Color*, 13 November 1998, 101.

146. "Libaneses se sienten perseguidos," *ABC Color*, 14 November 1998, 75; "Embajador de Líbano protesta por imputaciónes a ciudadanos árabes," *ABC Color*,

16 November 1998, 85; Brasemb Assunção, "Relações Paraguai-Líbano . . .," MRE, 25 January 1999.

147. Brasemb Assunção, "Assassinato do presidente da Câmara de Comércio de Ciudad del Este," MRE, 12 November 1998. Without basis, *ABC Color* alleged that the author of the crime was Ahmed Kassem. See "Supuesto autor moral del crimen de Taijén habria huido del país," *ABC Color*, 22 November 1998, 66; "Comerciante libanés implicado en el asesinato de Taijén," *ABC Color*, 21 November 1998, 77; "Libanés buscado por muerte de Taijén estaría en su país: Se trata del empresário Armando Kassen," *ABC Color*, 23 November 1998, 68.

148. "Recibió amenazas de activistas islámicos," *ABC Color*, 9 November 1998, 71; "Arabes demostraron dolor, pero no quisieron opinar sobre el crimen," *ABC Color*, 9 November 1998, 71; "Rastrean a árabe del Hizbullah que llegó del Líbano el viernes," *ABC Color*, 10 November 1998, 85.

149. Alexandre Palmar, "Depoimentos começam a esclarecer crime," *A Gazeta do Iguaçu*, 11 November 1998, 33; "Presos os matadores do empresário libanês," *A Gazeta do Iguaçu*, 12 November 1998, 29.

150. "Libanés duda de que Taijén haya sido asesinado por deudas," *ABC Color*, 13 November 1998, 101.

151. "Cubas pidió que se esclarezca el caso," *ABC Color*, 10 November 1998, 85.

152. "Caso Taijén no frena inversión en el Este: Vendrán empresarios brasileños," *ABC Color*, 13 November 1998, 12.

153. "Se deben redoblar las medidas de seguridad," *ABC Color*, 9 November 1998, 71; Efraín Martínez Cuevas, "El crimen del empresario Taijén," *ABC Color*, 11 November 1998, 29.

154. "Barreto insinuó que Hussein andaba en 'cosas raras,'" *ABC Color*, 12 November 1998, 28.

155. "Crimen de Taijén deriva en una investigación sobre algunos árabes," *ABC Color*, 19 November 1998, 29.

## CHAPTER 5

1. "PY faz rastreamento em busca de suspeitos," *A Gazeta do Iguaçu*, 14 September 2001, 27; "La Argentina, Brasil y Paraguay vigilan juntos la Triple Frontera," *La Nación*, 14 September 2001.

2. "O terror por aqui," *Revista Época*, 22 October 2001, 36.

3. Melani McAlister, "A Cultural History of the War without End," *Journal of American History* 89.2 (2002): 439–55; Amy Kaplan, "Violent Belongings and the Question of Empire Today: Presidential Address to the American Studies Association, October 17, 2003," *American Quarterly* 56.1 (2004): 1–18.

4. Grace Livingstone, "George W. Bush and the 'War on Terror,'" in *America's Backyard: The United States and Latin America from the Monroe Doctrine to the War on Terror* (London: Zed Books, 2013).

5. Edward Said, *Beginnings: Intention and Method* (New York: Basic Books, 1975), 373.

6. Media turned a blind eye to the authoritarian echoes of counterterrorist interventions in South America. See Gianpaolo Baiocchi, "Media Coverage of

9–11 in Brazil," *Television & New Media* 3.2 (2002): 183–89; Francisco F. Gutié-rrez Sanín, Eric Hershberg, and Monica Hirst, "Change and Continuity in Hemispheric Affairs: Latin America after September 11," in *Critical Views of September 11*, eds. Eric Hershberg and Kevin Moore (New York: New Press, 2002), 177–90; Antônio La Pastina, "The Self-Absorbed Bully: A Brazilian View of the US at War," in *War, Media, and Propaganda*, ed. Yahya Kamalipour (New York: Rowman and Littlefield, 2004), 199–206; Kathleen Tobin, "Threat or Ally: US-Latin American Relations and the Middle East Conflict," in *War, Media, and Propaganda*, ed. Yahya Kamalipour (New York: Rowman and Lit-tlefield, 2004), 207–18.

7.  Catherine Lutz, "Militarization," in *A Companion to the Anthropology of Poli-tics*, eds. David Nugent and Joan Vincent (New York: Blackwell, 2004), 318–31.

8.  Brasemb Assunção, "Paraguai-EUA. Visita do Comandante do Comando Sul," MRE, 8 September 2003; Gordon Adams and Shoon Murray, eds., *Mission Creep: The Militarization of US Foreign Policy* (Washington, DC: Georgetown University Press, 2015).

9.  Renato Dagnino, *A indústria de defesa no governo Lula* (São Paulo: Editora Expressão Popular, 2010).

10.  Lambert, "Dancing between Superpowers," 67–86.

11.  Isabela, 3 October 2008.

12.  "PF reforça vigilância entre muçulmanos e judeus," *O Estado de S. Paulo*, 13 September 2001; "Fronteira sob suspeita," *Isto É*, 26 September 2001.

13.  Mark Hosenball, "Fighting Terror by Attacking . . . South America?" *Newsweek*, 8 August 2004, www.newsweek.com/fighting-terror-attacking-south-america-126355.

14.  United States Department of State, *Patterns of Global Terrorism 2000* (Washington, DC: Office of the Secretary of State, 2001), 44, 53–54.

15.  "EUA preocupados com a Tríplice Fronteira," *O Estado de S. Paulo*, 15 October 2001.

16.  "Brasileiros na rede do terrorismo," *O Globo*, 3 November 2011, 22.

17.  Fernanda Odilla e Rubens Valente, "Tríplice Fronteira gerou atrito com EUA: Telegramas do Itamaraty obtidos pela Folha mostram que país reclamou de 'satanização' da região por americanos," *Folha de S. Paulo*, 29 August 2011.

18.  "Entrevista/Alberto Cardoso: Tríplice fronteira financia o terror," *Correio Bra-ziliense*, 9 November 2001, 16; "Não existe terrorismo na fronteira," *A Gazeta do Iguaçu*, 21 November 2001, 3.

19.  "Brasil-Estados Unidos, Visita do Comandante-em-Chefe, interino, do Comando Sul," 6 December 2001, folhaleaks.folha.com.br. For current web-site owner, see www.folha.uol.com.br.

20.  Vicente Nunes, "Beija-mão na Casa Branca," *Correio Braziliense*, 9 November 2001, 16.

21.  Rubens Antonio Barbosa, "Brasil-EUA, Terrorismo, Fronteira triplice, Con-versa no Departamento de Estado," 5 October 2001, folhaleaks.folha.com.br; Rubens Antonio Barbosa, *O dissenso de Washington: Notas de um observador privilegiado sobre as relações Brasil-Estados Unidos* (Rio de Janeiro: Editora Nova Fronteira Participações, 2011).

22.  "Sâmis nega presença de terroristas na fronteira," *Hoje*, 9 November 2001, 6.

23. Câmara Municipal de Foz do Iguaçu, "Moção No 016/2001—Solidariedade à comunidade árabe residente em Foz do Iguaçu," 19 September 2001, Câmara Municipal de Foz do Iguaçu.

24. "Câmara presta homenagem à colônia árabe," *A Gazeta do Iguaçu*, 14 November 2001, 26.

25. Patrícia Iunovich, "Árabes temem perseguição indiscriminada em Foz," *A Gazeta do Iguaçu*, 14 September 2001, 27.

26. "Gregori diz que foi pressionado a encontrar terroristas," *O Estado de S. Paulo*, 13 November 2001.

27. "Los árabes de la Triple Frontera se burlan de las sospechas," *Clarín*, 16 September 2001.

28. Emerson Dias, "Árabes de Foz lamentam atentados," *Folha de Londrina*, 15 September 2001.

29. Ibid.

30. Mhamad Mahmoud Ismail, 12 July 2007; Elvio Seibert, "Árabes não vivem em guetos," *Hoje*, 24 October 2001, 6.

31. "Tensão no Brasil Árabe," *Correio Braziliense*, 29 September 2001, 8.

32. "Árabes denunciam perseguição," *Jornal do Iguaçu*, 12 October 2001, 4; Patrícia Iunovich, "Segurança na fronteira continua reforçada," *A Gazeta do Iguaçu*, 13 September 2001, 28; "Conflito pode gerar nova onda de xenofobia," *A Gazeta do Iguaçu*, 14 September 2001, 27; "Paraguai sob tensão," *Jornal do Iguaçu*, 13 September 2001, 6–7.

33. Fawas, 26 August 2008.

34. "Paraguay no está contra los árabes," *ABC Color*, 30 October 2001, 40; "Segurança é tema de reunião na fronteira," *Hoje*, 10 November 2002, 6.

35. Mora and Cooney, *Paraguay and the United States*, 260.

36. "Ciudad del Este, la otra orilla del Islam," *ABC Color*, 2 October 2001, 28.

37. "En Ciudad del Este se preguntan si sus árabes son 'buenos' o 'malos,'" *Los Andes*, 2 October 2001.

38. "Antiterroristas realizan trabajos de inteligencia en Ciudad del Este," *ABC Color*, 2 November 2001, 53; "Árabes são discriminados, *Jornal do Iguaçu*, 7 November 2001, 9.

39. "Carta al director," *ABC Color*, 1 October 2001.

40. "CNN pratica terrorismo contra a fronteira," *A Gazeta do Iguaçu*, 9 November, 2001, 4.

41. Ibid.

42. "Ciudad del Este, la otra orilla del Islam," *ABC Color*, 2 October 2001, 28.

43. "Opinión de autoridades y líderes de la región," *ABC Color*, 12 November 2001, 61.

44. United States Department of State, *Patterns of Global Terrorism 2001* (Washington, DC: Office of the Secretary of State, 2002), 49.

45. "Árabes," *Vanguardia*, 26 September 2001, 30; "Árabes acusam polícia antiterrorista de praticar chantagem em Ciudad del Este," *A Gazeta do Iguaçu*, 27 September, 2001, 1, 2.

46. "Presidente de comerciantes árabes, buscado por Interpol," *Misiones Online*, 25 September 2001.

47. "En Ciudad del Este se preguntan si sus árabes son 'buenos' o 'malos,'" *Los*

*Andes*, 2 October 2001; Laura Vales, "Bagalleros y custodios," *Pagina/12*, 30 September 2001.

48. Denise Paro, "Comunidade árabe contesta investigação," *Gazeta do Povo*, 18 October 2001, 3; "Conexão brasileira," *Revista Época*, 17 September 2001, 44–45.

49. "Opinión de representante," *Diario Vanguardia*, 12 November 2001, 3; Opinión de autoridades y líderes de la región," *ABC Color*, 12 November 2001, 61.

50. Brasemb Assunção, "Paraguai. Tríplice Fronteira. Combate ao terrorismo," MRE, 31 October, 2001, 2; "Paraguay no está contra los árabes," *ABC Color*, 30 October 2001, 40.

51. Ali Said Rahal and son Fawas, 16 September 2008.

52. "Las huellas de Bin Laden que la SIDE encontró en la Triple Frontera," *Clarín*, 16 September 2001; Gerardo Young, "En la Triple Frontera siguen una pista que lleva a Bin Laden," *Clarín*, 17 September 2001.

53. "Refuerzan la seguridad en Comodoro Py," *La Nación*, 17 September 2001; Osvaldo Albano, "Cuestión judicial o de Estado," *Ámbito Financeiro*, 24 September 2001; "La seguridad en la Triple Frontera," *Clarín*, 27 September 2001.

54. Martín Rodríguez Yebra, "Fuerzas de elite en la Triple Frontera," *La Nación*, 26 September 2001; "Triple frontera: Argentina se queja de Brasil y Paraguay," *Clarín*, 28 September 2001; "Argentina reforça segurança na fronteira para cooperar com EUA," *Folha de S. Paulo,* 24 September 2001; "Misiones: Ejercicio militar con EE.UU.," *Clarín*, 28 September 2000.

55. Carlos Menem, "Somos parte de esta lucha," *Clarín*, 20 September 2001.

56. United States Department of State, *Patterns of Global Terrorism 2002* (Washington, DC: Office of the Secretary of State, 2003), 71.

57. Montenegro and Giménez Béliveau, *La triple frontera: Globalización y construcción*; Roberto Russell, "Argentina and the United States: A Distant Relationship," in *Contemporary US-Latin American Relations: Cooperation or Conflict in the 21st Century?*, eds. Jorge Domínguez and Rafael Fernández de Castro (New York: Routledge, 2010), 101.

58. Elvio Seibert, "Autoridades negam a presença de terroristas," *Hoje*, 31 October 2001, 6.

59. "Comitê tripartite descarta terrorismo na fronteira," *A Gazeta do Iguaçu*, 31 October 2001, 7.

60. Howell and Shryock, "Cracking Down on Diaspora," 443–62.

61. "Interpol investiga telefones de Foz," *A Gazeta do Iguaçu*, 16 October 2001, 4; "PF estoura duas centrais clandestinas," *A Gazeta do Iguaçu*, 20 October 2001, 29.

62. US Department of State, *Patterns of Global Terrorism 2001*, 49.

63. "Libanês diz que tarifas altas induzem às fraudes," *Hoje*, 25 November 2001.

64. José Paulo Netto, *Pequena história da ditadura brasileira (1964–1985)* (São Paulo: Cortez Editora, 2016).

65. Elvio Seibert, "Delegado descarta máfia do DDI com terrorismo," *Hoje*, 20 October 2001, 6.

66. "Cresce movimento pela Paz," *A Gazeta do Iguaçu*, 4 November 2001, 8.

67. Elvio Seibert, "Árabes não vivem em guetos," *Hoje*, 24 October 2001, 6.

68. "Lerner vem à Foz para ato pela paz," *Jornal do Iguaçu*, 2 November 2001, 10.

69.  Elvio Seibert, "Foz em Notas: Causa Árabe," *Hoje*, 6 November 2001, 4.

70.  "Evento pode reunir 3 presidentes," *A Gazeta do Iguaçu*, 16 October 2001, 4; "Foz é mais segura que Londres," *A Gazeta do Iguaçu*, 9 November 2001, 5.

71.  "Embajada de EE.UU en Brasil informará a Bush sobre el acto," *Avance*, 1 November 2001, 3.

72.  "Não devemos querer pagar com a mesma moeda," *A Gazeta do Iguaçu*, 9 November 2001, 2; "Pobladores de la zona dirán 'paz' ante acusaciones de terrorismo," *Diario Vanguardia*, 7 November 2001, 3.

73.  "Guerra a la mala imagem," *Diario Vanguardia* (Ciudad del Este), 10/11 November 2001, 2; "Multitudinaria convocatoria abogó por la paz y repudió propaganda contra la frontera," *Avance*, 12 November 2001.

74.  "Guerra a la mala imagem," *Diario Vanguardia*, 10/11 November 2001, 2.

75.  The presence of the state at the event was not uniform. The federal senators from the state of Paraná, Álvaro Dias (PDT) and Osmar Dias (PDT), criticized the absence of then president Fernando Henrique Cardoso, though his message of solidarity was read at the beginning of the event. Álvaro Dias declared: "This shows that the president of the Republic doesn't care at all about matters regarding the border region" ("Ausência do governo é criticada por senadores," *Jornal de Hoje*, 13 November 2001).

76.  "40 mil pessoas unidas pela paz: Brasil, Paraguai e Argentina disseram não ao terror no ato Paz Sem Fronteiras," *A Gazeta do Iguaçu*, 12 November 2001; Sônia Inês Vendrame, "Cerca de 40 mil pedem paz," *A Gazeta do Iguaçu*, 12 November 2001.

77.  "Ato em Foz do Iguaçu reúne 15 mil," *Folha de S. Paulo*, 12 November 2001.

78.  "40 mil clama pela paz na fronteira: Lideranças condenaram notícias sobre terrorismo na fronteira," *O Paraná*, 13 November 2001.

79.  "Políticos criticam condenação da fronteira," *A Gazeta do Iguaçu*, 12 November 2001, 4.

80.  "40 mil clama pela paz na fronteira: Lideranças condenaram notícias sobre terrorismo na fronteira," *O Paraná*, 13 November 2001.

81.  "Autoridades cuestionaron las acusaciones sobre la región," *Diario Vanguardia*, 12 November 2001, 3; "Triple Frontera se une para decir no 'al terrorismo y sí a la paz,'" *Ultima Hora*, 12 November 2001, 3.

82.  Ulf Hannerz, *Foreign News: Exploring the World of Foreign Correspondents* (Chicago: University of Chicago Press, 2004), 103. I was only able to locate one news story issued by the Associated Press: see Stan Lehman, "South American Tri-Border Region Said to Harbor Terrorists Stages Giant Peace Rally," Associated Press Online & Worldstream, 11 November 2001. European newswire services, such as Reuters and France Presse, gave greater news coverage.

83.  I was unable to locate any coverage of Paz sem Fronteiras in major Argentine newspapers, including *Clarín* and *La Nación*. For Brazilian and Paraguayan coverage, see "Tríplice Fronteira: Ato em Foz do Iguaçu reúne 15 mil," *Folha de S. Paulo*, 12 November 2001; "Árabes de Foz se dizem vítimas de conspiração," *Folha de S. Paulo*, 9 November 2001; Mauri Kônig, "Comércio faz manifestação de desagravo," *O Estado de S. Paulo*, 12 November 2001; "Movimento para resgatar imagem da região," *O Globo*, 4 November 2001; "Triple Frontera se une para decir no 'al terrorismo y sí a la paz,'" *Ultima Hora*, 12 November

2001; "Unas 30,000 personas claman por la paz, en Foz de Yguazú," *ABC Color*, 12 November 2001.

84. "40 mil pessoas unidas pela paz: Brasil, Paraguai e Argentina disseram não ao terror no ato Paz Sem Frontieras," *A Gazeta do Iguaçu*, 12 November 2001; Sônia Inês Vendrame, "Cerca de 40 mil pedem paz," *A Gazeta do Iguaçu*, 12 November 2001.

85. "Paz sin fronteras, un mensaje de comunión en Foz do Iguazu," *Misiones Online*, 12 November 2001.

86. "Guerra a la mala imagem," *Diario Vanguardia*, 10/11 November 2001, 2; "Multitudinaria convocatoria abogó por la paz y repudió propaganda contra la frontera," *Avance*, 12 November 2001.

87. Marcio Aith, "Powell elogia Brasil e critica Argentina," *Folha de S. Paulo*, 7 May 2002; "EUA insiste em paranóia terrorista," *A Gazeta do Iguaçu*, 4 May 2002, 4; Amaral, *A Tríplice Fronteira e a Guerra ao Terror*, 195.

88. "Jefe militar de EE.UU. considera a Paraguay un gran amigo antiterrorista," *ABC Color*, 18 October 2002, 20; Esteban Areco, "Las tres fronteras es propensa al terrorismo," *Noticias*, 23 October 2002, 35.

89. "Prefeito rechaça as declarações sobre terrorismo em Foz," *Hoje*, 8 May 2002, 9; Maurício Bevervanso, "Líderes refutam declarações americanas," *A Gazeta do Iguaçu*, 8 May 2002, 5.

90. Fawas, 7 September 2008.

91. Rogério Bonato, 26 August 2008.

92. Yahya, 3 October 2008.

93. Fawas, 4 December 2008.

94. "Bilal Mohsen Wehbe, Portaria N9 1.329," Brazilian Ministry of Justice, *Diário Oficial da União*, 30 December 1997, 22.

95. Fawas, 7 September 2008.

96. Ricardo Galhardo, "Árabes da fronteira denunciam perseguição," *O Globo*, 4 November 2001, 34.

97. "Comuna apoyaría demanda contra CNN por acusación de terrorismo," *Diario Vanguardia*, 11 December 2002, 3.

98. "Mais um comerciante árabe é preso," *A Gazeta do Iguaçu*, 11 November 2001, 42.

99. "Comuna apoyaría demanda contra CNN por acusación de terrorismo," *Diario Vanguardia*, 11 December 2002, 3.

100. "Acusaciones sobre terrorismo se originan en Ciudad del Este," *Diario Vanguardia*, 17 January 2005, 2; "Ordenan detención de ex intendentes," *ABC Color*, 19 October 2002.

101. "Ordenan detención de ex intendentes," *ABC Color*, 19 October 2002.

102. "Hoy se recuerda el Día Nacional de Independencia de República del Líbano," *Diario Vanguardia*, 22 November 2002, 9.

103. "Contrabando humano no Mercosul—Esquema para libaneses desmontado no Paraguai," *A Gazeta do Iguaçu*, 22 October 1997, 1, 8–9.

104. "'Fueron utilizados para acusarme', asegura el libanés Ali Zaioun," *ABC Color*, 16 April 2004.

105. "Acusaciones sobre terrorismo se originan en Ciudad del Este," *Diario Vanguardia*, 17 January 2005, 2.

106. Ibid. This Hijazi was mentioned in the United States Department of State's *Country Reports on Terrorism 2006*, not as a potentially duplicitous informant but rather for allegedly being a "Hizballah [*sic*] money launderer." See: United States Department of State, *Country Reports on Terrorism 2006* (Washington, DC: Office of the Coordinator of Counterterrorism, 2007), 2009–17. state.gov/j/ct/rls/crt/2006/82735.htm.

107. Ibid.

108. Mora and Cooney, *Paraguay and the United States,* 261.

109. "Niegan versión sobre presunta reunión de líderes terroristas," *Diario Vanguardia*, 9/10 November 2002, 3; "Informantes de la Policía Antiterrorista dan datos falsos sobre terrorismo," *Diario Vanguardia*, 23/24 November 2002, 3.

110. Andrés Colmán Gutiérrez, "Las contradictorias facetas de Marito," *Ultima Hora*, 15 September 2018.

111. "Antiterrorista destaca elogio de los EE.UU.," *ABC Color*, 2 May 2003.

112. "Denuncian a libanés de extorsionar a sus paisanos," *ABC Color*, 13 December 2003; "Abogado de libanés niega supuesta extorsión y chantaje," *ABC Color*, 15 December 2003.

113. "Fiscala investiga a asesor antiterrorista de la Corte," *ABC Color*, 29 August 2003.

114. José Maschio, "Acusado de terror preso no Brasil quer processar CNN," *Folha de S. Paulo,* 19 November 2002; "Paraguaios protestam contra acusações," *A Gazeta do Iguaçu*, 1 November 2002, 5; "Niegan versión sobre presunta reunión de líderes terroristas," *Diario Vanguardia*, 9/10 November 2002, 3; "Informantes de la Policía Antiterrorista dan datos falsos sobre terrorismo," *Diario Vanguardia*, 23/24 November 2002, 3.

115. Lourival Sant'Anna, "Briga comercial dá impulso a acusações," *O Estado de S. Paulo*, 22 June 2003.

116. "Denuncian a libanês de extorsionar a sus paisanos," *ABC Color*, 13 December 2003.

117. "Denuncian a libanês de extorsionar a sus paisanos," *ABC Color*, 13 December 2003; "Allanan negocio de Alí Zaioun," *ABC Color*, 2 December 2008.

118. Lourival Sant'Anna, "Briga comercial dá impulso a acusações," *O Estado de S. Paulo*, 22 June 2003.

119. "Abogado de libanés niega supuesta extorsión y chantaje," *ABC Color*, 15 December 2003.

120. "Paraguai quer Interpol em caso de libanês investigado," *Folha de S. Paulo*, 8 November 2001; "Mais um comerciante árabe é preso," *A Gazeta do Iguaçu*, 11 November 2001, 42; "Barakat rompe su silencio de fugitivo," *Diario Vanguardia*, 10/11 November 2001, 2.

121. US Department of State, *Patterns of Global Terrorism 2002*, 72.

122. Silvana de Freitas and José Maschio, "Brasil vai extraditar suspeito de terror," *Folha de S. Paulo*, 20 December 2002; Supremo Tribunal Federal, Acórdão no. 853 de Tribunal Pleno, 5 September 2003.

123. "Resck denunció ante la OEA y ONU al fiscal Carlos Cálcena por maltratos," *La Nación*, October 18, 2001; José Machio, "Paraguai mostra ligação Foz-Hizbollah," *Folha de S. Paulo*, 26 November 2001; "Ex fiscal Cálcena es procesado por apropriarse de dólares de un narco," *ABC Color*, 20 February 2004.

124. Stan Lehman, "Wanted by Paraguay, Hezbollah supporter is free in Brazilian town across the border," *Associated Press*, 12 December 2001; Lourival Sant'Anna, "Pedido de extradição paraguaio converteu Barakat de protegido em detido," *O Estado de S. Paulo*, 22 June 2003.

125. José Maschio, "Acusado de terrorismo, libanês de Foz vê 'ignorância,'" *Folha de S. Paulo*, 13 November 2001; José Maschio, "Paraguai mostra ligação Foz-Hizbollah," *Folha de S. Paulo*, 26 November 2001.

126. "Foz tenta se recuperar dos prejuízos de boato terrorista," *Agência Globo*, 21 December 2002.

127. "Zaioun y su grupo crean zozobras entre sus paisanos," *ABC Color*, 9 June 2005.

128. "Tribunal condenó a Barakat a 6 años de cárcel, por evasión," *Noticias*, 13 May 2004, 51; "Barakat responde por evasión pero lo involucran en terrorismo," *Noticias*, 12 May 2004, 51; "Por evasión, tribunal condena a Barakat a seis años de cárcel," *ABC Color*, 13 May 2004, 46.

129. "Libanés monopoliza comercio pirata," *ABC Color*, 21 February 2005; "Zaioun y su grupo crean zozobras entre sus paisanos," *ABC Color*, 9 June 2005.

130. "Niegan presiones contra los árabes," *ABC Color*, 9 June 2005.

131. United States Department of State, *Country Reports on Terrorism 2004* (Washington, DC: Office of the Coordinator of Counterterrorism, 2005), 85.

132. Lambert, "Dancing between Superpowers."

133. Mora and Cooney, *Paraguay and the United States*, 263.

134. Lambert, "Dancing between Superpowers."

135. "Barakat responde por evasión pero lo involucran en terrorismo," *Noticias*, 12 May 2004, 51; "Abogado denuncia manipulación judicial en el proceso a Barakat," *ABC Color*, 17 May 2004.

136. Lourival Sant'anna, "Caso Barakat," *O Estado de S. Paulo*, 22 June 2004, 18.

137. "Comunidad árabe de CDE está en zozobra," *Diario Vanguardia*, 21 March 2003, 3.

138. José Machio, "Agora, EUA descartam terror na Tríplice Fronteira, *Folha de S. Paulo*, 19 December 2002; "Agentes americanos confirman que no hay terroristas en triple frontera," *Diario Vanguardia*, 19 December 2002, 1, 15; "EEUU reconoció que no existen terroristas en las Tres Fronteras," *Noticias*, 19 December 2002, 15.

139. United States Department of State, *Patterns of Global Terrorism 2003* (Washington, DC: Office of the Coordinator of Counterterrorism, 2004) 78–79.

140. Brasemb Assunção, "Relatório do Departamento de Estado sobre terrorismo reflete postura mais moderada sobre a Tríplice Fronteira," MRE, 4 May 2004.

141. Maurício Bevervanso, "Monblatt pede transparência nas remessas," *A Gazeta do Iguaçu*, 4 August 2003, 7; "OEA pide 'transparencia' en la zona de las Tres Fronteras," *Noticias*, 2 August 2003, 22.

142. Cláudio Camargo and Eduardo Hollanda, "Donna Hrinak," *Isto É*, 31 August 2003; "'Não há terror em Foz,' afirma embaixadora," *A Gazeta do Iguaçu*, 1 September 2003, 5.

143. "Jefe militar de EE.UU. considera a Paraguay un gran amigo antiterrorista," *ABC Color*, 18 October 2002, 20; Esteban Areco, "Las tres fronteras es propensa al terrorismo," *Noticias*, 23 October 2002, 35; "Terrorists / South

America," *Voice of America News*, 9 January 2003.

144. Robert Mueller, "Predicting and Preventing Terrorist Attacks," speech given at Border Terrorism Conference, San Antonio, TX, 8 September 2003, www.fbi.gov/news/speeches/predicting-and-preventing-terrorist-attacks. For current website, see archives.fbi.gov/archives/news/speeches/predicting-and-preventing-terrorist-attacks.

145. "Bin Laden Reportedly Spent Time in Brazil in '95," *Washington Post*, 18 March 2003, 24.

146. Policarpo Júnior, "Ele esteve no Brasil," *Veja*, 19 March 2003. See also "Bin Laden esteve em Foz do Iguaçu e até deu palestra em mesquita," *O Estado de S. Paulo*, 16 March 2003; "Bin Laden esteve no Brasil, afirma 'Veja,'" *Folha de S. Paulo*, 17 March 2003.

147. "'Bin Laden nunca esteve em Foz,' diz Ali Rahal," *A Gazeta do Iguaçu*, 20 March 2003, 6.

148. "Se o vídeo existe, nós queremos vê-lo," *A Gazeta do Iguaçu*, 20 March 2002, 7; "Dirigentes islámicos de Foz desmienten afirmación sobre presencia de Bin Laden," *Diario Vanguardia*, 21 March 2003, 3.

149. Jackson Lima, "Os cristãos quase nada sabem sobre o islã," *Classe 10* 1.3 (1996), 14–15; Antônio França, "Árabes na fronteira," *A Gazeta do Iguaçu*, 16 February 1996, 1, 7, "Embaixador retribui hospitalidade de Foz," *A Gazeta do Iguaçu*, 27 March 1997, 8.

150. "'Bin Laden nunca esteve em Foz,' diz Ali Rahal," *A Gazeta do Iguaçu*, 20 March 2003, 6.

151. Shohat and Stam, *Unthinking Eurocentrism*, 48.

152. "Hospitalidade da Colônia Árabe impressiona o Ministro Hariri," *A Gazeta do Iguaçu*, 12 June 2003, 6.

153. "Gobierno de Lula decide esta semana suerte de Barakat," *ABC Color*, 23 June 2003.

154. Press release of Rafic Hariri, 13 June 2003, www.rhariri.net.

155. "Hospitalidade da Colônia Árabe impressiona o Ministro Hariri," *A Gazeta do Iguaçu*, 12 June 2003, 6.

156. "Foz: Uma casa libanesa, com certeza!" *A Gazeta do Iguaçu*, 10 September 2003, 9.

157. "Ministro libanês vem a Foz definir consulado," *A Gazeta do Iguaçu*, 6/7 September 2003, 9.

158. "Vice-ministro libanês elogia o civismo," *A Gazeta do Iguaçu*, 8 September 2003, 5.

159. Ibid.

160. "Lebanon to Re-open Embassy in Paraguay," press release of Rafic Hariri, 10 July 2003, www.rhariri.net.

161. "EE.UU. asesorará a Paraguay en leyes antiterroristas," *Diara Vanguardia*, 14/15 June 2003, 4.

162. "Líbano reabre embajada en Paraguay luego de 7 años," *ABC Color*, 17 January 2004; "Líbano reabre embajada y busca ser socio estratégico de Paraguay," *Nacion*, 17 January 2004; "Escaparon del horror en Beirut y ya están en la Argentina," *La Nación*, 24 July 2006.

163. "Embajador quiere saber por qué están detenidos dos libaneses," *ABC Color*,

17 January 2004.

164. Fawas, 29 May 2009

165. Agência Brasil, "Chefe do Gabinete de Segurança Institucional fala na Câmara sobre atribuições de sua Pasta," Agência Brasil, 4 June 2003, memoria.ebc.com.br/agenciabrasil/noticia/2003–06–04/chefe-do-gabinete-de-seguranca-institucional-fala-na-camara-sobre-atribuicoes-de-sua-pasta.

166. Nóbrega Júnior, "A militarização da segurança pública," 126; Jorge Zaverucha, "A militarização da Abin," *Folha de S. Paulo*, 9 January 2006.

167. Nóbrega Júnior, "A militarização da segurança pública," 126.

168. Márcio Paulo Buzanelli, Introdução, *II Encontro de Estudos: Terrorismo* (Brasília: Presidência da República—Gabinete de Segurança Institucional, 2004), 10–11.

169. Sérgio Leite Schmitt Correa Filho, Daniel Chiari Barros, Bernardo Hauch Ribeiro de Castro, Paulus Vinícius da Rocha Fonseca, and Jaime Gornszetjn, "Panorama sobre a indústria de defesa e segurança no Brasil," *BNDES Setorial* 38 (2013): 373–408.

170. "Palavras do Presidente Luiz Inácio Lula da Silva na conferência 'Combatendo o Terrorismo em Prol da Humanidade,'" Ministério das Relações Exteriores, 22 September 2003; "Lula critica política dos EUA," *Jornal do Iguaçu*, 23 September 2003, 3.

171. US Embassy Brasília, "Ambassador's Lunch with General Jorge Armando Felix, Minister for Institutional Security," Wikileaks, 6 May 2005.

172. Jessic Stern, "The Protean Enemy," *Foreign Affairs*, July/August 2003.

173. Rubens Barbosa and Jessica Stern, "Tri-Border Dispute," *Foreign Affairs*, January/February 2004.

174. Larry Luxner, "Ambassador Leila Rachid de Cowles: Paraguay's Long Evolution into Democracy," *Washington Diplomat*, May 2002.

175. "Rachid: 'En la triple frontera no hay células terroristas,'" *La Nación*, 16 March 2004.

176. Chalmers Johnson, *Nemesis: The Last Days of the American Republic* (New York: Palgrave Macmillan, 2007), 167–70.

177. Fermín Jara, "Unos 10 paraguayos están 'atrapados' en el sur del Líbano," *ABC Color*, 19 July 2006.

178. Fakih family, 22 July 2007

179. David Stout, "Bush Ties Battle with Hezbollah to War on Terror," *New York Times*, 31 July 2006; Gilbert Achcar and Michel Warschawski, *The 33-Day War: Israel's War on Hezbollah in Lebanon and Its Consquences* (New York: Routledge, 2007).

180. "Guerra no Líbano ecoa em Foz do Iguaçu," *Revista Painel*, August/September 2006, 227; "Véu e Alcorão integram cultura da fronteira," *Gazeta do Povo*, 1 December 2011; Diogo Bercito, "Brasileira morta no Líbano é enterrada em cerimônia pública," *Folha de S. Paulo*, 3 January 2014.

181. Fermín Jara, "Unos 10 paraguayos están 'atrapados' en el sur del Líbano," *ABC Color*, 19 July 2006.

182. "Paraguay: Hostilities in Middle East Raise Jewish Community Concerns about Safety," 06ASUNCION748, Wikileaks, 21 July 2006.

## CHAPTER 6

1. Franco Iacomini, "Um enclave libanês," *Veja*, 8 April 1998, 47.
2. Roberto Cosso, "Brasileiros ajudam a financiar terrorismo," *Folha de S. Paulo*, 18 November 2001; José Maschio and Ronaldo Soares, "Remessas do Brasil sob investigação," *Folha de S. Paulo*, 11 November 2001.
3. Mauro Albano, "Empresário árabe vê preconceito em declaração de diplomata da OEA," *Folha de S. Paulo*, 4 August 2003.
4. Bill Maurer, "Anthropological and Accounting Knowledge in Islamic Banking and Finance: Rethinking Critical Accounts," *Journal of the Royal Anthropological Institute* 8 (2002): 645–67; Tsing, *Friction*, 4, 120.
5. Goede, *Speculative Security*.
6. Goede, *Speculative Security*, 28; Marieke de Goede, "Hawala Discourses and the War on Terrorist Finance," *Environment and Planning D: Society and Space* 21.5 (2003): 513–32; Marieke de Goede and Gavin Sullivan, "The Politics of Security Lists," *Environment and Planning D: Society and Space*, 34.1 (2016): 3–13.
7. Hussein Abdul-Munim Amery, "The Effects of Migration and Remittances on Two Lebanese Villages," PhD diss., McMaster University, Hamilton, Ontario, 1992, 179–81.
8. Ibid., 175.
9. Zé Beto Maciel, "Árabes fazem ato pela causa palestina," *A Gazeta do Iguaçu*, 26 November 2000, 10.
10. "Investigação sobre dinheiro repatriado," *Hoje*, 15 April 1992, 1.
11. "Estados Unidos preocupado com a lavagem de dólares no Paraguai," *A Gazeta do Iguaçu*, 8 November 1992, 4.
12. "Ministros decidem intensificar controle na Tríplice Fronteira," *A Gazeta do Iguaçu*, 18 January 1998, 5; Zé Beto Maciel, "Brasil não foi ao encontro de Corach em Alto Paraná," *A Gazeta do Iguaçu*, 4 August 1998, 4.
13. "PF não encontra evidências de terror nas três fronteiras," *A Gazeta do Iguaçu*, 10 July 1998, 27.
14. "Contas criadas no regime militar," *A Gazeta do Iguaçu*, 7 December 1999, 27.
15. "Agência de Foz era usada para remessa ao Paraguai," *A Gazeta do Iguaçu*, 18 October 1995, 5; "Estabelece procedimentos e condições para abertura, movimentação e cadastramento no SISBACEN de contas em moeda nacional tituladas por pessoas físicas ou jurídicas domiciliadas ou com sede no exterior e dispõe sobre as transferências internacionais em reais," Circular n° 2.677, Banco Central do Brasil, 10 April 1996; Fátima Lessa, "Só em Foz existiam 25 contas frias," *A Gazeta do Iguaçu*, 19 June 1998.
16. Palácio Itamaraty, Rio de Janeiro, 14 November 2008.
17. "Foz é reduto de quadrilhas que lavam dinheiro," *A Gazeta do Iguaçu*, 7 December 1999, 27.
18. Ibid.
19. Ibid.
20. José Maschio and Ronaldo Soares, "Remessas do Brasil estão sob investigação," *Folha de S. Paulo*, 11 November 2001.

21. "Foz é considerada a 'matriz da lavagem.'" *A Gazeta do Iguaçu,* 17 November 2000.
22. Palácio Itamaraty, Rio de Janeiro, 14 November 2008.
23. Romero Sales, "RF quebra sigilo de 20 contas em Foz," *A Gazeta do Iguaçu,* 30 June 2001, 7; Marcelo Carneiro, "Mentor do fiasco," *Veja,* 22 December 2004, 64; "MPF pede documentos de casas de câmbio," *A Gazeta do Iguaçu,* 28 January 2005, 27; "Paraguaios foram acusados de lavagem," *A Gazeta do Iguaçu,* 28 January 2005, 27.
24. Sônia Inês Vendrame, "Ciudad del Este quer o retorno de turista verdadeiro na região," *A Gazeta do Iguaçu,* 24 January 1999, 4; "40 mil empregos estão ameaçados: Paraguai poderá implantar cota para compras que começam a ser feitas no Brasil (Entrevista com Charif Hammoud)," *A Gazeta do Iguaçu,* 24 January 1999, 5.
25. Sônia Inês Vendrame, "Preço do dólar deixa Ciudad del Este vazia," *A Gazeta do Iguaçu,* 17 January 1999, 5.
26. Romero Sales, "Dólar alto faz despencar vendas no PY," *A Gazeta do Iguaçu,* 22 April 2001, 5.
27. "Exportação cai à espera de definições," *A Gazeta do Iguaçu,* 19 January 1999, 5; Mônica Cristina Pinto, "Crise do dólar ressucita Vila Portes," *A Gazeta do Iguaçu,* 4 February 1999, 7.
28. Palácio Itamaraty, Rio de Janeiro, 14 November 2008.
29. Jailton de Carvalho, "Brasileiros na rede do terrorismo," *O Globo*, 2 November 2001.
30. Francis X. Taylor, speech given at Seminar on Preventing Terrorism and Organized Crime in the Tri-Border Area, Asunción, Paraguay, 19 December 2001, https://2001-2009.state.gov/s/ct/rls/rm/2001/7012.htm.
31. Esteban Areca, "Terroristas operan en Sudámerica" (Entrevista con Otto Reich), *Noticias*, 17 September 2002, 9.
32. Ricardo Mignone, "Brasil e Argentina unem forças para combater terrorismo," *Folha de S. Paulo*, 8 October 2001; "Brasil e Argentina querem evitar atos terroristas," *A Gazeta do Iguaçu,* 9 October 2001, 25.
33. "Entrevista: Alberto Cardoso," *Correio Braziliense,* 9 November 2001, 16.
34. "Lafer vê possibilidade de financiamento ao terrorismo no País," *O Estado de S. Paulo*, 23 November 2001; "Lafer admite que triple frontera puede financiar el terrorismo," *ABC Color*, 24 November 2001, 43.
35. "Por Paraguay habría pasado parte del dinero del terrorismo," *ABC Color*, 7 November 2001, 41.
36. "PF reforça investigação sobre saída de dinheiro," *O Paraná*, 31 October 2001, 7.
37. Edson Luiz, "Polícia fará devassa na Tríplice Fronteira," *O Estado de S. Paulo*, 12 November 2001, 12.
38. "Insisten en que nuestro país refugia a terroristas," *ABC Color*, 7 November 2001, 41.
39. "Por Paraguay habría pasado parte del dinero del terrorismo," *ABC Color*, 7 November 2001, 41; "Gobierno investiga a unas 40 entidades por supuesta conexión con el terrorismo," *Avance*, 7 November 2001, 3.
40. Reinaldo Penner, 15 April 2009.
41. Hector Guerín, 16 April 2009.
42. "Árabes no Paraguai são proibidos de enviar dinheiro para o exterior, *O Estado de S. Paulo*, 10 October 2001.

43. "Árabes são discriminados," *Jornal do Iguaçu*, 7 November 2001, 9.

44. "Lerner vem à Foz para ato pela paz," *Jornal do Iguaçu*, 2 November 2001, 10.

45. José Maschio e Ronaldo Soares, "Remessas do Brasil sob investigação," *Folha de S. Paulo*, 11 November 2001. In Portuguese, "passam pela Câmara de Compensação de Nova York e é preciso identificar o remetente e o beneficiário."

46. Léo Gerchmann, "Procurador afirma que terror lava dinheiro no país," *Folha de S. Paulo*, 18 November 2001; Claudio Carneiro, "Bancos enviaram R$602 milhões por contas CC5," *A Gazeta do Iguaçu*, 3 June 1999.

47. "Resck denunció ante la OEA y ONU al fiscal Carlos Cálcena por maltratos," *La Nación*, October 18, 2001; José Machio, "Paraguai mostra ligação Foz-Hizbollah," *Folha de S. Paulo*, 26 November 2001; "Ex fiscal Cálcena es procesado por apropriarse de dólares de un narco," *ABC Color*, 20 February 2004.

48. Município de Foz do Iguaçu, "Ação de reparação de danos contra CELSO TRÊS," Vara Cível da Comarca de Porto Alegre, Número 108665051, 28 November 2001.

49. "Município vai processar Celso Três," *A Gazeta do Iguaçu*, 28 November 2001, 28.

50. "Foz é mais segura que Londres," *A Gazeta do Iguaçu*, 9 November 2001, 5; "Rede hoteleira busca alternativas para compensar perdas," *Gazeta Mercantil —Paraná*, 5 November 2001, 1, 5.

51. Antônio Vanderli Moreira, "Por uma cidade mais humana," *Revista Painel*, July 1976, 12–13; Antônio Vanderli Moreira, "Nuvens negras pairam sobre a Pátria," *Revista Painel*, February 1977, 12–13; Antônio Vanderli Moreira, "Opinião," *Nosso Tempo*, 18 February 1981, 17; Antônio Vanderli Moreira, "'64: Um regime pecaminoso," *Nosso Tempo*, 7 April 1981, 11–12; "AI-5 de triste memória," *Nosso Tempo*, 22 December 1988, 12.

52. Antônio Vanderli Moreira, 11 August 2008.

53. "Município vai processar Celso Três," *A Gazeta do Iguaçu*, 28 November 2001, 28; "Foz está livre do terrorismo," *A Gazeta do Iguaçu*, 29 November 2001, 27; Maurício Bevervanso, "MP vai interpelar CNN sobre terrorismo," *A Gazeta do Iguaçu*, 12 November 2002, 5; Juliana Fontanella, "Procuradoria aciona rede CNN na justiça," *A Gazeta do Iguaçu*, 4 December 2002, 4; "Fracassa tentativa de conciliação com a CNN," *A Gazeta do Iguaçu*, 13 May 2004.

54. Harris Whitbeck and Ingrid Arnesen, "Terrorists Find Haven in South America," CNN transcript, 8 November 2001, www.cnn.com/2001/WORLD/americas/11/08/inv.terror.south/index.html.

55. Hannerz, *Foreign News*, 102–3.

56. J. Adelino Souza, "CNN pratica terrorismo contra a fronteira," *A Gazeta do Iguaçu*, 9 November 2001, 4.

57. "Terrorismo verbal preocupa Foz," *A Gazeta do Iguaçu*, 23 October 2001, 2; "Ministro da Justiça intervém na fronteira," *Jornal do Iguaçu*, 26 October 2001, 6.

58. "Gregori quer reverter prejuízos causados a Foz com suspeitas," *Gazeta do Paraná*, 25 October 2001, 7

59. Constança Tatsch, "Para FHC, há 'muito barulho' sobre terrorismo na tríplice fronteira," *Folha Online*, 8 November 2001; "Presidente responde à CNN e pede provas," *O Globo*, 9 November 2001, 27.

60. Coco Arce, 25 March 2009; see also Hannerz, *Foreign News*.

61. Magrão, 12 July 2007.

62. "CNN Newsnight with Aaron Brown," CNN Transcript, 16 November 2001, www.cnn.com/TRANSCRIPTS/0111/16/asb.00.html.

63. Mike Boettcher (with Ingrid Arnesen), "South America's Tri-Border Back on Terrorism Radar," CNN Americas, 8 November 2002.

64. Ibid.

65. "Cidade condena terrorismo da CNN contra a fronteira," *A Gazeta do Iguaçu*, 9–10 November 2002, 1; Rossana Schmitz, "CNN volta a atacar a tríplice fronteira," *Jornal do Iguaçu*, 9 November 2002, 4; "Terrorismo é o que faz a CNN," *Jornal Costa Oeste*, 15–21 November 2002; "Argentinos 'fabricaron' presunta reunión de los líderes terroristas," *Diario Vanguardia*, 11 November 2002; "Descartan reunión terrorista en Brasil," *Noticias*, 9 November 2002.

66. "Sâmis contra-ataca o 'terrorismo da CNN,'" *Jornal Hoje*, 9 November 2002, 21; Maurício Bevervanso, "Prefeito critica o 'terrorismo da CNN,'" *A Gazeta do Iguaçu*, 9–10 November 2002, 5; Luciana Barcellos, "Autoridades repudiam a CNN," *Gazeta do Paraná*, 9 November 2002.

67. Maurício Bevervanso, "PF nega e Câmara aprova moção de repúdio," *A Gazeta do Iguaçu*, 9–10 November 2002.

68. "Municipalidad del Este apoyaría demanda iniciada contra CNN," *ABC Color*, 11 December 2002.

69. "Municipalidad del Este apoyaría demanda iniciada contra CNN," *ABC Color*, 11 December 2002; "Comuna apoyaría demanda contra CNN por acusación de terrorismo," *Diario Vanguardia*, 11 December 2002, 3.

70. "Niegan versión sobre presunta reunión de líderes terroristas," *Diario Vanguardia*, 11 December 2002, 9–10.

71. "Imigrantes querem processar o Secretario de Turismo," *Folha de Londrina*, 11 May 2002; Mauri König, "Árabes vão à Justiça," *Globonews*, 22 May 2002.

72. Alberto González Toro, "Ciudad del Este, la más espiada del sur," *Clarín*, 30 March 2003.

73. Maristela do Valle, "Bin Laden vira garoto-propaganda de Foz do Iguaçu," *Folha de S. Paulo*, 24 March 2003.

74. Município de Foz do Iguaçu, "Ação de reparação de danos contra Turner International do Brasil Ltda. (cnn.com.br)," Vara Cível da Comarca de Foz do Iguaçu, Número 642, 4 December 2002; Maurício Bevervanso, "MP vai interpelar CNN sobre terrorismo," *A Gazeta do Iguaçu*, 12 November 2002, 5; "Fiscal de Foz iniciará demanda por acusaciones," *Diario Vanguardia*, 13 November 2002, 4; "Promotoria vai interpelar CNN," *Gazeta do Paraná*, 13 November 2002, 4; "MP 'compra briga' e interpelará CNN," *Jornal Hoje*, 13 November 2002.

75. Juliana Fontanella, "Procuradoria aciona rede CNN na justiça," *A Gazeta do Iguaçu*, 4 December 2002, 4.

76. "Foz aciona CNN por reparação de danos," *Gazeta do Paraná*, 4 December 2002, 4; "Foz aciona CNN por reparação de danos," *Jornal Hoje*, 4 December 2002.

77. "Audiência de ação da prefeitura contra a CNN será amanhã," *A Gazeta do Iguaçu*, 11 May 2004, 4.

78. "Sem acordo, segue ação de Foz contra a CNN," *Correio do Oeste*, 21–31 May 2004; "Fracassa tentativa de conciliação com a CNN," *A Gazeta do Iguaçu*, 13 May 2004; "Segue ação de Foz contra a CNN," *Jornal do Iguaçu*, 13 May 2004.

79. Antônio Vanderli Moreira, 11 August 2008.
80. "Testimony of Robert M. Mortgenthau, District Attorney of New York County, before the United States Senate Committee on Finance," 21 July 2004, www.finance.senate.gov/imo/media/doc/072104rmtest.pdf.
81. "City's D.A. Gets Tough on 4 Big," *New York Daily News*, 18 December 2005; Niles Lathem, "NYC's Terror Bank—DA Shuts $3B Acct," *New York Post*, 3 April 2006; "Jornal liga terror à Tríplice Fronteira," *Folha de S. Paulo*, 5 April, 2006; "Esquema que financiava Al-Qaeda tinha ramificação no Brasil," *O Estado de S. Paulo*, 4 April 2006; Alberto Armendáriz, "Revelan lazos entre la red Al-Qaeda y la Triple Frontera," *La Nación*, 6 April 2006.
82. Mario Cesar Carvalho, "Doleiros são acusados de enviar US$19 bi aos EUA," *Folha de S. Paulo*, 29 September 2006; Vannildo Mendes, "País recupera US$1,6 mi do caso Banestado," *O Estado de S. Paulo*, 2 November 2007.
83. "Países da Tríplice Fronteira negam suposta ligação com terror," *Folha Online*, 5 April 2006; "Leila defiende región y acusa a EE.UU.," *ABC Color*, 6 April 2006; "Câmara de Foz condena acusações dos EUA à fronteira," *H2Foz*, 8 April 2006, www.h2foz.com.br/noticia/camara-de-foz-condena-acusacoes-dos-eua-a-fronteira-8723; "Exigirán pruebas a los EE.UU. sobre supuesta presencia de terroristas," *ABC Color*, 19 July 2006; "33 brasileiros são indiciados nos EUA," *Gazeta do Povo*, 29 September 2006.
84. Office of Foreign Assets Control, Financial Institution Letter, 28 December 2006, www.fdic.gov/news/inactive-financial-institution-letters/2006/fil06113.pdf.
85. Executive Order 13224, *Federal Register: The Daily Journal of the United States Government*, 23 September 2001, 49,079–82, www.federalregister.gov/documents/2001/09/25/01-24205/blocking-property-and-prohibiting-transactions-with-persons-who-commit-threaten-to-commit-or-support.
86. Ibid.
87. "USA incluye a Barakat en su lista de financistas del extremismo islámico," *ABC Color*, 7 December 2006.
88. "Need for a Strategy on the TBA Terror Finance Designation Package," US Embassy in Brasília Cable, 17 November 2006, Wikileaks; "Post Supports Delay of Hezbollah Tri-Border Area Finance Designations," US Embassy in Buenos Aires, 20 November 2006, Wikileaks.
89. "Need for a Strategy on the TBA Terror Finance Designation Package," US Embassy in Brasília Cable, 17 November 2006, Wikileaks.
90. Ibid.
91. Ibid.
92. "Post Supports Delay of Hezbollah Tri-Border Area Finance Designations," US Embassy in Buenos Aires, 20 November 2006, Wikileaks.
93. Ibid.
94. Ibid.
95. Andréa Michael, "Brasil e EUA vão reformular acordo sobre extradição," *Folha de S. Paulo*, 9 February 2007, 8.
96. Eliane Cantanhêde, "Brasil e EUA debatem terror na tríplice fronteira," *Folha de S. Paulo*, 7 February 2007, 8.
97. "Editorial," *Revista Brasileira de Inteligência*, 3.4 (2007): 9.

98. Depoimento de Márcio Paulo Buzanelli, Audiência Pública da Comissão de Segurança Pública e Combate ao Crime Organizado, Câmara dos Deputados, República Federativa do Brasil, 21 August 2007.

99. "Treasury Targets Hizballah Fundraising Network in the Triple Frontier of Argentina, Brazil, and Paraguay," Press Release of the US Department of Treasury, 6 December 2006.

100. José Maschio, "Empresário nega ligação com Hizbollah," *Folha de S. Paulo*, 13 December 2006; "Paraguayos y árabes son los cráneos del lavado de activos en Tres Fronteras," *ABC Color*, 12 December 2007; "Triple Frontera: EE.UU. acusa a nueve personas de financiar a Hezbollah," *El Cronista*, 6 December 2006; Natasha Niebieskikwiat, "Triple Frontera: Desestiman en la región una denuncia de EE.UU.," *Clarín*, 7 December 2006.

101. Matheus Machado e Murilo Ramos, "Os terroristas estão aqui," *Revista Época*, 12 March 2007.

102. Lourival Sant'Anna, "Diplomata americano recomenda 'transparência' a doadores de Foz," *O Estado de S. Paulo*, 1 August 2003; Maurício Bevervanso, "Monblatt pede transparência nas remessas," *A Gazeta do Iguaçu*, 4 August 2003, 7; "OEA pide 'transparencia' en la zona de las Tres Fronteras," *Noticias*, 2 August 2003, 22.

103. United States Department of State, *Country Reports on Global Terrorism 2005* (Washington, DC: Office of the Coordinator of Counterterrorism, 2006), 38, 157.

104. Jimmy Gurulé, *Unfunding Terror: The Legal Response to the Financing of Global Terrorism* (Cheltenham: Edward Elgar Publications, 2009), 111.

105. "'Nosso interrogatório pode ser mostrado no tribunal,' alfineta diretor da polícia," *Folha de S. Paulo*, 17 September 2006, A30.

106. Brasemb Assunção, "Combate ao terrorismo e seu financiamento," MRE, 6 April 2006.

107. Machado e Ramos, "Os terroristas estão aqui"; "Treasury Targets Hizballah Fundraising Network," press release of the US Department of Treasury, 9 December 2010.

108. Mônica Resende, "Árabes constroem segunda escola em Foz," *A Gazeta do Iguaçu,* 9 January 2000, 7.

109. Shahimi, *Dirasat ightirabiyah*, 178–80.

110. Sheikh Khalil, 19 July 2007.

111. Joyce Carvalho, "Medo atinge muçulmanos em Foz do Iguaçu," *Paraná-Online*, 14 March 2007, www.parana-online.com.br/editoria/cidades/news/229892.

112. Sheikh Khalil, 19 July 2007.

113. "Edital: Clube União Árabe de Foz do Iguaçu," *A Gazeta do Iguaçu,* 21 January 1999, 19; "Nadia e Fadia Jebai" and "Turbante do Mohamed Ismail," *A Gazeta do Iguaçu,* 30 March 2000, 21.

114. Nasser, 17 August 2008.

115. Ibid.

116. Sheikh Khalil, 19 July 2007.

117. Ibid.

118. "La empresa electrónica Pioneer distingue a Samir Jaber," *Diario Fedecamaras*, 29 May 2012, www.diariofedecamaraspy.com/2012/05/pioneer-internacional-distingue-samir.html.

119. "Procesos por evasión iniciados en el Este significaron pingües ganancias," *ABC Color*, 4 May 2009.

120. "La empresa electrónica Pioneer distingue a Samir Jaber," *Diario Fedecamaras*, 29 May 2012, www.diariofedecamaraspy.com/2012/05/pioneer-internacional-distingue-samir.html.

121. "La semana nacional," *ABC Color*, 2 September 1974, 34; "Mision China a Stroessner," *ABC Color*, 6 September 1974, 8; "Intercambio con Sur Corea," *ABC Color*, 19 October 1974, 32. Bazas recalled that his uncle's business imported goods from China, but not directly, as early as the 1970s. Mihail Meskin Bazas, 17 September 2008.

122. Arjun Appadurai, *Modernity at Large: Cultural Dimensions of Globalization* (Minneapolis: University of Minnesota Press, 1996), 41; Khaled Ghotme, 18 September 2008.

123. Khaled Ghotme, 18 September 2008.

124. Maria Belen Servin, *Boletin de Comercio Exterior* (CADEP), vol. 1, 2011, cited in Birch, "Paraguay and Mercosur," 269–90.

125. Said Taijen, 16 June 2009.

126. Fouad Fakih, 9 December 2008.

127. Fouad Fakih, Mohamad Barakat, and relative, 17 August 2008.

128. Meeting with Vincente and Juan, Shopping del Este, 29 August 2008; "Initial S.A.," *Gaceta Oficial de la Republica del Paraguay*, 135, 15 December 2005, 1–2.

129. "Detectan dos cuentas bancarias usadas para remesas al exterior," *ABC Color*, 7 April 2006; "Comuna debe recuperar el predio usurpado," *ABC Color*, 21 November 2008; "Clan Zacarías privatizó millonario bien público," *ABC Color*, 22 October 2018.

130. Roberto Couto, "O lado sofisticado de Ciudad del Este," *Gazeta do Povo*, 15 July 2010.

131. "Afirma que no es investigado," *ABC Color*, 14 August 2008; "Clan Zacarías privatizó millonario bien público," *ABC Color*, 22 October 2018.

132. "Las perspectivas del Grupo Rahal," *5dias*, 26 February 2014.

133. "Horizonte de Ciudad del Este sumará otro edificio de altura," *Ultima Hora*, 22 September 2011.

134. "Soluciones innovadoras y exclusivas en el país," *5dias*, 16 August 2013.

135. "Horizonte de Ciudad del Este sumará otro edificio de altura," *Ultima Hora*, 22 September 2011.

136. Paula Rocha, "Luxo autêntico no Paraguai," *Isto É*, 26 August 2011.

137. SAX department store website, shop.sax.com.py (date of access: 28 August 2020).

138. Denise Paro, "Sai o ceular xing-ling, entra o vestido Dior," *Gazeta do Povo*, 22 November 2012; Paula Rocha, "Luxo autêntico no Paraguai," *Isto É*, 26 August 2011.

139. "Hyatt Announces Plans for a Park Hyatt Hotel in Brazil," Hyatt Investor Relations, 3 September 2014, investors.hyatt.com/investor-relations/news-and-events/financial-news/financial-news-details/2014/Hyatt-Announces-Plans-for-a-Park-Hyatt-Hotel-in-Brazil/default.aspx.

140. "Fiscal Anticorrupción imputó a 19 personas por supuesto perjuicio al fisco," Ministerio Público, República del Paraguay, 17 February 2017, www.ministeriopublico.gov.py/fiscal-anticorrupcion-imputo-a-19-personas-por-supuesto-perjuicio-al-fisco-n3715; "Más comerciantes entre posibles sobreseídos en caso Megaevasión," *ABC Color*, 18 April 2018.

141. Reinaldo Penner, 15 April 2009; Said Taijen, 16 June 2009.

142. "Zona franca, disponsible sin costo," *ABC Color*, 6 April 2008; "Miami quiere mejorar oportunidades de los negocios con el Paraguay," *ABC Color*, 27 July 2008; "Desean facilitar el intercambio comercial Paraguay-Miami," *ABC Color*, 21 September 2008.

143. Said Taijen, 16 June 2009.

144. "Lugo propone desmitificar Ciudad del Este como centro operativo terrorista," *ABC Color*, 10 August 2008.

145. "Barakat quedó en libertad," *ABC Color*, 27 June 2008; "Barakat viajó a Foz do Yguazú," *ABC Color*, 28 June 2008.

146. "Presunto extremista islámico es detenido en calle Palma," *ABC Color*, 30 October 2002; "Libanés condenado por evasión ya está recluido en la Agrupación," *ABC Color*, 23 November 2002.

147. "Recepção do Deputado Libanes Ali Khalil do partido AMAL," personal fieldnotes, 30 August 2008.

148. United States Department of State, *Country Reports on Terrorism 2007* (Washington, DC: Office of the Coordinator of Counterterrorism, 2008), 148; United States Department of State, *Country Reports on Terrorism 2008* (Washington, DC: Office of the Coordinator of Counterterrorism, 2009), 201; United States Department of State, *Country Reports on Terrorism 2009* (Washington, DC: Office of the Coordinator of Counterterrorism, 2010), 212.

149. "Avanza construcción de mezquita en el Este," *ABC Color*, 3 April 2013.

150. "Comunidad árabe inaugura mezquita como un símbolo de arraigo en CDE," *La Nación*, 3 November 2015.

151. "Comunidad árabe construye mezquita y fortalece presencia en la frontera," *Ultima Hora*, 30 April 2012.

152. "Comunidad árabe inaugura mezquita como un símbolo de arraigo en CDE," *La Nación*, 3 November 2015.

153. "Mezquita construida por la comunidad árabe va cobrando forma," *Ultima Hora*, 19 September 2012. In Spanish, "podrá entrar cualquier persona, chiita, sunita, como así como el musulmán puede entrar en cualquier iglesia."

154. "Cartes inaugura mezquita de USD 1 millón en CDE," *Ultima Hora*, 3 November 2015; "Prefeito participa da inauguração da mesquita Al-Rashdeen Alkhaulafa de Ciudad del Este," press release, Governo do Município de Foz do Iguaçu, 4 November 2015, www.pmfi.pr.gov.br/noticia/?idNoticia=39017; "Mesquita de Ciudad del Este, Paraguai," *Revista 100 Fronteiras* 138 (2017): 130.

155. Hugo Olazar, "Musulmanes en Ciudad del Este estrenan mezquita dispuestos a sacudirse estigmas," *La Nación*, 28 January 2016. In Spanish, "símbolo de la pluriculturalidad cosmopolita."

156. Dave McNary, "Bigelow, Boal reteam for 'Frontier,'" *Variety*, 9 August 2009; Peter Keough, *Kathryn Bigelow: Interviews* (Jackson: University Press of Mississippi, 2013).

157. "Brasil, Paraguai e Argentina recusam-se a apoiar filme de vencedora do Oscar," *Correio Braziliense*, 10 May 2010; "Senatur no colaborará con película de Bigelow sobre la Triple Frontera," *Ultima Hora*, 10 May 2010.

158. André Miranda, "'Tríplice fronteira': Brasil, Argentina e Paraguai se voltam contra Kathryn Bigelow," *O Globo*, 14 May 2010, oglobo.globo.com/cultura/triplice-fronteira-brasil-argentina-paraguai-se-voltam-contra-kathryn-bigelow-3008594. In Portuguese, "que não há elementos concretos para se afirmar qualquer conexão de empresários, entidades ou pessoas de ascendência árabe da fronteira com o financiamento de grupos terroristas islâmicos."

159. "Crámer insta a no colaborar con filme 'Triple Frontera,'" *ABC Color*, 7 May 2010.

160. Borys Kit, "'Elite Squad' Director, 'Gran Torino' Writer Tackle South America's 'Tri-Border,'" *Hollywood Reporter*, 25 May 2011, www.hollywoodreporter.com/heat-vision/elite-squad-director-gran-torino-192342.

161. José Padilha and Elena Suárez, *O Mecanismo (The Mechanism)*, Netflix, 1st and 2nd seasons, 2018–19.

162. Asunción-based media lauded the participation of Paraguayans in Padilha's production, overlooking the disturbing representation of the border that attributes lawlessness to Paraguay and generally downplays the complicity of Argentine, Brazilian, and US states.

163. In brief shots during the film, there are two signs, in Spanish, that make reference to Brazil and two verbal exchanges about Peru, along with treks through rainforests and across the Andes. So the border where Brazil, Colombia, and Peru meet may be among the many "triple frontiers" implied in the film. See Kaká Souza, "Tríplice fronteira não tem nada a temer com *Triple Frontier*," ClickFoz, 13 March 2019, www.clickfozdoiguacu.com.br/triplice-fronteira-nao-tem-nada-a-temer-com-triple-frontier.

164. "Pronunciamento de Roberto Requião em 30/09/2015," Senado Federal, 10 September 2015, www25.senado.leg.br/web/atividade/pronunciamentos/-/p/texto/417220.

## CONCLUSION

1. Guilherme, 24 July 2019.

2. Juan Poblete, Introduction to *Critical Latin American and Latino Studies* (Minneapolis: University of Minnesota Press, 2003), xxxv.

3. Saldívar, *Trans-Americanity*.

4. Walter Mignolo, *Local Histories / Global Designs: Coloniality, Subaltern Knowledges, and Border Thinking* (Princeton, NJ: Princeton University Press, 2000).

5. See Christina Cavedon, *Cultural Melancholia: US Trauma Discourses before and after 9/11* (Leiden: Brill, 2015); Amaney Jamal and Nadine Naber, eds., *Race and Arab Americans before and after 9/11: From Invisible Citizens to Visible Subjects* (Syracuse: Syracuse University Press, 2008); Patricia Molloy, *Canada, US, and Other Unfriendly Relations before and after 9/11* (New York: Palgrave Macmillan, 2012); Caryl Phillips, *Color Me English: Migration and Belonging before and after 9/11* (New York: New Press, 2013).

6. Shohat and Stam, *Unthinking Eurocentrism*, 48.

7. Conselho de Senhoras da Sociedade Árabe de Beneficência (Saben), *Árabes*

*no Paraná*, Lu Rufalco, director (Curitiba, 2016), YouTube, 22 November 2016, www.youtube.com/watch?v=qFEnXwHT3ns.

8. Mignolo, *Local Histories / Global Designs*; Aníbal Quijano, "Modernidad, colonialidad y América Latina," *Neplanta* 1.3 (2000): 533–80.

9. "Migración árabe en Paraguay," on the *Invisibles* RPC (Red Paraguaya de Comunicación, 2016), YouTube, 2 November 2016, www.youtube.com/watch?v=W8bauePMiYE.

10. Mohammed, 26 August 2008.

11. José Daniel Nasta, *Árabes en el Paraguay: Migrantes y descendientes* (Asunción: Garbo Producciones, 2016). See also José Daniel Nasta and L. Alberto Asbun Karmy, *La migración árabe y su descendencia en Paraguay* (Asunción: Publicitaria Nasta SA, 2007).

12. Ahmed, 22 July 2007.

13. Mohamad Barakat, Fouad Fakih, Hamad Rahal, 21 July 2007.

14. Hamad Rahal, 29 July 2007.

15. Ronildo Pimentel, "Definida programação da Cúpula das Américas em Foz do Iguaçu: Três mil pessoas são esperadas no evento; o presidenciável Jair Bolsonaro fecha o encontro falando de política," *Gazeta Diário*, 20 July 2018, 3.

16. Matias Spektor, "Bolsonaro lança sua mais ambiciosa iniciativa de política externa," *Folha de S. Paulo*, 5 July 2018.

17. "Entusiasta do Estado de Israel, Bolsonaro pedirá votos aos árabes," *Veja*, 5 July 2018, veja.abril.com.br/blog/radar/bolsonaro-acena-para-a-comunidade-arabe; Matias Spektor, "Bolsonaro lança sua mais ambiciosa iniciativa de política externa," *Folha de S. Paulo*, 5 July 2018.

18. Sociedade Beneficente Islâmica, Centro Cultural Beneficente Islâmico de Foz do Iguaçu, Sociedade Árabe Palestina Brasileira de Foz do Iguaçu, and Federação Árabe Palestina do Brasil, "Carta Aberta—Comunidade Árabe-Brasileira," Facebook, 25 July 2018, www.facebook.com/MesquitaFoz/photos/pcb.2039593079625667/2039593052959003.

19. Beatriz Bulla, "'A questão não é se, é quando,' diz Eduardo Bolsonaro sobre mudar embaixada para Jerusalém," *O Estado de S. Paulo*, 27 November 2018; Júlia Zaremba, "Eduardo Bolsonaro diz que mudança de embaixada brasileira para Jerusalém está decidida," *Folha de S. Paulo*, 27 November 2018; Júlia Zaremba, "Eduardo Bolsonaro vai a aniversário de Bannon, ex-estrategista de Trump," *Folha de S. Paulo*, 28 November 2018.

20. Ronildo Pimentel, "Extrema-direta das Américas testa sua popularidade em cúpula em Foz do Iguaçu," *Gazeta Diário*, 7 December 2018, 11; Mariana Haubert, "Cúpula divulga 'Carta de Foz,' documento com 'anseios dos conservadores da América Latina,'" *O Estado de S.Paulo*, 10 December 2018, politica. estadao.com.br/noticias/geral,cupula-divulga-carta-de-foz-documento-com-anseios-dos-conservadores-da-america-latina-leia,70002640409.

21. Gésica Brandino, "Apoio a Bolsonaro divide comunidade islâmica no Brasil," *Folha de S. Paulo*, 13 November 2018; "O Brasil só tem a perder com o distanciamento do mundo árabe," *Jornal Água Verde*, 5 November 2018.

22. "Marito desafió al bandidaje de las aduanas y al fraude altoparanaense," *Vanguardia*, 9 October 2017.

23. "Paraguay restablece su Embajada en Tel Aviv tras mudarse a Jerusalén,"

*Ultima Hora*, 5 September 2018; "Mario Abdo justifica traslado de embajada a Tel Aviv," *La Nación*, 5 September 2018.

24. Dante Quadra, "Argentina anuncia radares israelenses para monitorar fronteiras," *Rádio Cultura*, 4 December 2017, www.radioculturafoz.com.br/2017/12/04/argentina-anuncia-radares-israelenses-para-monitorar-fronteiras; Dante Quadra, "Argentina irá instalar sistema de vigilância de última geração na fronteira," *Rádio Cultura*, 21 May 2018, www.radioculturafoz.com.br/2018/05/21/argentina-ira-instalar-sistema-de-vigilancia-de-ultima-geracao-na-fronteira; "Argentina aumentará segurança nos rios Iguaçu e Paraná a partir de 6 de agosto," *Gazeta Diário*, 26 July 2018, 5; Guido Carelli Lynch, "Primer viaje oficial: En Israel, Alberto Fernández participó de un encuentro con líderes mundiales y le preguntaron por la deuda," *Clarín*, 22 January 2020; "El primer viaje al exterior de Alberto Fernández," *La Nación*, 19 January 2020.

25. "Sociedade Árabe Palestina faz ato público na Câmara Municipal de Foz," *Gazeta Diário*, 18 December 2017, 4.

26. Eva Muzzopappa and Ana Margarita Ramos, "Una etnografía itinerante sobre el terrorismo en Argentina: Paradas, trayectorias y disputas," *Antípoda: Revista de Antropología y Arqueología* 29 (2017): 123–42.

27. César Alfonso, "Represión y prevención del terrorismo en la República del Paraguay," in *Terrorismo y derecho penal*, eds. Kai Ambos, Ezequiel Malarino, and Christian Steiner (Berlin: EdPal and Konrad-Adenauer-Stiftung e. V., 2015), 89–112.

28. Veronica Tavares de Freitas, *Quem são os terroristas do Brasil? A Lei Antiterror e a produção política de um inimigo público* (Curitiba: Editora CVR, 2017).

29. Judith Butler, *Precarious Life: The Powers of Mourning and Violence* (New York: Verso, 2004), 56, 65.

30. Office of Foreign Assets Control, "Publication of the Hizballah International Financing Prevention Act of 2015 Related Sanctions Regulations; Counter Terrorism Designations Updates; Syria Designations Updates," US Dept. of the Treasury, 15 April 2016, home.treasury.gov/policy-issues/financial-sanctions/recent-actions/20160415.

31. "State Sponsors of Terrorism: An Examination of Iran's Global Terrorism Network," House Homeland Security Committee, 17 April 2018, homeland.house.gov/hearings-and-markups/hearings/state-sponsors-terrorism-examination-iran-s-global-terrorism-network.

32. Congressional testimony of Emanuele Ottolenghi, "State Sponsors of Terrorism: An Examination of Iran's Global Terrorism Network," House Homeland Security Committee, 17 April 2018, 8, 28–29, docs.house.gov/meetings/HM/HM05/20180417/108155/HHRG-115-HM05-Wstate-OttolenghiE-20180417.pdf.

33. Ibid, 37.

34. Ibid, 36–37.

35. Emanuele Ottolenghi, "The Mystery Martyr," *Weekly Standard*, 24 February 2018, www.weeklystandard.com/emanuele-ottolenghi/the-mystery-martyr; Emanuele Ottolenghi and José Luis Stein, "Trump Should Cut Hezbollah's Lifeline in the Americas," *Foreign Policy*, 12 December 2018, foreignpolicy.com/2018/12/12/trump-should-cut-hezbollahs-lifeline-in-the-americas; Emanuele Ottolenghi, "Paraguay Is a Fiscal Paradise for Terrorists," *Foreign*

*Policy*, 14 February 2019, foreignpolicy.com/2019/02/14/paraguay-is-a-fiscal-paradise-for-terrorists; "Experts: Iran, Hezbollah Have 'Radicalized Thousands of Latin Americans,'" Breitbart, 18 April 2018, www.breitbart.com/national-security/2018/04/18/experts-iran-hezbollah-radicalized-thousands-latin-americans.

36. The Argentine state released press releases in English and Spanish. See Unidad de Información Financiera, "Terrorist Financing," 13 July 2018, www.argentina.gob.ar/noticias/terrorist-financing; "Financiación del Terrorismo," 13 July 2018, www.argentina.gob.ar/noticias/financiacion-del-terrorismo.

37. "Statement by FinCEN Director Kenneth A. Blanco in Support of Recent Anti-Terrorism Financing Actions by Argentina's Financial Intelligence Unit," FinCEN, 14 July 2018, www.fincen.gov/news/news-releases/statement-fincen-director-kenneth-blanco-support-recent-anti-terrorism-financing.

38. Mariano Federici and Kenneth Blanco, "Luchar contra los delitos financieros, un objetivo común de la Argentina y EE.UU.," *La Nación*, 27 November 2018, www.lanacion.com.ar/opinion/luchar-delitos-financieros-objetivo-comun-argentina-eeuu-nid2196903; Mariano Federici and Kenneth Blanco, "US-Argentina Teamwork Is Battling Money Laundering and Illicit Finance," *Miami Herald*, 26 November 2018, www.miamiherald.com/opinion/op-ed/article222216265.html.

39. Butler, *Precarious Life*, 61.

40. Unidad de Información Financiera, "Terrorist Financing"; "Statement by FinCEN Director"; Federici and Blanco, "Luchar contra los delitos financieros"; Federici and Blanco, "US-Argentina Teamwork"; Lucía Salinas and Daniel Santoro, "AMIA: Descubren cómo lavaba dinero un libanés de la Triple Frontera para las finanzas del Hezbollah," *Clarín*, 17 July 2018.

41. "Emanuele Ottolenghi: "Triple Frontera sigue siendo lugar de refugio para terroristas y financiadores," *Ultima Hora*, 9 September 2018; "Afirman que hay prueba de financiamiento a terrorismo," *ABC Color*, 20 January 2019; "Funcionario antiterrorista de EE.UU. se reúne con canciller," *ABC Color*, 15 January 2019; "Canciller responde a Ottolenghi," *ABC Color*, 21 January 2019.

42. "Paraguay, 'paraíso' para el terrorismo," *ABC Color*, 15 February 2019. In Spanish, "el nivel muy bajo de integridad pública de los gobernantes en Paraguay."

43. "Canciller responde a Ottolenghi," *ABC Color*, 21 January 2019; "Gobierno reacciona y dice que actuó en los casos vinculados a Hezbollah," *Ultima Hora*, 21 January 2019; "Gobierno califica de hecho aislado y exagerado el informe de Ottolenghi," *ABC Color*, 21 January 2019; "Declaración negativa sobre el país no afectará ante examen," *La Nación*, 18 February 2019.

44. "Ordenan la captura de Barakat," *ABC Color*, 1 September 2018.

45. Butler, *Precarious Life,* 97.

46. Ibid., 67.

47. Peter Speetjens, "The Curious Case of Assad Barakat: Financial Evil Genius or Scapegoat?," *Executive Magazine*, 8 November 2018, www.executive-magazine.com/economics-policy/the-curious-case-of-assad-barakat.

48. "'Satanización' de comercio esteño y de la triple frontera," *ADN Paraguayo,* 5 November 2018, www.adndigital.com.py/satanizacion-comercio-esteno-la-triple-frontera.

49. Ibid. In Spanish, he and others came to "esta zona porque están cansados de los ataques terroristas que solo causan dolor, de la guerra, quieren paz, y decir que están alentando la violencia y el odio es algo que no entra en la cabeza de nadie. . . . No entendemos esto."

50. Butler, *Precarious Life*, xiv–xv.

51. "Antes de ser preso, Assad Barakat havia pedido refúgio ao Brasil," *Gazeta Diário*, 26 September 2018, 13.

52. João Adelino de Souza, "Na Toca do Leão," *Gazeta Diário*, 26 September 2018, 4; João Adelino de Souza, "Polícia Federal prende em Foz libanês procurado pela polícia dos três países," *Gazeta Diário*, 22/23 September 2018, 7.

53. "Parentes e amigos pedem a soltura de Assad Barakat," *Gazeta Diário*, 29/30 September 2018, 1, 8. In Portuguese, "Nós não somos terroristas. Nós somos parte desta cidade," adding that "Nós estamos aqui pedindo apoio à Embaixada Libanesa em Brasília e até ao presidente Michel Temer que é descendente de libaneses e cujo pai também veio do Líbano como refugiado."

54. Luiz Vassallo e Fabio Serapião, "Raquel vê 'risco de fuga' de libanês ligado ao terror," *O Estado de S. Paulo*, 21 September 2018, politica.estadao.com.br/blogs/fausto-macedo/raquel-ve-risco-de-fuga-de-libanes-ligado-ao-terror/.

55. Bronwyn Davies, ed., *Judith Butler in Conversation: Analyzing the Texts and Talk of Everyday Life* (New York: Routledge, 2008), 192.

56. "Assad Barakat fue ingresado al país con fuerte custodia policial," ABC, 17 July 2020, www.abc.com.py/este/2020/07/17/assad-barakat-fue-ingresado-al-pais-con-fuerte-custodia-policial; "Libanês suspeito de crime de falsidade ideológica é extraditado ao Paraguai, diz PF," *O Globo*, 17 July 2020, g1.globo.com/pr/oeste-sudoeste/noticia/2020/07/17/libanes-suspeito-de-crime-de-falsidade-ideologica-e-extraditado-ao-paraguai-diz-pf. ghtml; "Assad Barakat é extraditado ao Paraguai por ordem do STF," *Gazeta Diário*, 18 July 2020, gdia.com.br/noticia/assad-barakat-e-extraditado-ao-paraguai-por-ordem-do-stf.

# Acronyms

**ABIN:** Agência Brasileira de Inteligência (Brazilian Intelligence Agency)
**ACIFI:** Asociação Comercial e Industrial de Foz do Iguaçu (Commercial and Industrial Association of Foz do Iguaçu)
**AMIA:** Asociación Mutual Israelita Argentina (Jewish Argentine Mutual Association)
**ANR:** Asociación Nacional Republicana (National Republican Association)
**ARENA:** Aliança Renovadora Nacional (National Renewal Alliance)
**BB:** Banco do Brasil (Bank of Brazil)
**Banestado:** Banco do Estado do Paraná (Paraná State Bank)
**BC:** Banco Central (Central Bank)
**Cacex:** Carteira de Comércio Exterior (Foreign Trade Portfolio)
**CCPA:** Cámara de Comercio Paraguayo-Americana
**CET:** Common External Tariff
**CIA:** Central Intelligence Agency
**CICAP:** Centro de Importadores y Comerciantes del Alto Paraná (Center of Importers and Traders of Alto Paraná)
**CIEEP:** Cámara de Comercio de Electrónica y Electrodomésticos del Paraguay (Chamber of Commerce of Electronics and Household Appliances of Paraguay)
**CC5:** Carta Circular nº 5 (Circular Letter Number 5)
**CNN:** Cable News Network
**DAIA:** Delegación de Asociaciones Israelitas Argentinas (Delegation of Argentine Jewish Associations)
**DOPS:** Departamento de Ordem Política e Social (Department of Social and Political Order)
**FBI:** Federal Bureau of Investigation
**FDD:** Foundation for Defense of Democracies
**FEARAB:** Federación de Entidades Árabes (Federation of Arab Associations)

**FEPRINCO:** Federación de Producción, Industria y Comércio (Federation of Production, Industry, and Commerce)
**FinCEN:** Financial Crimes Enforcement Network
**FTAA:** Free Trade Association of the Americas
**MDB:** Movimento Democrático Brasileiro (Brazilian Democratic Movement)
**Mercosul:** Mercado Comum do Sul (Southern Common Market)
**Mercosur:** Mercado Común del Sur (Southern Common Market)
**MR8:** Movimento Revolucionário Oito de Outubro (October 8th Revolutionary Movement)
**NAFTA:** North American Free Trade Agreement
**OAB:** Ordem dos Advogados do Brasil (Bar Association of Brazil)
**OFAC:** Office of Foreign Asset Control
**PC do B:** Partido Comunista do Brasil (Communist Party of Brazil)
**PLO:** Palestine Liberation Organization
**PMDB:** Partido do Movimento Democrático Brasileiro (Party of the Brazilian Democratic Movement)
**PF:** Polícia Federal (Federal Police)
**PN:** Policia Nacional (National Police)
**PR:** Paraná
**PSDB:** Partido da Social Democracia Brasileira (Brazilian Social Democracy Party)
**PT:** Partido dos Trabalhadores (Workers' Party)
**RF:** Receita Federal (Federal Revenue Secretariat)
**SEPIT:** Secretaria de Prevención e Investigación del Terrorismo (Secretariat of the Prevention and Investigation of Terrorism)
**SIDE:** Secretaría de Inteligencia del Estado (State Intelligence Secretariat)
**SNI:** Serviço Nacional de Informações (National Intelligence Service)
**TBA:** Tri-Border Area
**UIF:** Unidad de Inteligencia Financiera (Financial Intelligence Unit)

# References

## ARCHIVES

Arquivo Nacional (Rio de Janeiro, Brazil)
Arquivo Público do Estado de São Paulo (São Paulo, Brazil)
Arquivo Público do Paraná (Curitiba, Brazil)
Biblioteca del Congreso de la Nación (Buenos Aires, Argentina)
Biblioteca Nacional de Argentina (Buenos Aires, Argentina)
Biblioteca Nacional del Paraguay (Asunción, Paraguay)
Biblioteca Pública Municipal Elfrida Engel Nunes Rios (Foz do Iguaçu, Brazil)
Câmara Municipal de Foz do Iguaçu (Foz do Iguaçu, Brazil)
Centro de Documentación y Archivo para la Defensa de los Derechos Humanos—
    CDyA (Asunción, Paraguay)
Centro de Documentación y Estudios (Ciudad del Este, Paraguay)
Centro Nacional de Información y Documentación Educativa–CeNide (Buenos
    Aires, Argentina)
Fouad Fakih, personal archive (Foz do Iguaçu, Brazil)
Gazeta do Iguaçu, A (Foz do Iguaçu, Brazil)
Itamaraty (Ministério de Relações Exteriores), Arquivo Histórico (Brasília, Brazil)
Library of Congress (Washington, DC, United States)
Ministerio de Relaciones Exteriores del Paraguay, Documentación e Archivo
    (Asunción, Paraguay)

## SECONDARY SOURCES

Abbot, Philip. "Terrorist Threat in the Tri-Border Area." *Military Review*, Fall 2004,
    51–55.
Aboud, Brian. "Re-reading Arab World—New World Immigration History: Beyond
    the Prewar/Postwar Divide." *Journal of Ethnic and Migration Studies* 26.4
    (2000): 653–73.

Achcar, Gilbert, and Michel Warschawski. *The 33-Day War: Israel's War on Hizbullah in Lebanon and Its Consequences.* New York: Routledge, 2007.

Adams, Gordon, and Shoon Murray, eds. *Mission Creep: The Militarization of U.S. Foreign Policy.* Washington, DC: Georgetown University Press, 2015.

Agamben, Giorgio. *State of Exception.* Chicago: University of Chicago Press, 2005.

Aizenberg, Edna. "Argentine Space, Jewish Memory: Memorials to the Blown Apart and Disappeared in Buenos Aires." *Mortality* 12.2 (2007): 109–23.

Albuquerque, José Lindomar C. *A dinâmica das fronteiras: Os brasiguaios na fronteira entre o Brasil e o Paraguai.* São Paulo: Annablume, 2010.

Alfonso, César. "Represión y prevención del terrorismo en la República del Paraguay." In *Terrorismo y derecho penal*, edited by Kai Ambos, Ezequiel Malarino, and Christian Steiner, 89–112. Berlin: EdPal and Konrad-Adenauer-Stiftung, 2015.

Almeida, Paulo Roberto de. "Brazilian Studies in the United States: Trends, Perspectives, and Prospects." In *Envisioning Brazil: A Guide to Brazilian Studies in the United States, 1945–2003*, edited by Marshall Eakin and Paulo Roberto de Almeida, 3–29. Madison: University of Wisconsin Press, 2005.

Alsultany, Evelyn, and Ella Shohat, eds. *Between the Middle East and the Americas: The Cultural Politics of Diaspora.* Ann Arbor: University of Michigan Press, 2013.

Álvarez, Sonia, Arturo Árias, and Charles Hale. "Re-visioning Latin American Studies." *Cultural Anthropology* 26.2 (2011): 225–46.

Amar, Paul. *The Security Archipelago: Human-Security States, Sexuality Politics, and the End of Neoliberalism.* Durham, NC: Duke University Press, 2013.

———, ed. *The Middle East and Brazil: Perspectives on the New Global South.* Bloomington: Indiana University Press, 2014.

Amaral, Arthur Bernardes do. *A Tríplice Fronteira e a Guerra ao Terror.* São Paulo: Apicuri Editora, 2009.

Amery, Hussein Abdul-Munim. "The Effects of Migration and Remittances on Two Lebanese Villages." PhD diss., McMaster University, Hamilton, Ontario, 1992.

Antunes, Priscila Carlos Brandão. *SNI e Abin: Uma leitura da atuação dos serviços secretos brasileiros ao longo do século.* Rio de Janeiro: Fundação Getúlio Vargas Editora, 2002.

———. "Establishing Democratic Control of Intelligence in Argentina." In *Reforming Intelligence: Obstacles to Democratic Control and Effectiveness*, edited by Thomas Bruneau and Steven Boraz, 195–218. Austin: University of Texas Press, 2007.

Anzaldúa, Gloria. *Borderlands/La Frontera.* San Francisco: Aunt Lute Books, 1987.

Appadurai, Arjun. *Modernity at Large: Cultural Dimensions of Globalization.* Minneapolis: University of Minnesota Press, 1996.

Arsan, Andrew. *Interlopers of Empire: The Lebanese Diaspora in Colonial French West Africa.* Oxford: Oxford University Press, 2014.

Arsan, Andrew, Akram Khater, and John Tofik Karam. "Editorial Forward." *Mashriq & Mahjar: Journal of Middle East and North African Migration Studies* 1.1 (2013): 1–7.

Awad, Yousef. *The Arab Atlantic: Resistance, Diaspora, and Trans-Cultural Dialogue in the Works of Arab British and Arab American Women Writers.* Berlin: Lambert Academic Publishing, 2012.

Baer, Werner. *The Brazilian Economy: Growth and Development.* 7th Edition. Boulder, CO: Lynne Rienner, 2013.

Baer, Werner, and Melissa Birch. "The International Economic Relations of a Small Country: The Case of Paraguay." *Economic Development and Cultural Change* 35.3 (1987): 601–27.

Baer, Werner, and Luis Breur. "From Inward- to Outward-Oriented Growth: Paraguay in the 1980s." *Journal of Interamerican Studies and World Affairs* 28.3 (1986): 125–40.

Baiocchi, Gianpaolo. "Media Coverage of 9-11 in Brazil." *Television & New Media* 3.2 (2002): 183–89.

Balloffet, Lily Pearl. "A Digital History of the Arab Argentine *Mahjar.*" Paper presented at the symposium "The Middle East in Latin America," Duke University, 21 October 2016.

_____. "Argentine and Egyptian History Entangled: From Perón to Nasser." *Journal of Latin American Studies* 50.3 (2018): 549–77.

_____. *Argentina in the Global Middle East.* Stanford: Stanford University Press, 2020.

Bandeira, Luiz Alberto Moniz. *Relações Brasil-EUA no contexto da globalização: I—Presença dos EUA no Brasil.* São Paulo: Editora SENAC, 1998.

_____. *Relações Brasil-EUA no contexto da globalização: II—Rivalidade emergente.* São Paulo: Editora SENAC, 1999.

_____. "Las relaciones en el Cono Sur: Iniciativas de integración." In *El Cono Sur: Una historia común,* edited by Mario Rapoport and Amado Luiz Cervo. Buenos Aires: Fondo de Cultura Económica, 2001.

_____. *Brasil, Argentina e Estados Unidos: Conflito e integração na América do Sul: Da tríplice aliança ao Mercosul, 1870–2003.* Rio de Janeiro: Editora Revan, 2003.

_____. "Política Exterior do Brasil—De FHC a Lula." *Projeto História* 31 (2005): 109–30.

Barbosa, Rubens Antonio. *O dissenso de Washington: Notas de um observador privilegiado sobre as relações Brasil-Estados Unidos.* Rio de Janeiro: Editora Nova Fronteira Participações, 2011.

_____. *The Washington Dissensus: A Privileged Observer's Perspective on US-Brazil Relations.* Translated by Anthony Doyle. Nashville, TN: Vanderbilt University Press, 2014.

Barreto, Fernando de Mello. "Olavo Setúbal." In *A Política Externa após a redemocratização.* Brasília: Fundação Alexandre Gusmão, 2012.

_____. "Roberto de Abreu Sodré." In *A Política Externa após a redemocratização.* Brasília: Fundação Alexandre Gusmão, 2012.

Bartolomé, Mariano. "A tríplice fronteira: Principal foco de insegurança no cone sul americano." *Military Review* (Summer 2003): 22–35.

Basch, Linda, Nina Glick Schiller, and Cristina Szanton Blanc. *Nations Unbound: Transnational Projects, Postcolonial Predicaments, and Deterritorialized Nation-States.* New York: Routledge, 2005.

Beeman, William O. *The Great Satan vs. the Mad Mullahs: How the United States and Iran Demonize Each Other.* Chicago: University of Chicago Press, 2005.

Bejarano, Ramón César. *El Paraguay en busca del mar.* Asunción: Casa Editorial Toledo, 1965.

Belnap, Jeffrey, and Raúl Fernandez, eds. *José Martí's 'Our America': From National to Hemispheric Cultural Studies*. Durham, NC: Duke University Press, 1998.

Bennassar, Bartolomé. "Tordesillas: El primer reparto del mundo." *Política Exterior* 6.25 (1992): 151–59.

Beraba, Ana Luiza. *América aracnídea: Teias culturais interamericanas*. Rio de Janeiro: Civilização Brasileira, 2008.

Berger, Mark. "After the Third World? History, Destiny, and the Fate of Third Worldism." *Third World Quarterly* 25.1 (2004): 9–39.

Bethell, Leslie. "Brazil and 'Latin America.'" *Journal of Latin American Studies* 42.3 (2010): 457–85.

Bidaseca, Karina Andrea. *Los sin tierra de Misiones: Disputas políticas y culturales en torno al racismo, la 'intrusión' y la extranjerización del excluido en un espacio social transfronterizo*. Buenos Aires: CLACSO, 2012.

Bigelow, Allison Margaret, and Thomas Miller Klubock. "Introduction to Latin American Studies and the Humanities: Past, Present, Future." *Latin American Research Review* 53.3 (2018): 573–80.

Birch, Melissa. "Paraguay and Mercosur: The Lesser of Two Evils?" *Latin American Business Review* 15.3–4 (2014): 269–90.

Blanc, Jacob. *Before the Flood: The Itaipu Dam and the Visibility of Rural Brazil*. Durham, NC: Duke University Press, 2019.

_____. "The Last Political Prisoner: Juvêncio Mazzarollo and the Twilight of Brazil's Dictatorship." *Luso-Brazilian Review* 53.1 (2016): 153–78.

Blanc, Jacob, and Frederico Freitas, eds. *Big Water: The Making of the Borderlands between Brazil, Argentina, and Paraguay*. Tucson: University of Arizona Press, 2018.

Brafman Kittner, Cristiana. "The Role of Safe Havens in Islamist Terrorism." *Terrorism and Political Violence* 19.3 (2007): 307–29.

Brennan, James. *Argentina's Missing Bones: Revisiting the History of the Dirty War*. Berkeley: University of California Press, 2018.

Briceño-Ruiz, José, and Andrés Rivarola Puntigliano. *Brazil and Latin America: Between the Separation and Integration Paths*. Lanham, MD: Lexington Books, 2017.

Brito, José Maria de. *Descoberta de Foz do Iguaçu e fundação da colônia militar*. Curitiba: Travessa dos Editores, 2005 [1907].

Brooks, Stephen. *Producing Security: Multinational Corporations, Globalization, and the Changing Calculus of Conflict*. Princeton, NJ: Princeton University Press, 2005.

Brown, Jacqueline. "Black Liverpool, Black America, and the Gendering of Diasporic Space." *Cultural Anthropology* 13.3 (1998): 291–335.

Bruckmayr, Philipp. "Syro-Lebanese Migration to Colombia, Venezuela and Curaçao: From Mainly Christian to Predominantly Muslim Phenomenon." *European Journal of Economic and Political Studies* 3 (2010): 151–78.

Butler, Judith. *Precarious Life: The Powers of Mourning and Violence*. New York: Verso, 2004.

Buzanelli, Márcio Paulo. Introdução. *II Encontro de Estudos: Terrorismo*. Brasília: Presidência da República—Gabinete de Segurança Institucional, 2004.

Cabán, Pedro. "The New Synthesis of Latin American/Latino Studies." In *Borderless Borders: U.S. Latinos, Latin Americans, and the Paradox of Interdependence*, edited by Frank Bonilla, Edwin Meléndez, Rebecca Morales, and María de los Angeles Torres, 195–215. Philadelphia: Temple University Press, 1998.

Call, Charles T. "War Transitions and the New Civilian Security in Latin America." *Comparative Politics* 35.1 (2002): 1–20.

Cancian, Nadir Aparecida. *Cafeicultura paranaense (1900–1970)*. Curitiba: Grafipar, 1981.

Cardozo, Poliana Fabíula. "O Líbano ausente e o Líbano presente: Espaço de identidades de imigrantes libaneses em Foz do Iguaçu." PhD diss., Universidade Federal do Paraná, 2012.

Carneiro, Camilo Pereira. *Fronteiras Irmãs: Transfronteirizações na Bacia do Prata*. Porto Alegre: Ideograf—Gráfica e Editora, 2016.

Carvalho, Francione Oliveira. "Fronteiras instáveis: Inautenticidade intercultural na escola de Foz do Iguaçu." PhD diss., Universidade Presbiteriana Mackenzie, 2011.

Carvalho, Vinicius Mariano de. "Brazilian Studies and Brazilianists: Conceptual Remarks." *Brasiliana: Journal for Brazilian Studies* 5.1 (2016): 344–66.

Causarano, Mabel. *Dinâmicas metropolitanas en Asunción, Ciudad del Este y Encarnación*. Asunción: UNFPA/ADEPO, 2006.

Cavalcante, Antonio Nilson Quezado, and Etienne F. Cracco. "Os incentivos às exportações de manufaturados: Analise e sugestão." *Revista de Administração de Empresas* 12.1 (1972): 63–69.

Cavedon, Christina. *Cultural Melancholia: U.S. Trauma Discourses before and after 9/11*. Leiden: Brill, 2015.

Chakrabarty, Dipesh. *Provincializing Europe: Postcolonial Thought and Historical Difference*. Princeton, NJ: Princeton University Press, 2000.

Chatterjee, Partha. *The Nation and Its Fragments: Colonial and Postcolonial Histories*. Princeton, NJ: Princeton University Press, 1998.

Civantos, Christina. "Ali Bla Bla's Double-Edged Sword: Argentine President Carlos Menem and the Negotiation of Identity." In *Between the Middle East and the Americas: The Cultural Politics of Diaspora*, edited by Evelyn Alsultany and Ella Shohat, 108–29. Ann Arbor: University of Michigan Press, 2013.

———. "Orientalism and the Narration of Violence in the Mediterranean Atlantic: Gabriel García Márquez and Elias Khoury." In *The Global South Atlantic: Region, Vision, Method*, edited by Kerry Bystrom and Joseph Slaughter, 165–85. New York: Fordham University Press, 2017.

Clausing, Kimberly. *Open: The Progressive Case for Free Trade, Immigration, and Global Capital*. Cambridge, MA: Harvard University Press, 2019.

Collier, David, ed. *The New Authoritarianism in Latin America*. Princeton, NJ: Princeton University Press, 1979.

Comaroff, Jean, and John Comaroff. *Theory from the South: Or How Europe Is Evolving toward Africa*. Boulder, CO: Paradigm Publishers, 2011.

Conniff, Michael. *Panama and the United States: The End of the Alliance*. Athens, GA: University of Georgia Press, 2001.

Corach, Carlos, and Mario Baizán, eds. *La respuesta Argentina Frente al terrorismo*. Buenos Aires: Fupomi Ediciones, 2002.

Correa Filho, Sérgio Leite Schmitt, Daniel Chiari Barros, Bernardo Hauch
    Ribeiro de Castro, Paulus Vinícius da Rocha Fonseca, and Jaime Gornszetjn.
    "Panorama sobre a indústria de defesa e segurança no Brasil." *BNDES Setorial*
    38 (2013): 373–408.
Costa, Thomaz Guedes da, and Gastón Schulmeister. "The Puzzle of the Iguazu
    Tri-Border Area." *Global Crime* 8.1 (2007): 26–39.
Costa e Silva, Alberto da. "Da Guerra ao Mercosul: Evolução das relações
    diplomáticas Brasil-Paraguai." In *A Guerra do Paraguai: 130 anos depois*,
    edited by Maria Eduarda Castro Magalhães Marques, 165–74. Rio de Janeiro:
    Relume Dumará, 1995.
Costigan, Lúcia Helena, and Leopoldo M. Bernucci. "O Brasil, a América
    Hispânica e o Caribe: Abordagens comparativas." *Revista Iberoamericana*
    68.200 (2002): 871–74.
Cunha, Ciro Leal M. da. *Terrorismo internacional e política externa brasileira após
    11 de setembro*. Brasília: Fundação Alexandre de Gusmão, 2010.
Dabène, Olivier. *The Politics of Regional Integration in Latin America: Theoretical
    and Comparative Explorations*. New York: Palgrave Macmillan, 2009.
Dagnino, Renato. *A indústria de defesa no governo Lula*. São Paulo: Editora
    Expressão Popular, 2010.
Davies, Bronwyn, ed. *Judith Butler in Conversation: Analyzing the Texts and Talk of
    Everyday Life*. New York: Routledge, 2008.
Dávila, Jerry. *Hotel Trópico: Brazil and the Challenge of African Decolonization,
    1950–1980*. Durham, NC: Duke University Press, 2013.
_____. *Dictatorship in South America*. Malden, MA: Wiley-Blackwell, 2013.
Dirlik, Arif, ed. *What Is in a Rim? Critical Perspectives on the Pacific Region Idea*.
    Boston: Rowman and Littlefield Publishers, 1998.
Dilla Alfonso, Haroldo. "Los complejos urbanos transfronterizos en América
    Latina." *Estudios fronterizos* 16.31 (2015): 15–38.
Dolan, Catherine, and Dinah Rajak, eds. *The Anthropology of Corporate Social
    Responsibility*. New York: Berghan Books, 2016.
Domínguez Dibb, Humberto. *Presencia y vigencia Arabes en el Paraguay*.
    Asunción: Editorial Cromos, 1977.
_____. *La evasión de divisas: Historia del mayor fraude al país*. Asunción:
    Ediciones HOY, 1986.
Dorfman, Adriana, and Arthur Borba Colen França. "Estudos fronteiriços no
    Brasil: Uma geografia da produção científica." In *Geografia política, geopolítica
    e gestão do território*, edited by Augusto César Pinheiro da Silva, 65–84. Rio de
    Janeiro: Gramma, 2016.
Eakin, Marshall. *Becoming Brazilians: Race and National Identity in Twentieth-
    Century Brazil*. Cambridge, UK: Cambridge University Press, 2017.
_____. "Does Latin America Have a Common History?" *Vanderbilt e-Journal of
    Luso-Hispanic Studies* 1.1 (2004): 29–49.
Edwards, Brian, and Dilip Parameshwar Gaonkar, eds. *Globalizing American
    Studies*. Chicago: University of Chicago Press, 2010.
Escudé, Carlos, and Beatriz Gurevich. "Limits to Governability, Corruption, and
    Transnational Terrorism." *Estudios interdisciplinarios de America Latina y el
    Caribe* 14.2 (2003): 127–48.

Estévez, Eduardo. "Intelligence Community Reforms: The Case of Argentina." In *Intelligence Elsewhere: Spies and Espionage Outside the Anglosphere*, edited by Philip Davies and Kristian Gustafson, 219–38. Washington, DC: Georgetown University Press, 2013.

Fahrenthold, Stacy D. "An Archaeology of Rare Books in Arab Atlantic History." *Journal of American Ethnic History* 37.3 (2018): 77–83.

_____. *Between the Ottomans and the Entente: The First World War in the Syrian and Lebanese Diaspora, 1908–1925*. Oxford: Oxford University Press, 2019.

Farah, Douglas. "Iran in Latin America: An Overview." In *Iran in Latin America: Threat or 'Axis of Annoyance'?* edited by Cynthia Arnson, Haleh Esfandiari, and Adam Stubits, 13–25. Washington, DC: Woodrow Wilson International Center for Scholars, 2009.

Fares, Seme Taleb. "O pragmatismo do petróleo: As relações entre o Brasil e o Iraque." *Revista Brasileira de Política Internacional* 50.2 (2007): 129–45.

Feldstein, Pablo, and Carolina Acosta-Alzura. "Argentinean Jews as Scapegoat: A Textual Analysis of the Bombing of AMIA." *Journal of Communication Inquiry* 27.2 (2003): 152–70.

Fernandes, Ananda Simões. "A política externa da ditadura brasileira durante os 'anos de chumbo' (1968–1974): As intervenções do 'Brasil Potência' na América Latina." *História Social* 1.18 (2010): 157–76.

Fernández-Armesto, Felipe. *The Americas: A Hemispheric History*. New York: Random House, 2005.

Ferradás, Carmen Alicia. *Power in the Southern Cone Borderlands: An Anthropology of Development Practice*. Westport, CT: Bergin and Garvey, 1998.

_____. "Security and Ethnography on the Triple Frontier of the Southern Cone." In *Borderlands: Ethnographic Approaches to Security, Power, and Identity*, edited by Hastings Donnan and Thomas Wilson, 35–53. New York: University Press of America, 2010.

Fleischman, Luis. "The Case of the Bombing of the Jewish Headquarters in Buenos Aires (AMIA): A Structural Approach." *MACLAS Latin American Essays* 12 (1999): 119–34.

Flores, Juan, and Renato Rosaldo, eds. *A Companion to Latina/o Studies*. Malden, MA: Blackwell, 2007.

Flores, Juan, and George Yúdice. "Living Borders/Buscando America: Languages of Latina/o Self-Formation." *Social Text* 24 (1990): 57–84.

Fluck, Winfried, Donald Pease, and John Carlos Rowe, eds. *Re-framing the Transnational Turn in American Studies*. Lebanon, NH: Dartmouth College Press, 2011.

Fogel, Ramón. "La region de la triple frontera: Territorios de integración y desintegración." *Sociologias* 10.20 (2008): 270–90.

Fojas, Camilla, and Rudy P. Guevarra, Jr., eds. *Transnational Crossroads: Remapping the Americas and the Pacific*. Lincoln: University of Nebraska Press, 2012.

Folch, Christine. "Surveillance and State Violence in Stroessner's Paraguay: Itaipú Hydroelectric Dam, Archive of Terror." *American Anthropologist* 115.1 (2013): 44–57.

_____. *Hydropolitics: The Itaipu Dam, Sovereignty, and the Engineering of Modern South America*. Princeton, NJ: Princeton University Press, 2019.

Franco, Alejandro Hamed. *Los árabes y sus descendientes en el Paraguay: Un largo recorrido histórico.* Asunción: Arandurã Editorial, 2002.

Freitas, Veronica Tavares de. *Quem são os terroristas do Brasil? A Lei Antiterror e a produção política de um inimigo público.* Curitiba: Editora CVR, 2017.

Galemba, Rebecca. "'Corn Is Food, Not Contraband': The Right to 'Free Trade' at the Mexico–Guatemala Border." *American Ethnologist* 39.4 (2012): 716–34.

Galsze, George. *Die fragmentierte Stadt: Ursachen und Folgen bewachter Wohnkomplexe im Libanon.* Opladen: Leske + Budrich, 2003.

Gebara, Ademir, Herib Caballero Campos, and Leandro Baller, eds. *Leituras de fronteiras: Trajetórias, histórias e territórios.* Jundiaí: Paco Editorial, 2018.

Gilroy, Paul. *The Black Atlantic: Modernity and Double Consciousness.* London: Verso, 1993.

Goede, Marieke de. "Hawala Discourses and the War on Terrorist Finance." *Environment and Planning D: Society and Space* 21.5 (2003): 513–32.

_____. *Speculative Security: The Politics of Pursuing Terrorist Monies.* Minneapolis: University of Minnesota Press, 2012.

Goede, Marieke de, and Gavin Sullivan. "The Politics of Security Lists." *Environment and Planning D: Society and Space* 34.1 (2016): 3–13.

Goldstein, Daniel. "Toward a Critical Anthropology of Security." *Current Anthropology* 51.4 (2010): 487–517.

_____. "Decolonialising 'Actually Existing Neoliberalism.'" *Social Anthropology / Anthropologie Sociale* 20.3 (2012): 304–9.

Gordon, Lincoln. *A New Deal for Latin America: The Alliance for Progress.* Cambridge, MA: Harvard University Press, 1963.

"Gran Hotel Casino Acaray." *Cataratas: A Rainha do Turismo* 1.5 (1969).

Greenberg, Nathaniel. "Amia and the Triple Frontier in Argentine and American Discourse on Terrorism." *A Contracorriente* 8.1 (2010): 61–93.

Grewal, Inderpal. *Transnational America: Feminisms, Diasporas, Neoliberalisms.* Durham, NC: Duke University Press, 2005.

Grimson, Alejandro. "Fronteras, estados e identificaciones en el Cono Sur." In *Estudios Latinoamericanos sobre cultura y transformaciones sociales en tiempos de globalización* 2. Buenos Aires: CLACSO, 2001.

_____. "Nations, Nationalism and 'Borderization' in the Southern Cone." In *A Companion to Border Studies*, edited by Thomas M. Wilson and Hastings Donnan, 194–213. Malden, MA: Blackwell, 2012.

Gualtieri, Sarah M. A. *Between Arab and White: Race and Ethnicity in the Early Syrian American Diaspora.* Berkeley: University of California Press, 2009.

_____. *Arab Routes: Pathways to Syrian California.* Stanford: Stanford University Press, 2020.

*Guia Assalam del comercio sirio-libanes en la República Argentina.* Buenos Aires: Empresa Assalam, 1928.

Gupta, Akhil, and James Ferguson. "Discipline and Practice: 'The Field' as Site, Method, and Location in Anthropology." In *Anthropological Locations: Boundaries and Grounds of a Field Science*, edited by Akhil Gupta and James Ferguson, 1–46. Berkeley: University of California Press, 1997.

Gupta, Pamila, Christopher Lee, Marissa Moorman, and Sandhya Shukla. Introduction to special issue "The Global South: Histories, Politics, Maps." *Radical History Review* 131 (2018): 1–12.

Gurevich, Beatriz. "After the AMIA Bombing: A Critical Analysis of Two Parallel Discourses." In *The Jewish Diaspora in Latin America and the Caribbean: Fragments of Memory*, edited by Kristin Ruggiero, 86–112. Sussex: Sussex Academic Press, 2005.

Gurulé, Jimmy. *Unfunding Terror: The Legal Response to the Financing of Global Terrorism*. Cheltenham: Edward Elgar Publications, 2009.

Gutiérrez Sanín, Francisco, Eric Hershberg, and Monica Hirst. "Change and Continuity in Hemispheric Affairs: Latin America after September 11." In *Critical Views of September 11*, edited by Eric Hershberg and Kevin Moore, 177–90. New York: New Press, 2002.

Gutmann, Matthew, and Jeffrey Lesser, eds. *Global Latin America: Into the Twenty-First Century*. Berkeley: University of California Press, 2016.

Han, Clara. *Life in Debt: Times of Care and Violence in Neoliberal Chile*. Berkeley: University of California, 2012.

Hannerz, Ulf. *Foreign News: Exploring the World of Foreign Correspondents*. Chicago: University of Chicago Press, 2004.

Hassan, Waïl. "Brazil." In *The Oxford Handbook of Arab Novelistic Traditions*, edited by Waïl Hassan, 543–57. Oxford: Oxford University Press, 2017.

———. "Carioca Orientalism: Morocco in the Imaginary of a Brazilian *Telenovela*." In *The Global South Atlantic: Region, Vision, Method*, edited by Kerry Bystrom and Joseph Slaughter, 274–94. New York: Fordham University Press, 2017.

Hewamanne, Sandya. *Stitching Identities in a Free Trade Zone: Gender and Politics in Sri Lanka*. Philadelphia: University of Pennsylvania Press, 2008.

Hirst, Mónica. "MERCOSUL Politics: Between Fragmentation and Integration." In *Paths to Regional Integration: The Case of Mercosur*, edited by Joseph Tulchin and Ralph Espach with Heather Golding, 135–51. Washington, DC: Woodrow Wilson Center Reports on the Americas, 2002.

Ho, Engseng. "Empire through Diasporic Eyes: A View from the Other Boat." *Comparative Studies of Society and History* 46.2 (2004).

Hoganson, Kristin, and Jay Sexton, eds. *Crossing Empires: Taking US History into Transimperial Terrain*. Durham, NC: Duke University Press, 2020.

Howell, Sally, and Andrew Shryock. "Cracking Down on Diaspora: Arab Detroit and America's War on Terror." *Anthropological Quarterly* 76.3 (2004): 443–62.

Hudson, Rex. *Terrorist and Organized Crime Groups in the Tri-Border Area (TBA) of South America*. Washington, DC: Federal Research Division—LOC and Central Intelligence Crime Center, 2003.

Hull, Matthew. *Government of Paper: The Materiality of Bureaucracy in Urban Pakistan*. Berkeley: University of California Press, 2012.

Hunter, Wendy. *Eroding Military Influence in Brazil: Politicians against Soldiers*. Chapel Hill, NC: University of North Carolina Press, 1997.

Hyland, Steven. *More Argentine Than You: Arabic-Speaking Immigrants in Argentina*. Albuquerque: University of New Mexico Press, 2017.

Jackson, K. David. "History of the Future: Luso-Brazilian Studies in the New Millennium." *Luso-Brazilian Review* 40.2 (2003): 13–30.

Jamal, Amaney, and Nadine Naber, eds. *Race and Arab Americans before and after 9/11: From Invisible Citizens to Visible Subjects*. Syracuse, NY: Syracuse University Press, 2008.

Johnson, Chalmers. *Nemesis: The Last Days of the American Republic*. New York: Palgrave Macmillan, 2007.

Jusionyte, Ieva. *Savage Frontier: Making News and Security on the Argentine Border*. Berkeley: University of California Press, 2015.

Kaplan, Amy. "Violent Belongings and the Question of Empire Today: Presidential Address to the American Studies Association, October 17, 2003." *American Quarterly* 56.1 (2004): 1–18.

Kaplan, Amy, and Donald Pease, eds. *Cultures of United States Imperialism*. Durham, NC: Duke University Press, 1993.

Karam, John Tofik. *Another Arabesque: Syrian-Lebanese Ethnicity in Neoliberal Brazil*. Philadelphia, PA: Temple University Press, 2007.

_____. "Fios árabes, tecido brasileiro." *Revista de História da Biblioteca Nacional* 4.46 (2009): 22–24.

_____. "Belly Dancing and the (En)Gendering of Ethnic Sexuality in the 'Mixed' Brazilian Nation." *Journal of Middle East Women's Studies* 6.2 (2010): 86–114.

_____. "Historias musulmanas en América Latina y el Caribe." *Istor: Revista de Historia Internacional* 12.45 (2011): 22–43.

_____. "On the Trail and Trial of a Palestinian Diaspora: Mapping South America in the Arab-Israeli Conflict." *Journal of Latin American Studies* 45.4 (2013): 751–77.

_____. "I, Too, Am the Americas: Arabs in the Redrawing of Area and Ethnic Studies." *Journal of American Ethnic History* 37.3 (2018): 93–101.

_____. "Romancing Middle Eastern Men in North and South America: Two Mid-Century Texts." In *Constructions of Masculinity in the Middle East and North Africa: Literature, Film, and National Discourse*, edited by Mohja Kahf and Nadine Sinno. Cairo: American University in Cairo Press, 2020.

_____. "The Levant in Latin America." In *Global Middle East: Into the Twenty-First Century*, edited by Asef Bayat and Linda Herrera, 253–66. Berkeley: University of California Press, 2021.

Karam, John Tofik, María del Mar Logroño Narbona, and Paulo G. Pinto. "Latino America in the *Umma* / The *Umma* in Latino America." In *Crescent over Another Horizon: Islam in Latin America, the Caribbean, and Latino USA*, edited by María del Mar Logroño Narbona, Paulo G. Pinto, and John Tofik Karam, 1–21. Austin: University of Texas Press, 2015.

Karim, Jamillah. *American Muslim Women: Negotiating Race, Class, and Gender within the Ummah*. New York: New York University Press, 2009.

Kearney, Michael. *Changing Fields of Anthropology: From Local to Global*. Lanham, MD: Rowman & Littlefield, 2004.

Kelly, Phil, and Thomas Whigham. "La geopolítica del Paraguay: Vulnerabilidades regionales y respuestas nacionales." *Perspectivas Internacionales Paraguayas* 3 (1990): 41–78.

Keough, Peter. *Kathryn Bigelow: Interviews*. Jackson: University Press of Mississippi, 2013.

Khan, Aisha, ed. *Islam in the Americas*. Gainesville: University Press of Florida, 2015.

Khater, Akram Fouad. *Inventing Home: Emigration, Gender, and the Middle Class in Lebanon, 1870–1920*. Berkeley: University of California Press, 2001.

Knauft, Bruce. "Provincializing America: Imperialism, Capitalism, and Counterhegemony in the Twenty-First Century." *Current Anthropology* 48.6 (2007): 781–99.

_____. "Reply." *Current Anthropology* 48.6 (2007): 799–803.

Lambert, Peter. "Dancing between Superpowers: Ideology, Pragmatism, and Drift in Paraguayan Foreign Policy." In *Latin American Foreign Policies: Between Ideology and Pragmatism,* edited by Gian Luca Gardini and Peter Lambert, 67–86. New York: Palgrave Macmillan, 2014.

_____. "The Myth of the Good Neighbour: Paraguay's Uneasy Relationship with Brazil." *Bulletin of Latin American Research* 35.1 (2016): 34–48.

Landau, Jacob. *The Politics of Pan-Islam: Ideology and Organization.* Oxford: Oxford University Press, 1990.

La Pastina, Antônio. "The Self-Absorbed Bully: A Brazilian View of the US at War." In *War, Media, and Propaganda,* edited by Yahya Kamalipour, 199–206. New York: Rowman and Littlefield, 2004.

Lee, Rensselaer. "The Triborder-Terrorism Nexus." *Global Crime* 9.4 (2008): 332–47.

Leonard, Thomas. "Colón Free Trade Zone (CFTZ)." In *Historical Dictionary of Panama,* 85. Lanham, MD: Rowman and Littlefield, 2015.

Lesser, Jeffrey. *Negotiating National Identity: Immigrants, Minorities, and the Struggle for Ethnicity in Brazil.* Durham, NC: Duke University Press, 1999.

_____. *Immigration, Ethnicity, and National Identity in Brazil.* Cambridge, UK: Cambridge University Press, 2013.

Levander, Caroline F., and Robert S. Levine, eds. *Hemispheric American Studies.* Rutgers, NJ: Rutgers University Press, 2008.

Lewis, Paul. *Paraguay under Stroessner.* Chapel Hill: University of North Carolina Press, 1980.

Lima, Jackson. "Os árabes da fronteira." *Classe 10* 1.3 (1996): 11–13.

_____. "Os cristãos quase nada sabem sobre o islã." *Classe 10* 1.3 (1996): 14–15.

Linz, Juan, and Alfred Stepan. *Problems of Democratic Transition and Consolidation: Southern Europe, South America, and Post-Communist Europe.* Baltimore, MD: Johns Hopkins University Press, 1996.

Livingstone, Grace. "George W. Bush and the 'War on Terror.'" In *America's Backyard: The United States and Latin America from the Monroe Doctrine to the War on Terror,* by Grace Livingstone, 120–66. London: Zed Books, 2013.

Logroño Narbona, María del Mar, Paulo G. Pinto, and John Tofik Karam, eds. *Crescent over Another Horizon: Islam in Latin America, the Caribbean, and Latino USA.* Austin: University of Texas Press, 2015.

Lomas, Laura. *Translating Empire: José Martí, Migrant Latino Subjects, and American Modernities.* Durham, NC: Duke University Press, 2008.

Loveman, Brian. *For La Pátria: Politics and the Armed Forces in Latin America.* Wilmington, DE: Scholarly Resources, 1999.

Lutz, Catherine. "Militarization." In *A Companion to the Anthropology of Politics,* edited by David Nugent and Joan Vincent, 318–31. New York: Blackwell, 2004.

Maksoud, Clovis. "Redefining Non-Alignment: The Global South in the New Global Equation." In *Altered States: A Reader in the New World Order,* edited by Phyllis Bennis and Michael Moushabeck, 28–37. New York: Olive Branch Press, 1993.

Manzetti, Luigi. "The Political Economy of Mercosur." *Journal of Interamerican Studies and World Affairs* 35.4 (1993–94): 101–41.

Marcus, George. "Ethnography in/of the World System: The Emergence of Multi-Sited Ethnography." *Annual Review of Anthropology* 24 (1995): 95–117.

Marcus, George, and James Faubion, eds. *Fieldwork Is Not What It Used to Be: Learning Anthropology's Method at a Time of Transition*. Ithaca, NY: Cornell University Press, 2009.

Margolis, Maxine. "The Coffee Cycle on the Paraná Frontier." *Luso-Brazilian Review* 9.1 (1972): 3–12.

Marini, Ruy Mauro. "Brazilian 'Interdependence' and Imperialist Integration." *Monthly Review* 17.7 (1965): 10–29.

_____. "Brazilian Subimperialism." *Monthly Review* 23.9 (1972): 14–24.

Martí, José. "Nuestra América." In *Nuestra América*, edited by Juan Marinello, 30–31. Caracas: Ayacucho, 1977.

Martins, Etiene Coelho. *Direito internacional e segurança pública*. São Paulo: Biblioteca 24 Horas, 2011.

Masco, Joseph. *The Theater of Operations: National Security Affect from the Cold War to the War on Terror*. Durham, NC: Duke University Press, 2014.

Mattar, Ahmad. *Guia social de la colonia de habla arabe en Bolivia, Colombia, Ecuador, Peru, Venezuela y las islas holandesas de Curacao y Aruba*. Barranquilla: Empresa Litográfica S.A., 1945.

Maurer, Bill. "Anthropological and Accounting Knowledge in Islamic Banking and Finance: Rethinking Critical Accounts." *Journal of the Royal Anthropological Institute* 8.4 (2002): 645–67.

Mazzarollo, Juvêncio. *A taipa da injustiça: Esbanjamento econômico, drama social e holocausto ecológico em Itaipu*. Curitiba: Comissão Pastoral da Terra do Paraná, 1980.

McAlister, Melani. "A Cultural History of the War without End." *Journal of American History* 89.2 (2002): 439–55.

McSherry, J. Patrice. "Strategic Alliance: Menem and the Military-Security Forces in Argentina." *Latin American Perspectives* 24.6 (1997): 63–92.

_____. *Incomplete Transition: Military Power and Democracy in Argentina*. New York: Macmillan, 1997.

_____. *Predatory States: Operation Condor and Covert War in Latin America*. Lanham, MD: Rowman & Littlefield, 2005.

Meehan, Howard. "Terrorism, Diasporas, and Permissive Threat Environments." MA thesis, Naval Postgraduate School, 2004.

Mendel, William. "Paraguay's Ciudad del Este and the New Centers of Gravity." *Military Review* (March 2002): 51–57.

Menegotto, Ricardo. *Migrações e fronteiras: Os imigrantes brasileiros no Paraguai e a redefinição da fronteira*. Santa Cruz do Sul: EDUNISC, 2004.

Menezes, Alfredo da Mota. *La Herencia de Stroessner: Brasil-Paraguay 1955–1980*. Asunción: Carlos Schauman Editor, 1990.

Menjívar, Cecilia, and Néstor Rodríguez, eds. *When States Kill: Latin America, the US, and Technologies of Terror*. Austin: University of Texas Press, 2001.

Mignolo, Walter. *Local Histories / Global Designs: Coloniality, Subaltern Knowledges, and Border Thinking*. Princeton, NJ: Princeton University Press, 2000.

_____. "Decolonial Reflections on Hemispheric Partitions: From the 'Western Hemisphere' to the 'Eastern Hemisphere.'" In *The Routledge Companion to Inter-American Studies*, edited by Wilfried Raussert, 59–67. New York: Routledge, 2017.

Miranda Silva, Fidel. *Historia de Alto Paraná.* Ciudad del Este: AGR, 2007.

Miyamoto, Shiguenoli. "O Brasil e as negociações multilaterais." *Revista Brasileira de Política Internacional* 43.1 (2000): 119–37.

Molloy, Patricia. *Canada, U.S., and Other Unfriendly Relations before and after 9/11.* New York: Palgrave Macmillan, 2012.

Montenegro, Silvia. "La inmigración árabe en Paraguay." In *Los árabes en América Latina*, edited by Akmir Abdeluahed Akmir, 281–317. Madrid: Siglo XXI, 2009.

Montenegro, Silvia, and Veronica Giménez Béliveau. *La triple frontera: Globalización y construcción social del espacio.* Madrid: Miño y Dávila, 2006.

Montenegro, Silvia, and Veronica Giménez Béliveau, eds. *La triple frontera: Dinámicas culturales y procesos transnacionales.* Buenos Aires: Editorial Espacio, 2011.

Mora, Frank O. "Paraguay: From the *Stronato* to the Democratic Transition." In *Small States in World Politics: Explaining Foreign Policy Behavior*, edited by Jean A. K. Hey, 13–31. Boulder, CO: Lynne Rienner Publishers, 2003.

_____. "Paraguay: The Legacy of Authoritarianism." In *Latin American and Caribbean Foreign Policy*, edited by Frank O. Mora and Jeanne A. K. Hey, 309–27. Lanham, MD: Rowman and Littlefield, 2003.

Mora, Frank O., and Jerry W. Cooney. *Paraguay and the United States: Distant Allies.* Athens, GA: University of Georgia Press, 2007.

Moraes, Ceres. *Paraguai: A consolidação da ditadura de Stroessner, 1954–1963.* Porto Alegre: EdiPUCRS, 2000.

_____. "Interesses e colaboração do Brasil e dos Estados Unidos com a ditadura de Stroessner." *Diálogos* 11 (2007): 55–80.

Moura, Vasco Graça. *O Tratado de Tordesilhas / The Treaty of Tordesillas.* Lisbon: CTT Correios, 1994.

Muzzopappa, Eva, and Ana Margarita Ramos. "Una etnografía itinerante sobre el terrorismo en Argentina: Paradas, trayectorias y disputas." *Antípoda: Revista de Antropología y Arqueología* 29 (2017): 123–42.

Naber, Nadine. *Arab America: Gender, Cultural Politics, and Activism.* New York: New York University Press, 2012.

Nasta, José Daniel. *Árabes en el Paraguay: Migrantes y descendientes.* Asunción: Garbo Producciones, 2016.

Nasta, José Daniel, and L. Alberto Asbun Karmy. *La migración árabe y su descendencia en Paraguay.* Asunción: Publicitaria Nasta S.A., 2007.

Nelson, Marcel. *A History of the FTAA: From Hegemony to Fragmentation in the Americas.* New York: Palgrave Macmillan, 2015.

Netto, José Paulo. *Pequena história da ditadura brasileira (1964–1985).* São Paulo: Cortez Editora, 2016.

Newcomb, Robert Patrick. *Nossa and Nuestra América: Inter-American Dialogues.* West Lafayette, IN: Purdue University Press, 2012.

Nóbrega Júnior, José Maria Pereira da. "A militarização da segurança pública." *Revista de Sociologia Política* (Curitiba) 18.35 (2010): 119–30.

Nickson, Andrew. "Brazilian Colonization of the Eastern Border Region of Paraguay." *Journal of Latin American Studies* 13.1 (1981): 111–31.

_____. "The Itaipu Hydro-Electric Project: The Paraguayan Perspective." *Bulletin of Latin American Research* 2.1 (1982): 1–20.

_____. "Tyranny and Longevity: Stroessner's Paraguay." *Third World Quarterly* 10.1 (1988): 237–59.

_____. "The Overthrow of the Stroessner Regime: Re-establishing the Status Quo." *Bulletin of Latin American Research* 8.2 (1989): 185–209.

_____. "Reestablishing the Status Quo." In *The Paraguay Reader: History, Culture, Politics*, edited by Peter Lambert and Andrew Nickson, 326–330. Durham, NC: Duke University Press, 2013.

_____. "Gustavo Saba (1950– )." In *Historical Dictionary of Paraguay*. 3rd edition. Lanham, MD: Rowman and Littlefield, 2015.

_____. "Brazil and Paraguay: A Protectorate in the Making?" *Mural Internacional* 10 (2019): 1–14.

O'Donnell, Guillermo. *Modernization and Bureaucratic Authoritarianism: Studies in South American Politics*. Berkeley: University of California Press, 1973.

O'Dougherty, Maureen. *Consumption Intensified: The Politics of Middle-Class Daily Life in Brazil*. Durham, NC: Duke University Press, 2002.

O'Keefe, Thomas Andrew. *Latin American and Caribbean Trade Agreements: Keys to a Prosperous Community of the Americas*. Leiden: Koninklijke Brill, 2009.

Oelsner, Andrea. "Consensus and Governance in Mercosur: The Evolution of the South American Security Agenda." *Security Dialogue* 40.2 (2009): 191–212.

_____. "Mercosur's Incipient Security Governance." In *The Security Governance of Regional Organizations*, edited by Emil Kirchner and Roberto Domínguez, 190–217. New York: Routledge, 2011.

Ong, Aihwa. *Flexible Citizenship: The Cultural Logics of Transnationality*. Durham, NC: Duke University Press, 2001.

_____. *Neoliberalism as Exception: Mutations in Citizenship and Sovereignty*. Durham, NC: Duke University Press, 2006.

Osava, Mário. "Triple frontera de Brasil, Argentina y Paraguay es un barril de pólvora." In *Estados Unidos en Guerra: El miedo a la libertad vigilada*, edited by Kintto Lucas, 165–68. Quito: Ediciones Abya-Yala, 2001.

Palmar, Aluízio. *Onde foi que vocês enterraram nossos mortos?* Curitiba: FotoLaser Gráfica e Editora Ltda., 2007.

Paniago, Paulo de Tarso Resende. "O papel dos serviços de inteligência na prevenção e no combate ao terrorismo internacional." *Revista Brasileira de Inteligência* 3.4 (2007): 23–28.

Paredes, Roberto. *Stroessner y el stronismo*. Asunción: Servilibro, 2004.

Parquet, Reinerio. *Las empresas transnacionales en la economia del Paraguay*. Santiago de Chile: Comisión Economica para America Latina y el Caribe de las Naciones Unidas, 1987.

Pastor, Camila. *The Mexican Mahjar: Transnational Maronites, Jews, and Arabs under the French Mandate*. Austin: University of Texas Press, 2017.

Pease, Donald. "Exceptionalism." In *Keywords for American Cultural Studies*, edited by Bruce Burgett and Glenn Hendler, 108–11. New York: New York University Press, 2007.

_____. "Re-thinking 'American Studies after U.S. Exceptionalism.'" *American Literary History* 21.1 (2009): 19–27.

Penna Filho, Pio. "O Itamaraty nos anos de chumbo: O Centro de Informações do Exterior (CIEX) e a pressão no Cone Sul (1966–1979)." *Revista Brasileira de Política Internacional* 52.2 (2009): 43–62.

Pereira, Anthony. "Brazilian Studies Then and Now." *Brasiliana: Journal for Brazilian Studies* 1.1 (2012): 3–21.

Pereira, Anthony, and Diane Davis. "Introduction: New Patterns of Militarized Violence and Coercion in the Americas." *Latin American Perspectives* 27.2 (2000): 3–17.

Perrone, Charles A. "Fred P. Ellison and Interamerican Imperatives." *Hispania* 99.4 (2016): 526–29.

Phillips, Caryl. *Color Me English: Migration and Belonging before and after 9/11.* New York: New Press, 2013.

Piazza, Maria de Fátima Fontes. "A arte estadunidense no suplemento *Pensamento da América,* do jornal *A Manhã.*" *Revista FSA* 11.2 (2014): 247–62.

Pinheiro-Machado, Rosana. "A ética confucionista e o espírito do capitalismo: Narrativas sobre moral, harmonia e poupança na condenação do consumo conspícuo entre chineses ultramar." *Horizontes Antropológicos* 13.28 (2007): 145–74.

_____. *Counterfeit Itineraries in the Global South: The Human Consequences of Piracy in China and Brazil.* New York: Routledge, 2018.

Pinto, Paulo Gabriel Hilu da Rocha. "Ritual, etnicidade e identidade religiosa nas comunidades muçulmanas no Brasil." *Revista USP* 67 (2005): 228–50.

Pinto, Paulo Gabriel Hilu da Rocha, and Silvia Montenegro. "As comunidades muçulmanas na tríplice fronteira: Identidades religiosas, contextos locais e fluxos transnacionais." Paper presented at the 26a Reunião Brasileira de Antropologia, Porto Seguro, 2008.

Poblete, Juan, ed. *Critical Latin American and Latino Studies.* Minneapolis, MN: University of Minnesota Press, 2003.

_____. Review of *Between the Middle East and the Americas,* edited by Evelyn Alsultany and Ella Shohat. *Mashriq & Mahjar: Journal of Middle East and North African Migration Studies* 2.1 (2015): 174–78.

_____. Introduction to *New Approaches to Latin American Studies: Culture and Power,* edited by Juan Poblete, 1–13. New York: Routledge, 2018.

Portes, Alejandro. "Towards a New World: The Origins and Effects of Transnational Activities." *Ethnic and Racial Studies,* 22.2 (1999): 463–77.

Prado, Maria Ligia Coelho. "O Brasil e a distante América do Sul." *Revista de História* 145 (2001): 127–49.

Prashad, Vijay. *The Darker Nations: A Biography of the Short-Lived Third World.* New Delhi: Leftword Books, 2007.

_____. *The Poorer Nations: A Possible History of the Global South.* London: Verso Books, 2014.

Preiss, José Luiz Silva. "As Relações Brasil-Irã: Dos antecedentes aos desdobramentos no século XXI." *ANMO: África del Norte y Medio Oriente* 1.1 (2011): 45–60.

_____. "Brasil e Argentina no Oriente Médio: Do Pós-Guerra Mundial ao Final da Guerra Fria." PhD diss., Pontifícia Universidade Católica do Rio Grande do Sul, 2013.

Preuss, Ori. *Bridging the Island: Brazilians' Views of Spanish America and Themselves, 1865–1912*. Madrid: Iberoamericana-Vervuert, 2011.

Quijano, Aníbal. "Modernidad, colonialidad y América Latina." *Neplanta* 1.3 (2000): 533–80.

Quijano, Aníbal, and Immanuel Wallerstein. "Americanity as a Concept, or the Americas in the Modern World-System." *International Journal of Social Sciences* 134 (1992): 583–91.

Quintão, Aylê-Salassié Filgueiras. *Americanidade: Mercosul—Passaporte para a integração*. Brasília: Senado Federal, 2010.

Rabossi, Fernando. "Nas Ruas de Ciudad del Este: Vidas e vendas num mercado de fronteira." PhD diss., Universidade Federal do Rio de Janeiro, 2004.

_____. "Árabes e muçulmanos em Foz do Iguaçu e Ciudad del Este: Notas para uma re-interpretação." In *Mundos em movimento: Ensaios sobre migrações*, edited by Giralda Seyferth, Helion Póvoa Neto, Maria Catarina Chitolina Zanini, and Miriam de Oliveira Santos, 287–312. Santa Maria: Editora UFSM, 2007.

_____. "Terrorist Frontier Cell or Cosmopolitan Commercial Hub? The Arab and Muslim Presence at the Border of Paraguay, Brazil, and Argentina." In *The Middle East and Brazil: Perspectives on the New Global South*, edited by Paul Amar, 92–116. Bloomington: Indiana University Press, 2014.

Rein, Raanan, María José Cano Pérez, and Beatriz Molina Rueda, eds. *Más allá del Medio Oriente: Las diásporas judías y árabes en América Latina*. Granada: Editorial de la Universidad de Granada, 2012.

Ricardo, Cassiano. *Marcha para Oeste*. Rio de Janeiro: Livraria José Olympio, 1942.

_____. *Marcha para Oeste*, vol. 2. São Paulo: Editora da Universidade de São Paulo, 1970.

Riquelme, Marcial. "Dificultades para la transición en Paraguay." *Investigación Económica* 186 (1988): 165–201.

_____. "Toward a Weberian Characterization of the Stroessner Regime in Paraguay (1954–1989)." *European Review of Latin American and Caribbean Studies* 57 (1994): 29–51.

_____. "Notas para el estudio de las causas y efectos de las migraciones brasileñas en el Paraguay." In *Enclave sojero, merma de soberanía y pobreza*, edited by Ramón Fogel and Marcial Riquelme, 113–39. Asunción: Centro de Estudios Rurales Interdisciplinarios, 2005.

Rodríguez Vignoli, Jorge. *Distribución espacial de la población de América Latina y el Caribe: Tendencias, interpretaciones y desafíos para las políticas públicas*. Publication 32. Santiago de Chile: CEPAL, 2002.

Rojas, Isaac Francisco. *Intereses argentinos en la Cuenca del Plata*. Buenos Aires: Ediciones Líbera, 1969.

_____. *La ofensiva geopolítica brasileña en la Cuenca del Plata*. Buenos Aires: Ediciones Nemont, 1979.

Rowe, John Carlos. "Areas of Concern: Area Studies and the New American Studies." *Alif: Journal of Comparative Poetics* 31 (2011): 11–34.

Roy, Olivier. *Globalized Islam: The Search for a New Ummah*. New York: Columbia University Press, 2004.

Russell, Roberto. "Argentina and the United States: A Distant Relationship." In *Contemporary US-Latin American Relations: Cooperation or Conflict in the 21st Century?*, eds. Jorge Domínguez and Rafael Fernández de Castro (New York: Routledge, 2010), 101–23.

Saddy, Fehmy, ed. *Arab-Latin American Relations: Energy, Trade, and Investment.* New Brunswick: Transaction Books, 1983.

_____, ed. *The Arab World and Latin America: Economic and Political Relations in the Twenty-First Century.* London: I. B. Tauris, 2016.

Said, Edward. *Beginnings: Intention and Method.* New York: Basic Books, 1975.

_____. *Orientalism.* New York: Vintage, 1979.

Said, Edward, and Christopher Hitchens, eds. *Blaming the Victims: Spurious Scholarship and the Palestinian Question.* New York: Verso, 2001.

Sakr, Ahmad H. "The First Islamic Conference of South America." *Muslim Standard* 25 (November): 1977.

Saldívar, José David. *The Dialectics of Our America: Genealogy, Cultural Critique, and Literary History.* Durham, NC: Duke University Press, 1991.

_____. *Trans-Americanity: Subaltern Modernities, Global Coloniality, and the Cultures of Greater Mexico.* Durham, NC: Duke University Press, 2011.

Santana, Carlos Ribeiro. "O aprofundamento das relações do Brasil com os países do Oriente Médio durante os dois choques do petróleo da década de 1970: Um exemplo de ação pragmática." *Revista Brasileira de Política Internacional* 49.2 (2006): 157–77.

Santos, Luis Cláudio Villafañe Gomes. *O Brasil entre a América e a Europa.* São Paulo: Editora Unesp, 2003.

Santos, Emanuelle, and Patricia Schor. "'Brazil is Not Traveling Enough': On Postcolonial Theory and Analogous Counter-Currents. An Interview with Ella Shohat and Robert Stam." *Portuguese Cultural Studies* 4 (2012): 13–40.

Sarlo, Beatriz. "Argentina under Menem: The Aesthetics of Domination." *NACLA Report on the Americas* 27.2 (September/October 1994): 33–37.

Sarto, Ana del, Alicia Ríos, and Abril Trigo, eds. *The Latin American Cultural Studies Reader.* Durham, NC: Duke University Press, 2004.

Schilling, Paulo. *O expansionismo brasileiro: A geopolítica do General Golbery e a diplomacia do Itamarati.* São Paulo: Global, 1981.

Schmitt, Carl. *The Concept of the Political.* Chicago: University of Chicago Press, 2007.

Schwartz, Jorge. "Abaixo tordesilhas." *Estudos Avançados* 7.17 (1993): 185–200.

Shaheen, Jack. *Reel Bad Arabs: How Hollywood Vilifies a People.* Northhampton: Interlink Publishing Group, 2001.

Shahimi, Muhammad Ayyub. *Dirasat ightirabiyah: Al-intishar al-lubnani fi al-baraghway.* Beirut: al-Tab'ah, 2000.

Sheinin, David. *Argentina and the United States: An Alliance Contained.* Athens: University of Georgia Press, 2006.

_____. "El judío en la mina de carbón: El inconfundible, dictadura e identidad en Argentina." In *Más allá del Medio Oriente: Las diásporas judías y árabes en América Latina*, edited by Raanan Rein, María José Cano Pérez, and Beatriz Molina Rueda, 163–96. Granada: Editorial de la Universidad de Granada, 2012.

Shohat, Ella. *Taboo Memories, Diasporic Voices.* Durham, NC: Duke University Press, 2006.

_____. "The Sephardi-Moorish Atlantic: Between Orientalism and
Occidentalism." In *Between the Middle East and the Americas: The Cultural
Politics of Diaspora*, edited by Evelyn Alsultany and Ella Shohat, 42–62. Ann
Arbor: University of Michigan Press, 2013.

_____. *On the Arab-Jew, Palestine, and Other Displacements: Selected Writings*. New
York: Pluto Press, 2017.

Shohat, Ella, and Robert Stam. *Unthinking Eurocentrism: Multiculturalism and the
Media*. New York: Routledge, 1994.

_____. *Flagging Patriotism: Crises of Narcissism and Anti-Americanism*. New York,
Routledge, 2007.

Simón, José Luis, ed. *Política exterior y relaciones internacionales del Paraguay contemporáneo*. Asunción: Centro Paraguayo de Estudios Sociológicos, 1990.

Skidmore, Thomas. *Politics in Brazil, 1930–64: An Experiment in Democracy*.
Oxford: Oxford University Press, 1968.

_____. *The Politics of Military Rule in Brazil, 1964–1985*. Oxford: Oxford University
Press, 1989.

Slocum, Karla. *Free Trade and Freedom: Neoliberalism, Place, and Nation in the
Caribbean*. Ann Arbor: University of Michigan Press, 2006.

Soares, Samuel Alves. *Controles e autonomia: As Forças Armadas e o sistema
político brasileiro (1974–1999)*. São Paulo: Editora Unesp, 2006.

Sochaczewski, Monique. "Palestine-Israel Controversies in the 1970s
and the Birth of Brazilian Transregionalism." In *The Middle East and
Brazil: Perspectives on the New Global South*, edited by Paul Amar, 75–91.
Bloomington: Indiana University Press, 2015.

Sondrol, Paul. "Totalitarian and Authoritarian Dictators: A Comparison of Fidel
Castro and Alfredo Stroessner." *Journal of Latin American Studies* 23.3 (1991):
599–620.

_____. "The Emerging New Politics of Liberalizing Paraguay: Sustained Civil-
Military Control without Democracy." *Journal of Interamerican Studies and
World Affairs* 34.2 (1992): 127–63.

Soprano, Germán. "La reforma de la defensa nacional y las fuerzas armadas
argentinas en democracia durante la década de 1990." *Cadernos Prolam/USP*
14.133 (2015): 133–56.

Spanos, William V. *Redeemer Nation in the Interregnum: An Untimely Meditation on
the American Vocation*. Oxford: Oxford University Press, 2016.

Sprandel, Marcia Anita. "Brasileiros na fronteira com o Paraguai." *Estudos
Avançados* 20.57 (2006): 137–56.

Steiger, William Raymond. "What Once Was Desert Shall Be a World: Getúlio
Vargas and Westward Expansion in Brazil, 1930–1945." PhD diss., UCLA, 1995.

Steinz, Mark. *Middle East Terrorist Activity in Latin America: Policy Papers on the
Americas*. Washington, DC: Center for Strategic and International Studies,
2003.

Stites Mor, Jessica. "The Question of Palestine in the Argentine Political
Imaginary: Anti-Imperialist Thought from Cold War to Neoliberal Order."
*Journal of Iberian and Latin American Research* 20.2 (2014): 183–97.

Stoler, Ann Laura. "Imperial Formations and the Opacities of Rule." In *Lessons
of Empire: Imperial Histories and American Power*, edited by Craig Calhoun,
Frederick Cooper, and Kevin Moore, 48–60. New York: New York University
Press, 2006.

Stolke, Verena. *Cafeicultura: Homens, mulheres e capital (1850–1980)*. São Paulo: Brasiliense, 1986.

Sullivan, Mark. *Latin America: Terrorism Issues*. Washington, DC: CRS Report for Congress, 2005.

Sverdlick, Ana. "Terrorists and Organized Crime Entrepreneurs in the 'Triple Frontier' among Argentina, Brazil, and Paraguay." *Trends in Organized Crime* 9.2 (2005): 84–93.

Taffet, Jeffrey. *Foreign Aid as Foreign Policy: The Alliance for Progress in Latin America*. New York: Routledge, 2007.

Tawil Kuri, Marta, ed. *Latin American Foreign Policies toward the Middle East: Actors, Contexts, and Trends*. New York: Palgrave Macmillan, 2016.

Tobin, Kathleen. "Threat or Ally: US-Latin American Relations and the Middle East Conflict." In *War, Media, and Propaganda*, edited by Yahya Kamalipour, 207–18. New York: Rowman and Littlefield, 2004.

Torres, Lourdes. "Editorial: Imagining the Future of Latino Studies." *Latino Studies* 11.3 (2013) 269–70.

Tota, Antonio Pedro. *O imperialismo sedutor: A americanização do Brasil na época da segunda guerra*. São Paulo: Companhia das Letras, 2000.

Tsing, Anna. *Friction: An Ethnography of Global Connections*. Princeton, NJ: Princeton University Press, 2005.

United Nations Economic Commission for Latin America and the Caribbean (Cepal). *América Latina: Urbanización y evolución de la población urbana, 1950–2000*. Santiago de Chile: Centro Latinoamericano y Caribeño de Demografía (CELADE), 2005.

United States Department of State. *Patterns of Global Terrorism 1992*. Washington, DC: Office of the Secretary of State, 1993.

_____. *Patterns of Global Terrorism 2000*. Washington, DC: Office of the Secretary of State, 2001.

_____. *Patterns of Global Terrorism 2001*. Washington, DC: Office of the Secretary of State, 2002.

_____. *Patterns of Global Terrorism 2002*. Washington, DC: Office of the Secretary of State, 2003.

_____. *Patterns of Global Terrorism 2003*. Washington, DC: Office of the Coordinator of Counterterrorism, 2004.

_____. *Country Reports on Terrorism 2004*. Washington, DC: Office of the Coordinator of Counterterrorism, 2005.

_____. *Country Reports on Terrorism 2005*. Washington, DC: Office of the Coordinator of Counterterrorism, 2006.

_____. *Country Reports on Terrorism 2007*. Washington, DC: Office of the Coordinator of Counterterrorism, 2008.

_____. *Country Reports on Terrorism 2008*. Washington, DC: Office of the Coordinator of Counterterrorism, 2009.

_____. *Country Reports on Terrorism 2009*. Washington, DC: Office of the Coordinator of Counterterrorism, 2010.

Valdés, Juan Gabriel. *Pinochet's Economists: The Chicago School of Economics in Chile*. Cambridge, UK: Cambridge University Press, 1995.

Veblen, Thorstein. *The Theory of the Leisure Class: An Economic Study of Institutions*. New York: Macmillan Company, 1902.

Vianna, Luiz Werneck. *A revolução passiva: Iberismo e americanismo no Brasil*. Rio de Janeiro: Editora Revan, 1997.

Vila, Pablo. *Crossing Borders, Reinforcing Borders: Social Categories, Metaphors, and Narrative Identities on the US-Mexico Frontier*. Austin: University of Texas Press, 2000.

Vizentini, Paulo Gilberto Fagundes. *Relações Internacionais do Brasil: de Vargas a Lula*. São Paulo: Editora Fundação Perseu Abramo, 2003.

_____. *A política externa do regime militar brasileiro: Multilateralização, desenvolvimento e a construção de uma potência média (1964–1985)*, 2nd ed. Porto Alegre: UFRGS Editora, 2004.

_____. *O regime militar e a projeção internacional do Brasil: autonomia nacional, desenvolvimento econômico e potência média, 1964–1985*. São Paulo: Almedina Brasil, 2020.

Wachowicz, Ruy. *Norte Velho, Norte Pioneiro*. Curitiba: Vicentina, 1987.

Wagner, Carlos. *Brasiguaios: Homens sem pátria*. Rio de Janeiro: Vozes, 1990.

Warren, Harris Gaylord. *Rebirth of the Paraguayan Republic*. Pittsburgh, PA: University of Pittsburgh Press, 1985.

Wegner, Robert. *A conquista do Oeste: A fronteira na obra de Sérgio Buarque de Holanda*. Belo Horizonte: Editora UFMG, 2000.

Wiarda, Howard, and Hilary Collins. "Constitutional Coups? Military Interventions in Latin America." *Security and Defense Studies Review* 12.1&2 (2011): 189–98.

Williams, Mary Wilhelmine. "The Treaty of Tordesillas and the Argentine-Brazilian Boundary Settlement." *Hispanic American Historical Review* 5.1 (1922): 3–23.

Wilson, Rob, and Arif Dirlik, eds. *Asia/Pacific as a Space of Cultural Production*. Durham, NC: Duke University Press, 1995.

Wilson, Thomas, and Hastings Donnan. "Border and Border Studies." In *A Companion to Border Studies*, edited by Thomas M. Wilson and Hastings Donnan, 1–25. Malden, MA: Blackwell, 2012.

Winant, Howard. *Racial Conditions: Politics, Theory, Comparisons*. Minneapolis: University of Minnesota Press, 1994.

Wolf, Eric. *Europe and the People without History*. Berkeley: University of California Press, 1982.

Ynsfrán, Edgar. *Un giro geopolítico: El milagro de una ciudad*. Asunción: Instituto Paraguayo de Estudios Geopolíticos e Internacionales, 1990.

Zaverucha, Jorge. "The Degree of Military Political Autonomy during the Spanish, Argentine and Brazilian Transitions." *Journal of Latin American Studies* 25.2 (1993): 283–99.

_____. "Poder militar: Entre o autoritarismo e a democracia." *São Paulo em Perspectiva* 15.4 (2001): 76–83.

Zimbalist, Andrew, and John Weeks. *Panama at the Crossroads: Economic Development and Political Change in the Twentieth Century*. Berkeley: University of California Press, 1991.

# Index

www.ingramcontent.com/pod-product-compliance
Lightning Source LLC
Chambersburg PA
CBHW021126270326
41929CB00009B/1064